The Highway War

Related Titles from Potomac Books

A Carrier at War: On Board the USS Kitty Hawk *in the Iraq War*
Richard F. Miller

Command Legacy: A Tactical Primer for Junior Leaders of Combat Units
Lt. Col. Raymond A. Millen, USA

Heavy Metal: A Tank Company's Battle to Baghdad
Capt. Jason Conroy, USA, with Ron Martz

The Iraq War: As Witnessed by the Correspondents and Photographers of United Press International
Edited by Martin Walker

Marine Rifleman: Forty-Three Years in the Corps
Col. Wesley L. Fox, USMC (Ret.)

War and Destiny: How the Bush Revolution in Foreign and Military Affairs Redefined American Power
James Kitfield

An AUSA Book

The Highway War

A Marine Company Commander in Iraq

Maj. Seth W. B. Folsom, USMC

Potomac Books
An imprint of the University of Nebraska Press

Library of Congress Cataloging-in-Publication Data

Folsom, Seth W. B., 1972–
The highway war : a marine company commander in Iraq / Seth W. B. Folsom.— 1st ed.
p. cm.
Includes index.
ISBN 1-57488-988-5 (hardcover : alk. paper)
1. Folsom, Seth W. B., 1972– 2. Soldiers—United States—Biography. 3. Iraq War, 2003—Personal narratives, American. 4. United States—Armed Forces—Biography. I. Title.
DS79.76.F65 2006
956.7044'342092—dc22

2005037340

Printed in the United States of America on acid-free paper that meets the American National Standards Institute Z39-48 Standard.

First Edition

NOTE
The opinions or assertions contained in this work are those of the writer and are not to be construed as official or reflecting the views of the Marine Corps, the Department of the Navy, or the Department of Defense.

[**For the Marines and sailors of Delta Company—**
the men to my left and right—and for their families,
who shared an equally difficult burden.]

The villainy you teach me I will execute, and it shall go hard . . .
But I will better the instruction.
—William Shakespeare, *The Merchant of Venice*

But I've a rendezvous with Death at midnight in some flaming town,
When Spring trips north again this year and I to my pledged word am true,
I shall not fail that rendezvous.
—Alan Seeger, *I Have a Rendezvous with Death*

One must wait until the evening to see how splendid the day has been.
—Sophocles

Think where man's glory most begins and ends,
And say my glory was I had such friends.
—William Butler Yeates

Contents

Illustrations

Maps

Diagram

Photographs

Author's Note

During the course of writing this book, I used several different resources. The primary foundation for the writing was my combat journal, a battered notebook filled with more than 150 pages of detailed daily entries and accounts. I began the journal the day I arrived in Kuwait in February 2003, and concluded it once Delta Company returned to Ad Diwaniyah in late April 2003. Most of the incidents described in this book come directly from this journal. I supplemented my notes with audio recordings and video footage, more than 500 photographs, official award summaries of individual actions, and informal interviews and emails exchanged between the Marines of Delta Company and me. Most major actions by Delta Company—and other major incidents within First Light Armored Reconnaissance Battalion—are described in 1st LAR Battalion's official command chronology.

This book is not a work of fiction. It is written from the often short-sighted perspective of a young company commander struggling to make sense of the chaotic events that surrounded him. Since then I have matured, and my outlook has broadened. As this account of my thoughts and feelings at the time is candid, I have chosen to change or delete the names of certain individuals in order to protect their privacy.

Accounts of actions that were taken by other units within RCT-5 and that I did not personally witness were drawn from an official account of the regiment's exploits during the war. They are meant to provide the reader a greater perspective of the "bigger picture" during the first month of the war.

Finally, it is important for the reader to understand that many of the conversations described in this book are reported only as precisely as my journal entries and my memories allow. The only way it would have been possible to recount conversations word-for-word in this book is if I had constantly carried a voice recorder with me in Iraq. However, although I believe it is a fair and accurate retelling, the story within this book is *my* story, told from *my* perspective. I commanded 130 Marines and sailors in Delta Company; 131 different accounts of our actions therefore exist. Numerous other recollections no doubt exist among the hundreds of other young men who belonged to 1st LAR Battalion at the time. Regardless, it is with great pride that I write about the Marines and sailors of Delta Company, 1st Light Armored Reconnaissance Battalion. I hope my retelling of our adventures properly conveys our story.

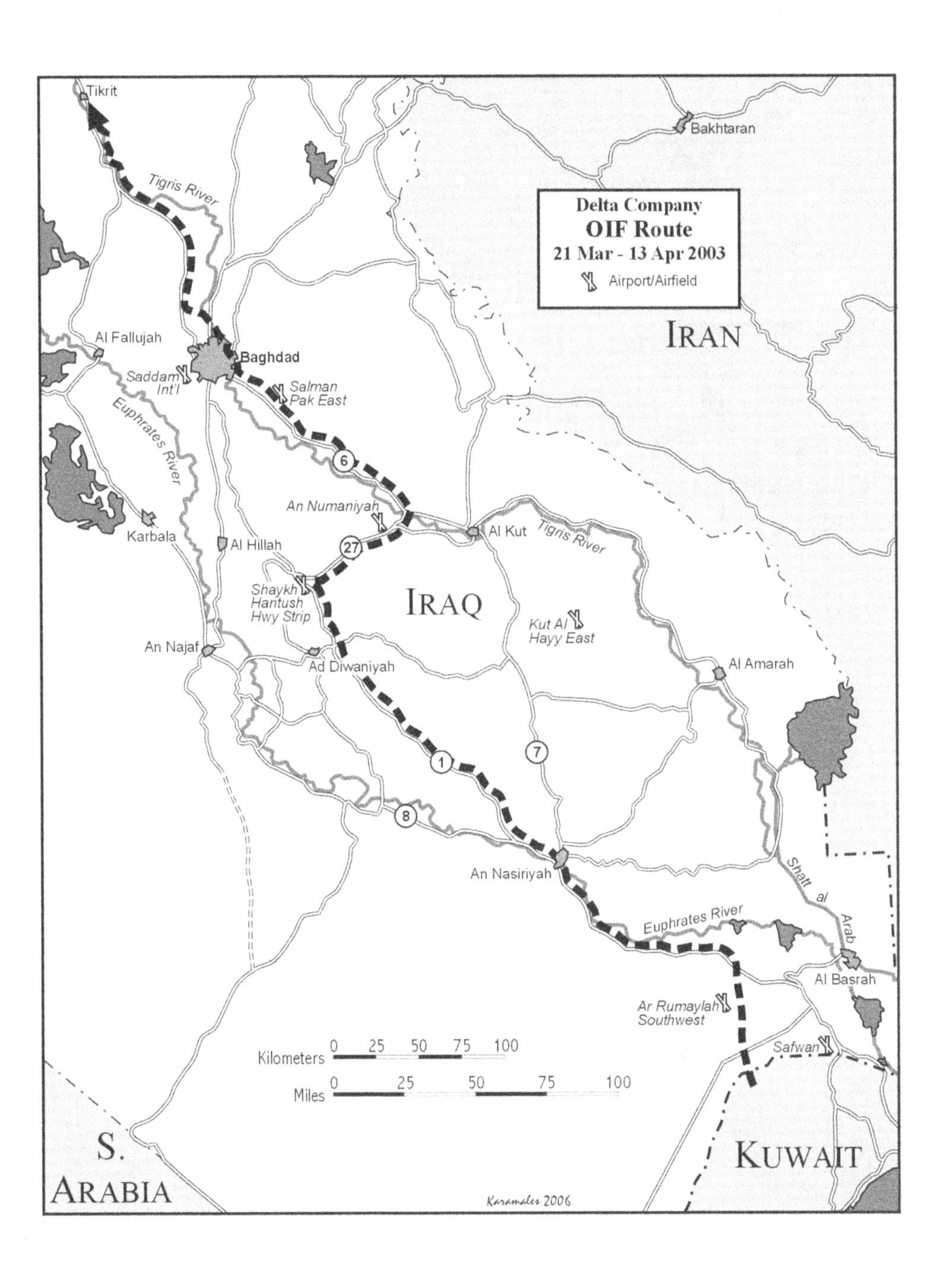

Delta Company
OIF Route
21 Mar - 13 Apr 2003
Airport/Airfield
Tikrit
Bakhtaran
Tigris River
IRAN
Al Fallujah
Baghdad
Saddam Int'l
Salman Pak East
Euphrates River
6
An Numaniyah
Karbala
Al Hillah
27
Al Kut
Tigris River
Shaykh Hantush Hwy Strip
IRAQ
Kut Al Hayy East
An Najaf
Ad Diwaniyah
Al Amarah
7
1
8
An Nasiriyah
Shatt al Arab
Euphrates River
Al Basrah
Ar Rumaylah Southwest
Kilometers 0 25 50 75 100
Miles 0 25 50 75 100
Safwan
S. ARABIA
KUWAIT
Karamales 2006

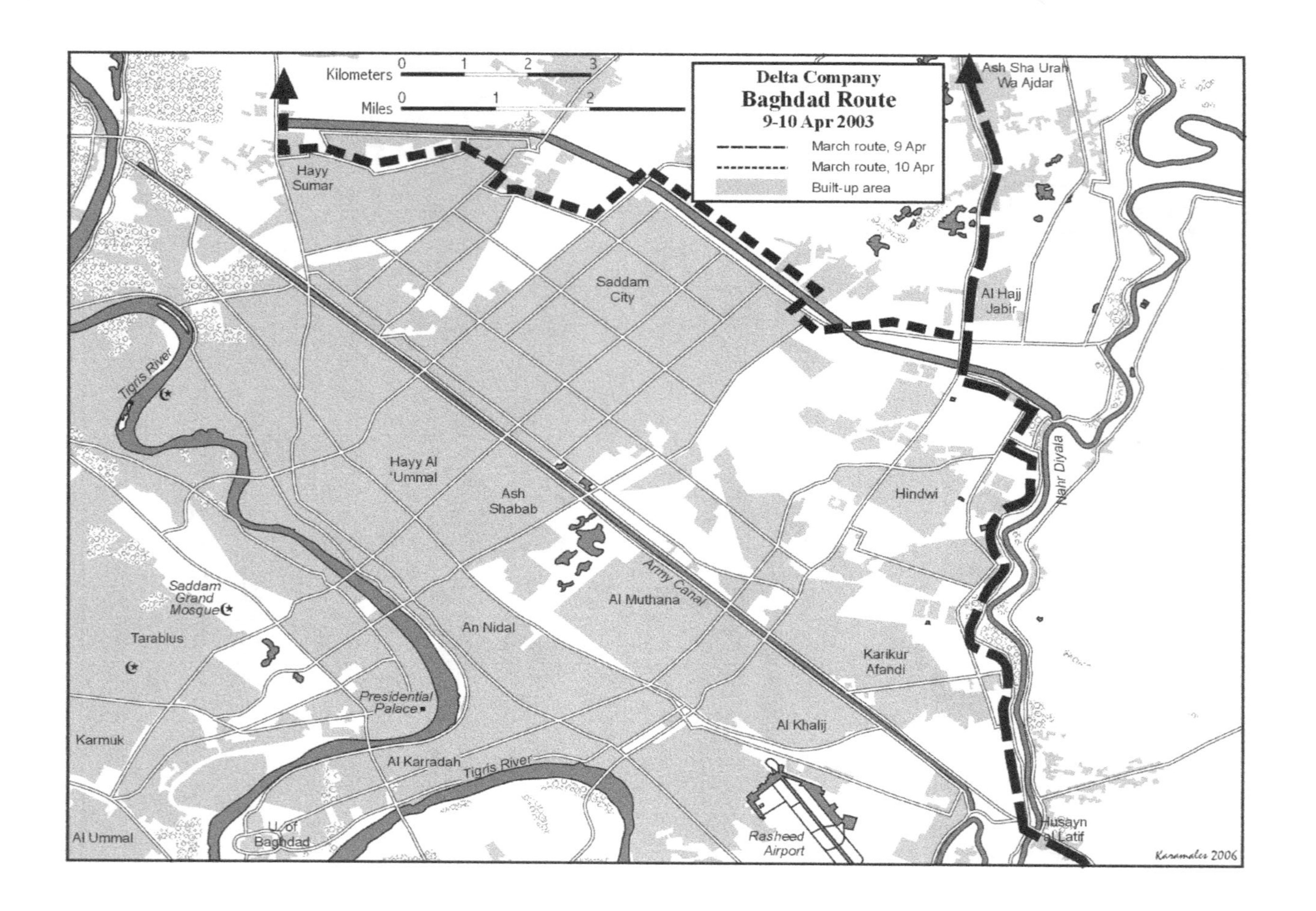

Delta Company
Baghdad Route
9-10 Apr 2003
March route, 9 Apr
March route, 10 Apr
Built-up area
Kilometers 0 1 2 3
Miles 0 1 2
Ash Sha Urah Wa Ajdar
Hayy Sumar
Saddam City
Al Hajj Jabir
Tigris River
Hayy Al 'Ummal
Ash Shabab
Hindwi
Nahr Diyala
Army Canal
Al Muthana
Saddam Grand Mosque
An Nidal
Tarablus
Karikur Afandi
Presidential Palace
Al Khalij
Karmuk
Al Karradah
Tigris River
U. of Baghdad
Al Ummal
Rasheed Airport
Husayn al Latif
Karamales 2006

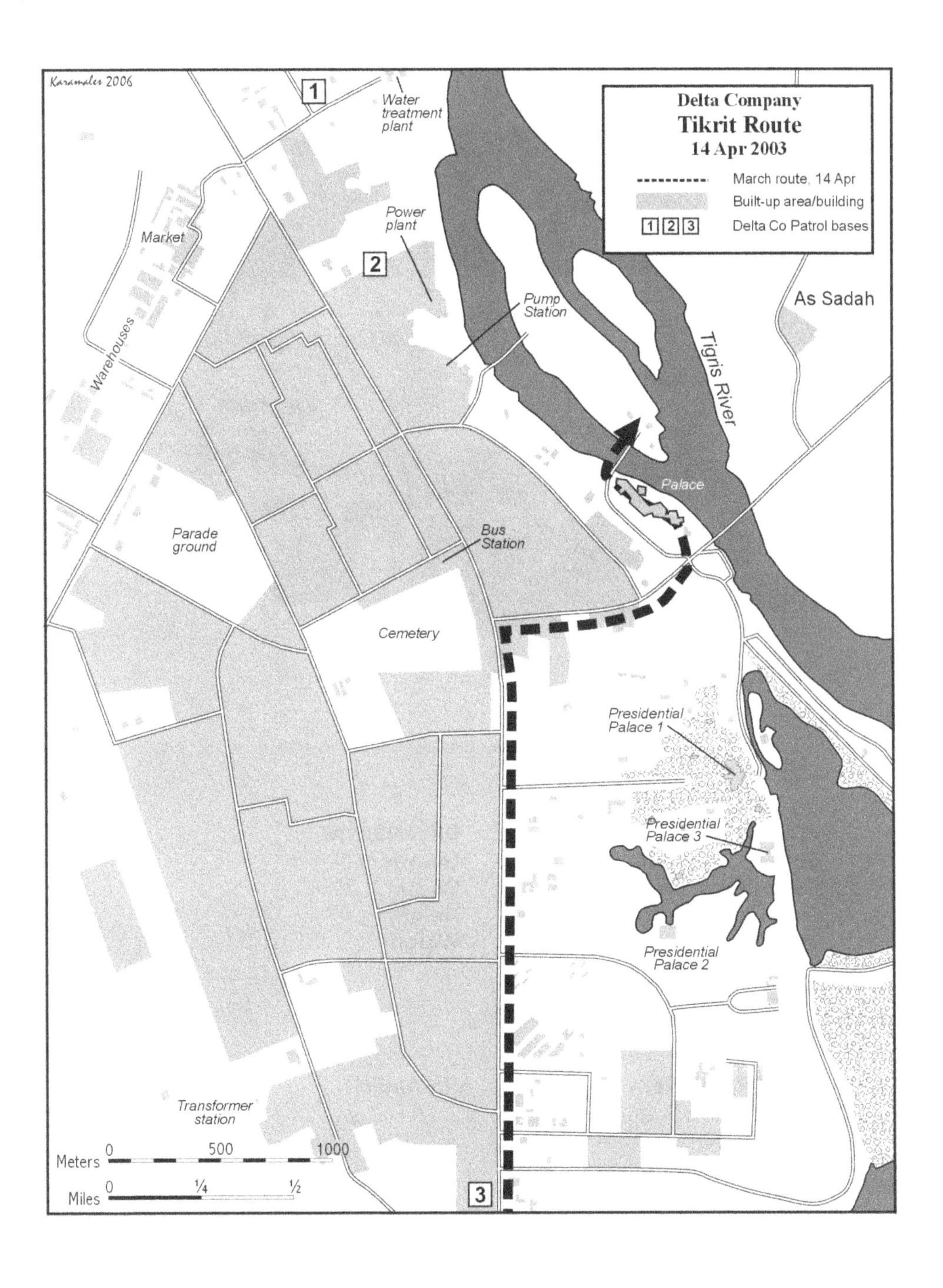
Karamales 2006
Delta Company
Tikrit Route
14 Apr 2003
March route, 14 Apr
Built-up area/building
Delta Co Patrol bases
1
2
3
Water treatment plant
Power plant
Market
Warehouses
Pump Station
As Sadah
Tigris River
Palace
Parade ground
Bus Station
Cemetery
Presidential Palace 1
Presidential Palace 3
Presidential Palace 2
Transformer station
Meters 0 500 1000
Miles 0 ¼ ½

LAV–25

INFORMATION:
Designation: LAV-25
Contractor: Diesel Division, General Motors of Canada
Country: United States
Service Date: 1983
Type: Light Tank
Accommodation: 3 + 6

DIMENSIONS:
Length: 6.39 m
Width: 2.50 m
Height: 2.69 m
Weight: 10,932 kg

PERFORMANCE:
Powerplant: 1 x General Motors Detroit Diesel 6V-53T 6-cylinder diesel engine delivering 275 hp.
Max Speed: 100 km/h
Max Range: 668 km

ARMAMENT:
1 x 25 mm gun
1 x 7.62 mm coaxial machine gun
1 x 7.62 mm AA machine gun
8 smoke grenade dischargers

Prologue

Highway 1, Tikrit, Iraq

I awoke to the canvas-ripping *whoosh* of rocket fire followed by the sound of explosions to the north. From where I had been dozing on the warm grill cover of my light armored vehicle (LAV), I spotted an AH-1W Cobra gunship helicopter circling overhead. It wheeled away from its target—an S-60 anti-aircraft artillery gun—and swiftly egressed to the south. The S-60 and its ammunition had ignited, and secondary explosions rocked the surrounding area. I watched as a Second Platoon scout team that had been spotting for the helicopters, began to move away from the exploding ammunition cache and toward the relative safety of their vehicle hidden in defilade. Angry that the scout team was so close to the impact area in the first place, I contemplated radioing their platoon commander to ask him why he was putting his Marines at risk over something as benign as an unmanned AAA piece. My train of thought was broken by a yell from my gunner, Lance Corporal Josh Davis. Second Platoon was in contact with the enemy to our northwest. The Marines were receiving small arms and rocket propelled grenade (RPG) fire from the tree line.

Still groggy from my nap—a result of the previous evening's arduous 150-kilometer road march from Baghdad—and unsure of the seriousness or veracity of the report, I yelled for my crew to mount up so we could check out 2nd Platoon's report. The LAV-25 lumbered across the rolling grassy terrain of our screen (picket) south of the city of Tikrit and towards the asphalt of Highway 1, where 2nd Platoon had tied in with First Platoon. Earlier I had directed First Lieutenant Chad Parment, the commander of 1st Platoon, to array his vehicles across the highway and control traffic leading into and coming out of Tikrit. His platoon was likewise tied in with our battalion's Weapons Company to the west. The enemy contact reported by 2nd Platoon appeared to have died down by the time I arrived. Although the Marines and corpsmen were treating an Iraqi who had been shot in the leg, the scene around the roadblock was, as I had guessed, not as urgent as first reported.

Observing the apparent lack of attention being paid to the roadblock mission by 1st Platoon, I redirected my ire towards Lt Parment. He stood in his LAV's turret, looking intently up the highway to the north. Walking across the paved asphalt and over to his vehicle, I motioned for him to jump down to brief me on the situation. As he approached me, I pointed to the Marines and vehicles scattered around the checkpoint and the absence of organization. With an unmistakable note of irritation in my voice I confronted him.

"You call this a check-point?" I demanded. "What the hell is going on over here, anyway?" Before he could formulate an answer, a burst of AK-47 fire erupted from the tree line to the north, the rounds zipping over our heads and impacted around us. To our left one of Parment's scout teams stationed along the road dropped to their knees and immediately returned fire into the trees where the enemy rounds had originated. The *pop, pop, pop* of the scouts' rifles competed with the noise from the tree line and the helicopter loitering high above. As I stood frozen in the middle of the road, Parment slowly shook his head and looked at me with an expression that said *You idiot . . . Haven't you been listening to the radio?* My decision to get the hell out of the open and start taking care of business was hastened when, to my disbelief, an explosion sounded to our front. Our feet rooted in place, we watched a rocket propelled grenade screech from the trees and slam into the flank of an LAV-25 from Weapons Company.

Oh shit, I thought, as oily black smoke billowed from the side of the vehicle. *They're dead.* But rather than seeing secondary explosions rip through the steel skin of the vehicle's hull as expected, I watched in awe as the LAV dropped down into reverse and began screaming backward at forty miles an hour. The column of smoke trailed crazily behind it as the vehicle bounced up and down over the bumpy earth. As I ran back to my vehicle, Davis yelled down to me.

"Holy shit, sir! Did you see that!"

Climbing into the turret I nodded and brusquely added, "Fire it up. Get ready to roll." Throwing on my helmet and keying the headset to the battalion tactical radio network, I radioed Captain David Hudspeth, the commander of Weapons Company.

"Warlord-Six, this is Dragon-Six. I just saw an RPG hit one of your vehicles. Is everyone alright?"

A moment passed, and I began to think the worst. Already our regimental combat team had lost at least two M1A1 Abrams tanks to RPG fire in the preceding weeks, and the Abrams was the most heavily armored vehicle in the world. Surely the armored hulls of our LAVs would be no match for the explosive molten jet produced by an RPG. I imagined the crew of the stricken Weapons Company vehicle dismembered and burning alive as the driver frantically attempted to escape from the killing zone. Instead, the radio crackled to life with the sound of Dave's deep North Carolina drawl.

"Dragon-Six, this is Warlord-Six. Roger, they're all right. Looks like it hit the muffler."

In an incredible piece of luck, the baffles lining the muffler's inside had served to dissipate the molten jet of the RPG. The vehicle crew had been spared. My astonishment at the LAV's ability to absorb the punishment of a direct hit from an RPG quickly gave way to raging anger. I was pissed. For weeks our battalion, along with the rest of the regiment, had endured hit and run ambushes by the Iraqis. Each time it slowed our movement to a crawl, sometimes to a dead halt. We were sick of it. *I* was sick of it. I keyed my headset again.

"Roger that Warlord-Six, I'm glad to hear it." I thought for a moment, staring north up the length of Highway 1. I keyed the headset again.

"Don't worry. We're gonna go get those motherfuckers right now."

PART I

The Road to War: Camp Pendleton to Kuwait

14 December 2002–20 March 2003

1
Start Point

My path to becoming a company commander during war did not begin on September 11, but my course was set that morning, after four hijacked airliners crashed into the World Trade Center, the Pentagon, and a lonely field in Pennsylvania. The United States was suddenly at war, and for me it couldn't have come at a more inopportune time.

I had been married barely forty-eight hours, and my new wife and I were honeymooning in Oxford, Mississippi, when I saw the events of that terrible morning unfold on television. Silently we packed our bags—the honeymoon was over. Ashley and I sat in silence as we drove the back roads to her family's home in Memphis and listened to the story rapidly unfold over the radio. Oddly, I remembered the words my company commander had spoken on my first day at Officer Candidates School (OCS) nine years earlier.

"Life as you know it is about to change," he had said. "From this point on, you will never look at anything again the same way you have up until now." Those words rang true after September 11, 2001. Nothing would ever really be the same for me again.

I was still relatively naïve, even though I had been a company commander for nearly five months at the time of the hijackings. Until that point, my career in the Marine Corps had been unremarkable. After scraping by in OCS during the summers of 1992 and 1993 (my final class standing in 1993 was a stellar 114 out of a class of 124), my performance as a second lieutenant at The Basic School (TBS) was similarly mediocre. Student officer peer evaluations (what the venerated biographer, historian, and former Marine William Manchester appropriately referred to as "fuck your buddy night") described me as everything from "gung-ho" to "abusive."

My first assignment as a second lieutenant and an infantry officer in the Fleet Marine Force, in 1995, was as a platoon commander in the First Marine

Division's First Light Armored Reconnaissance Battalion. Despite its successful trial by fire during operations Desert Shield and Desert Storm in 1990 and 1991, 1st LAR Battalion continued to suffer from an identity crisis within the division. Based around companies of eight-wheeled light armored vehicles (LAVs), the battalion regularly changed names over the years following its creation in the mid-1980s, even if its wartime mission did not. Originally First Light Armored Vehicle Battalion, it switched to First Light Armored Infantry Battalion prior to the 1991 Gulf War. Several years later, First Light Armored Infantry Battalion and First Reconnaissance Battalion merged to form First Reconnaissance Battalion (Light Armored). And finally, in 1994, the battalion was renamed First Light Armored Reconnaissance Battalion. Its mission was—and remains—to conduct reconnaissance and security operations and, within capability, limited offensive, defensive, and economy-of-force operations. A mouthful. What the LAR battalion is, and was designed to be, is the vanguard force for the Marine division. It is a swift, mobile, and deadly unit capable of conducting self-sustained reconnaissance and combined arms operations well forward of the division's main body.

The centerpiece of the LAR battalion is the LAV-25, so named for its M242 25-millimeter Bushmaster cannon. The Bushmaster (or simply "main gun," as it is known) can fire up to 200 rounds of high explosive or armor-piercing projectiles per minute. The effects on humans and light-skinned and other lightly armored vehicles are devastating. The LAV-25 also comes equipped with two M240 machine guns. One is coaxially mounted to the main gun (referred to as the "coax"), and the second is supported on a pintle arm for the vehicle commander. Supporting the LAV-25 in the LAR battalion are five other variants utilizing the same basic chassis. The LAV-M (mortar) houses an 81-millimeter mortar, and the LAV-AT (antitank) has an elevating "hammerhead" turret to fire TOW (tube-launched, optically tracked, wire-guided) missiles. The LAV-C2 (command and control) is the heart of the LAR company's communications network. With four VHF radios, one HF radio, one UHF radio, and other modular communications assets, the LAV-C2 also serves as the principal vehicle for controlling external fire support. The LAV-L (logistics) is typically referred to as "the Log"; its spacious cargo bay can haul most everything the LAR company requires. Finally, the LAV-R (recovery) comes equipped with a massive hydraulic crane, a 30,000-pound test winch, a welding kit, and various other tools to keep the maintenance-intensive LAVs up and running.

Still, regardless of 1st LAR Battalion's success in Desert Storm, its focus following that war shifted to providing LAR companies to Marine Expeditionary Units (MEUs) for their six-month western pacific (WestPac) deployments. As the number of deployments and tempo of operations both continued to increase, the battalion's ability to fight as a cohesive team began to deteriorate. Imagine a football coach constantly sending away large portions of his team for months on end, while seldom having practice for the remaining players in their absence. The focus was clearly on supplying and supporting the MEUs, which were predicted to be the Marine units most likely to be involved in future combat operations. Even the division commander wanted more emphasis on training 1st LAR Battalion as a unit, yet the demand to deploy companies of LAVs in MEUs continued.

Most of this was transparent to me as a second lieutenant. As one of the most junior officers in a battalion that numbered close to one thousand Marines and hundreds of vehicles of all types, I was more concerned with trying to manage and lead a platoon of thirty Marines and four light armored vehicles. Several of my men were combat veterans from Kuwait and Somalia, and I faced the daily challenge of trying to find my place as their leader without making a total asshole out of myself. William Manchester was correct when he said there is no job less enviable than that of a green second lieutenant taking over a platoon of veterans. It doesn't help when you are a temperamental perfectionist with a confidence problem and deficient in the TBS-inspired ideal of "command presence." At least that was how I thought of myself at the time. Sometimes I look back and wonder how I made it through my tenure as a platoon commander without my Marines mutinying.

My trials and tribulations as a new lieutenant aside, one thing remained constant in nearly all of our platoon, company, and battalion training: preparing to fight Iraq again. For the most part, all classwork on armored fighting vehicle identification focused on models operated by the Iraqi army. Through hours of repetitive drills, the silhouettes of these Russian-produced armored hulks were burned like photo-negatives into all of our brains. Maneuver training against enemy threat doctrine in southern California's Camp Pendleton and in the Marine Corps' desert stronghold of Twentynine Palms always employed the Iraqi model. The major training exercises during my 1997 WestPac deployment were in Jordan and the United Arab Emirates—desert countries situated near Iraq with comparable terrain and climates. No matter how much the establishment preached that we should not focus on "fighting the last war," it was generally accepted that one day we would go up against Iraq again and finish what our predecessors had begun in 1990.

◆ ◇ ◆

After graduating from the U.S. Army's Armor Captains Career Course, I returned to 1st LAR Battalion in April 2001. Upon assuming command of Delta Company, I committed myself to accomplishing two objectives. I wanted to be a better captain than I had been a lieutenant. As a lieutenant I had been prone to angry, emotional outbursts when I didn't get my way. Everyone knew I wore my heart on my sleeve, and that was probably my greatest weakness. But as a captain at age twenty-nine, I knew my personality and limitations. The chances of this tiger changing its stripes seven years into his career were slim.

Above all, I committed myself to training my Marines for war. But in April 2001 the prospects for participation in armed conflict seemed as remote as they had been when I was a platoon commander. Sure, tension had periodically bubbled in the Persian Gulf and Southwest Asia, but it was nearly always met by the United States with a barrage of cruise missiles and empty diplomacy. Despite a U.S. refusal to commit the time and resources to permanently address the problems in the Persian Gulf, I always remembered something one of my colleagues had said to me while I was assigned as an instructor at OCS. I had been complaining about the laziness and general unmilitary attitude displayed by many of the personnel who worked at OCS. A fellow staff member, formerly a drill instructor and a prior Force Reconnaissance Marine, rolled his eyes and simply said, "Hey, lighten up, man. We're not going to war anytime soon." I couldn't believe someone who had so much experience could have such an attitude about the subject. From then on, I knew that even if war didn't seem to be on the horizon, we had to train as if it was right around the corner, waiting to ambush us. That sounds like a cliché, but it is for that reason the Marine Corps has always performed so well.

September 11 confirmed this. Ashley and I sat at her parents' house for two days, unable to get a flight home because of flight restrictions immediately following the attacks or rent a car because there were none to be had anywhere. The tension in her family's household resulting from the attacks was matched only by my restlessness, which my new wife knew she could calm only by taking me out to the local bar for a drink and to discuss options for getting me back with my company. First LAR Battalion was conducting desert training in Twentynine Palms, and the most important thing on my mind after seeing two airliners slam into the World Trade Center was to get my ass out of Tennessee to be with my men. I didn't feel safe sitting in America's heartland; I felt safer with my Marines. My father-in-law offered his car, and on the evening of September 12 Ashley and I left Memphis. Twenty-seven hours later we were in Carlsbad, California, just south of Camp Pendleton. Along the way, I mused to Ashley, "Man, if they link Iraq to 9/11 in any way, we are gonna total that country."

Much to the surprise of my Marines and the entire battalion—who couldn't believe I had found my way back so quickly under such chaotic circumstances—by September 14 I was in the desert with my company. I was where I belonged.

That was where Delta Company's road to war began.

2

First Class to Kuwait

On December 14, 2002, Delta Company returned home to Camp Pendleton after its six-month WestPac (Western Pacific deployment) with Battalion Landing Team 3/1 (Third Battalion, First Marine Regiment) and the Eleventh Marine Expeditionary Unit. Homecoming from a WestPac is supposed to be a glorious affair. Ours was not. According to many our deployment, in a word, sucked. I spent most of my time battling my own company staff and the friction I myself had generated with them, while at the same time attempting to reduce the negative impact the deployment had on my Marines. In that respect, I failed miserably. After the rigors of a six-month training "work-up" period and a six-month deployment—most of which was spent sweltering on a thirty-year-old amphibious landing ship—nearly every Marine in the company hated me. As much as I tried to do the right thing and be the hard-but-fair leader I always wanted to be, my efforts always resulted in personality conflict and what my men surely perceived as hegemony replete with micromanagement. More simply put, they were sick of my shit, and I was sick of theirs. After twenty months as a company commander I was ready to pack it in, turn over the unit to the next schmuck in line, and execute my impending duty orders to the Naval Postgraduate School in Monterey to begin my preparations to be a South Asian foreign area officer (FAO).

More important, I just wanted to be home again with Ashley. Since our abbreviated honeymoon in Oxford and subsequent nonstop journey across the country, we had spent very little time together as husband and wife. Training requirements, long days with the company, and the deployment itself kept us apart for the majority of that time. I was fortunate enough to have daily email access while I was on ship, and our communication didn't suffer too much while I was gone. Still, six months away is six months away. Marriages break up all the time, no matter how much Internet connectivity or bandwidth you have. The fact of the matter is that the guy is not there, and neither is the girl. People just grow apart sometimes.

Ashley and I weren't too worried about that. But the closer my company got to home, the closer the United States and Iraq seemed to get to a showdown. I had followed events closely while deployed, and even as our MEU approached Camp Pendleton's coastline in December, advance units from First Marine Expeditionary Force (I MEF—First Marine Division's parent unit) were making their way to Kuwait for a build-up that had been underway for several months.

No sooner did I dump my field gear in my office than Major Byron Harper, the battalion operations officer (S–3), walked in to welcome me back. I asked him what was on the battalion's plate, and he shot me a knowing look.

"Get ready to swim," he said. His cryptic message directing me to prepare my LAVs for water operations signaled that the battalion would be expected to cross several rivers during a march to Baghdad. I begged for more information, in particular, whether Delta Company would redeploy with the battalion if the division were ordered to Kuwait.

"Talk to the CO," he merely said. "There will be a staff meeting on Monday. See you there."

✦ ✧ ✦

What I discovered was that 1st LAR Battalion was indeed slated to deploy to Kuwait for the approaching hostilities with Iraq. The plan called for transporting nearly the entire MEF to Kuwait. This would be accomplished by offloading vehicles and equipment from two maritime prepositioning force (MPF) squadrons and flying in the personnel to operate them. Additionally, amphibious task forces (ATF) would sail from San Diego, California, with personnel from Camp Pendleton, and from Morehead City, North Carolina, with personnel from Camp Lejeune.

Further, the plan called for 1st LAR Battalion to send four companies to war. Three would go with their own vehicles via the amphibious task force, and the remainder would fly in and rendezvous with LAVs from one of the MPF squadrons. By the time I returned from WestPac, the battalion's planning process for the deployment was already well underway. Headquarters and Service (H&S) Company, Weapons Company, and Charlie Company would sail to Kuwait with the ATF. Alpha Company was out of the equation because they were already locked into deploying with 15th MEU, which was scheduled to depart less than a month after we returned. That left Delta Company and Bravo Company.

Captain Lance Dowd, Bravo's company commander, had been recently tapped to prepare his company as the battalion's MPF element. Despite the fact that they were scheduled to begin work-up training with 13th MEU, Lance and his company had completed all requirements to be the battalion's fly-in echelon of the MPF; they were prepared to fly away to Kuwait at a moment's notice and marry up with the mothballed vehicles and equipment that would be awaiting them. That was where I came into the picture.

Lance and I had been friends ever since we deployed together in 1997. He was a really solid guy, a prior-enlisted reconnaissance Marine who knew his job and was just nice as hell. But I still bristled when I heard the decision that had to be made: one of our companies would serve as the fly-in echelon, and the other would begin work-up training with the MEU and deploy in June. The Marine Corps had decided that the upcoming Iraq conflict would not interrupt the MEU deployment cycle or the unit deployment program to Okinawa. In other words, some units were going to have to miss the "Big Show." Lance and I immediately began butting heads over who should get assigned the fly-in echelon job. For each of us the answer was simple: we felt our own company deserved to go to Iraq.

With the benefit of hindsight, I can easily understand why Lance thought Bravo Company should be selected. He had spent the previous eight or nine months preparing his Marines to deploy. They had recently finished a combined arms exercise (CAX), and they were tactically proficient. They were hungry, motivated, and fully equipped with personnel. Bravo Company seemed to be the leading candidate for the fly-in job.

Delta Company, on the other hand, was exhausted. There was little doubt about it. The company had been up and running since September 11—over a year—and the strain was beginning to wear on all of us. Several Marines within the company were scheduled to rotate to other jobs within the Marine Corps, and others were ready to complete their service obligations and move on to civilian life. Among the latter, several had already extended their enlistment contracts in order to deploy with us six months earlier, on the condition that they be allowed to leave the Corps as soon as humanly possible after we returned to Camp Pendleton. Not the least of our problems was that we were all pissed off at each other after spending so much time together in the close confines of the ship. I was, no doubt, the least popular of the bunch.

But what Delta Company's Dragons lacked in the energy and motivation department, they more than made up for it in tactical performance. Despite all of our flaws—mine included—the company had molded itself into an organization fully capable of running itself. We had put tremendous energy into our tactical training, and the results had been phenomenal. We had been cold together. We had been miserably hot together. We had even shared the harrowing experience of seeing three of our own seriously injured in a training mishap. I believed the old adage that collective misery creates unbreakable bonds. And for better or worse, we were the most experienced company in 1st LAR Battalion. I had no doubt that, when the time came, the company would kick ass on the battlefield. But now it was looking like we wouldn't get that chance.

Few Marines within the company were wild about the notion of boarding a plane and heading back overseas to the same sand-encrusted dungheap we had just left. There were also older Marines within the company—veterans of Desert Storm and Somalia—who weren't jumping up and down at the idea of going back to war.

My own feelings on the subject were mixed. I had always emphasized to the Marines that we were executors of policy, not makers of it. But privately I questioned whether all had been done at the highest levels to exhaust every diplomatic option short of war. In my estimation I just didn't think the United States had built a strong enough case to go to war. Then again, I knew this was my last chance to do what I had been training for since I was a second lieutenant in TBS. I wasn't foaming at the mouth over the prospect of getting my ass shot off in Iraq, but I didn't want to sit on the sidelines and watch the whole thing on CNN. As far as I was concerned, the decision was simple. Delta Company was the best-trained company within the battalion, and there could be no other choice for who would fly in and meet the battalion in Kuwait—we were it.

The unfortunate victim in this crisis of personalities and personal desires was Ashley. Each evening I would come home from work and fume about the situation. No one seemed able to make a decision, and the anxiety was driving me up the wall. Ashley was fond of saying sympathetically, "The pain of uncertainty is worse than the certainty of pain." True, but as far as I was concerned it was all bullshit. The only thing that would make me happy, or at least provide some measure of relief, was for Delta Company to be selected as the fly-in company. Ashley, meanwhile, had to put up with my ranting and raving about how Delta Company *deserved* that assignment as compensation for all the ways we had been jammed in the past year. Ashley's vision of a nice settled life following my deployment quickly dissolved, and she realized that the only way she could be happy was if I was happy. The only way that was going to happen was if I was able to take my company to Iraq. I had put her in a position of praying I would go to war.

On 6 January I got a call indicating that the battalion commander wanted to see me. *This is it,* I thought. *It's one way or another. You are going or you are staying.*

"The division staff won't make a decision, Seth," my battalion commander told me. "So I'm just going to make it myself and deal with the consequences. As far as I'm concerned, Delta Company is going to be the fly-in echelon and Bravo Company will deploy with Thirteenth MEU. Start getting your advance party ready."

So I got my wish, at least for the time being. I had been home fewer than three weeks, and now I was getting ready to return to the Persian Gulf and whatever lay beyond that.

✦ ✧ ✦

Planning for the battalion's departure with "Amphibious Task Force West" accelerated about the same time the decision was made to insert Delta Company into the MPF slot. The battalion had had a basic plan on the table for several months, and the only thing left was to get the Marines and all of the battalion's vehicles and equipment from Camp Pendleton down to the naval base in San Diego. That in itself was no small task, and I was relieved not to have to deal with it, since Delta Company's MPF vehicles would be waiting for us when we flew into Kuwait.

Because Delta Company would be receiving all of the major equipment necessary to fight with once we arrived in Kuwait, our biggest headache was preparing the Marines to redeploy once again. We began the frustrating drills of updating everyone's service record books, verifying next-of-kin information, updating wills and powers of attorney, performing personal gear inspections, and receiving immunizations. The company was fortunate, however, for two reasons. Because we had just returned from deployment, there was little administrative work required within the company; we had gone through the same routine six months earlier, and overall, our records were pretty clean. Additionally, during the course of our previous deployment, Ashley and several wives within the company's Key Volunteer Network (KVN) had worked hard to ensure there was a smooth channel of communication among the Delta Company wives. The families may not have wanted us to go back overseas, but at least in this regard they were better prepared than the other wives within the battalion.

Still, each level of preparation seemed to come with its own set of hurdles. The regimental personnel and administrative office and Camp Pendleton's legal office had to update service record books and legal paperwork. Several Marines within the company had chosen to get married before we left, and we needed to jump through hoops to get their new wives entered into the Marine Corps' administrative system. One sergeant married a girl he had met on-line and corresponded with via email during our WestPac. Although we all thought this a recipe for disaster, the two of them proved us wrong after we left for Kuwait. He received more mail from her than any twenty or thirty

Marines combined during the time we were deployed to Kuwait and Iraq. Each time there was a mail call he would receive dozens of letters from her. She faithfully wrote him every day, sometimes more than once.

Preparing our personal gear and equipment was no piece of cake, either. Marines began heading out into town to purchase countless pieces of gear to complete their lists. When I pontificated to my company first sergeant on the fact that they were missing so much personal equipment, he bluntly informed me that many of the men had had half of their personal gear stolen while they were on ship. Sadly, rampant theft by fellow servicemen had taken money out of their pockets.

But the men weren't just buying required items, and it wasn't just the enlisted Marines who were purchasing what we called "queer gear" as fast as their paychecks would allow. Each morning someone on the company staff would show off his new, often high-tech, piece of equipment. I myself bought a personal global positioning system (GPS), a high-speed flashlight that could shine in visible light or infrared, a new Camelbak drinking system, and dozens of map pens in different colors. Shortly before we left, one staff sergeant within the company came in toting a telescoping aluminum baton like the type police officers were beginning to carry. I asked him what in the hell he planned to use it for. He said, "In case I have to beat the shit out of someone, sir." Roger that.

Most distressing for all of us as we prepared to redeploy was the news that we were required to get immunized for smallpox. We had already suffered though a series of shots to protect us from anthrax during our WestPac, and questions were raised about the safety of the smallpox immunizations. The usual rumors began floating around about how it would sterilize all of us, drive us crazy, and kill every millionth person injected. But what made everyone *really* nervous was hearing that there was a chance we could pass the virus on to our families. Nevertheless, we all stood in line and got our left shoulders pricked. Several days later everyone developed dime-sized boils where we had been injected. They were sickening, especially when the boils shriveled to thick, black scabs that peeled and flaked around the edges and threatened to come off prematurely every time we showered. It wasn't until we had been in Kuwait for several weeks that everyone's scabs had naturally fallen off and we were declared "home free" by the company's chief hospital corpsman.

✦ ✧ ✦

There were other important aspects of our preparation that filled the days before our departure. Most exasperating was the cataloging and loading of the major equipment we would haul with us to the Kuwaiti assembly area, such as weapons, communications gear, and accessory items. The MPF squadron provides most, but not all, of the equipment required for an LAV company to operate. Much of our company's maintenance expertise had departed with the advance party shortly after the company was designated as the fly-in echelon, but that didn't matter much anyway. As each day passed, the battalion gradually assumed control of Delta Company's vehicles one by one to supplement the other companies. Those LAVs that did not get signed over to the other companies were slowly raped to provide spare parts for the vehicles within the battalion that weren't operational. By the time the battalion boarded its ships, the few remaining LAVs within Delta Company were mere skeletons of their former selves, missing tires, main guns, alternators, and everything else that had made them run. It was a depressing end to the vehicles the Marines had worked so hard to keep running over the previous year and a half of training.

There were mandatory briefings, too. Most of them were planning meetings at Fifth Marine Regiment, the unit 1st LAR Battalion would fall under for the duration of the deployment. With the attachment of 1st LAR Battalion, Second Tank Battalion, a combat service support company, a combat engineer company, and an assault amphibian company, Fifth Marines quickly transformed into Regimental Combat Team Five (RCT-5). It was a hell of a force, comprising approximately six thousand personnel and nearly two thousand vehicles of all types—M1A1 Abrams tanks, amphibious assault vehicles (AAVs, or "amtracks"), LAVs, humvees (or HMMWVs—high mobility, multipurpose wheeled vehicles), seven-ton trucks, bulldozers, and fuel tankers. For division planning rehearsals, the commanding general had devised the idea of "Lego drills," in which each unit would bring a mat to which Lego blocks had been affixed to represent every vehicle in each RCT. Only that way could the commanders get an idea of the magnitude and scope of the operation ahead, as well as the space considerations involved in housing a regimental combat team's allotment of vehicles and Marines and allowing room for them to maneuver. I saw the Lego set for RCT-5 one day while I was at their headquarters. It was staggering. As I stood there staring at it, one of the regimental operations officers came up to me.

"What do you think?" he asked, motioning to the thousands of tiny, plastic icons arrayed before me. I nodded my head and looked back at him.

"That's a shit-ton of vehicles," I replied.

Another dose of reality came one day as I attended a regimental planning session for what would become the war's first operation. Intelligence had indicated that Saddam Hussein would likely attempt to destroy his oil infrastructure in southern Iraq as soon as the United States invaded. Of particular importance was a series of gas-oil separation plants (GOSPs) located in the

Rumaylah oil fields north of the Iraq-Kuwait border. It would be one thing for Hussein to ignite his oil wells as he had done in Kuwait in 1991. Such sabotage could be dealt with relatively easily (if you call recapping a flaming oil well "easy"). The GOSPs, however, were complicated, high-dollar facilities that weren't easily replaced if destroyed. Part of the overall plan called for seizing Iraq's oil infrastructure intact so that it could be used to help pay for reconstruction after hostilities ended. Continued oil production would further enable Iraq to capitalize on its major source of revenue once its government was functioning. RCT-5 had been given the task of seizing four of these GOSPs. To the east, RCT-7 had a similar mission. At the time of the planning session little was known about these GOSPs. How big were they? Would they explode if a firefight occurred while securing them? And just how big would that explosion be? There were a lot of unknowns at the time, but the original plan for the "Opening Gambit," as the operation came to be called, would require the efforts of nearly every unit within 1st Marine Division.

There were more personal things to be attended to as well. I hadn't seen my parents since before I had left for WestPac the previous April. As soon as the company got the word that we would re-deploy I informed them, and they arranged to fly out to San Diego for a weekend. Their trip was hastily planned, and they were adamant that it should not interfere with my preparations with the company for our departure. Normally Ashley and I would have planned activities for the four of us, but there was no time or desire for that on this occasion. After they arrived we spent a lot of time talking about my past deployment, but very little time talking about the impending one. A noticeable tenseness permeated the atmosphere around our house, and when I was called in to work one day that weekend I was relieved to be able to get away from everyone for a couple of hours.

My father had spent twenty-seven years as a naval aviator, during which he had done several tours in Vietnam. There was a period of about five years in my childhood when he was deployed about six months out of every year. I had never analyzed it too much—I just thought it sucked, and I knew there was nothing I could do about it. But now here I was, thirty years old and preparing to leave my family for what would probably become a war halfway around the world. I realized that I was putting my father through the same thing he had put his family through years earlier, and he wasn't handling it well. The day they were supposed to fly back east, I had to say my farewell to my parents before heading to work. I said good-bye to my mother, who as always showed a brave face and gave solid support.

"Keep your head down," she said as she hugged me. "Don't be a hero."

This was nothing new to her. She had done it numerous times with my father even before I was born. As my father walked me out to my car that last morning I realized it was going to be very emotional for him. I told him several times, "Dad, I'm just like you were—I'm bullet-proof. I'll be back soon." His eyes filled with tears, and I could see what a struggle it was for him.

✦ ✧ ✦

We all complained about a lot of things in the final days leading up to our departure from Camp Pendleton. But there was one thing that was without a doubt worse than anything else: the waiting. Several days after the company was designated as the fly-in echelon, we sent twenty Marines ahead of us to serve as our advance party. They were the lucky ones. The rest of us began a period of intense frustration during which we never knew if each approaching weekend would be the last one home with our families. One week after the advance party left, the company was placed on twenty-four hour alert.

Delta Company suffered in this purgatory for over three weeks, and it was horrible. The greatest victims during this period were the wives. Like many others, Ashley and I felt we had to treat each weekend as if it would be the last one in which we would be together for a long time. There were trips to places where we had never been, there were errands to run, and there were tasks that had to be completed. Was the will updated? Was the power-of-attorney current? Where the hell was all my income tax paperwork?

Then there were the unpleasant "talks" that we had to have. *Don't expect to know where I am for quite a while. No, I have no idea how long I will be gone. If I die, this is how much money you are going to get from the government.*

It was agony for my wife. Six months earlier, when I left for WestPac, she knew there was little chance I would get into any trouble. For this trip, however, she wasn't so sure. But I was surprised one evening about a week before I departed when she said, "I'm done. I am not going to cry anymore before you leave." And she didn't.

There was one other significant incident in my personal life before I left, and it was completely unexpected. The last week in January I received a phone call from the man who had been my best friend since high school. He and his fiancée wanted us to meet them in Las Vegas that weekend so he could see me before I left. I agonized over the decision. How could I drive five hours each way to see a friend when I frowned on my Marines doing the same thing? I told him I would think about it and left it at that. As much as I wanted to see this guy who had been such an important part of my life for nearly seventeen years, I was having difficulty making the decision to leave the San Diego area for an entire weekend. Once my company staff caught wind of it, they were adamant.

"Are you crazy, sir?" my company first sergeant said. "Go! Now!"

"What if the recall comes while I am away?" I asked nervously.

"We'll call you and cover for you until you get back here."

Ashley was equally supportive.

"If you don't do this you'll regret it all weekend, and well after that," she told me that Friday night. "Let's go now while we have the chance." Five hours later we were in Las Vegas with our friends.

That was my last weekend in the States. Two days later, after leaving work I received a call from the first sergeant.

"Sir, we just got a call from the division embark officer. We're leaving tomorrow."

Delta Company mustered at the company area in Las Flores just before midnight on Tuesday, 4 February. Before any deployment there is always a lot of speculation about how many and who will not show up for the final accountability formation. For some reason that was one of those things that I didn't worry about this time. The men all knew it was our time to get the job done, to earn our pay. I was sure everyone would show up.

I was wrong, but there were extenuating circumstances. As soon as I had walked through the company office's door we received a call telling us that the infant daughter of Staff Sergeant Thomas Reeves, the platoon sergeant for 2nd Platoon, had been seriously injured in a terrible automobile accident earlier in the evening. She was in critical condition. I spoke over the phone with her doctor, and I was faced with my first leadership decision of the deployment.

Should I make him go with us or not?

Staff Sergeant Reeves was one of my best. A Gulf War veteran and former tanker, he was the epitome of a staff non-commissioned officer (SNCO). Direct, intense, and passionate about his work, he also was sincere and thoughtful. I cringed at the thought of leaving him behind. But before I could open my mouth my first sergeant appeared behind me and opened his.

"Sir, we can get the remain-behind personnel to fly Staff Sergeant Reeves in with Lance Corporal Weise in a couple of weeks." Chad Weise, a scout from 1st Platoon, had been diagnosed a week earlier with some sort of phantom bowel condition. His doctor was convinced that if he spent even one day in the field his colon might rupture. Weise was non-deployable until the results of his medical tests came back, which would be at least another two or three weeks. First Sergeant Ruben Guzman, a quick-talking veteran of both

Desert Storm and Somalia who sported a magnetic, Cheshire cat smile, had proven his worth to me once again. As I told the doctor to take care of SSgt Reeves and his child and to keep us informed, I knew I would be in good hands with men like 1stSgt Guzman looking after me.

Meanwhile, the atmosphere around the company barracks was somber. Scattered about the parade deck were small clusters of Marines huddled together in the chill night air and chain-smoking like there was no tomorrow. Also spread around in groups were Marines with their wives, girlfriends, and children. There was little laughter. Ashley had driven me to the company area, and after less than an hour's waiting around I finally had to put her in the car and send her away. Dragging out the inevitable was painful, and I couldn't take it anymore. Any longer and I feared I would break down. She would have enough tears for the both of us, and I felt it was best to say my good-byes to her and get on with the deployment. She knew that the final good-bye at the base was coming—I had done the same thing six months earlier when she took me to the naval base in San Diego. Now, standing there in the parking lot, I told her I loved her and that I would be back soon. She sat in the car, looking very small behind the steering wheel, and slowly drove away with tears welling up in her eyes. I later found out that she made it about two blocks before she had to stop the car. Her tears were blurring her vision.

As I watched her car turn the corner, I stood motionless. Looking down at the asphalt, I suddenly wondered if I would ever see her again. Despite previous deployments, it was a feeling I wasn't used to. I slowly walked back to the barracks and the smoking pit, where ten or fifteen Marines were puffing away. Reaching into my pocket, I pulled out a pack of Marlboro Lights and my Zippo lighter. As I lit a cigarette and gazed at the legend etched into the lighter's face—"Instant Gratification"—one of the Marines piped up.

"Hey sir, I thought you quit!"

"Yeah," I replied, exhaling smoke. "So did I."

◆ ◇ ◆

Soon the baggage trucks arrived, followed shortly after by three chartered tour buses. We loaded our baggage and began piling into the buses for the ninety-minute drive to March Air Reserve Base (ARB). While several Marines had done the same thing I had and sent their significant others away earlier, there were still many loved ones watching us as we boarded the buses. Good-byes were painful for everyone. I was the last one to board, and after making one last accountability check of all the buses, I was suddenly faced with a crowd of sobbing wives, girlfriends, and children. Not really knowing what to say, I simply told them that we would all be back soon. I seemed to be saying that a lot lately, but what the hell else was there to say? This time I said it with some doubts, however. The division had been planning for a year-long deployment, and the likelihood of everyone coming back alive and in one piece was dim.

The trip across the dark Southern California countryside was quiet. Only the slight buzz of a couple of Marines chatting in the back of the bus filled the cold air, but I don't think anyone slept despite the early hour darkness. Each man was too wound up in his own personal thoughts. The company arrived at March ARB at 0330 and stepped off the buses into the freezing cold. The hangar was already packed with the Marines waiting for flights, so we had to wait outside until our turn came. Although our flight was scheduled for 1000, we quickly learned it would be delayed, and everyone began passing the time dragging on cigarettes in the smoking pit or sleeping on the cold concrete. *This is no way to begin a war*, I thought, but the Gulf War vets among us ensured me that they had played the same "hurry up and wait" game twelve years earlier. As darkness turned into daylight, and the frigid night air was replaced with heat shimmers rising in waves off the tarmac, the company grew restless. But we waited. And waited. After stewing on the flight line for nearly twelve hours and enduring several false alarms for boarding call, we finally climbed aboard a United Airlines 747 for the ten-hour flight to Frankfurt, Germany. *About damn time,* I thought. *Let's get this show on the road.*

My staff and I were fortunate enough to fly in first class, which made the flight bearable. Having never traveled first class in my life, I had always wondered what it would be like. Now there I was, but the presence of all of our combat gear and the complete absence of in-flight drinks seemed to detract from the whole "first class experience." Throughout the trip the flight attendants and crew were incredibly nice—almost too much so. They kept running their mouths on the plane's public address system about how proud they were to be flying us and how they wished us the best. By the flight's end it felt like we were being led to our executions, and the aircrew was administering us the last rites.

We stopped in Frankfurt for a one-hour layover that quickly turned into a two-hour stop. I called Ashley to tell her how far we had made it, but our conversation was cut short when my flight was suddenly announced. Five hours later Delta Company landed at Kuwait City International Airport.

3
LSA–5

We landed in the early morning darkness in Kuwait feeling like a dirty secret being smuggled into the country. After one last good-bye from our flight attendants we gathered our combat gear and were escorted off the flight line to a staging area outside the airport. As we sat there basking in the glow of generator-powered floodlights and freezing our asses off at the same time, everyone remarked how the last time we were in Kuwait it had been hotter than hell. With nothing to do but wait for buses to arrive to shuttle us to our camp, the Marines sat around in groups, talking and smoking. A gunnery sergeant appeared with vats of coffee and hot chocolate, and the Marines began filing through the line to grab Styrofoam cups of steaming liquid.

Our ride finally showed up at around 0400. After piling in, we endured another two hours of being transported by the civilian-contracted buses to Camp Coyote, where 1st Marine Division was located. We ended up at Logistics Support Area Five (LSA-5), a swath of nearly empty terrain alongside the U.S. Army's Udairi Range training complex. Our arrival in Udairi was like returning to the scene of a crime, as we had been in the same training area for three weeks the previous September and October, during our WestPac. The Marines spent most of the day lazing around outside and suffering from jet-lag. It really hit me around 1600. After lumbering around in a stupor for two hours, I curled up in my sleeping bag and slept straight through the night until 0600 the next morning.

I awoke having to piss like a racehorse. I donned all my gear and made the five hundred-yard trek to the closest Port-a-Jons around, only to find most of them already overflowing with shit, piss, and blue water. Life in LSA-5 had gotten off to a great start.

After returning to our company area, I suddenly realized I had no idea what the date was. Counting days on my fingers, I finally settled on 8 February, though I still was not completely sure. I hadn't experienced jet-lag in a long time, and the extended flight and the time change were really screwing with my head. As I sat there trying to gather my bearings, 1stSgt Guzman sized me up.

"Man, you look like shit, sir," he said, grinning.

"Thanks." He was nothing if not honest. My skin was pale, and big bags had formed under my eyes. A throbbing headache pulsed behind my eyes.

Later, as I picked at an MRE (Meal, Ready to Eat—what passed for our field rations), Spool—Captain Mike Peitz, our company's forward air controller (FAC)—appeared at my side. He told me a leader's reconnaissance north to the Iraqi border had been scheduled for 0900. Spool had earned his call sign (or familiar radio code name) as a UH-1N Huey helicopter pilot by being high-strung and getting easily spun-up about a lot of things. Sometimes he would get so agitated that he would spit inadvertently while talking. That didn't bother me. He had real-world experience from flying in Afghanistan, and in the month he had been with Delta Company he had taught the Marines more about close air support and aerial medical evacuations (medevacs) than I would have guessed there was to know.

He went on to tell me our battalion commander would be at the meeting, and he asked me if I wanted to go. I met up with everyone at the RCT headquarters, but I was unable to find Lieutenant Colonel White. Duffy White, our battalion commander, had left Camp Pendleton with the rest of 1st LAR Battalion as part of ATF West. He and the principal members of the battalion staff had flown from Singapore in order to arrive in theater for planning with the RCT. Rather than looking for him and getting lost, we ended up grabbing a humvee and a driver ourselves. Captain Christian Portiss (my company executive officer, or XO), and First Lieutenant Andrew Manson, the battalion's intelligence officer (or S-2) appeared, and we piled into the vehicle. We followed a convoy of humvees, which consisted mostly of battalion commanders and operations officers from the RCT, and headed north through the training area towards Iraq. Five kilometers south of the border stood a fifteen-foot-high sand berm, which we skirted along, heading west, for five or ten kilometers, stopping occasionally to look over the barrier into Iraq. We joked that if Saddam had only known what we were up to, one good artillery round could have taken out the entire leadership of RCT-5.

When we returned to the LSA, we found that the Port-a-Jon flooding still had not been resolved. Quality of life in the camp was already becoming an issue. Shaking my head in disgust at the human waste spilling from the portable chemical toilets, I jumped into my humvee again and drove to an adjacent camp to find Staff Sergeant Jason Kappen and Staff Sergeant Brian

Monroe. Kappen, the company operations chief, and Monroe, the company's maintenance chief, were heading up the preparation of all the vehicles and equipment that had arrived earlier in the week. I was anxious to link up with them and get a look at the vehicles and equipment they had taken delivery of from the MPF ships. I spoke briefly with Kappen and Monroe, but I still wasn't up to full power after my jet-lag. I headed back to LSA-5. With no electricity in our tent (and thus no lights) I crawled into my sleeping bag and racked out. As I was falling asleep, I groggily thought to myself, *We are fewer than fifty kilometers from the Iraqi border, but so far this seems like just another field exercise at Twentynine Palms. When does it get exciting?*

The next morning I awoke to the sound of Marines relieving themselves all over the place outside our tent. After voicing my displeasure to 1stSgt Guzman at the mass voiding of bladders outside, I spent an hour or so listening to Delta Company's SNCOs yelling at Marines to stop pissing in the dirt and to walk their lazy asses to the overflowing Port-a-Jons.

Later that evening I watched as the company corpsmen began issuing auto-injecting syringes of atropine, 2-pam chloride, and Cana—a cocktail of nerve agent antidotes. It was sobering to sit there and hold in my hands those seven injectors, knowing that we might be forced to use them on ourselves. If the reality of what we were about to do had not yet set in with each of my Marines, it would very soon.

✦ ✧ ✦

On the morning of 10 February, 1stSgt Guzman, two of the platoon commanders, and I jumped into a bashed-up humvee and headed over to the arrival and assembly area where the company's vehicles were being serviced. On our first day in camp, Guzman and his driver had been rear-ended by a 7-ton truck from another unit. Now we were bouncing around the desert in a vehicle whose doors would not close all the way. Holding on as tightly as I could, I feared I would be thrown out and killed even before the war began. At the arrival area we found all twenty-five of the company's "new" vehicles, many in states of repair or assembly. Spare parts were everywhere, hanging out of wooden shipping crates and cardboard boxes, and the company's mechanics were running around under SSgt Monroe's direction. He told me the vehicles were coming along well, with only minor problems detected so far. I was pleased—it had seemed at first glance like the LAVs we had taken custody of from the MPF squadron weren't too bad off. As soon as I said that aloud, a mechanic approached Monroe and told him they needed to pull the engine out of the LAV-C2 because of a transmission leak. Unbeknown to us, the tip of a maintenance iceberg had just surfaced.

✦ ✧ ✦

The next day I learned that Delta Company would be attached to First Battalion, Fifth Marines (1/5) for the Opening Gambit. One-Five's mission was to secure four GOSPs to keep the Iraqis from destroying them. Delta's piece of this mission was to secure GOSP-1 and then screen two high-speed avenues of approach to the east in order to catch any enemy personnel who were withdrawing from RCT-7's zone of action. It was a good mission, and together with our Weapons Platoon, Delta Company was more than up to the task. Until just before we left for Kuwait Delta Company hadn't even included a Weapons Platoon. Before the 2003 deployment to Kuwait, all companies within the battalion had operated "under-strength." Because MEUs never wanted to deploy with an entire twenty-five vehicle company, a deal was struck between 1st LAR and its two parent organizations, 1st Marine Division and the MEF: MEUs would deploy with sixteen-vehicle companies. The remaining nine LAVs from each line company consolidated and formed the battalion's Weapons Company. But as the battalion began to form for deployment, the decision was made that all companies would fight as twenty-five-vehicle entities. I couldn't have been happier when I heard the news. Prior to leaving Camp Pendleton the battalion attached six LAV crews to Delta—enough Marines to man four antitank and two mortar variants—to bring the company up to full strength. There had been some friction integrating the Weapons Marines into the company, but we were happy to have them.

✦ ✧ ✦

Some Marines tend to think that once the word is given that they are going to war, the bureaucracy and administrative restrictions of peace-time will go out the window. In Kuwait, it became clear to Delta Company that this is not the case. We discovered early that things get just as screwed up, if not more so, once everyone begins ratcheting down for combat. The company's first live-fire shoot on 12 February at the regimental firing range—dubbed "Grizzly Range"—was cancelled because of improper coordination for the ammunition. It wasn't the last training "SNAFU" we experienced during our lead-up to the war.

In place of attending the cancelled range, I sat in the troop tent and analyzed the intelligence summary and satellite imagery 1/5 had provided me. The GOSP facility was a hairy place to be. It had three large oil storage tanks filled with raw crude, and one or two gas-oil separation vessel compounds. If these were hit with small arms fire, or if any booby-traps planted by the Iraqis were triggered, they would go up in flames like fireworks on the Fourth of July. If that happened and we were close by, or worse, actually *in* the compound, the flames would likely incinerate us instantly.

Mulling over the volatile objective, I glanced over at First Lieutenant

Chad Parment and began watching him with interest. Parment, 1st Platoon's commander, was a prior-enlisted scout-sniper who generally only spoke when he felt he had something important to say. Pensive and subdued, he was clearly the most intelligent officer in the company; but I also often considered him the laziest. He had spent the better part of the day constructing a gun-bag for his M-4 carbine using a foam sleeping mat. As he sat there determinedly cutting and binding the contraption with duct tape, it began to take the shape of the old saddle holsters cowboys used to carry their rifles in when they rode their horses. Parment was totally focused on it, swearing to all of us that it would work.

As I alternated between scribbling in my journal and watching Parment wrestle with his Frankenstein's monster, Kuwaiti contractors roamed around in our tent, installing lights. Two of them were behind me putting up one of the long fluorescent tubes, and I got that weird feeling of someone looking over my shoulder. I slowly realized that the Kuwaiti wasn't looking at me, but was instead ogling a picture of Ashley I had placed next to my journal. I was trying to keep an open mind and be tolerant, but the longer I was away from home and closer to danger, the less tolerance I had. Part of me was tempted to hold the picture up to his face and say, "Take a closer look, asshole!" Another part wanted to stand up and knock his block off.

My attention was diverted by the sounds of Parment completing his gun bag. He placed his carbine in it and withdrew it, testing it out. I had to admit, it looked good. He stood up, held up his creation triumphantly to everyone as if to say "Kiss my ass," and walked out of the tent to go mount it on his turret. It worked perfectly, and I suddenly found myself wishing I had thought of it first.

On the morning of 13 February, as I sat on my campstool copying operational graphics and typing checkpoint grid coordinates into my GPS, Corporal James Thyden cornered me and told me my LAV was down with a broken fuel pump. One of the best mechanics in the company, Thyden had an incredible passion for his job. I appreciated his directness, and because of that he knew he could always come right to me and tell me about maintenance problems within the company. However, this frequently led others to accuse him of insubordination and disregard for the chain of command.

"How long will it be down?" I asked him, knowing a spare parts shortage had already developed in-country.

"Don't worry, sir," he told me, turning the broken piece over in his grimy hands. "We'll get it up and running." I expected my vehicle to be sidelined for quite a while, but two hours later SSgt Monroe appeared with a new fuel pump. A new air compressor also sat in a box behind him.

"Where did you get those?" I asked, raising an eyebrow. "Or do I want to know?"

He looked at me and said, "I've got contacts. Don't worry about it, sir." His resourcefulness never ceased to amaze me; but sometimes I wondered.

◆ ◇ ◆

On the afternoon of 14 February, Delta Company began staging for its movement to Range 4. Ironically, Range 4 was the same location where, the previous October, one of the company's Marines had stepped on a 40-millimeter grenade that critically injured him and sprayed two others with dozens of tiny slivers of shrapnel. It had been the first time anyone in Delta Company was seriously injured during training under my watch. The Marines and corpsmen at the scene had performed superbly as they applied first aid to their three injured comrades, and Capt Portiss had executed a flawless aerial medevac request. Later I was beside myself with guilt because the Marines had wandered downrange not knowing where the impact area began. I had accepted responsibility for the incident, but this did nothing to erase the fact that those three Marines would carry around shrapnel in their bodies for the rest of their lives. Had the mishap not been overshadowed by an Al Qaeda terrorist attack on 3/1's Lima Company the day before on Faylaka Island—resulting in the death of one of its Marines—I'm positive I would have been relieved of command for the entire incident. Instead, I got a lesson in ensuring my men were informed, and I saw first-hand the value of making certain that all Marines were properly trained in combat first aid.

Delta Company departed LSA-5 at sunset for a night road march to Range 4. For nearly five hours the company's column slowly snaked across Udairi Range, and we made it to our release point exhausted but without incident. The vehicles arrayed in a wide circle, forming a tactical assembly area, and I ordered everyone to dig in for the night. There was some grumbling and groaning in the cold darkness, but because the sand was so soft the Marines had no trouble digging deep holes. After completing my own sleep trench, I spent the evening freezing two feet below the surface as dirt sifted down on top of me all night.

The Marines awoke before sunrise the next morning and prepared to calibrate the company's main guns. We quickly discovered that our firing position was right in the middle of an adjacent unit's surface danger zone (SDZ), and it took precious time to solve this geometry problem. Shortly after that there was a medevac called in somewhere in Udairi Range, which shut down all training until the emergency was resolved. Just as they had so many times back home in Camp Pendleton, our training plans were quickly going to hell because of events beyond our control. Fortunately, Capt Portiss had a contingency plan, and he directed the company to begin "round robin" instruction that covered most of our functional areas. Stations were set up around the assembly area for communications procedures, GPS and map reading, weapons assembly and disassembly, and calling for, observing, and adjusting supporting arms. Portiss was an outstanding officer. He and I had bumped heads many times since we had begun working together, but there was no doubt in my mind that he knew what he was doing. I was happy to have him as an XO. He had been a sergeant in the Reserves before he was commissioned, and his maturity was far beyond my own. Even when he was promoted to the same rank as I while we were aboard ship, he never took advantage of it. To him I was always "CO," "Captain Folsom," or sometimes even "sir." Many officers might opt for a new XO once their old one was promoted to the same rank, but there was no way in hell I was going that route. When it came to training and fire support planning, he was my right-hand man.

Delta Company didn't finish its weapons calibration until after 1600. As night approached, the company trundled south to a secondary range to shoot some 25-millimeter high explosive incendiary tracer (HEI-T) rounds and to test-fire all eight of our TOW missile launchers. The company was ready to shoot shortly after sunset, and after the TOWs fired, the LAV-25s began sending rounds downrange. My vehicle's gun immediately developed problems. Even after Lance Corporal Davis and I disassembled it and attempted to fire again, it still refused to function properly. Josh Davis was a slow-talking good ol' boy from Booneville (pronounced "Boon-vul"), Mississippi, who tended to hide his significant intelligence behind a redneck personality. He was a good gunner, and we had grown close in the past year.

We called over the company's turret technician, Staff Sergeant Leslie Ryan, and he went to work on the gun system. As he and Davis were pulling the weapon apart and reassembling it, I stood on the muffler deck next to the turret, talking to Chief Warrant Officer Joe Day. Joe was 1st LAR Battalion's coalition/foreign military exchange officer, and he and I had developed a quick friendship once he had been temporarily attached to Delta Company for the flight to Kuwait. We were still uncertain whether or not his country's military would permit him to go to war as part of our battalion, but everyone was keeping his fingers crossed. Down in the turret Davis and Ryan attempted to fire the main gun, but I didn't hear him yell out the standard warning "On the way." The cannon went off next to me with a thundering, metallic *ka-chunk,* the concussion knocking me over and almost off the vehicle. Without hearing protection the blast was deafening, and it was so painful that I thought it had ruptured my eardrum. My right ear continued to ring for weeks afterward, a constant reminder of my dangerous, momentary carelessness.

The two Marines in the turret worked on the gun for several hours, alternately cursing and laughing with each other the entire time. By 2230 the only thing we had to show for their efforts was Davis's blood all over the inside of the turret from when he had pinched his finger between the gun's feeder assembly and the thermal sight housing. I was beginning to tire, and the temptation to have the company bed down for the night there at the range was growing stronger. I weighed the options. I could put the company to sleep where we were, or I could inflict the long night drive on them. As much as I was screaming to myself, *Screw it! Go to sleep and drive back in the morning!* I knew that, beginning very soon, there would be times when the company would be expected to drive for long periods while everyone was tired. I finally made the call to take the company back across the training area to LSA-5. They surely hated me for it, but I also knew they would appreciate the night of sleep in a tent rather than on the cold, sandy ground.

The trip was excruciating. Standing in my turret, exhausted and shivering violently, I cursed myself again and again for deciding to return to camp. I developed a splitting headache from having fastened my CVC (combat vehicle crewman) helmet too tightly, and the depthless, green luminescence of my night vision goggles (NVGs) began to give me double vision. We moved at a crawl, the LAVs visible only as blurry, two-dimensional images through the tubes of our NVGs and thermal sights. The company finally pulled into camp at 0300, and 1stSgt Guzman approached me to ask what time he should announce reveille. He didn't have to work hard to convince me to allow the company to sleep late. They had earned it.

Late in the afternoon on 16 February, the MEF Commanding General showed up at LSA-5 to talk to all of the Marines and sailors. Lieutenant General James Conway was a Marine's Marine, and an exemplar for other generals. Tall, with a deep, booming voice, he inspired everyone around him. The man had my utmost respect and admiration, and that of many others. Many among us believed he was in line to be the next Commandant of the Marine Corps.

Lieutenant General Conway gathered the RCT's entire officer corps and spoke privately to us first. He urged us not to be foolish in combat. He went on to say that when a unit loses an officer the Marines take it very hard. I wondered just how hard Delta Company would take it if I bought the farm. *Not too much, I'll bet,* I thought. After speaking with us, Conway jumped up on a podium and addressed the RCT over a public address system. While he spoke, he described how the MEF was going to hit the Iraqi army like a football linebacker.

"Marines, it's not going to be a fair fight," he growled. "And we don't intend it to be." On that cue, two F/A-18 Hornet jets screamed 100 feet above our heads, trailing earsplitting sonic booms in their wakes. Four AH-1W Cobra helicopter gunships followed immediately at the same altitude. The regiment's Marines raised their fists and cheered mightily. It was a motivating sight. Clearly the general was trying to impart to us that we wouldn't be alone out there, that we would have all the firepower the Marine Corps had to offer looking after us.

✦ ✧ ✦

On the morning of 18 February I decided to go with the lieutenants to Camp Mathilda for a round of new training they had started the previous day. Several days earlier, the vehicles belonging to Delta Company's officers had been designated to have the Marine Data Automated Communications Terminal (MDACT) installed on each. A small, shoebox-sized computer equipped with a GPS tracker, the MDACT was also pre-programmed with digitized maps. Controlled by a digital network, it was designed to track friendly and enemy units on the battlefield. It had been heralded as one of those inventions that would revolutionize the battlefield. The lieutenants had returned from their training the previous night claiming the MDACT was the greatest thing since canned beer. It was important for me to learn more about this piece of equipment, especially since an MDACT was scheduled to be installed on my vehicle. The classes lasted all day, and I was frustrated by the time it was over. I wasn't grasping the system as quickly as the others, and I didn't fully trust it. The more I pondered it, the less I liked the idea of test-driving the new, unfamiliar device into combat.

We returned to the LSA, our vehicles rolling onto the makeshift LAV maintenance ramp in the sand. Before I could climb down from the turret, 1stSgt Guzman came up to me and announced he had news that wouldn't make me happy. A television crew from Music Television (MTV) had been in the camp earlier in the day, interviewing Marines around the area. During the course of the interviews, the TV crew asked a Marine from Third Platoon if he was scared. Supposedly he had said "yes." Months earlier, the division commander had emphasized to the Marines that, when confronted by the media, they were not to show any personal weakness in front of the camera. Guzman went on to tell me that a corporal from Weapons Company who had been detached from the battalion to be the commanding general's mechanic had wrecked the general's LAV *and MTV filmed the entire thing.* He had driven it into a wadi (dry riverbed), bending a strut and breaking off the machine-gun mount in the process. After that televised jackassery, the battalion decided that Delta Company would provide another mechanic to replace the corporal, who would then come to Delta. I immediately got a chip on my shoulder about it. My anger at the first Marine's loss of bearing on camera was quickly overridden after I learned about the personnel switch. I grudgingly agreed to swap Marines as directed, but stipulated that the transfer would only be temporary.

The operations officer then cornered me and told me he wanted Delta Company to provide Sergeant Jeremy Osborn to teach a motorcycle course that would equip each company with at least two scout riders. I began discussing it at length with Osborn, but I wasn't sold on the idea. It was but one more example of how the battalion had been leaning heavily on Delta Company to support it with manpower, training, and equipment, and it was aggravating me.

The problem was compounded when Fourth LAR Battalion's Alpha Company, a reserve unit from Las Flores, arrived in camp later that afternoon. Their LAVs were aboard cargo ships and wouldn't show up until sometime in mid-March. Having Alpha Company with us in Kuwait was a mixed blessing. Their presence took some of the heat off Delta Company, but suddenly we were expected to facilitate their training because they had no vehicles. At the risk of others in the battalion thinking I was "one-way," I expressed concern that Alpha's significant requirements would affect Delta's training.

The longer I stayed with the battalion, the more I began to question much of what its staff was doing in preparation for battle. I think by that time I was experiencing feelings about the battalion staff probably not atypical of those that hard-working junior officers often feel: basic respect for them and their positions, but a frustration that they were merely on "cruise control" and not responding to the needs of the company commanders. In considering decisions that the battalion staff were making, I wondered if they really realized what the line companies might be about to head into: multiple casualties; chemical attacks leading to contaminated remains of Marines being left on the battlefield; decisions about what kind of information to pass back to our families; and so on. The bottom line, I guess, was that I felt like the battalion was somehow too eager to put us in harm's way.

At the same time, I may have been second-guessing my own level of readiness, as I wondered constantly if we had crossed every *t* and dotted every *i* in our frantic, last-minute training and preparation for the coming war. The irony of my situation was that any doubt I felt was a double-edged sword. Two persistent thoughts plagued me deep down: one, it was my duty to support the battalion commander and his staff's legal orders, and two, I had fought hard to get Delta Company on the short list for war. Was I just as eager to put my Marines and myself in harm's way? I figured time would tell on that issue.

◆ ◇ ◆

On the morning of 19 February I briefly addressed the men of Delta Company. I wanted to impart to them the importance of getting in the right mindset for what we were about to do, as well as the importance of ensuring that our weapons and equipment were as ready as our minds. During my entire time as their commander I had never been very good at giving motivational talks. It comes easily to some people, but not me. Usually when I tried to do so, whatever came out of my mouth sounded insincere, falsely optimistic, or downright stupid. The company knew I usually relied on quotes from famous people or from movies. This time was no exception.

"Our time is coming," I told them, quoting William Manchester. "And coming very fast." Before we knew it we would get the order to cross into Iraq, I told them, and we had to be ready to do it at a moment's notice. I went on to give them a brief overview of the Opening Gambit and the company's planned role in its execution. After the Marines were dismissed, I stood there and wondered, as I often did, if my words had had any meaning or effect on them. Was I making a difference, or was I simply white noise droning on and on?

After the sun set on 20 February, Delta Company stepped off from camp to establish a tactical assembly area (TAA) in preparation for a regimental breach rehearsal scheduled for the following morning. By that point many of the Marines had begun to get sick with some sort of upper respiratory infection. We called it "the crud," and the best explanation we could come up with was the desert itself. For centuries men and animals had been pissing and shitting in the sands around us, and after several weeks of inhaling the blowing dust, that shit had settled in our lungs and was making us ill. I was among the ailing. I coughed and hacked continuously, and fatigue was setting in. To make matters worse, what should have been a one-hour administrative movement to the assembly area turned into a four-hour excursion. By the time the company arrived in the TAA and I finished scraping out my shallow sleep trench in the rock-hard ground, I was exhausted. The battalion staff was supposed to rendezvous with us at 2200, but that time came and went and they were nowhere in sight. I crawled into my bag and fell sound asleep.

After midnight a Marine woke me up and told me that the battalion command element's convoy had arrived at our assembly area. I looked at him and mumbled, "Good for them," and rolled over back to sleep. Five minutes later he returned and shook me awake again.

"Sir, the S-3 needs to see you ASAP."

"Man, what the hell," I murmured to myself, crawling out of my hole. I donned all of my gear and walked across the darkened assembly area to where the command element's humvees had parked. Major Harper gave me some checkpoints for the rehearsal, and then gruffly called me aside, away from everyone else. He got on my case about the company not having its camouflage vehicle nets up, and he chided me for not being around when the battalion commander showed up.

"You aren't out with the MEU anymore," he said sharply. "So get off your own program. If you want me to be an asshole, I can be one." I couldn't tell if those were the CO's words coming out of his mouth or not. After all, I didn't work for the S-3—I worked for the battalion commander. But I suspected Maj Harper was the messenger in this case. There's an old saying that "shit flows downhill," so I wrote the incident off to experience. I respected Harper; he was incredibly intelligent, and he knew what he was doing. But I was pissed off that he was pulling that kind of crap. If I had ever been "on my own program," it was because the battalion had pushed me that way. As I had led Delta Company over the course of the previous year and a half, I had had to fight for the battalion staff's support. Since the company's return from deployment in 2002 and our re-attachment back to the battalion earlier in the year, things had not changed. As Maj Harper stood there chewing my ass off, I had only one thought: *Walk a mile in my shoes.* I stomped back to my vehicle, severely agitated and mumbling countless expletives to myself.

The breach rehearsal the next morning went relatively smoothly despite some degree of friction with the engineers conducting the breach. The engineers had erected a huge mock-up of the two earthen berms and the electrified fence we would have to pass through as we rolled from Kuwait into Iraq. We still encountered problems trying to properly integrate Weapons Platoon and convince its Marines to employ the company's standard operating procedures (SOPs), but I tried to give them the benefit of the doubt. Dave Hudspeth ran a tight ship in Weapons Company, but the Marines who had come from his company to Delta didn't want to give up their old ways. One of the qualities that had made Delta so outstanding in the field was its strict adherence to the SOPs we had developed over the previous year and a half. It had always been a case of everyone jumping into his vehicle and knowing exactly what to do. But integrating the Weapons Platoon was like starting over, and I frequently heard Marines in the company complaining about the Weapons personnel "doing their own thing." Their talk reminded me of my episode with Maj Harper.

The evening rehearsal on 21 February was delayed until 2030, and once it kicked off, it lasted much longer than anyone had anticipated. Visibility through our night vision devices was poor, the going was slow, and the engineers ran into problems marking the breach lanes properly. Three breach lanes were supposed to be carved out for the RCT to pass through, but at the last minute the engineers radioed and said the far right lane was fouled and impassable. I radioed 2nd Platoon, the element designated to pass through it, and informed them that an obstacle blocked their path. After my vehicle had passed about 200 meters through the opening in the berm, I glanced off to my right to see 2nd Platoon's vehicles driving down the fouled lane. I radioed them and told them to back up, but instead the LAVs simply turned left out of the lane and crossed over the notional minefield all around us and into my lane. I started shouting at them over the radio, but it was too late. The rest of the passage through the breach lanes was quick, but Weapons Platoon failed to properly mark their vehicles with the infrared strobes as I had told them to do earlier in the afternoon. When the rehearsal was over I voiced my displeasure over the foul-ups with several ass-chewings. The Marines glumly mounted their vehicles for the road march back to LSA-5, their spirits sinking.

I awoke the next morning hacking up big green globs of mucus. My upper respiratory infection was in full swing, and I wasn't the only one whose chest felt as if a heavy dumbbell was resting on it. Throughout the tent Marines coughed and wheezed. It sounded like a tuberculosis ward. Lying in my sleeping bag with my eyes closed, I heard a deep, familiar voice above me.

"Look at this guy. You sorry piece of shit." I opened my eyes to see Captain Don Tomich—Alpha Company's commander from 1st LAR Battalion, who was currently deployed with 15th MEU—standing over me. He slowly shook his head, feigning disappointment. The two of us sat around the tent, shooting the shit for a while. Our reunion was interrupted when Spool walked in, jittery and excited as usual. He had arranged seats for us on a reconnaissance flight to the crossing points at the Iraqi border. By 1030 we were aboard a UH-1N Huey flown by Captain Jim Isaacs, an old OCS buddy of mine from 1992. We flew around the southern berm for close to an hour, observing the crossing points and the land beyond, in Iraq. I had carried a borrowed camcorder with me, and as I filmed the ground the company would cross on the way to and from the breach I thought, *Man, this is an unreal feeling: looking at the ground we will eventually travel across and into Iraq.* As Jim circled around and headed back toward the LSA, he took us over the camps of 1st Marine Division and the U.S. Army's Third Infantry Division. Below us thousands of armored vehicles of all types massed around the camps as tiny figures moved about, preparing them for the moment when we would all get the order to go. The panorama of the armored juggernaut amassing beneath us was breathtaking, and I thought, *If ol' Saddam knew what was coming for him, he would just crap in his pants.* The Iraqis would be out of their minds to oppose a force like the one assembling in the rippling desert sands beneath us.

✦ ✧ ✦

On 23 February Delta Company mounted its vehicles and drove to Grizzly Range to continue test-firing and calibrating our numerous weapons systems. Because we were sharing the range with several other units, training didn't get underway until several hours after our arrival. It was a long day, and the company didn't return to camp until after sunset. I sat down with the company staff, and together we mapped out a plan to get all of the LAV-25s to Range 4 later that evening. The scouts and mortar teams would return to Grizzly the next morning for more small arms firing.

After attending an after-action conference with the regimental staff, I hitched a ride to Grizzly Range to watch the Marines throw grenades and fire our 81-millimeter mortars. But by the time I arrived the scouts were in a check-fire status because a Marine from another unit had thrown a grenade without pulling the thumb-clip safety device. The range was shut down until personnel from explosive ordnance disposal (EOD) could come to our location and blow the grenade in place.

While the Marines waited on EOD, SSgt Kappen shuttled the Delta Company scouts back to the LSA, and I walked over to the mortar position to watch the crew shoot. After they fired a couple of times, I asked Second Lieutenant Brad Stiller and his mortar platoon sergeant, Staff Sergeant Vince Peralta, how quickly the mortar crews could get "fire-capped" (ready to fire a mortar mission). Having only joined the company with his Weapons Platoon in January, Stiller still stood out from the other lieutenants in the company. He had come highly recommended from Dave Hudspeth, but I was beginning to think Stiller was not only arrogant, but also a know-it-all—two qualities a second lieutenant definitely should *not* possess. Stiller and Peralta boasted that their crews could get fire-capped in a minute and a half.

"Prove it," I said. The first attempt took their mortar crews six and a half minutes—a far cry from a minute and a half. Peralta fumed and begged for a second chance for his crews to prove themselves. The second time around they did it in one minute and thirty-four seconds. *Not too bad,* I thought, nodding approvingly.

While I waited for the rest of the company to return from Range 4 late in the evening, SSgt Kappen pulled me aside. He had heard some Marines from Weapons Platoon talking and knew I needed to hear what they had said. The previous evening as the company was leaving Grizzly, Lt Stiller had backed his LAV-AT into another LAV in his platoon. The collision had dented up both vehicles. It was the first time I had heard about the mishap. I was furious but chose not to wake the lieutenant. Instead I decided to let him get a good night's sleep before I laid into him the next day.

✦ ✧ ✦

Shortly after sunrise on 25 February a sandstorm rolled in, smothering the camp. The stinging sand and reduced visibility restricted the Marines to their tents for most of the day, but as the afternoon wore on, the weather began to clear up. I walked Lt Stiller out to his vehicles and read him the Riot Act for not telling me about his vehicle accident. After yelling at him for five minutes, I figured he had gotten the point.

Later that afternoon at the battalion staff meeting I was surprised to hear the news that Delta Company was no longer to secure GOSP-1 during the Opening Gambit. Though disappointed that the company wouldn't get to execute such an important, strategic mission, I also felt some measure of relief that I wouldn't be compelled to place my men into such a volatile area. That feeling was amplified when intelligence reported that the Iraqis had begun reinforcing the GOSPs with artillery and infantry. Going into that situation could cause a bloodbath. When I told the company staff about the mission change they all exhibited disappointment, but I think some of them were secretly comforted as well. Doing your job is one thing. Going on a potential suicide mission is something altogether different.

I exited the company meeting wondering about the company's morale level. As a company commander—as an officer—I often found it difficult to gauge how the men felt. Despite the closeness I felt to them after all we had endured, the bottom line was crystal clear: I just was not one of them. They were never going to come up to me and tell me that they were pissed off and why. They aren't supposed to, and sometimes that makes it difficult for an officer to really know what is going on inside his unit. My father had often told me about the "loneliness of command," and I was beginning to understand it well. Most of the time I relied on my first sergeant to provide me with the pulse of the company, but I also liked to sneak out on my own and find Marines who I knew would tell me the truth just as Guzman would. As I wandered around the ramp, watching the Marines work on their vehicles, I found SSgt Monroe and Staff Sergeant Ramon Navarro sitting and talking in the rear compartment of Monroe's vehicle. Navarro, the platoon sergeant for 3rd Platoon, was short and built like a fire-plug, and usually had the temper to match. He was the company's martial arts instructor, and there was a general consensus that no one would want to fuck with him. At the same time, he was a conscientious Marine, and you could tell he wanted his men to be the best they could be. He always spoke from the heart, and I enjoyed listening to him.

The two SNCOs talked with me. Or rather, they complained to me for an hour. But I needed to hear it, and I kept my mouth shut and listened to them vent. Among other things, SSgt Navarro confided in me about some of the discipline problems he was having among his scout teams. Two of his corporals in particular were giving him problems. Navarro was relatively new to the job as a platoon sergeant, and many of the Marines were fond of neither him nor his hard-assed approach to the job. Their attitude hadn't changed since our return to Kuwait.

"Sir, these motherfuckers got no idea what they're in for," Navarro vented. "We're getting ready for combat. Fucking *combat*! And they're still acting like fucking bitches. So I told them, you want to act like bitches, I'll treat you like bitches. You want to play 'Who's the Alpha Male?' I'll play with you, motherfuckers."

He was on a roll, and I didn't dare interrupt him. But I could see his point. Here we were, fifty kilometers from the Iraqi border, and reality wasn't setting in for many of the Marines. I had never been in combat, and that fact kept me on edge every minute of every day. It seemed to me the Marines must feel the same. But then I began to realize what the problem really was. We had been idling in the desert for twenty days. It's difficult to get excited about something when you are going through the same boring routine all day, every day. Our time in the desert had come on the heels of a stress-filled month wondering if and when we were even going to re-deploy. Suddenly it seemed like we were just sitting on our asses and repeatedly playing the same stupid games. A well-trained company was withering on the vine. With no firm date for the beginning of the war, I began to realize that my greatest challenge wasn't preparing my Marines for combat. Instead, it was keeping Delta Company from tearing itself apart before the war even began.

4

Stir Crazy

Several hours after our conversation by the LAV, SSgt Navarro stormed into the troop tent. He cursed loudly and dropped an armful of long, silvery blades next to his gear. I watched intently as he knelt down next to his platoon commander, First Lieutenant Doug Cullins, and told him that one of their Marines had just been stabbed in the leg. Because of that, Navarro had confiscated all personal knives from the men in his platoon. Cullins, a quiet but intense officer with the driest sense of humor I had ever heard, wasn't one to go off half-cocked about anything. Once he got Navarro to calm down, he asked to hear the whole story, and Navarro related what had happened.

I sat listening to SSgt Navarro explain how the Marine in question had been stabbed "accidentally" while another Marine was sharpening his knife. While trying to get to the bottom of the injured Marine's bullshit story, Navarro met significant resistance from several of his non-commissioned officers (NCOs), who attempted to cover up the real cause of the incident. Navarro demanded that everyone in his platoon hand over their personal knives, and when one corporal refused, there was a scuffle between the staff sergeant and the corporal.

That evening I read statements written by Marines who had witnessed the episode. Clearly, trouble was brewing, and Navarro and Cullins obviously had problems with their NCOs. Yet I hesitated to get involved. I pulled Cullins aside and talked with him about the incident.

"Well," I asked him, as we stood outside the tent, smoking. "What's going on?" He looked at me, shook his head slowly, and thought for a moment. He then answered.

"I've got some fucking problems in my platoon, sir."

"What do you want to do?" I replied. "I don't want to impose any command influence here, but I can see at least two charge sheets coming out of this."

"No doubt about it, sir. I'm sick of these guys' crap. They're acting like shitheads."

Grinding out my cigarette, I turned to head back into the tent. "Well, just let me know what you want to do. It's up to you. In the meantime, unfuck your platoon. This is the last goddamned thing we need right now."

I went searching for 1stSgt Guzman. My ears led me to the troop tent, where he stood inside yelling at the top of his lungs. He was ordering the entire company of Marines to hand over their personal knives.

"You want to act like fucking kids?! Fine! We're gonna treat you like kids!" The Marines walked up to him one by one and dropped their knives in a growing pile at his feet. *What the hell?* I thought. *Has it gotten this bad?*

I had thought the fact that the men were heading into combat soon would sharpen their edge. Instead, the farther we went—the longer we waited—the duller that edge seemed to get. A malaise was settling over the company, and all at once the problem's *real* source hit me. It wasn't just our stagnation in the desert—the company was tired. No, they were beyond tired—they were burnt out.

And as I sat in the tent attempting to find a solution to the problem, I realized something else: I was just as fried as they were. It was difficult for me to get motivated about anything. The only excitement I could generate came from my famous ass-reaming explosions at the company staff—excitement and agitation over things that were probably of little significance. But there was nowhere I could go to vent my frustrations. This wasn't Vietnam; there was no officer's club where I could go drink my warm beer ration and stew by myself. We were in the Middle East, a region where alcohol is strictly off-limits to U.S. troops. But there was tobacco, and so instead I spent much of my time chain-smoking Marlboros and chewing tobacco as if it was part of my job description. The long days, weeks, and months of the last year and a half were finally taking their toll. I was afraid the finely-tuned machine Delta Company had crafted itself into would soon begin to unravel like a cheaply-made sweater.

✦ ✧ ✦

Captain Portiss and I scheduled platoon and company maneuver training for 26 February. That morning, while the company was out rolling around in the desert, my crew and I drove around the training area to observe each platoon. After watching 2nd and 3rd Platoons, we headed west in search of 1st Platoon. As a company commander I missed the days when it was just me and a platoon with four vehicles, and I got nostalgic whenever I watched the lieutenants working closely with their Marines. As we drove in circles trying to find Parment and his Marines, the battalion radio net beeped to life. First

Lieutenant Tom McGee, the battalion communications officer (S-6) called for me, but before I could answer he began yelling into the radio.

"Gas! Gas! Gas! This is not a drill!"

Holy shit!

Up in the turret LCpl Davis and I snapped our heads and looked at each other, our eyes as big and round as tea saucers.

"*This is not a drill!*" McGee yelled the alert again over the radio net. We dropped everything we were doing as we scrambled to don our gas masks.

Ten seconds, man, I kept saying to myself. *Remember your training. Get it on in ten seconds. Open the mask carrier, pull out the mask, now pull the mask out of its waterproof bag. Fuck! Why did I put it inside the waterproof bag? There's no water out here! Jam it on your face, blow out and clear the mask. Test it. Are you breathing? Good. Pull the straps around your head and cinch them down. Is it comfortable? Hell no, but it's on and it's working. Now call the rest of the company, asshole!*

While I radioed the company and repeated McGee's alert to mask up, Davis leaned down inside the turret. He began yelling at Private First Class Bryce Gurganus in the driver's compartment and Corporal Kevin Harter, our communication technician, in the scout compartment.

"Get your fucking masks on!" he yelled, his order muffled by his own mask. "Corporal Harter, wake the fuck up back there! Gurganus, get your fucking mask on!"

"Are you up?" I called over the intercom. "Everybody sound off!"

"I'm good," said Davis.

"Up," replied Harter.

"I'm okay," added Gurganus.

As the initial rush of adrenaline took hold of my system, I keyed my headset and attempted to locate the platoons. One by one the platoon commanders reported that their men were all masked up. Soon the S-3 radioed and directed me to move the company to a position ten kilometers west of LSA-5, away from any potential area of contamination. After a great deal of confusion I finally rallied the majority of the company, and our column made its way to a hasty assembly area along the 36 easting (north-south-running gridline). Once in place I jumped down from my vehicle and ran to the XO's position. There I learned we were still missing the vehicles commanded by the first sergeant, SSgt Monroe, and Sergeant William Lyman, who were all stuck at the outlying camps. A few minutes later, the S-3 radioed again and directed me to execute a fifty-percent "selective unmasking" procedure. I turned around and ordered the platoons to perform the unmasking process on half of each vehicle crew and monitor the Marines for signs of a nuclear, biological, or chemical (NBC) attack. Normally the unmasking procedure is performed on a select few junior Marines (actually the most junior men in the unit). It is a long, complicated process in which, little by little, the subject is exposed to the environment by breaking the seal of his mask a certain number of times over a certain period. But we were being ordered to unmask half our number at once. *Either someone is pretty confident this is a false alarm,* I thought wryly. *Or the battalion NBC officer doesn't know what he's doing.*

Twenty minutes passed with no symptoms of an NBC attack among the unmasked Marines, and the battalion radioed the "all clear" signal. Walking around during the alert and finding Marines hiding in vehicles and not wearing masks, I grew unhappy with the company. Many platoons hadn't taken the alert seriously, and their leaders bore the brunt of my displeasure. I passed the order to return to camp, but as we approached the outskirts of LSA-5 the battalion radioed again.

"Gas! Gas! Gas! This is not a drill!" the voice on the other end repeated. *Okay, this is getting ridiculous.* We masked up again, and once more the battalion directed Delta Company to return to its previous position. The Marines took the alert more seriously the second time, but I suspected it was only because I had thrown such a fit the first time. Not too far under the surface they were all telling themselves it was just another bullshit false alarm. Twenty minutes later their suspicions were confirmed when the "all-clear" signal was relayed.

We returned to the LSA, tired, sweaty, pissed off, and frustrated at the false alarms. Needless to say, after all the disorder and selective unmasking, no one looked forward to the real thing.

✦ ✧ ✦

First LAR Battalion's main body had been appearing in force over the preceding several days. As the battalion's vehicles began arriving from Ash Shubayh (the main port in Kuwait) so too did Marines from the other companies. Many were bitching and talking trash about the condition Delta Company had left its vehicles in after returning from its WestPac. First Sergeant Guzman approached me one day soon after, confiding in me that the sergeant major had told the battalion commander I should be relieved of command. I laughed out loud.

"Whatever! He doesn't know a friggin' thing about LAV maintenance aboard ship." My coolness suddenly turned to anger. "Besides, we didn't even have a chance to work on the vehicles before the battalion started taking them away from us after we got back! *Jesus Christ!*"

Guzman paused and replied, "I know, sir, but I'm just telling you that's what he said. The master guns don't like you either."

"I can fight my own battles, First Sergeant."

"Yes, sir, I know you can. I just wanted to let you know what people are saying about you behind your back."

"Whatever. Screw them. Next time you hear someone talking smack, tell them I said to eat shit." I stormed outside and fired up a cigarette. As I stood there fuming to myself, Staff Sergeants Kappen and Monroe approached me.

"Hey sir," Monroe asked. "Did battalion really say that shit about the company?"

"I guess so," I replied, exhaling smoke. "According to the first sergeant."

"Those motherfuckers!" he yelled. The only thing Monroe cared about more in the company than the maintenance of the LAVs was the Marines themselves. "Battalion maintenance told me the vehicles were fine when we signed them over to 'em. That's fucking bullshit!"

Kappen joined in. "Man, screw them bitches, sir. They're just jealous because they know Delta does everything better than they do."

I paused and looked at him. *"Do* we? After all, *I* sent the company out on leave after we got back from WestPac instead of turning-to immediately on corrosion control. *I* knew the battalion was ramping up for Iraq by that point."

"Yeah, but you'd cleared that with the CO months before," Kappen replied. "The battalion never told you to change the plan, and rather than jam the Marines who had all already made vacation plans, you let them go on leave. What's the problem with that?"

Monroe jumped in. "I'll bet those sumbitches didn't do jack shit with the vehicles while they were floating over here."

I appreciated their support, but I also knew they were unable to give objective opinions. The rumors flying around weren't just a slight on me—they reflected on the entire company. The two SNCOs were simply defending the honor and reputation of their own organization.

◆ ◇ ◆

After picking through an MRE, I sat down, put a wad of tobacco in my lower lip, and began writing in my journal. As I recounted the events of the previous days, the tent flaps sailed open and a breathless Marine ran in.

"Gas! Gas! Gas!" he screamed, pulling his mask from its carrier strapped to his hip.

Goddammit! Not again!

Everything went flying. Papers, MREs, weapons cleaning gear, you name it. Marines desperately searched for their gas masks, tearing through their equipment as it lay in piles around the tent. I was so concerned with donning my own mask that I forgot about the plug of Copenhagen in my mouth. Only after I had obtained a good seal and was breathing correctly did I realize the dilemma I now faced. We had no idea what was going on, so we had to take the alert seriously. That meant that once I had my mask on, it had to stay on. Soon my mouth filled up with bitter, brown tobacco juice, and I faced a sickening choice: I could either swallow the crap slowly filling up my cheeks or else just let it all out. If I swallowed it, I risked puking inside my mask, which would ruin not just *my* day, but probably the day of everyone around me. The alternerative was to face the consequences of my actions, keep my mask on, and empty the contents of my mouth into my mask. I chose the latter, and little by little my mask filled with tobacco spit. *Man, this is gross,* I thought to myself. *This is about enough to get me to quit dipping for good.*

As my gas mask slowly became an aquarium, I walked over to the battalion's combat operations center (COC) tent to find out what was going on. No one knew, and I returned to the tent after receiving the order to begin selective unmasking within the company. First Sergeant Guzman pulled aside four junior Marines and sat them down for the procedure. After he explained how it worked, we both sat down with the Marines and talked to them while we monitored them for symptoms of an NBC attack. Soon the false alarm ended. I walked outside, broke the seal of the mask around my jaw, and leaned over. Several mouthfuls of stringy brown saliva inside the mask poured out onto the sand. I was thoroughly disgusted with myself.

As I went to work cleaning out my mask with a box of wet-wipes, I wondered about the potential repercussions of the false alarms we had been experiencing. They were more severe than the possibility of my drowning in my own nasty, brown dip-spit. I feared that if the false alarms continued the Marines would cease taking the NBC alerts seriously or, worse, would begin refusing to selectively unmask when ordered to do so. The young enlisted Marines were learning that they were considered expendable because they were the ones required to unmask first. It was a shitty deal all the way around, but the only way we could do it. Imagine someone you trust in your chain of command coming up to you, taking away your weapon, and ordering you to break the seal of your gas mask and inhale the possibly contaminated air around you. Now imagine other Marines guarding you at gunpoint while all this is going on. It had been one of those things as lieutenants we used to joke about in Quantico. Now it wasn't funny at all.

The evening of 27 February, while I attended a battalion staff meeting, the company stepped off for a road march while wearing gas masks. We were getting all the NBC training we needed, and at the rate we were going I was sure the Marines would all be duty experts by the time the war eventually came. Shortly before the company rolled out of the camp I was in the head. I heard the now-familiar scream signaling another NBC alert. Like Clark Kent in his transformation into Superman, I jumped out of the phone booth–like Port-a-Jon, gas mask in hand. As I scrambled to don it I began laughing uncontrollably. Marines were exploding from the Port-a-Jons in various states of undress, all desperately trying to don masks whether their trousers were pulled up or not. Already in their masks for the road march, Delta Company was unfazed by the mayhem of Marines running around yelling "Gas! Gas! Gas!," and one by one the vehicles departed camp for the evening's exercise.

I walked to the COC to see what was going on, but all that greeted me was general confusion. Picking up a radio handset, I directed Capt Portiss to take the company ten kilometers west back to the position we had occupied during the first false alarm. While the company displaced, the battalion commander walked into the tent and began passing routine administrative information to all of us. In between his words I started hearing over the radio what sounded like Portiss saying there had been a vehicle accident, but we couldn't confirm this because the quality of the communications relay was so poor. I suddenly found it difficult to concentrate on the meeting as I wondered if anyone had been hurt.

After the meeting and the false alarm both ended, I returned to the troop tent just as the company slowly rolled up the gravel road into camp. Portiss jumped down from his vehicle and told me that as the company waited at the assembly area during the NBC alert, the floodlights from a nearby airfield began blinding the vehicle commanders (VCs) wearing NVGs and the drivers staring through their AN/VVS-2 "fishbowl" night vision viewers. Sergeant Cesar Rocha, a quiet Marine from 1st Platoon, angled his LAV-25 too close to one of the LAV-ATs, and the spare tire on the starboard side of his vehicle clipped the front of the TOW vehicle. The damage was minimal, and with my initial concern about personnel casualties alleviated, I became angry about the carelessness of the vehicle commander. When the VC loses visibility, he is supposed to stop or slow down his vehicle and let the vehicles around him know he is doing so. Clearly Rocha hadn't done so.

After informing the battalion commander of the mishap, I returned to our tent to speak to the company staff. Restraining myself as much as possible, I told them how disappointed I was by the company's recent chain of vehicle mishaps. I used to repeat a colorful phrase I had learned as a lieutenant: "You can build a thousand bridges, but if you suck one cock you won't be remembered as a great bridge-builder but instead, just a cocksucker who builds bridges." With Delta Company's growing list of antics, 1st LAR Battalion was quickly forgetting about all the bridges we had built in the last year and a half.

◆ ◇ ◆

On 28 February, following a battalion formation, I followed LtCol White to his tent to express my maintenance concerns to him. My report complete, I took the opportunity to apologize for the relative crappiness of Delta Company's recent performance. He looked at me for a moment and then spoke.

"Just peak at the right time, Seth." I was unsure what that implied, and in the end I convinced myself it meant, "Yeah, you've been screwing the pooch, buddy. But I don't care as long as you do your job once we're in Iraq."

After the evening battalion staff meeting, one of the platoon commanders approached me, wanting to get one of his platoon corpsmen a call home to check on his dying grandmother. I went in search of Major Mike Bodkin, the battalion executive officer, and asked him to let me use the battalion's coveted satellite cell phone. It didn't take much convincing. Mike Bodkin was a genuine guy, someone who you could tell really cared about doing the right thing. With his approval I sought out the S-6 for the cell phone, and after wandering in circles looking for him I finally cornered him in the COC tent. He handed me the phone, and I was so frustrated and irritated that I said "to hell with it" and called Ashley first. *I'm just testing it out, making sure it works*, I convinced myself. I limited my conversation with her to two minutes, but hearing her voice for even that tiny bit of time drastically improved my outlook on life. I found the "doc" (as it seems all Navy corpsmen are known to their Marine counterparts), and together we made about thirty attempts to get an adequate satellite signal. As we were about to give up hope, a signal finally came on line and he got in touch with home.

While talking to Maj Bodkin earlier, I broached the subject of possibly authorizing use of the satellite phone by Delta Company to make morale calls. My Marines had been out in the desert longer than any of the others with no communications home, while the men from the battalion who had sailed with ATF West had at least had some access to either email or shipboard satellite phones. He agreed to my request and promised to raise the issue with the chain of command. But deep down I already knew the answer: there would be no morale calls for the company.

But I had bigger fish to fry. I had lost nearly all confidence in the vehicles Delta Company had drawn from the MPF squadron. Day after day they continued to break down, and nine of the twenty-five LAVs weren't operating correctly. To make matters worse, the spare parts shortage in-country had worsened. There was no relief in sight, and each night the battalion maintenance officer, a young chief warrant officer named Jerry Copely, would read from a laundry list detailing the inoperable vehicles in the battalion and the deficiencies in critical parts. It was infuriating, particularly in light of the fact that Delta Company was to be entrusted as the main effort if the battalion were ordered to cross the line of departure immediately. I knew that our equipment was not ready to accomplish the mission. And I wasn't the only one. The Marines knew it as well, and they were getting restless. Roaming the camp, I would hear the men grumbling in private.

"How the fuck do they expect us to fight a war if we don't have the parts to fix the fucking LAVs?"

"I guess we're gonna have to tow our vehicle into combat!"

My ability to mitigate this lack of confidence was declining. After all, I agreed with them. Just how in the hell *were* we supposed to go into combat without spare parts? I began to wonder at what point I would have to go to the battalion commander and announce that Delta Company wasn't mission-capable.

◆ ◇ ◆

On the afternoon of 1 March, Delta Company returned to the training area south of LSA-5 for more maneuver training. Over the radio I drilled the platoon commanders in calling for air support and for indirect fire while their platoons engaged the notional enemy. In a typical drill, Capt Portiss would coordinate fire support with Spool and the rest of his fire support team (FiST), and then they would hand control of the supporting fires over to the platoon commanders one after another. For the platoon commanders it was one more opportunity to prove they knew how to employ their platoons quickly and efficiently. More important to me, however, was that they had demonstrated the ability to *calmly* call for and control supporting fires over the radio. That was the first step. None of us knew if it would turn out that way under fire or not, but having long observed the lieutenants in training I was confident of their abilities. Even before the company re-deployed to Kuwait, when I was having misgivings about the leadership abilities of two of the platoon commanders, I opted to keep them in the company for the war. Despite my opinions of them as persons, in my heart I knew they were technically and tactically proficient. I had finally begun to realize that you don't have to share the same views or philosophy as your subordinates to be an effective leader. It was one of those myriad lessons I wish I had learned years before I became a company commander.

Delta Company returned to camp. An hour later, the XO walked into the tent and told me Lance Corporal Quezada from 2nd Platoon had collapsed while exercising. The corpsmen had treated him and had then taken him to the battalion aid station to get a bag of intravenous fluid into him. After telling me this, Portiss paused and gave me a knowing look.

"The whole thing seems kind of sketchy to me," he said. First Lieutenant Brandon Schwartz stood nearby, and I turned to him.

"It's a heart problem, sir," Schwartz said. "He doesn't have any. He was straggling earlier when my scouts were rushing the objective during training." That was easy for him to say. First Lieutenant Schwartz was the biggest Marine in the company, a real monster who stood well over six feet, weighed close to 250 pounds, and sported biceps the size of softballs. I had the feeling that he usually classified people into two broad categories: "good-to-go" or "wussy." I directed both officers to look into it as I departed for the COC to check in from training. By the time I returned, Lt Schwartz had investigated the matter, and he briefed his findings to me. A corporal from his platoon—a notorious goldbricker and spotlight performer—had ordered two younger Marines to take Quezada on a run with his rucksack as punishment, but failed to go himself to supervise. Initially the corporal denied the accusation, but when the hulking lieutenant suddenly towered over him he came clean. As Schwartz relayed this to me, it was obvious that he had changed his tune about Quezada, and instead was angry that one of his men had been abused. I thought he would blow a gasket; unless, that is, I blew one first.

We discussed it with the first sergeant, and having considered statements made by two Marines who corroborated the story, we decided to charge the corporal in question with cruelty and maltreatment of a subordinate. First Sergeant Guzman read the corporal his rights, and as we had predicted the Marine refused to make a statement and demanded to see an attorney. I viewed this particular corporal as a "sea-lawyer," the kind of guy other Marines knew they could go to if they were in trouble because he always knew some legal loophole to escape justice. His mere presence chapped my ass, and I believed that there wasn't an officer or a SNCO in the company who didn't feel the same. In my opinion he was an embarrassment to his fellow NCOs, and I had wanted nothing more than to see him get knocked down a peg by losing a stripe. Now it looked like he had finally fallen on his sword.

The next morning my crew saddled up, and with SSgt Monroe's vehicle in tow we moved out to re-calibrate our LAV's main gun at Udairi's Range 9. The weapon problems we experienced on Range 4 two weeks earlier had prevented us from getting a good "zero" on the main gun; it was imperative that we confirm the battlesight setting on the Bushmaster. The tedious process of aligning the gun barrel with the sights and then test-firing it on a known-distance target gives the only true indication of where a round will go when you pull the trigger. Without it you can be sure you won't hit what you're aiming at. Our two vehicles linked up with Weapons Company around 0900, and Dave Hudspeth gave me a belt of 25-millimeter ammunition to zero the Bushmaster. We rolled onto the firing line to confirm our zero, but after one round the gun jammed again. Staff Sergeant Monroe and LCpl Davis went to work on it, and together they ended up completely dismantling the gun's complicated feeder assembly. With the weapon in pieces, Monroe installed a sprocket modification to the high explosive feed shoot, all the while explaining to Davis what he was doing step by step. His expertise with the gun—as well as other facets of maintenance—was simply phenomenal. It was like watching an artist at work. My level of respect for him continued to grow more each day.

When we got back from the range Capt Portiss and 1stSgt Guzman called me into the tent for a briefing. Portiss told me two Marines in the division had drawn their weapons on each other. In another incident closer to home, two Marines in 1st LAR Battalion's H&S Company had an argument over, of all things, a spaghetti MRE. The confrontation escalated, and one Marine pulled a knife and stabbed the other in the stomach. It seemed the monotony of our desert isolation was getting to everyone.

Portiss then told me a division-directed maintenance stand-down had been put in effect to allow all units to make sure their equipment was operational. There was a genuine concern that division units would break too much gear before the war began. But the higher headquarters failed to take into account the situation Delta Company and every other unit that came from the MPF squadrons faced: our vehicles had been stored on ships for so long that they were now beginning to fall apart. Seals and gaskets had rotted, electrical connections had corroded and broken, and weapons systems were missing routine modifications. We needed to operate the vehicles in the field for a while to work the bugs out, but we weren't going to get the chance.

The XO turned over the briefing to 1stSgt Guzman, who told me the results of the corporal's visit to the legal section that afternoon. The lawyer believed it was simply a case of an NCO administering extra military instruction (EMI, also called "NCO justice") to a subordinate. The battalion adjutant later told me that if the NCO requested a court-martial in lieu of nonjudicial punishment, the case would likely be dismissed. We felt strongly enough about the case that we were willing to take that chance. My only concern was whether the battalion commander would back me up if the Marine requested a court-martial.

✦ ✧ ✦

The S-2 forecasted another sandstorm for 4 March, and it rolled in early, confining the Marines to their tents once again. I began proofing the operational graphics created by the battalion staff, but even after an hour trying to marry the list of checkpoints to the overlay graphics I had received, I couldn't make them match. Throwing up my arms in frustration, I went to the S-3 tent to get some answers. There the staff told me they knew the list was incorrect, yet they had published it anyway. I was furious. Hours had been wasted trying to process information the operations staff had known was incomplete and inaccurate. The ops officers had no answers for me, which made me that much angrier. I knew what would end up happening: I would end up writing my operations order for the company at the last minute, which is a bad way to do business if you have the time to do it beforehand. Who was responsible for this problem? Was it the battalion, or was it at a level higher than that?

That afternoon I spoke with LtCol White about the escalation of the suspected hazing incident. Earlier in the day the offending Marine had indeed demanded a trial by court-martial, and Guzman had forwarded the request up the chain of command. After pleading with the battalion commander for his support in the case, I was pleasantly surprised by his reaction. White had told the division legal officer that he planned to appoint an investigating officer for a preliminary inquiry of the case. If the results of the investigation warranted it, he would hold a competency review board and administratively reduce the NCO's rank to lance corporal. Confiding in me that he thought the corporal in question was a "turd" who knew how to beat the system, White also agreed the Marine shouldn't be an NCO. Like me, the battalion commander believed strongly in the importance of leadership within the noncommissioned officer ranks. Anyone who couldn't cut the mustard as an NCO didn't deserve to wear that second stripe.

Yet even with the battalion commander's vocal support, I was upset. This was what it had come to for me. My focus of effort had somehow shifted from preparing Delta Company for war to busting down one of my men. I felt as if I was losing control not only of my Marines, but also of my own ability to lead them in peacetime. If that was the case, how could I possibly show them the way when the bullets started flying?

5
All Times Zulu

The ultimate symbol of our self-induced friction and aggravation came at the battalion staff meeting the evening of 4 March. Major Harper announced that the MEF would switch to Zulu time that evening for the remainder of the operation. In real terms, the change meant we would shift our clocks three hours back to coincide with Greenwich Mean Time (GMT, or "Zulu," the same worldwide common clock time on which aviators base their operations). Practically it meant that taps, which normally went at 2200 each evening, would now go at 1900. Similarly, reveille (normally occurring at 0530) now went at 0230. Of course, there was no *real* time change—we weren't starting the day in the middle of the night, nor was everyone hitting the rack just after sunset. But a lifetime of conditioned behavior is not easily unlearned, and our instincts told us that certain things happened at a certain time on the clock. You would wake up at 0200 and think *Great, I still have over three hours to sleep,* and then thirty minutes later someone would shout "Reveille!" You would look at your watch at 1900 and think, *It's too early for me to be this tired.* Soon, whenever someone announced a time for a meeting, another person would immediately pipe in and say, "Is that Zulu time or local time?"

A mandate was finally issued to all hands: all times given are Zulu times.

◆ ◇ ◆

On 5 March, while Delta Company remained heavily occupied with the division's maintenance stand-down, LtCol White pulled me aside and told me I needed to call Ashley to clear up some misunderstandings within the company's KVN. A mistake had led the families to believe Delta Company was operationally attached to another RCT-5 battalion, and LtCol White wanted Ashley to hear directly from me the situation as it actually was. The confusion was, in fact, mostly of my doing. As we prepared to leave Camp Pendleton I had told her it appeared Delta Company would work with RCT-5 instead of

Delta Company in LSA-5, 5 March 2003.
Official Marine Corps photo by LCpl Andrew P. Roufs.

1st LAR Battalion. I had never updated what I had said. I tracked down the satellite cell phone and after several attempts I connected with her at her parents' home in Memphis. As soon as she spoke I knew she was miserable, and I hated myself for putting her through this. My constant absence over the course of the previous year and a half was beating her down. How much longer could she take it? She was strong, but how much was too much? I didn't know.

Meanwhile, media personnel were appearing around the regiment, and the teams designated to "embed" with 1st LAR Battalion arrived that day. A news crew from ABC News—including a reporter I had never heard of named Bob Woodruff and a journalist and photographer from the *San Diego Union-Tribune*—showed up. I cringed at the thought of my family seeing me on television, knowing that the odds of this would now increase. Ashley and her mother were fans of Peter Jennings, ABC's anchorman, and I secretly hoped they would decide instead to get their news from CNN.

On 6 March, as the maintenance stand-down dragged on, the Marines began stenciling names on their vehicles. Walking around the ramp, I noticed 2nd Platoon had named an LAV *Sodomizer*, and 3rd Platoon had christened one *Blue Balls*. Here now was the dilemma of the modern Marine officer: how to foster pride for their vehicles amongst your troops without allowing them to go overboard. Personally I didn't give a hoot *what* the Marines named their vehicles. One of my favorite movie lines was Marlon Brando in *Apocalypse Now* lamenting, "They train young men to drop fire on people, but their commanders won't allow them to write *fuck* on their airplanes because it's obscene." How true. Nothing is more obscene than training every day to kill people, yet we were bound by regulations that compelled us to be politically correct. We couldn't name our vehicles anything offensive. Unable to pretend the vehicle names had slipped past me, I did one of the things I hated more than just about anything in the world: I toed the party line. I found both Lieutenants Schwartz and Cullins and let them know their crews had chosen unacceptable names, and that changes were in order. It felt as if I was endorsing the greatest hypocrisy possible. We expected these young men to risk their lives, yet they were allowed to neither name their vehicles as they wished nor put Playboy pin-ups inside their vehicles. It was "chickenshit" like this that made Marines want to leave the Corps in droves.

Later in the afternoon, the company's officers attended the operations order brief for 1st LAR Battalion. The order was still incomplete and continued to change daily, but as it stood at that moment, Delta Company's mission was to provide security for the combat engineers as they reduced the western portion of the Iraqi berm. We would then conduct a zone reconnaissance to a major oil pipeline and establish a screen (picket) to the north. Second Tank Battalion and Second Battalion, Fifth Marines (2/5) would pass through our lines, and then First Reconnaissance Battalion would link up with us. From there we would guide them through the Ar Rumaylah oil fields to a highway "cloverleaf" about forty-five kilometers to the north.

Listening to the complicated op-order, everyone knew one thing was certain: the old saying, "No plan survives enemy contact" would apply for sure. But the lieutenants and I were excited. If the plan remained unchanged, Delta Company would be the first unit to cross the border from Kuwait into Iraq.

The next morning the Marines awoke beneath a fine blanket of powder, the result of a howling dust storm the previous evening. Our gear was filthy, but we were worse. Everyone was experiencing horrible, rasping coughing fits from the dust that had spent all night settling in their lungs. *Jesus,* I thought. *How do people live out here?* Storm or no storm, it was a constant battle to keep our equipment presentable and functioning. Oiling weapons only attracted more dust and grit, and no matter how clean you got your gear you could be sure that five minutes later it would be covered in a chalky film. We established a routine: each morning after reveille, before doing anything, the

Marines would sit and clean their weapons and magazines. No one wanted his rifle or pistol to jam at the moment of truth.

After dark, as I prepared for the nightly staff meeting, the normal buzz in the troop tent was interrupted by the burp of a machine-gun burst to the south. The word soon filtered down that a Marine from Charlie Company had discharged his M249 squad automatic rifle (SAW) while on guard duty. It was the first negligent discharge for the battalion since we had been in-country, and LtCol White was understandably hacked off. It's not difficult to observe the weapons safety conditions, and I continued to knock on wood that none of my Marines would do something so stupid and dangerous. There was worse news, though. Two nights earlier, a mishap had occurred when a Marine from the regiment had been checking a generator's fuel level. He didn't have a flashlight with him, so he used his Zippo lighter to peer down into the generator's gas tank. The flame ignited the fuel vapors, and he burst into flames from the chest up. The sturdy Kevlar of his body armor protected his torso, but he inhaled the burning fumes and sustained third degree burns to his neck, face, and arms. He was medically evacuated to Germany and wasn't expected to survive his injuries. Months later I learned that miraculously he did. The Marine and the generator were but one example of the numerous mishaps resulting in personal injury that had plagued the division since its arrival in-country. Several days earlier, we had been told that a Marine had been cleaning his pistol and negligently fired off a round. The bullet passed through his tent and the one next door, finally seating itself in another Marine's collarbone. Then we heard that during the MPF equipment offload a woman had lost both legs when she was pinned to a tractor-trailer by an errant amtrack. To cap it off, it was reported that a Marine from one of the division's battalions was hit in the face by the falling tailgate of a 7-ton truck. The tailgate's edge amputated the tip of the man's nose, both lips, his top and bottom rows of teeth, and the tip of his chin. He was flown to Germany to get a new face. All this, and the division hadn't even crossed the line of departure and faced the enemy. Following Delta Company's grenade mishap at Range 4 the previous October, I learned few things were worse than peacetime mishaps that injured Marines. In combat you could understand wounds incurred facing the enemy. In peacetime there was no justification, period.

✦ ✧ ✦

On the evening of 7 March, LtCol White personally spoke to the battalion and company staffs about casualty evacuation procedures, combat awards criteria, and mortuary affairs. The mortuary affairs brief was a sobering experience. The only death the battalion had dealt with in the recent past had been a young Marine named Private First Class McMillan. In January 2002, after his company returned from field training, he was crushed to death against a loading dock on the battalion maintenance ramp at Camp Pendleton. It had been difficult for everyone to handle, but time had faded our memories. As we discussed the procedures for bagging and tagging a Marine who had been killed in action, I sat there wondering how I would react if one of my Marines was killed. I had few illusions about everyone making it out of Iraq alive—there were just too many obstacles that could trip us up along the way. Would I be prepared if I lost one? Just what *would* I do? The nature of our job could result in horrific injury and destruction of the human body. How would I be able to ask Marines to pick up commingled body parts that used to be their friends? I knew I had to stop thinking that way or I would psych myself out before the war even began. I took to heart what White said as he discussed this grim subject with us.

"How you react," he said, "how your company's leadership reacts when a Marine is killed will set the tone for the rest of your men for the remainder of the war. If you collapse, they will collapse." His words resonated in my head as I made the long walk through the night back to the tent. Later, as I lay staring at the ceiling of our tent trying to fall asleep, I realized that the same sleeping bag I was lying in would also serve as my body bag if I were killed in action.

On the morning of 8 March the Marines formed up outside, and I walked out into the chill morning air to reenlist SSgt Monroe and 1stSgt Guzman. The two men had approached me several days earlier and announced that they wanted me to be the person to re-enlist each of them. The surge of pride this simple request instilled in me was remarkable. Guzman had more than seventeen years' experience in the Marine Corps, a veteran of both Desert Storm and Somalia. Monroe had much less time in the organization, but his request meant just as much to me. He had been adamant about getting out of the Marines once his enlistment contract expired, yet one day, out of the blue, Guzman had come up to me and announced that Monroe planned to re-enlist. Both were individuals upon whom I knew I could always depend, and I was so proud of them that I determined to make a big deal out of their ceremony. I spoke to the company at great length about each man's accomplishments and his contributions to the Marine Corps, and after realizing the embarrassment I had caused them, I told each one to raise his right hand as I read the oath of enlistment.

The emotional high of watching the two SNCOs reaffirm their oaths as Marines was quickly overshadowed by my sudden realization that it was Ashley's birthday. I was in a funk all day because I couldn't be home for her special day, particularly because her grandfather had passed away recently. My constant absence was surely wearing on her, and I wondered how long this roller-coaster ride would last before I would be allowed to get off and restart my life again.

Taking a walk around camp, I saw SSgt Kappen and his crew roll onto the ramp with more ammunition for the company. The Marines spent the afternoon happily cramming it all into their LAVs. As I walked from vehicle to vehicle asking the Marines if they had enough ammunition, the general response was along the lines of "I don't know how the hell I'm going to fit it all in here!" But while walking through 3rd Platoon's area I heard a different response from Sergeant Kevin Cole.

"You think we have enough ammo, Sergeant Cole?" I asked him as I pulled out a cigarette. He looked at me soberly. Cole had always been serious about his job in the company. He had spent most of his time as Lt Cullins's senior scout, and when, months earlier, it had appeared that he would have to execute orders to recruiting duty instead of deploying with the company for the war, he approached me in private to plead his case.

"Sir, you're not going to let them make me go to recruiting duty, are you?" he had asked one day. "You got to let me go with the company." I knew just how he felt—at the time I was unsure whether I would stay with the company or remain behind to execute my own orders to graduate school at Monterey.

"Sergeant Cole, if I have my way we'll both go with Delta to Iraq." We got our wish. A last-minute personnel change before the company left Camp Pendleton placed him as a vehicle commander in his platoon, but he didn't care. He was just glad to be with his comrades. Now here he was again, showing me just how serious he was taking our build-up to the war.

"No, sir. We still need more," he said, referring to my sarcastic joke about the ammunition. He paused, and then said, "A lot more. It will never be enough."

"You're ready for this thing to get started, aren't you?"

"Yes, sir. Let's get this shit over with so we can go home."

"I hear you," I said. "It won't be long now." But I was lying. I had no idea how long it would be. We listened to the BBC every day and I received the daily intelligence summary every night, but we were no closer to knowing when the war would begin. There was little discussion among the company officers about whether the war was right or wrong. All anyone really seemed to care about was when would it start and when would it be over. It was as if the coming war was an interlude between two acts of our lives and we just wanted to get on with the show.

Pondering my brief conversation with Sgt Cole, I wandered across the ramp to check on my vehicle crew. They worked hard, and I often felt guilty that I didn't put in nearly as much time as they did maintaining the LAV. As I approached the vehicle, LCpl Davis proudly pointed to the freshly stenciled name across the LAV's hull: *No Leaf Clover.* I laughed out loud, voicing my pleasure that he and Gurganus had named the vehicle after a song by Metallica. Davis explained that he had given it that particular name because, until recently, the vehicle (especially the main gun) had seemed plagued by bad luck.

"I'll tell you guys what," I said to both Davis and Gurganus. "Before we cross the line of departure into Iraq we'll play *No Leaf Clover* over the company's radio net for everyone to hear."

I walked back to the tent and found SSgt Monroe standing by himself, smoking a cigarette and staring aimlessly at the Marines loading their vehicles. I stopped to talk to him.

"We're really getting close to going, aren't we, sir?" he asked, dragging on his cigarette. He absently reached into his pocket and handed me a crumpled pack of Marlboros.

"Yeah, looks like it, doesn't it?" I replied, taking one. "You sure look serious today."

"I'll tell you what, sir," he said, almost to himself. "I don't know what I'm gonna do if one of these guys dies. That's why I refuse to get close to them, after what happened to Spanky." Corporal Spankenburg had been one of Monroe's best friends in the company. A year before I arrived in the company, Spanky had been killed in a brawl in Tijuana. It devastated Monroe, and by his own admission he had never been the same since his friend's untimely death.

"You know what you'll do," I said, matter-of-factly. "You're gonna keep your shit together just like the rest of the staff will. You heard what the battalion commander said . . . if we can't keep it together, our Marines won't be able to."

"I know, sir. But the company is tight. *Really* tight."

"Yeah," I said, thinking for a moment. I wondered if that fact would hurt us when someone got it. We didn't say too much after that. We just stood in silence and watched the Marines go about their work.

Despite the topic of discussion between Monroe and me, my mood had taken a turn for the better after talking with the Marines. It was further elevated later that afternoon. As most of the company staff sat in the tent shooting the shit, one of the Marines spoke up.

"Well goddamn, will you look at that?"

We turned our heads to see Staff Sergeant Reeves strolling in toward us. A big, shit-eating grin was plastered across his face.

"Anybody miss me?"

The Marines jumped up and grabbed hold of him, alternately shaking his hand and clapping him on the back. I remembered reading stories about Marines wounded in combat and being evacuated, then months later being reunited with their units in the field. This seemed like one of those times. Everyone was genuinely excited to see Reeves again, and he looked the same. It was as if he was home with us, back where he belonged. After more than a month he had finally made his way to Kuwait, and it was good to have him back.

"Did you bring Weise?" asked Lt Parment.

"I sure did, sir. His ass checks out okay."

"How's your daughter?" I asked.

"She's doing well, sir. Thanks," he replied. "Oh yeah, brought this for you." He reached into his sea bag and pulled out a crumpled, fat manila envelope. He handed me a package Ashley had put together at the last minute. As I tore it open, all kinds of candy fell onto the floor. On her birthday—from halfway around the world—she had given *me* a gift.

On 9 March Capt Portiss taught a class for the company on the standing rules of engagement (ROE), and soon every Marine seemed to be asking a situational question. As I stood back in the corner observing, Portiss patiently answered each question until I finally stepped in and told the company two things. I paraphrased what General Wilhelm had said when he was the commanding general. "If the enemy initiates contact with you, the question is proportionality of your return fires. If you initiate contact with the enemy, the question is what collateral damage you may cause."

I looked around momentarily, trying to read their faces. I continued.

"Marines, this is the important thing. If you perceive yourselves to be in danger, then you either return fire or initiate fire on the enemy. Period." I thought it was a simple matter, but it had been legally complicated over the previous ten years or more. The Marines feared they would be punished for shooting at the wrong time.

"Don't get me wrong. You know as well as I do that you can't shoot up anyone you want. You will use your best judgment, and I will trust you to do so. But remember something. To win this war, we also have to win the hearts and minds of the Iraqi people. They're the ones we're dedicated to liberating. We're not going to have any 'My Lai massacres' out here."

The following morning, 10 March, there was an orders walk-through for all officers in the battalion. The S-2 had built a massive terrain model, and we spent several hours standing around it as the S-3 walked everyone through the phases of the plan and the company commanders briefed their schemes of maneuver. I had yet to write my own company order, and the only thing that prevented me from being a total clusterfuck was the fact that Dave Hudspeth,

Gil Juarez (Charlie Company's CO), and I had all developed a basic plan together over the previous several weeks. However, with the refinements to the battalion's plan complete, I was now free to complete my own company op-order. Supposedly less than a week away from offensive operations, the battalion's plan was finally beginning to solidify.

✦ ✧ ✦

As March inched along, 1stSgt Guzman and I became increasingly dissatisfied with the performance of the NCOs in the company. Together we felt like the mythological Sisyphus, forever pushing the boulder up the hill. We would sense that the company was making great progress, then something stupid would happen that sent everything back to square one. As in the cases of the stabbing and the hazing incidents, many of the NCOs had been getting in trouble recently. The more Guzman and I felt they were acting like turds, the more we realized something had to be done. Guzman proposed the idea of holding an evaluation board to determine if all the eligible lance corporals were ready to become NCOs. I fully concurred, remembering that when LtGen Conway was the division commanding general he had directed a similar board system be implemented in all battalions. Guzman and the platoon sergeants held the board on 10 March while the platoon commanders and I were out, and upon returning he told me that the majority of the lance corporals had performed miserably. Those who failed weren't recommended for promotion.

Later Lt Schwartz approached me and told me he didn't agree with the board; he thought several of his lance corporals deserved to be promoted. Standing there listening to him make his argument, I began to lose patience. I might have been more receptive to his argument had he not approached it in what I perceived as the whiny manner that he did. For such a big guy, Schwartz had a habit of looking and sounding pathetic when he was arguing for something about which he felt strongly. Schwartz was a fine leader. He could always be counted upon to lead from the front, and as a motivational figure for the men he was unsurpassed. But I believed his chief deficiency was that he loved his Marines too much. That trait distorted his judgment when he argued on their behalf, and if I didn't agree with him *I* always ended up looking like the bad guy. As he pleaded his case he ended up making me so angry that I started to raise my voice with him. I finally cut him off, telling him there would be no further discussion of the matter. The two Marines he was fighting for would not be promoted to corporal if I had anything to say about it.

✦ ✧ ✦

Lieutenant Schwartz and 2nd Platoon departed at 0600Z (Zulu Time) to rehearse establishing the TAA with the rest of the battalion's quartering party. The remainder of Delta Company spent until 1200Z preparing for the field before finally driving out to the TAA. The company occupied the western flank of the position, and once in my place I spent an hour inside my turret messing around with the MDACT. It was a complicated piece of equipment, and I thought *If this is so tedious to operate now, how the hell am I going to work it in combat?* I wasn't the only one experiencing difficulty with it. Constant problems plagued the digital network designed to support it, and ultimately once we crossed into Iraq the MDACT failed to operate as anything more than a glorified digital map and GPS receiver. Our only assurance that anyone outside the battalion would know where Delta Company was on the battlefield was the electronic signal sent by the "Blue Force Tracker" mounted in the XO's LAV-C2. Blue Force Tracker (or the "horse-dick tracker," as Dave Hudspeth had christened it) was a similar system the Army had implemented in many of its units to improve Blue Force situational awareness. On digital maps it displayed icons of all friendly units in blue. Icons for enemy units appeared in red. Because of persistent VHF radio problems that developed, the Blue Force Tracker ended up being the only way we could tell the location of adjacent units once the war began in Iraq. I slammed the MDACT shut, ready to throw the piece of junk out of my turret and drive the LAV over it. I later found out that I wasn't the only person who felt that way about the MDACT.

Delta Company's plan was beginning to come together. On the morning of 12 March I had the company's scouts build a terrain model of our area of operations for the Opening Gambit. When the model was complete, the company showed up and the Marines situated themselves around it. The terrain model was built inside an amphitheater-like cut in a berm near camp, and the Marines all sat around the lip of the berm looking down on to the model and me. I thought back to the spring of 1995 when I was a second lieutenant at TBS and I had to give my first operations order to my platoon. I remembered how uneasy I was, dictating an order to forty of my peers for a platoon-level exercise. Now there I was, almost nine years later, briefing a combat operations order to a company of 130 Marines and sailors for a mission that would soon become a reality. But rather than nervous, I felt strangely excited. Though I had planned for the order to last about an hour, it ended up going for two. I was moving the entire time. I began with a brief history of Iraq since Saddam Hussein and the Ba'ath Party had seized power, and I highlighted the foreign policy strategy and general reign of terror he had conducted since becoming president. After providing an overview of the U.S. strategy in Iraq, I issued the order, walking the company through the terrain model step-by-step as I frenetically chain-smoked Marlboros.

Once the op-order was complete, I brought forward the staff. They gave their back-briefs to me, demonstrating their understanding of the plan. We conducted a walk-through of the operation with the terrain model, and in the process changed and refined the plan as necessary. When I was confident they all knew the drill, we brought forward all of the vehicle commanders and conducted a larger-scale walk-through of each phase of the operation. The company moved out to link-up with the combat engineers and conducted a full-scale rehearsal of the breach phase. We used the same berms we had rehearsed on three times previously, and the platoons performed perfectly. Everything seemed to be falling into place.

After the rehearsal, the engineer officer and I coordinated a time to link up for an evening rehearsal later that night, and the company returned to camp for a hot meal in the regiment's chow hall. We loaded up and headed back out to the link-up point two hours later. As we drove across the rolling desert landscape in the dark, we enjoyed the good lunar visibility and a slight, warm breeze. The LAVs rolled up to the rehearsal start point, and as the Marines sat in their vehicles waiting for the engineers to arrive, I dropped down inside the turret and eavesdropped on the battalion radio net. Captain Gil Juarez was talking to Maj Harper about his company's training for the evening. Suddenly Harper told Juarez he recommended Charlie Company stay put and not leave the LSA.

"Charlie-Six, this is Highlander-Three," Maj Harper radioed. "The weather has really turned to shit out here. I recommend you stay put for the evening and we'll get the rehearsals started in the morning once this clears up."

"Roger that, Highlander-Three," Juarez replied. "Good call. I'll check in once we all make it back in to battalion. It may take a while." I had no idea what they were talking about. The weather was fine—we were only a couple of kilometers away from camp. Harper then called me and recommended the same course of action.

"Dragon-Six, did you copy my last to Charlie-Six?"

"Highlander-Three, this is Dragon-Six," I replied. "Roger, I copied all. But the weather is fine where I am. Stand by." *What the hell is going on?* I thought. I popped up to check out the weather I'd been enjoying not five minutes earlier. As my head emerged from the turret I suddenly felt as if I had been hit in the face by a two-by-four. The worst sandstorm I had ever seen was whipping the desert around me into stinging needles that assaulted every inch of exposed skin. The hurricane-like winds and vicious sand of the Kuwaiti *shamal* blinded and choked me immediately, and even with my night vision goggles visibility was reduced to absolute zero. I dropped back down into the turret and keyed my headset.

"Roger, Highlander-Three," I tried calmly to report, my eyes burning and watering heavily. "I think we're going to stay put for the evening like you recommended." I then participated in a confusing radio conference call among Juarez, Hudspeth, Harper, and an assistant operations officer named Captain Bob Whalen. Afterward I radioed to the Marines to stay put.

"All Dragon Victors [vehicles]," I transmitted, addressing each vehicle crew in the company. "We aren't going anywhere tonight. Hunker down, and we'll weather this thing out for the evening." As the platoon commanders acknowledged my orders, I listened to the battalion net with interest as a company reported that one of its Marines was unaccounted for in the storm.

I radioed the company again. "One last thing. Don't let your Marines go any more than five feet away from your vehicles. We don't want anyone getting lost out there in the storm tonight." I remembered as a kid reading stories about people wandering away from their homes in blizzards and dying fewer than fifty feet from their front doors. I had thought it was impossible at the time, yet now as my vehicle seemed under attack by the blowing desert I knew it could happen. If anyone moved far enough away from the vehicle column that he could no longer see it, chances were he would become disoriented and would never find his way back. It was that bad out there.

I spent several minutes attempting to sleep in my seat in the turret, but the cramps that ratcheted my knees got too bad. I tried to stretch my legs out by hanging them down into the vehicle's hold, but sleep still evaded me. Even with the turret's hatches closed and locked the storm's gale continued to inject sand and dust into every crevice. A fine mist of powder gently rained down all over me inside the turret, and I finally figured I would be better off just hiding in my sleeping bag outside in the maelstrom. I repeated my earlier orders to the Marines on my crew: stay next to the vehicle, no matter what. In the blowing wind we had to yell to be heard, and the crewmembers all howled like banshees as the stinging sand needled their exposed flesh. Lance Corporal Davis leaned in close and shouted a question in my ear.

"What if we have to piss?!"

"Do it in a bottle like you always do!"

Gurganus heard us, and shouted another question. "Sir, what if I have to take a shit?!"

For some reason he always had to move his bowels at the most inopportune times. I laughed.

"Then you're fucked! Hold it until morning!" We rolled out our sleeping bags and bedded down along the leeward side (opposite the wind) of the LAV. With my *shemagh* wrapped tightly around my face, I climbed inside the shelter of my bag and attempted to hide from the raging wind and pelting sand. It was one of the worst evenings I had ever spent in the field, and I felt like I was suffocating all night.

At 0100Z I felt a nudge as Corporal Harter woke me for radio watch. As I attempted to sit, I found myself buried under a mountain of sand. I finally sat up and looked around, realizing the storm had ended. As I climbed out of my sleeping bag I picked it up and turned it upside down. Sand and dust poured out of it forever. My eyes burned fiercely and were nearly sealed shut with dust and dried tears. Both nostrils were likewise crusted over with a gritty paste of sand and snot. I was glad to be free from the stuffy confines of my bag and in the fresh air, but relief gave way to misery as I spent the next two hours on radio watch shivering in the icy metal cage of the turret. As the sun broke the horizon I peered up and down at the column of vehicles. Dozens of mounds of sand shuddered and came to life as the Marines sleeping beneath them awakened and realized they too had been buried alive the night before. As my crew sat around the vehicle that morning commiserating about the lousy evening we had all spent getting sandblasted, LCpl Davis stumped me with a question.

"Sir, what are we gonna do if a storm like that happens in combat?" It was a good question, one for which I didn't have an answer.

"I don't know, Davis. I imagine we'd do exactly the same thing. If we can't see, neither can the Iraqis."

An hour later the company departed the scene of our miserable night, and we set up a field refueling point for Charlie and Weapons Companies to use once they finished their own rehearsals with the engineers. We ran through the station and refueled first, and the company managed to fill all twenty-five vehicles in as many minutes. The battalion was pushing for each company to be able to refuel in twenty minutes, but that seemed impossible. I watched closely as the Marines raced their vehicles through with the same speed and skill as pit stop teams fueling Formula One racecars. I couldn't envision them doing it any faster without someone getting run over. There was also the fact that we weren't filling empty tanks. Most vehicles only took on several gallons, and I knew it would take a company longer to fuel vehicles that were starving for gas. I became very interested to hear how long it took the other companies after we left for camp.

To my dismay, the rehearsal with the engineers scheduled for that evening was cancelled, and instead the battalion scheduled a meeting. I was unhappy that we had lost one more chance to rehearse the plan. Although I was confident the Marines knew what to do, the closer we got to the real thing the more I wanted everything perfected. I donned my gear and walked to the dining hall tent reserved for the meeting, but found only Dave Hudspeth, Gil Juarez, and a couple of staff officers. They stood in a circle smoking, and one of the staff officers repeated to me the same thing he had been passing to everyone: the meeting had been cancelled. I turned to Dave and Gil.

"Man, this is bullshit. Nine out of ten meetings are cancelled in this joint. I'm sick of getting my rope jerked around here."

Gil laughed disdainfully, and Dave handed me a cigarette and his lighter.

"Hey, man," he joked. "What do you expect?"

"Yeah," Gil added, sarcastically. "Who needs to rehearse at night anyway?"

Dave, Gil, and I continued our conversation for a while, and it was apparent that we collectively felt the same about the situation at the battalion-level. The common thread was that we believed we were ready to go, but would in some ways be "on our own" when the shooting started. We grumbled about the battalion staff and how it seemed at odds with what we as commanders wanted and needed to do in order to prepare our companies for war. At that point, needless to say, if I had known any of my Marines were saying the same sort of things about *me,* I would have gone ballistic. Without saying so, I think the three of us probably reached the same intended conclusion. Shoulders were shrugged, and we walked together back to our troop tents. Put Marines together and they will figure out something to complain about at some point—officers are no different.

The next morning Chris Portiss and I headed out to the field to link up with the battalion "Main." During field operations, the battalion headquarters was divided up into two parts: the "Forward," headed by the battalion commander and S-3, and the Main, headed by the battalion XO and the S-3A. Major Harper had planned a communications exercise and radio rehearsal of the Opening Gambit, and it was as close to a final dress rehearsal as we would probably get. Portiss and I spent close to three hours with the other company commanders and XOs, reacting to notional enemy updates handed to us on index cards by Alpha Company's staff. The exercise wasn't without merit, but I knew the same thing everyone else did: the real deal wouldn't go as smoothly. Radio rehearsals are fine for establishing procedures, but sitting inside your vehicle when it's not bouncing up and down and you're not struggling to keep your map from blowing away tends to give a false sense of security and effectiveness. But how many more times could we scrimmage the Opening Gambit before it started hurting rather than helping us? While I wanted another opportunity for Delta Company to conduct a night rehearsal of the breach operation, that was purely out of a desire to work out any last minute bugs. *Well,* I finally realized. *I guess that's what the battalion is trying to do as well.*

✦ ✧ ✦

Upon learning that they wouldn't be recommended for promotion because of their lousy performance at the evaluation board, two lance corporals from 2nd Platoon requested mast (an opportunity to plead their case, a right of every Marine) to the battalion commander. On 14 March 1stSgt Guzman began processing the paperwork for the two Marines' meeting with LtCol White.

After Guzman submitted the paperwork, the sergeant major told him that the corporal involved in the hazing incident would be transferred to another work section in the battalion. Guzman demanded to know why. He was as possessive of the Marines as I was, and one thing he couldn't stand was the sergeant major making personnel decisions for our company without even consulting him. The sergeant major replied by accusing Guzman of collaborating with me to "head-hunt" for the NCO in question. Despite Guzman's protests, the sergeant major was adamant. He ended the conversation by voicing his personal dislike of me and suggesting that Guzman "get a hold of his company commander."

After hearing this from 1stSgt Guzman, I stormed outside the troop tent to cool off. At about that time SSgt Monroe approached me.

"Sir, I just wanted you to know there's crap written about you in the Port-a-shitters."

I laughed and told him not to worry about it. "I'm a big boy, Staff Sergeant. But thanks." Itching to see how I ranked in the ongoing graffiti war waging between the Texan cowboys and Los Angelino gangbangers, I walked over to the Port-a-Jons. It didn't take long to find something written about me. In black magic marker someone had written on the plastic wall of the toilet:

> I hope for the safety of many Marines in this battalion that Delta Company has improved since their CAX. Delta 'CO' on the net: "Blue Platoon, do I need to come down there and set your vehicles in for you? What the fuck is taking so long?!"
> I hope you have improved gentlemen.

The ponderous declaration was true. I had said that exact thing over the radio nearly a year and a half earlier. I chuckled, figuring a Marine from Weapons Company who had been attached to Delta Company for our CAX in 2001 had written it. Later in the afternoon I ran across the very original legend "Delta fucking sucks" scrawled across the inside of another toilet.

That evening I saw a toilet that proclaimed:

> I'll never be happy, I'll never be free,
> Until I've fucked Delta Company
> Like they fucked me

Another angry, albeit more succinct, memo announced: "Capt Folsom → FAG." It wasn't my job to be liked, but what irritated me was that none of the individuals who wrote these things had the intestinal fortitude to do anything about it except write on a shitter wall. My father had once told me, "You know you've arrived as a commander when you find graffiti written about you on the shithouse walls." If that was the case, then the literature decorating the toilets truly heralded great things to come. Yeah, right.

I thought it was strange how Delta Company could be so good at the tactical level, yet so many problems seemed to plague us at the personal and leadership levels. The same night I learned about the graffiti in the heads, I shared a smoke with Bob Whalen. For much of the time I had known him I had thought he was pompous and immature, but within the last couple of months he had changed. Since returning from WestPac I tended to listen more to what he had to say. As we talked he told me he had been constantly impressed with Delta Company's performance. Major Bodkin gave me the same compliment a little while later. Little did they know what lay beneath the tranquil surface of Delta Company. Portiss, Guzman, Kappen, and Monroe openly supported me, but I constantly fought against my platoon commanders and platoon sergeants over things I considered to be basic discipline and leadership issues. The company staff often sat around and bragged about how much better Delta Company was than everyone else in the battalion, yet they were frequently unwilling to make the extra effort required to truly ensure the company was a cut above the rest. Despite my endless bitching at them to supervise and enforce the standards set by the first sergeant and me, they seemed to me either unable or unwilling to fulfill their leadership roles.

The most unsettling thing about the situation was that this was a reflection of *my* own leadership ability. Whether the Marines were just fed up with the long wait in the desert or whether they really had no confidence in my abilities was irrelevant. I feared I was failing my job as a company commander. All I had ever wanted was to command troops in combat. I had been in the Marine Corps long enough to have forgotten what life was like as a civilian. Yet there I was, doubting my capacity to lead and command the company. Worse, I questioned why I had ever had a desire to do that which I had dreamed of since childhood. I even contemplated for a while going to the battalion commander to request re-assignment back to the States. It wasn't a decision I wanted to make when I was as bound up as I was at the time, but believe it or not, I did think about it.

Early the following afternoon, after fuming to myself all day, I was finally fed up with hearing about my crappy reputation in the battalion. I walked to LtCol White's tent and asked to speak with him. He put down the book he was reading.

"What's on your mind, Seth?"

"Sir, I need you to give me a performance counseling," I said, very matter-of-factly. "I need you to tell me what I'm doing wrong and what I'm not doing that I should be." He looked taken aback for a moment, and then he proceeded to tell me that he had all the confidence in the world in me and Delta Company.

"You've got the most experienced company out here. I'm glad Delta is with us," he added. Understanding and very much appreciating the fact that he didn't have any complaints about the company, I redirected the conversation to my reputation among the battalion staff.

"I appreciate that, sir. But I have another concern. I'm not happy about the rumors going around about me among your staff. You are the only person I work for in this battalion; I don't make a habit of going around spouting off that other people should be relieved. It pisses me off that others are saying that very thing about me."

"Who's saying that?"

"Your sergeant major, for one. And he's saying it to my first sergeant. I have enough problems in the company without having to worry about the sergeant major running his mouth to my first sergeant about what a shitty company commander I am."

He thought for a moment, and then spoke. "Well, don't worry about it. I'll talk to the sergeant major about it." Then he added, "Just remember what you said: you work for me. Don't worry about what others are saying." We then discussed the request mast issue concerning the two lance corporals. He told me he had decided to allow both Marines to be promoted because the company hadn't been consistent in conducting the evaluation boards. I tried to argue my case, but it was clear that his mind was made up. I was angry. Such a decision potentially set a precedent that whenever I didn't recommend a Marine for promotion all he would have to do would be to request mast to the battalion commander. It was a hit on my credibility and authority, but it was a battle I was sure to lose if I continued to contest it with the CO. Moreover, I recognized the ultimate judgment call was always the prerogative of the commander.

Later that evening I returned from the battalion meeting to lay down the law with my own staff. I was still pissed off from an altercation with Lt Schwartz earlier in the afternoon. First Sergeant Guzman and the platoon sergeants had all been in a circle yelling at each other about the promotion issue when Schwartz had jumped in. He had begun shouting at Guzman.

"That's fucked up, First Sergeant! You put the Marines on the board after I had already recommended them for promotion! And the CO had already signed off on it! You can't do that!"

"The fuck I can't, Lieutenant!" Guzman shouted back. "The CO approved it. Besides, if you and your fucking platoon sergeant had been doing your jobs and counseling your Marines the right way and training them to be NCOs, none of this would be happening right now!"

"That's fucking bullshit, and you know it!" I was outside, leaning against the tent and writing in my journal. Their every word was clearly audible, but I had been determined not to get involved and to let them fight it out for themselves. Schwartz continued. "You've just got it in for my Marines!"

Determined or not, I had heard enough. Dropping my journal in the sand, I stormed around the corner and into the tent. The SNCOs and Lt Schwartz stopped shouting and looked at me.

"Lieutenant," I said sharply. "Get your ass outside right now." I turned around and exited the tent. A minute later Schwartz stood in front of me with his arms casually by his sides. He looked down at me, an angry expression on his face.

"Goddammit!" I yelled. "Lock your fucking body up and look straight ahead!" I had chewed ass on Schwartz before, more so probably than any of the other lieutenants. But this time I had well and truly had enough. I lost control.

"I am sick and tired of your fucking shit!" I yelled up at him. He towered over me, and I wondered if he might just haul off and knock me down. "The first sergeant doesn't work for you! He works for me! I gave him the go ahead for that board! Your Marines don't rate to be promoted! They don't know *shit!"*

"Sir, you . . ." he began. I instantly cut him off.

"This is a one-way conversation, Lieutenant!" I shouted. "I'm talking and you're listening. I'm sick of your whining and complaining. Your loyalty is zero! If you continue to undermine my authority you are fucking *done* in this company, war or no war. Do I make myself clear?"

"Yes, sir."

I turned to walk back toward my camp stool next to the tent where I had been writing. "You are dismissed," I said curtly. He performed an about face and walked back into the tent as I sat down and fought to get a cigarette in my mouth without dropping it. I was so angry my hands trembled. *You totally lost it,* I told myself. *You won't recover from that. They wouldn't follow you to the shitter now, even if they had diarrhea.*

But it wasn't just my earlier meltdown with Schwartz that had me primed for my evening encounter with the company staff. As I had returned from the battalion staff meeting I stopped off to use one of the Port-a-Jons. On the wall in front of me was the recommendation "Buy a strap-on for your wife. She'll love it . . . just ask Purple-6." On the other side was another announcement that said "Delta CO → Purple-6!" "Purple-6" was an obvious reference to the color of my Harley Davidson back home. I didn't give a shit about the homosexual insinuation. That was nothing. But what set me off as I returned to my tent for the company staff meeting was the reference to Ashley. I fell for the bait. When the officers and SNCOs had assembled I blew up at them.

"I failed my job today because you failed to do *your* jobs," I told them. "You failed to properly counsel and instruct your Marines. Now I'm requiring you to be everywhere your Marines are. *Everywhere.* That will teach you how to supervise and give you the observation time you need to properly evaluate your Marines for promotion." I looked around at them and continued.

"Let me be clear," I said in closing, looking directly at Lt Schwartz. "There is a chain of command for a reason. If any of you undermine my authority, I will fire you. War or no war." I went outside and sat down in the sand. *This is what it has come to,* I thought. *You just lost them for good.* Most experienced unit or not, I suddenly knew that if we didn't get some traction soon the wheels would fall right off the company.

I spent most of 17 March walking the company area, observing the Marines as they prepared for my scheduled inspection on 19 March. The previous night we had learned that the entire division would execute a full-dress rehearsal on 20 March. The expectation was that we would not return to the LSA. In other words, the sand had almost run out of the hourglass. We were getting ready to go.

That morning I talked to Capt Portiss about the problems in the company. In general I tended not to seek personal advice from him—we just didn't have that kind of relationship. But time had proven him to be one of the few among my staff in whom I could confide.

"Don't worry about them," he said, referring to the staff. "They're just being babies."

"I've about had it. I'm ready to go to the CO and request reassignment." I was serious.

"What are you talking about?" he asked, surprised.

"You want the company?" I had finally realized my problem. "I think I'm too burnt out to make rational decisions or properly lead the Marines."

"No," he said quickly. "Don't do that. That isn't a good idea."

"Then what's the problem with the company?"

"Look, sir, the Marines haven't had an honest-to-God day off since we got to this shithole. Yeah, they've had 'light training days,' but no *real* days off. Let's give them tomorrow off. You can inspect their gear on the nineteenth, and we'll head to the field on the twentieth as planned."

"What if they fail the inspection? There won't be time to correct the problems before we go to the field."

He smiled and continued. "If you promise them a day off, I guarantee you they'll pass the inspection."

I considered it for a moment. "Okay, let's do it."

Later, as I roamed the company area I noticed a total lack of NCOs helping the junior Marines work on their vehicles and equipment. Wandering into a troop tent, I found SSgt Kappen having a discussion with the NCOs about the problems in the company. I began to walk out, knowing he would want to speak with them without any officers around. But I really wanted to hear what he had to say, so instead I stood in the corner and just listened. He repeated the same things I had ranted and raved about, and although I initially planned to keep my mouth shut the temptation was too great. Like so many other officers, sometimes I tended to have diarrhea of the mouth. I stepped in and asked him if I could say a few things.

"Gents, here's the deal. You just heard it all from Staff Sergeant Kappen. Everything he said came straight from me. He is supporting my intent here. But now I want to give *you* the chance to ask *me* questions about what is going on here. Go ahead, anything. Particularly regarding my policies in the company." (In reflecting upon this incident much later, I realized that I had unwittingly put myself at considerable risk when I had invited the Marines to ask me questions—unconditional questions about my leadership and command policies. Fortunately I dodged a bullet, but I learned a new lesson: be careful what you ask for.)

The Marines began venting many of their frustrations, but I provided a solid answer for each question. The episode was productive, and I gave it to them straight about the leadership issues I thought we had in the company. By the time the session ended I had a feeling that, at the very least, the stronger NCOs in the company still supported me. I knew it wasn't a popularity contest, but near the end I added one more thing.

"The staff has recommended to me that the company get tomorrow off." I looked around. "Here's the catch: my inspection goes on the nineteenth. Everybody better be ready, or I'm holding you NCOs responsible. Good to go?"

"Yes, sir," they all replied.

"Okay, good to go. Everyone gets tomorrow off."

6

On the DMZ

"Seth," the voice whispered in the darkness of our tent. "Wake up." Normally it took me several minutes and someone practically kicking me to wake up. Marines hated waking me because it took so long for me to get out of the bag. But for some reason this time I snapped my eyes open immediately. Major Bodkin was silhouetted in the entrance of the tent.

"Huh?" I asked, disoriented. "Whazzat?"

"We need you in the COC." *What in the hell?* I thought, looking at my watch. It was 2230Z (0130 local time).

"What's going on, sir?" I asked, awake now.

"We're going." He turned around and walked away.

✦ ✧ ✦

I threw on my uniform and thought about the events of earlier in the evening. The company commanders, the operations officer and the battalion commander had all walked together to the regimental CO's tent to present our final back-briefs detailing our plan for the breach of the Kuwaiti and Iraqi barriers. As we walked across the dimly lit camp, LtCol White said something that made no sense to any of us.

"Looks like the Division is having a mustache-growing contest," he said to no one in particular. We looked at each other, puzzled.

"Are you kidding, sir?" I asked.

"Nope," he replied. "General Mattis wants all men in the Division to grow their mustaches." We prodded him for details, but that was all he would say. As we waited around to talk to the RCT CO, I began talking with another officer from the regiment. He had more details on the mustache issue, and after I pressed him he secretively told me intelligence reports indicated that Iraqis had stolen Coalition uniforms. It was believed they planned to commit atrocities and blame the acts on U.S. soldiers. To counter this, a plan was implemented for all men in the Division to grow their mustaches until a designated time when we would be told to shave them off. You rarely see an Iraqi Arab without a mustache, and this way any "atrocities" reported would show mustachioed men committing them, but by then our mustaches would have been shaved off. There was another theory that claimed the mustache idea would also be a way of identifying Iraqis attempting to infiltrate our lines, but either way I raised my eyebrow. It sounded pretty far-out to me.

Still confounded over the mustache mystery, we had returned to 1st LAR's briefing tent for the evening battalion staff meeting. The S-2 briefed that there were reports of rioting in Baghdad, and some members of the Ba'ath Party had been targeted by drive-by shooters. Manson's report produced rumblings around the staff table of "Yeah," and "Get some." He also announced that President Bush planned to address the nation the following morning around 0100Z—8:00 P.M. eastern standard time on 17 March, prime time. Everyone was eager to hear it, and I set my watch's alarm so I could listen to the speech on the BBC. Back at the tent, I gave the company staff the run-down from the evening's meeting, including the directive to grow the mustaches. They were incredulous, and I had to tell them several times I was serious.

"Sir," SSgt Monroe laughed, shaking his head. "You have got to be shitting me."

"I wouldn't shit you, Staff Sergeant. You're my favorite turd."

"You aren't making this up?" asked 1stSgt Guzman. "No bullshit?"

"No bullshit. This is straight from Division."

"That's it," said Monroe, nodding his head knowingly and looking around for support. "We're going soon."

"Don't get your hopes up," I said, rolling out my sleeping bag. "Besides, the Division commander has no idea how difficult it is for a pale white guy like me to grow a mustache."

Hours later, as I buckled my web gear and headed out of the tent into the darkness I wasn't so sure. I ran to the COC only to discover it had been moved to another tent—no one wanted to alert the media teams to what was going on. Once everyone on the battalion staff had crammed himself into the tent, LtCol White walked in with Maj Harper.

"Gents," White began. "The Division just ordered us to occupy the regimental dispersal area. The first elements of the battalion need to be moving within three hours." Everyone started chattering, and Maj Harper stepped in.

"Quiet down and listen up," he said, pointing to a list of instructions taped to a map board. "The S-3 section will hash out a quick 'frag' [fragmentary, or basic information only] order for the battalion's movement to the DA.

1st LAR company commanders the night we got the order to move out to the Iraqi border. (L to R: Capt Gil Juarez, Capt Seth Folsom, Capt Dave Hudspeth.)

Everyone else, here is the rough timeline. If there are no questions, be back here in one hour for the detailed order."

I left the COC still skeptical it was the real thing. *This is probably just a drill,* I thought. *I bet General Mattis wants to see how fast the Division can get to the field on short notice.* Then I started to put the pieces together: the mustache directive, the intelligence briefings by the S-2, the speech by the President, and the secrecy of the op-order in the middle of the night. *Yep,* I thought. *This is it.* I rounded the corner to Delta Company's tent and walked in. With a click of a button on one of the support posts, the fluorescent tubes crackled and popped to life. They flooded the darkened tent with unnatural white light.

"Everyone get up. Pack your shit. We're going," I announced loudly. "Company staff, I need you in the back of the tent ASAP." I walked down the length of the tent as the Marines hurriedly rolled up their sleeping bags and packed their rucksacks. There was little conversation among them. The company staff assembled on the far side of the tent, each man rubbing his eyes and trying to wake himself up. Once they were standing in a circle around me I gave the news to them as succinctly as I could.

"We got the word. First elements of the battalion have to be out of here in less than three hours now. I have to go right back to battalion for more information."

"Sir," SSgt Kappen asked. "What order are we leaving in?" It was a good question.

"I don't know," I replied, turning to leave. "Just plan on us leaving first. Anything else will mean that much more time we have to get ready." Then I turned back to all of them.

"In the meantime, get this place cleaned out. Finish loading all the ammo and gear into the vehicles, and do it quickly. Assholes and elbows, okay?" Everyone nodded his head, many smiling. There were grunts of "Ooh-rah" and "Let's do it." I added one last thing.

"Gents, let's do this right, and let's do it safe. The last thing we need to do is run over someone out there in the dark because we aren't paying attention. Don't let anybody get stupid. I'll be back soon with more details."

I headed out of the tent into the cold night air and walked back to the COC. Once there we discovered the timeline had been bumped up. Suddenly Delta Company had only one hour to load up its vehicles, break out ammunition from its packing containers, and get the hell out of Dodge. I ran back to the tent to pass the schedule change to the staff, and the activity suddenly erupted throughout the camp. What before had been shadowy figures running around in ones and twos in the dark were now great masses of people and vehicles racing all over the place. The early morning darkness was replaced with floodlights that illuminated motor pools and mustering points. The entirety of LSA-5 was alive and buzzing. I made my way over to the ramp where the company mechanics continued to work feverishly on an LAV's engine they had removed earlier in the day. Staff Sergeant Monroe stood there, supervising closely as the Marines connected fittings and hoses. The engine was perched precariously over them, suspended from the recovery vehicle's massive hydraulic crane. The mechanics had been working all night.

"How long is it gonna take?" I asked Monroe.

"Maybe an hour and a half, maybe less."

"You've got an hour, or else we're leaving it behind. They bumped the timeline on us." Corporal Thyden heard us from inside the vehicle and spoke up.

"Don't worry, sir," he yelled over the noise. "We'll get her up!"

"Yeah," Monroe added, looking at their progress. "We'll get it, sir. We're not leaving her behind." Forty minutes later they were securing the engine inside the hull and attaching a tow bar to the LAV to tow it out to the dispersal area. *Unbelievable,* I thought.

Back in the tent I hastily packed up my personal gear. Rolling up my sleeping bag and stuffing it into my rucksack, I eyed the bag of dirty laundry hanging next to my equipment. A laundry service had been established soon after we arrived in camp, but it had proved unreliable. If you sent your clothing out with the infrequent service you could be guaranteed at least one of two things: either your clothes would come back wet and dirty, or they wouldn't come back at all. Since my first experience with the service I had refused to send my clothing out, opting instead to wash it myself in empty ammunition containers with detergent brought from home. I had planned to do my laundry the following day. Cursing my procrastination, I crammed the mesh bag into my rucksack. My delay in doing laundry meant I would be hauling my dirty underwear into combat.

Amid the organized chaos of the ramp, President Bush addressed the nation. Every vehicle crew with a personal radio blared his speech.

"Peaceful efforts to disarm the Iraqi regime have failed again and again—because we are not dealing with peaceful men," the President said. "Yet, some permanent members of the Security Council have publicly announced they will veto any resolution that compels the disarmament of Iraq. These governments share our assessment of the danger, but not our resolve to meet it. Many nations, however, do have the resolve and fortitude to act against this threat to peace, and a broad coalition is now gathering to enforce the just demands of the world. The United Nations Security Council has not lived up to its responsibilities, so we will rise to ours." *In other words,* I thought. *If no one else is going to have the backbone to stand up to this asshole, we will do it ourselves.*

All around camp, as George Bush said these words the Marines stopped what they were doing and positively roared with delight. The air was electric. You could feel the excitement all around, and the news crews began moving from vehicle to vehicle, filming the Marines as they broke open ammunition crates and mounted weapons systems and burned classified documents. There was shouting everywhere.

"I need a fourteen-millimeter wrench!"

"Where the hell is the platoon battle roster?!"

"Hey, you dumb motherfucker! Get away from that ammo with that cigarette in your mouth!"

I had nothing to do but walk around and watch them—they were on auto-pilot, and they needed no guidance or interference from me. The company had moved out hastily in the past, and as far as the Marines were concerned this was no different from any other drill we had performed before. But it wasn't a drill, and by 0215Z the company had moved from the ramp to the staging area one kilometer away. As the sun rose and we waited for the call from the battalion to step off for the dispersal area, the Marines had a chance to wind down some after the initial exhilaration of the evening. Staff Sergeant Monroe continued to direct his mechanics as they worked to bring

SSgt Kappen's LAV on-line, and the news crew from ABC showed up. Bob Woodruff started talking to me, asking questions about what was going on and what would happen next.

As I attempted to closely monitor what came out of my mouth during the informal interview, Woodruff's crew pulled out cans of black spray-paint and attempted to camouflage the tan civilian "Hummer" provided to them by ABC. I shook my head, remarking the difference between the military and the civilian world. In the military you would never see anyone randomly painting up a government owned vehicle. I took a closer look at the Hummer. It had been fully outfitted to suit the news crew's needs. Along with amenities like air conditioning and bucket seats, it also sported hook-ups for their satellite relays and digital equipment. They planned to drive the Hummer right into combat with us and report from the frontlines. *Fat chance,* I thought. *They're gonna get wasted if they try that.*

"So," Woodruff asked me. "Where's the best place for us to travel?" I looked at him for a moment, then at the Hummer, then back at him.

"Well, I guess you want to be up front where the action is."

"Yeah, that's what we want," he replied.

"Well, I usually alternate which platoon is going to be the company's main effort, so you can travel with whichever platoon is the main effort for the mission," I went on. "Or you and your crew can travel with my section. I always travel with the company's main effort, so you can be guaranteed a good view of whatever happens."

"Do you have space for me in your vehicle?" he asked, looking derisively at the cramped conditions in the scout compartment. Corporal Harter was sprawled out across the narrow bench-seats, sleeping with his mouth open.

"Yeah, we've only got Harter back there. And the combat cameraman the battalion just gave us last night," I continued, pointing back into the hole. "Plenty of room."

I walked around the other side of the vehicle to find LCpl Davis talking with some other Marines. He turned to me when he saw me coming.

"Hey sir," he said. "I thought we were supposed to get today off." I looked at my watch—it was 18 March.

"Tough shit, Davis. You got a war instead."

"Does that mean we don't get today off?" asked another.

"I'll tell you what," I replied. "If you want to stay here while we go kick Iraq's ass, you're welcome to." The Marines all started laughing. Their responses told me that after almost two years of preparation and months of mind-numbingly repetitious training none of them would pass up what we were about to do for anything.

◆ ◇ ◆

At 0500Z we received radio traffic from the battalion. "Move out," the order said. "Rendezvous with the quartering party and the battalion at the dispersal area [DA]." Captain Portiss yelled to me from his vehicle.

"CO! Did you hear that?"

"Yeah," I replied, climbing into my turret and donning my helmet. "Let's get moving."

"Mount up!" Portiss yelled. "Short count, two minutes!" The Marines repeated the XO's command up and down the column of vehicles. "Short count, two minutes!" The short count was the synchronized starting or stopping of all vehicles' engines at once, a practice designed to disguise the true number of vehicles to a listening enemy. It was always the first and last transmission over the company radio net when we were training. Woodruff climbed into the back of the LAV, and minutes later the column was rolling along a dirt trail leading to our route into the dispersal area.

The main route north to the dispersal area was a crumbling asphalt road the Iraqi army had built in 1990 after it had invaded Kuwait. They had constructed it as a logistics pipeline to facilitate the bringing-in of supplies and the bringing-out of loot. Everyone simply referred to it as the "log road," and as the company traveled north along it we dodged vehicles whose crews all seemed to have the exact same goal: getting to their assembly areas as fast as they possibly could. Occasionally swerving to avoid humvees, trucks, and people loitering along the sides of the route, I had a thought that would become a constant worry as the war progressed: *If we don't watch what the hell we are doing out here someone is going to get killed in this traffic jam.* The drive to the dispersal area began to drag out, and the build-up of traffic soon turned the ride into a start-and-stop evolution. As the initial anticipation of the morning wore off, I began to doubt whether it was for real or not. *Surely this is just an exercise,* I began to rationalize. *The Division needs to see how long it takes to get everyone out here.* But we had all heard the President's speech the night before—*that* certainly was real. Maybe we were just doing this to show Iraq we were serious. Maybe Saddam Hussein would back down. *Bullshit,* I finally told myself, realizing I had been in denial. *You don't put this much equipment, this many people, this much SHIT out here on the border unless you plan to use it.* Thousands of vehicles were assembling before my eyes. *This is happening.*

Two hours later Delta Company pulled into the dispersal area. Before leaving the staging area I had dispatched Lt Schwartz and his platoon as our quartering party, and he guided the company via radio into the DA and arranged the vehicles on-line, facing north. As we went about erecting our camouflage nets, the rest of the battalion slowly lumbered into the assembly area. Woodruff and his crew pulled out their cameras and filmed us as we set up the netting and readied the vehicle.

After I bored Woodruff with canned, uninteresting answers to his questions, he moved on to interview Cpl Harter. It was exactly what I wanted to happen. I didn't oppose the media embed program. It was a good way to get the word to the folks back home about what we were doing. But already I wasn't impressed with our particular embed team. Riding in the comforts of a fully loaded Hummer did not put the news team "in our shoes." It wasn't in line with the original intent of the embed program, that is, to fully incorporate the media teams with the units they were supposed to cover. Instead, it isolated the ABC team, and it had the potential to create bad blood between the Marines and the news crew. Even when Woodruff and his crew were forced by higher headquarters to abandon their Hummer just before crossing the border into Iraq, they chose to ride in SSgt Kappen's LAV-L—the most spacious and comfortable vehicle in the company. That fact, among other things, would become an issue over which Woodruff and I would lock horns throughout the war.

Once the nets were raised, the battalion radioed all companies to hold tight. *No movement expected for seven to eight hours.* Staying up all night had finally caught up with everyone, and the movement delay was just what we wanted to hear. I moved around to the front of the vehicle and sat down in the shade, and soon I was out cold next to one of the tires.

✦ ✧ ✦

I had been asleep one hour, maybe two. I was in that half-sleep, half-awake zone, and in that haze I heard someone say, "Where is Captain Folsom?" Seconds later I was brought back into consciousness by a yell from Lance Corporal Andrew Roufs, the combat cameraman who had been assigned to the company.

"Sir," he called down from the turret where he stood radio watch. "The battalion is calling for you."

"What do they want?"

"They need you at the COC." Mumbling to myself, I climbed up on the turret and took the radio's handset from Roufs.

"Highlander, this is Dragon-Six. Say again your last." The radio beeped back at me.

"Dragon-Six, this is Highlander," the voice on the other end replied. "Need you at the COC in five mikes." *Five minutes?* I thought. *It will take me ten just to walk over there!*

"Roger, I copy," I acknowledged. Pulling the handset away from my ear, I yelled down to the crew bagged out around the tires. "Let's go. Get me over to the COC." I threw on my gear and sped over to the COC, where I found the battalion staff and the company commanders assembled around a small terrain model alongside one of the command vehicles. No sooner had I walked up than Maj Harper began talking.

"We're occupying the attack position tonight," he told everyone. He looked at the company commanders. "And you have to be there by fifteen-hundred Zulu. Delta, you're the first out of here." I glimpsed my watch. *Shit, that's ninety minutes,* I thought. *We haven't even broken down our nets yet.* As I turned to run back to my LAV, Dave Hudspeth, Gil Juarez, and I momentarily stopped and looked at each other.

"Well, see you on the other side," said Gil, emotionless. Dave nodded and grunted.

"Yeah," I said to both of them. "Be careful." There was no time for melodramatic movie bullshit. We were in a rush. I sprinted across the COC and yelled to Davis to get the vehicle started.

"Back to our pos, Gurganus," I said into the intercom as I pulled on my helmet. The company had already begun breaking down their nets. "Davis, call the company, tell them to set RedCon-One." When we weren't on the move the company observed readiness conditions, or "RedCons," that dictated the amount of time they had to get ready if we got the word. RedCon-4 was one hour; RedCon-3 was thirty minutes; RedCon-2 was fifteen minutes; and RedCon-1 was five minutes or less. As Davis passed the word over the radio, I plotted our route to the attack position south of the Kuwaiti berm. As long as there wasn't a traffic jam we would be able to make it there on time.

Soon we were filing out of the DA, and the company sped up the log road to its assigned attack position. I could see the berm clearly, and there were breaches already cut into it. With no other information available, we sat in our vehicles in march formation for several hours, waiting for word to go. Supposedly, elements of a Kuwaiti tank battalion were forward of us, screening along the berm and watching for any signs of an Iraqi spoiling attack across the border. But after scanning through our thermal imaging sights no one in the company could see them. I wondered if they were there at all. The battalion radioed and directed me to link up with the Kuwaitis to obtain solid position reports on all of their vehicles. I balked at the order—there was no way I was going to send any of my vehicles wandering around in the dark, looking for a Kuwaiti tank that might or might not be out there. As jittery as everyone was, there were bound to be some itchy trigger fingers, American *and* Kuwaiti. I managed to convince the battalion that it wasn't a good idea, and we continued to wait for orders to move to the berm.

At 1800Z the battalion radioed that we probably would not cross the border that evening. I thought for a minute, and then reduced the company's alert status to RedCon-4. It was going to be a long couple of days if this hurry up and wait nonsense continued. With the crew rotating on radio watch, I crawled in the back of the vehicle in search of sleep. The LAV's scout compartment is not designed for a person to stretch out, and as packed as the vehicle was with ammunition, MREs, and personal equipment, I had to spend the night on my back with my legs up, resting against the back hatch. It was incredibly uncomfortable, and I didn't get much sleep. But discomfort wasn't the only thing keeping me awake. Something didn't seem right. *Why aren't they attacking us?* I thought to myself, *They have to know we are here. Why aren't they lobbing artillery at us?*

I awoke the next morning and plopped down next to the vehicle to dust off my weapon. Lance Corporal Davis sat atop the turret, monitoring the radio. He leaned over and called down to me.

"Hey sir, you think this is it?"

"I don't know. Let's go find out." We drove to where the battalion had established its COC, and I walked into the operations tent to find the S-3. Everyone began showing up, and Maj Harper tasked the companies to screen along the electrified fence sandwiched between the northern, Iraqi berm and the southern berm inside Kuwait. The electrified fence was the final barrier before the no man's land just south of the Iraqi border. Dave Hudspeth and I agreed to rotate our companies through eight-hour shifts along the fence line, and I volunteered Delta Company to take the first shift. The screen would require at most only one platoon to cover its observation sector, and I called up 1st Platoon for the mission. They would be observing the exact area the company was designated to travel through once we crossed the border, and I wanted to get a better look. I followed Parment's platoon through the passage point in the Kuwaiti berm to the heavy chain-linked fence that ran east to west across the demilitarized zone in front of us. I anchored the screen on a Kuwaiti border outpost, and once 1st Platoon was set in place I moved my own vehicle next to the tall observation tower behind the compound. The skies were overcast, and it was difficult to see very far to the north beyond the electrified fence. The Iraqi border in the distance was a fuzzy line in the mid-afternoon gloom, and no visible movement caught our eyes.

Soon after our LAV arrived next to the border post a group of Kuwaitis formed up outside. They ambled over to our vehicle to see what we were all about, and once they realized we were friendly and willing to talk to them, they all began laughing and cutting jokes with each other. Several of them would point at us, say "Saddam," and then run their fingers across their throats.

Then, as if to clarify their meaning, they would say, "Bush, good!" and start laughing again. Later our new friends brought out tea and coffee, and they asked to take pictures with us and our vehicle. It was good to see that these guys seemed to like and support us. I suspected they had spent a long time, maybe years, at this border post, fearful that the Iraqi army would come pouring south across the border again as it had twelve years earlier.

◆ ◇ ◆

Bright skies continued to evade us along the screen, and while the crew talked with the locals, the Kuwaiti captain who ran the post came out to see us. I was around the back of the vehicle when I heard LCpl Davis yell for me.

"Sir," he said, walking around the LAV with a tiny glass of Kuwaiti tea in his hand. Davis and Gurganus had become big fans of hot *chai* tea the last time we were in Kuwait. "This guy sounds like he wants to tell you something." I stood up and walked over to the captain, who began talking in broken English.

"Soldier. Iraqi," he said, holding up his hands and making like he was looking through binoculars. "Morning." He pointed to his watch.

"Sounds like he saw Iraqis this morning, sir," offered Gurganus.

"Where?" I asked the captain, holding up my hands and imitating the binocular motion he had just made. He turned and pointed toward the United Nations border post that sat along the Iraqi berm next to a dirt road running to the north. The road, called "Bravo Road" on our UN border maps, was one of the three routes Delta Company was assigned to move along when we passed through the border. It would be the route on which I would travel behind 2nd Platoon once the Opening Gambit kicked off.

"Tanks?" I asked, patting the LAV for emphasis. "Did you see tanks?" He shook his head, and began making a digging motion. Then he began acting like he was putting something in the imaginary hole. He made a booming noise like an explosion.

Oh shit, I thought to myself. *Land mines. He saw them putting in a minefield.*

"Sounds like land mines, sir," Roufs said.

"Yeah," I replied. "Keep him talking." I climbed up onto the turret and tore through my map case hanging from it. A moment later I jumped down with my map and a land mine handbook the S-2 had distributed several weeks earlier. I had planned on tossing it before we left the LSA, but something had told me to keep it. I was glad I had made that decision. Walking back over to the captain, I pointed to the map.

"Show me." He examined the map and pointed to a location along Bravo Road about 100 meters north of the UN outpost and the berm.

"Goddamn," said Davis, looking over our shoulders. "That's our route!" The captain began describing the mines through gestures with his hands, and I pulled out the handbook. As I flipped through it page after page, he kept saying, "No," to each mine I pointed out to him. Halfway through the handbook he pointed to one, and then tilted his hand back and forth, indicating that the mines he had seen were similar to it. I continued to flip pages for him, and suddenly he exclaimed, "Ah-ha!" and pointed to an antitank mine called a TC-6.

"TC-6?" I asked. "You saw a TC-6?" I looked back down at the picture of the Italian-made antitank land mine. It fit his earlier description perfectly: as big around as a basketball, with a fluted plastic casing and a rope carrying handle. He nodded his head emphatically, and I turned to Davis next to us. "You got that?"

"Got it, sir," he replied, scribbling in his notebook. I handed him the handbook and knelt down with the captain. I had to be sure.

"One more time," I asked. "What did you see?" Drawing in the dirt he described seven to nine soldiers, supervised by an officer, laying about fifteen mines across the road and burying them. He pointed to the map again, and then pointed back north toward the border. That was it. I had what I needed, and I stood back up with him.

"Let's go," I said to my crew. "Mount up." As the Marines packed up their equipment and boarded the LAV, I turned to the Kuwaiti.

"Shukram," I said in Arabic, firmly shaking his hand. *Thank-you.* As I climbed aboard the vehicle and we turned south toward the battalion COC, the Kuwaiti waved and smiled at us. Whether he understood it or not, he had just saved the lives of many Marines in 2nd Platoon. He may have saved mine, too. As the vehicle moved across the desert toward the COC, Davis continued to study the land mine handbook. He keyed his intercom.

"Sir, those mines are big sons o' bitches."

Gurganus's voice came across the intercom from down inside his driver's compartment. "Hey sir, what would happen if we drove over one of those things?"

I thought about his question for a moment, and then looked back at the picture Davis had in his hand. After all, the mine was designed to take out a tank. "I don't know. I reckon it would tear our vehicle apart." No one said much after that.

Back at the COC I walked into the briefing tent to submit the mine report to the S-2 and the S-3. Seeing both Maj Harper and LtCol White standing inside, I bypassed the S-2 and went right to them.

"Sir," I said to LtCol White. "We might have a problem."

"What do you got?" he asked, turning from the situation map he and Harper were studying.

"I just talked with the head honcho who runs the border post. He told me there are land mines on Bravo Road." I pointed to the CO's map, and then referred to the notes Davis had made for me. "This grid right here, Quebec Uniform one-eight-six, two-six-eight. It's about five meters deep and goes all the way across the road, about one hundred meters north of the UN post." Lieutenant Manson and one of his intel clerks joined us, and I repeated the information to them.

"And you're sure about this?" Harper asked me. I nodded.

"Yes, sir. I haven't seen them up close, but the Kuwaiti was pretty adamant about it. His description perfectly matched what I showed him in the mine book."

"Good job, Seth," LtCol White said.

"Wish I could take the credit, sir. That Kuwaiti is the one who just saved my ass."

"S-2," Maj Harper said. "Submit this mine report to the RCT."

"What are we going to do to get around it, sir?" I asked Harper. "That's Delta Company's route."

"Don't worry about it right now. We'll wait to see what RCT-Five has to say." As it turned out, the report made its way up the chain of command to Division, and that changed the rules. Division declared that mine-laying by Iraqis would be considered a hostile act. If we observed it occurring again we would be authorized to engage the mine-layers.

It was dark by the time I left the COC with Delta Company's new mission. The next morning Kuwaiti bulldozers were scheduled to cut breaches into the Iraqi berm. It would be Delta Company's job to provide security for the dozers as they reduced the obstacle for us. We were also required to clear out the UN outpost to ensure that no observers still manned their posts. I returned to the company's attack position and briefed the staff on the mine-laying issue and the new task for the next morning. Shortly after that I fell sound asleep inside my sleeping bag.

Unbeknown to me, the war had just begun.

✦ ✧ ✦

At 0100Z on 20 March, 1st Marine Division ordered all units to assume mission-oriented protective posture level one (MOPP-1). The company was up and moving at 0115Z, the Marines already cursing and complaining as they cut open the foil packaging containing their chemical protective suits. Even with a slight chill in the air, the heavy, charcoal-impregnated MOPP suit made you overheat quickly, and it was a challenge to stay hydrated in it. More annoying for me was my suit's size once I put it on. The company had been fitted for the suits while we were still in Camp Pendleton. After nearly a month and a half in the field I weighed significantly less than I did when I was sized. I'd lost close to ten pounds, and my MOPP suit now fit me about as well as an extra-large Hefty Bag. It was necessary to wrap green duct tape around the material below my knees to keep the suit from billowing out like clown pants and dragging on the ground behind me.

Delta Company stepped off for the border to reoccupy the screen and conduct the security mission for the bulldozers. As we waited next to the Kuwaiti border post, LtCol White showed up in his LAV to get a closer look at the area. The two of us began talking.

"Well, I just heard they launched forty Tomahawks into Baghdad early this morning," he told me.

"No shit? Holy cow."

"Yeah," he continued. "It looks like H-hour is going to end up being either twenty-one or twenty-two March at zero-three Zulu. The battalion may head out tonight."

"Good to go, sir. It's on."

"Yep," he replied. "Game on." He seemed as eager as we all were to get the job over with, or at least to get it started.

I placed 2nd Platoon on the screen and directed Lt Schwartz to move his scouts in and clear the UN border outpost. Covering the scouts' advance on the outpost were 2nd Platoon's LAVs and an artillery forward observer. Additionally, one of 3rd Platoon's sniper teams had situated itself in an observation tower to the south. Bob Woodruff and his media crew followed Corporal Chris Stoia and Lance Corporal Jésus Suarez del Solar—the two snipers—as they lugged their .50-caliber sniper rifle up into the run-down tower. Woodruff began asking the two Marines questions.

"How do you feel about all this, Jésus?" he asked.

"Hopefully we'll get this done soon, so we can come home and see our families . . . safe," Suarez del Solar replied.

"Are you nervous, being up here so high in the open?" Woodruff asked.

"No, not at all," Suarez del Solar answered as he knelt down behind the massive weapon. He aimed it downrange toward the outpost.

"Why? The Iraqis . . . can't they get you from here?"

"Nah," Suarez replied, looking around. "They can't get us from this high."

The bulldozers arrived, and the mission went without a hitch. For years the Marine Corps had planned to conduct an opposed breach of the Iraqi border. It would be dangerous, and it would likely result in numerous casualties. But suddenly there were no Iraqis anywhere within sight across the border. Again I wondered *Where are they? We just cut a hole into their country and there's no one here to stop us.* I continued to think about it as I pulled my vehicle off the line and returned to the company's new attack position inside the DMZ and southwest of the Kuwaiti border post.

The chill from the morning burned off, and as afternoon approached, the temperature in the desert began to rise. We all started to sweat in our MOPP suits. Around 0930Z, as the Marines moved about in our assembly area attempting to refuel and rest, we heard the transmission over the battalion net everyone most feared.

"*Lightning! Lightning! Lightning!*" a nameless voice from battalion yelled. The brevity code "lightning," when announced over the radio, meant a Scud launch had been detected. Such a report required everyone to go to MOPP-4 (chemical suit, thick rubber over-boots and gloves, and gas mask) and hope like hell the incoming missile didn't fall on our heads. The initial Scud warning produced the same results our first NBC alarm did a month earlier in LSA-5: a brief moment of panic as we all fumbled to don our protective gear, followed by a period of self-induced stress as everyone wondered whether the missile would land on top of us and whether our equipment would work after so much time in the sand and dust. In my case, that sense of panic skyrocketed when I suddenly couldn't breathe inside my gas mask. The dust and grit had sealed shut the mask's paper-thin rubber diaphragms, and no air was getting into the mask. I looked around frantically, trying to decide between removing the mask (and risking a lungful of something nasty) and attempting to fix it on my face before passing out from lack of oxygen. Preparing to tear my mask off, I made one last desperate attempt. I grabbed it by the sides and gave it a final, forceful blow of air. There was a popping sound as the diaphragms un-seized themselves. *If I don't keep this thing clean and we get gassed, I'm a goner,* I thought, gasping heavily.

Scud alarms continued throughout the day—four within five hours—and already the Marines were failing to take them seriously. It was difficult to fault them. There was no indication anywhere around us that a Scud had landed. More importantly, though, everyone realized that the time delay from a Scud launch to when the information actually trickled down to us severely lessened our chances for survival if a missile was headed right for us. Whoever detected the launch had to notify the MEF, who had to notify the division, who had to notify the regiment, who had to notify the battalion, who had to notify the companies. I had no idea what a Scud missile's time of flight was before it hit its objective, but I had a pretty good clue how long it would take the information to make its way down the chain of command: too long.

By afternoon the constant Scud warnings and moving around in MOPP-

4 had exhausted everyone, myself included. I sat down in the sand and leaned up against one of the vehicle's tires, my gas mask in my lap and my galoshes and rubber gloves sitting next to me. I began to nod off. Inside the LAV our radio crackled to life once again.

"Dragon-Six, this is Highlander," the voice called. "Your presence is requested at the COC." There was a pause, and then the familiar shout from inside the vehicle.

"Sir, did you hear that?" It sounded like Davis. We were on the move again.

Activity around the battalion COC had picked up since my last visit. All of the companies had moved their assembly areas north of the Kuwaiti berm and into the DMZ with Delta Company, and some of the COC appeared to have been disassembled. I found Maj Harper, who was wandering around in his shorts, trying to find someone to give him one last haircut before kick-off time. He told me to devise a plan to provide security for the combat engineers as they swept the mined portion of Bravo Road and marked a route around it for the battalion. I fumbled with a hasty plan for an hour, and as I left to relay the plan to my staff, LtCol White appeared. A Marine and a soldier stood behind him.

"Seth, here are your psyops [psychological operations] guys and EOD snipers," he began. "Take them up to the border." I looked at the Marine from explosive ordnance disposal and laughed.

"EOD sniper? What's that all about, sir?" White turned to the staff sergeant, who stepped forward.

"It's something new EOD has been working on, sir," the staff sergeant told me, completely serious. "Detonating ordinance from a distance with a rifle."

"Oh, well I *have* to see this," I said, incredulously. I turned back to the battalion commander and pointed to the soldier. "Sir, what do I do with this guy?"

"Just take him up near the border," White replied. "They'll blast surrender messages to the Iraqis with their P.A. system." I followed the psyops soldier, a young kid who looked barely out of high school, to his tan humvee. His psychological operations unit had outfitted the vehicle with two gigantic speakers that seemed designed to broadcast over a distance roughly equal to the space between Maine and California.

"You guys ever blast music out of that thing?" I asked them.

"Sometimes. We've played Metallica on it before."

The two humvees followed my vehicle to the border, and we parked fifty meters from the berm. The border was deserted, and the protection of the dirt berm afforded us a clear view of Bravo Road and the area that had been mined. After looking through my binoculars I pointed out the row of freshly dug holes stretched across the dirt road. The contrast between the weatherworn road and the dark patches of recently moved earth clearly gave away the position of the mines, but that didn't matter. A minefield was a minefield. If we didn't clear them out, we weren't going through that route. One sniper set up his spotting scope and began making range calculations while the other uncased and mounted his scoped rifle on its bipod legs. Behind us the psyops team initiated its broadcast, and deafening streams of Arabic echoed over our heads and across the border. Unfazed by the noise, the spotter relayed distance and wind conditions to his partner, and the two debated which mine to shoot first. They finally decided on the mine farthest left, and as we all held our breath, the sniper fired off a round. An instant later a huge explosion cooked off across the road with a cracking *whumpf,* sending an enormous mushroom cloud of dirt and debris into the air. Everyone around the snipers cheered, but I was speechless. The force of the explosion made me realize that we had perhaps just cheated death. Had a vehicle from Delta Company detonated one of those mines, everyone inside would have been torn apart. I couldn't believe the twist of fate that had resulted in the Kuwaiti captain telling me about that minefield. What I had suspected before was now confirmed: I owed the lives of many of my Marines, and possibly myself, to that nameless man.

The two snipers remained calm and icily professional as they methodically calculated the range for each subsequent mine. But after shooting for close to an hour they only managed to detonate two more mines. The lane was fouled—Delta Company and RCT-5 would not be able to use it to cross the border into Iraq. I reported the bad news to the battalion and headed south to the company's assembly area.

Time seemed to accelerate shortly after I returned to the attack position. To the east, enemy artillery impacts thundered inside the division's lines, and a long volley of counter-battery fire from one of our own artillery battalions answered them. As I radioed the company and briefed the general situation, all around me there were shouts of "Look at that!" and "What is that? *What the hell is that?*" Far to the southwest, a dozen pinpoints of light crested the horizon and approached our position. The glowing orbs grew into bright orange fireballs trailing long, snake-like plumes of white exhaust smoke. It was a volley of rockets from an Army multiple-launch rocket system (MLRS), and as they arced across the sky their angle of flight made it seem as if they would land on top of us. Instead, they screamed high over our heads one after another, landing somewhere in Iraq and hopefully ruining someone's day. We all knew that the more of those they sent, the less resistance we were bound to meet on the way up.

I continued my interrupted transmission to the company. As I finished speaking, a pair of Cobra gunships and a Huey helicopter flying from the south passed 100 feet above us and continued north toward the border. Moments later the tearing-burlap report of a Hellfire missile and a 2.75-inch rocket barrage from the Cobras echoed back toward us. Captain Portiss was still up on the screen with one of the platoons, and I radioed him to find out the situation at the border.

"Black-Five, this is Black-Six," I called. "What the hell is going on up there?"

"Black-Six, they just hit the Iraqi observation post on the other side of the border," he began. Portiss was normally a bastion of calmness on the radio, but I sensed from his voice that he was clearly agitated. "Those bastards just fired right over the top of us without warning."

"Roger that," I replied. *It's beginning,* I thought. *And it's beginning right now.* I re-keyed my headset. "Head back this way. Collapse the screen and rally with the company at the assembly area." Their attack complete, the helicopters wheeled around and headed south again. As they returned, all three aircraft dipped down to fifty feet and performed a low-level, high-speed pass right above our vehicles. They seemed close enough to reach up and touch with our bare hands, and in the deafening *whup-whup-whup* of the helicopters' rotor blades the Marines raised their arms, pumped their fists, and cheered. The air in the assembly area practically sizzled from the Marines' elation. They ran from vehicle to vehicle, shouting to each other, smoking cigarettes, and pointing to the horizon. No one really knew what was going on, but whatever it was it sure was exciting.

I soon learned exactly what the situation was. Only hours before, the regiment had finalized the plan to send 1st LAR Battalion across the border later that evening, with the rest of the RCT to follow the next morning. But shortly after the final coordination meeting with all of the battalion commanders, Major General James Mattis—1st Marine Division's commanding general—radioed RCT-5's commanding officer, Colonel Joe Dunford. Mattis, who was known over the radio by his call sign "Chaos," asked Col Dunford how quickly RCT-5 could be prepared to attack. Intelligence had just indicated that the Iraqis planned to sabotage and destroy their oil-producing infrastructure in the Rumaylah oil fields. It was exactly what we were trying to avoid, and the division had to act immediately to counter it. Dunford immediately replied that his Marines could be ready in four hours. But it happened sooner than that. In less than three hours RCT-5 was on the move.

The sun began its dive toward the horizon, and a call from the S-3 came across the radio telling me the battalion was getting ready to go. But the plan had changed. Delta Company and 1st LAR Battalion wouldn't lead the reconnaissance we had meticulously planned for months. Instead, to protect the oil infrastructure in the Rumaylah oil fields RCT-5 would push 2nd Tank Battalion and 2/5 forward to seize the GOSPs. Delta Company and a combat engineer platoon would be responsible for providing security for the far western breach lane, designated "Red 1," while simultaneously passing 2nd Tanks and 2/5 forward of us and through Red 1. The regiment had determined the middle and eastern lanes—Red 2 and Red 3—were impassable, and both attacking battalions would funnel through Red 1. The S-3 ended the transmission by informing me that H-Hour was scheduled for 1730Z. I looked at my watch: 1630Z. The company was spread to the winds; vehicles were still returning from the screen, needing fuel, and the clock was ticking. *There is no way I'm going to be able to get us there in time,* I thought, keying the radio.

"Guidons [the company code used for addressing all principle company staff members], this is Black-Six," I said, trying to maintain my composure. "We're moving out, time: now. Rally in column on Bravo Road, south of the Kuwaiti border post." The platoon commanders acknowledged the order, and LAVs immediately began pulling out of the assembly area and heading west to the rally point. As I raced the clock to corral the combat engineers and direct them to our rally point, Lt Stiller keyed his radio.

"Black-Six, this is Green-One," his deep voice said. "One of my Marines has lost his rifle."

Carl von Clausewitz and other war theorists have talked about friction during war. Clausewitz said, "The easiest things become difficult, and the difficult things become nearly impossible." Old Uncle Carl had apparently decided to test his hypothesis on me. Unfortunately, my response was not, as my wife was fond of saying, *well done.*

"You have got to be shitting me!" I yelled into the microphone. "Where is it?"

"I don't know, Six. He left it in the field while he was taking a shit."

Left it in the field while he was taking a shit?!

"Green-One, you have fifteen minutes to find it." I said curtly. "Black-Six, *out.*" But I already knew the end of that particular story. It was past sundown. The clouds blotted out all light from the moon, and soon the sky would be as dark as ink. He would never locate the rifle. There were few things I deemed as unforgivable as losing a weapon. You just don't do it. In minutes Stiller radioed me again.

"Black-Six, we can't find it," he said, his voice dejected.

"Fuck it. It's too late," I said, looking at my watch. "We have to roll *now.* Red-One, we're Oscar Mike [*on the move*] to the support by fire position." The company slowly drove in column along Bravo Road and through the gaping holes cut in the electrified fence. As we moved toward our hasty battle positions overlooking the berm and the passage point, the radio net came alive with people yelling and screaming on both the company and battalion frequencies. It was chaos.

"Dragon-Six, this is Highlander-Six," LtCol White called over the radio. "Is your company out of the way for Second Tanks and Two-Five?"

"Highlander-Six, affirmative. We are set to provide security at this time." The company was oriented into the area north of the border, but suddenly I realized we weren't in the correct position after all. We were oriented on lane Red 2—the center, impassable breach lane—and we still needed to be more than a kilometer to the west, oriented on lane Red 1.

"Negative, Dragon-Six," White yelled into his headset. "I can see you. Your company is in the way. Second Tanks is going to run right over your company!" Things were about to get bad.

"Roger, I copy," I replied, my voice breaking. I cleared my throat, but it cracked again. I had never totally recovered from the mysterious upper respiratory infection of several weeks before, and since leaving LSA-5 I had become sicker and sicker. The war was beginning in front of me, and I was losing my voice over the radio. It sounded like I was crying. "I copy, Six. We are Oscar Mike, time: now." I radioed the shift in location to the company.

"We're in the wrong place," I yelled over the commotion on the radio. "We're in Second Tanks' way. Displace west two klicks." I gave the platoons the rally point, and we were on the move once more. In the midst of it all, as I attempted to manage the pandemonium while pathetically croaking out orders over the radio, the same question repeated itself in my head: *Man, what in the fuck happened?*

The battalion commander's voice returned to the radio.

"Dragon-Six, are you clear yet?" he demanded.

"Roger, Six," I said, my voice raspy over the radio net. "We're moving as fast as we can. There's a lot of confusion out here right now." I paused, and then added, "It's like herding cats out here." There was what sounded like a chuckle on the other end of the radio.

"Roger, Dragon-Six, I copy," LtCol White said. "Just get your people out of the way. Highlander-Six, *out.*"

The company made it to the rally point. I glanced at my watch again: 1730Z. Standing high up in the turret, I focused my night vision goggles toward the southeast where the company had originally set up. Scores upon scores of blinking infrared beacons, each atop a darkened M1A1 tank or an amtrack, charged forward like a pack of angry fireflies. The frigid night air echoed with the shrill whine of a hundred armored vehicles blazing a wide, dusty trail across the DMZ and through the passage point.

Before long, the column of armored vehicles was beyond the breach and moving north into Iraq toward the GOSPs. Delta Company and the rest of 1st LAR Battalion were set at their rally points, and the S-3 radioed for the companies to reduce their alert levels. We wouldn't be moving again until the next morning. With the drama over, energy seemed to leak from my body like a faucet. I knew I would be useless the next morning if I didn't try to get some sleep. Exhausted, I crawled into the back of the vehicle and assumed the normal cramped position on my back. Rather than sleep, though, I lay in the dark and listened to the roar of MLRS artillery soaring far above us outside. I replayed in my head the events of the evening.

I thought about the disorder and how badly things had turned out. No rounds had been fired in anger at me yet, and already I had gooned up the first operation. In the confusion as the company moved from its assembly area I had given the wrong grid coordinates for the company's support by fire position—we had ended up two kilometers shy of where the battalion had assigned us. When the crucial time came, the company wasn't where it was supposed to be to provide security for 2nd Tanks and 2/5. If those two units had sustained any casualties as they traversed the passage point it would have been my fault. I started thinking about friction again, and about what Uncle Carl had said about the "fog of war." He sure as shit wasn't kidding. You could have practically cut it with a knife as the company struggled to get into position in the darkness.

Along with the disappointment I felt in my performance, I was further crushed by another reality: Delta Company had just lost the chance to be the first unit into Iraq. With all the confusion and havoc of that night it may have been a blessing in disguise that we weren't out there. But I was frustrated nonetheless. All night long, as I attempted to get some sleep the same bitter thought raced through my head.

So much for 1st LAR Battalion being the "Tip of the Spear."

PART II

The Other Shoe Drops: Highway 7/8 to the Tigris River

21–30 March 2003

7

Across the Border

Throughout the night I passed in and out of consciousness, listening to the rumble of artillery and bombs impacting across the border. In the darkness of the LAV's scout compartment the explosions were muffled and far away. The adrenaline-fueled dash to get the company to the border on time had exhausted me, but real sleep continued to evade me. I would slowly drift off, listening to what James Webb had once described as "someone else's war," only to be awakened minutes later by the radio beeping to life as some far away voice passed traffic over the net. Squirming around inside the cramped, overloaded compartment I somehow managed to find a position perfectly conducive to sleep. The noise of the radio and the artillery thudding on the horizon gradually faded. Eventually I slept.

I don't know how long I dozed, but I was awakened around 0100Z by the vehicle vibrating around me. The enormous *thu-wump* of an explosion outside immediately followed. The concussion rattled the LAV's hull back and forth momentarily, and then there was silence again. I bolted upright and kicked open the scout hatch. The pitch black of earlier had been replaced by shimmering moonlight, which illuminated the company's vehicles, arrayed in a semicircle around my own. One of the LAV-Ls was parked behind my vehicle, and perched atop it were Corporal Andrew Martin and Lance Corporal William Schaffer. The two Marines watched the MLRS as it continued to shriek high above our heads.

"Hey!" I yelled to them. "What the hell was *that?*" They both started laughing.

"Holy shit, sir! You shoulda seen it!" Cpl Martin called back to me. "A fucking rocket just landed, like, less than a klick from us!" A short round from an MLRS volley had impacted near our position. Someone else's war or not, things were getting dangerous very quickly. Sleep eluded me for the rest of the night as the battle raged on to the north.

RCT-5 had assumed the role of 1st Marine Division's main effort. As it pushed through the berm and across the border nine hours ahead of everyone else, it became the first conventional ground unit in the war to enter Iraq. Second Tank Battalion and 2/5 sped north, with 1/5 and 3/5 following in the east. The RCT quickly reached its objective and overcame the Iraqi defenders. In the oilfields the RCT discovered abandoned positions that had been previously occupied by more than a brigade of enemy soldiers. However, 1/5 encountered stiff resistance at Pumping Station Two in the southern oilfield, and the RCT lost its first Marine when Second Lieutenant Therrel Childers was killed in the fighting. We listened to reports over the radio of enemy tanks and armored vehicles, surface to air missiles, artillery, and mortars, but despite the warnings of what lay ahead for us, we all knew the same thing. The loss of the RCT's first Marine was sobering, but the war wouldn't be real for Delta Company until we crossed the border.

✦ ✧ ✦

Before sunrise on 21 March Maj Harper radioed me.

"Dragon-Six, prepare to cross the LD [line of departure] at zero-six Zulu. Continue mission as planned; provide flank security for RCT-Five north along Axis Edith. Lead First LAR and First Recon north to Southwest Rumaylah airfield. There, detach one platoon to provide security for battalion Main, and escort First Recon to the cloverleaf."

I keyed my helmet switch. "Roger Highlander-Three, I copy. Moving to passage point now." I radioed the company and directed them to rally on X-Ray Road, a paved route south of the border that ran parallel to the berm. The crews pulled the vehicles out of their positions from the previous night and moved toward X-Ray in column. Once on the road, the company automatically positioned the column into a herringbone formation. In the herringbone, one of the most common procedures we performed as a company, the first vehicle pulls off the road to the right at a forty-five degree angle. The second vehicle pulls off the road to the left, the third to the right, and so on until the column of vehicles literally resembles a herringbone pattern. It orients the company to the flanks while at the same time getting the vehicles off the road in case other units need to move through the formation. Once the word is given it is easy for the company to resume moving.

I called for the final company radio check before we stepped off across the border. This was not only standard procedure, it had become a company ritual. Over time, the Marines had come to use the first radio check as a gauge to predict how the day would be. It was well known that if the company botched the radio check I would be pissed off from the very beginning of the exercise.

"All Dragon Victors, this is Black-Six," I radioed, looking back down the long column. "Radio check, respond in sequence."

As each vehicle commander acknowledged with a simple "Roger," I thought about the voice on the other end of the radio and the crew of Marines and sailors sandwiched inside the confines of each LAV. When the last vehicle commander signaled his acknowledgment, I yelled down inside the cabin of my own vehicle.

"Is everyone up?"

"Up!" yelled back Cpl Harter and LCpl Roufs in unison.

"Up," replied Davis on the intercom.

"Gurganus, can you hear me?" I asked into my microphone.

"I've got you, sir," he said. I craned my neck around to look up and down the herringboned column of twenty-five vehicles one last time, and then acknowledged the company's transmissions.

"Roger, Black-Six copies all." I directed Lt Parment to move out. "Red-One, we are Oscar Mike. You are clear to cross the line of departure at this time."

Crossing the border into Iraq during the daytime was strangely "underwhelming," a term Lt Cullins was fond of using when he wasn't impressed. It fit our situation, as I expected more than the great clouds of dust churned up by the RCT's tracked vehicles the previous night. But the only thing ahead of the company was rolling, empty desert. Behind us, the entire battalion was parked and waiting for our column to navigate the narrow breach cut into the berm. Behind them, 1st Reconnaissance Battalion did the same. Delta Company followed Bravo Road as it wound north through the DMZ until it turned into a route called "Juliet Road." Several kilometers beyond that, the route ended and the terrain opened up into a flat expanse with few identifying features. On my radio signal to assume a modified "V" formation, the company column broke apart and 1st and 2nd Platoons effortlessly moved up and abreast of each other to take the lead for the company. My vehicle section continued to travel in trace of the two lead platoons, and Headquarters Platoon and the mortar section moved along behind me. Providing trail security, 3rd Platoon brought up the rear. The transition from a column to the "V" formation was an effortless dance that took seconds. To the uninitiated, it seemed a simple maneuver. Only those who had spent countless hours performing the same action over and over again could appreciate the training, skill, and time required to perform the drill without it looking like a circus.

We continued north, inching along at twenty-five kilometers per hour. The LAV-25 gunners rhythmically scanned their gun turrets back and forth, searching for any signs of the enemy. At first it was nerve-wracking. It was, after all, the real thing, not an LAV gunnery skills test. In combat a gunner's overlooking a tank didn't mean he lost points—it meant he lost one of our vehicles. But after an hour we still found nothing but an occasional rusted tank-hulk decorated with fresh holes. It looked like the two units that had swept through the previous night had put an antitank round into every hulk just to ensure it was destroyed. We also ran across an M1A1 from 2nd Tanks sitting off to the side of our route. It had broken down the night before, and as we rolled past, the tank's crew sat glumly on the turret. They ignored our waves. I felt a perverse pleasure that at least *someone* was crossing the border after us.

The Ar Rumaylah oilfields weren't completely empty. We passed several Bedouin camps, and the inhabitants all scrambled out of their ramshackle tents to wave at us as we passed by. Blank looks filled most of their faces, but some smiled. Still unsure about the Bedouins' intentions, I radioed the company to keep a close eye on them. Aside from the periodic position reports from Lt Parment, the radio was quiet. It was a far cry from the confusion of the previous evening. I didn't even realize LtCol White and the battalion forward were behind me until I heard his voice sound over the radio.

"Dragon-Six, this is Highlander-Six. Whoever it is in the LAV ahead of me has a flat tire." I looked to my rear and saw him standing in the turret of the vehicle behind me. *Oh man, he's talking about me.* I leaned out of the turret and looked down, trying to examine the damage to the tire.

"Six, this is Eight," 1stSgt Guzman called. "Your number three right tire is out." Throughout Delta Company's training our SOP had always emphasized utilizing the "bump plan" if a key leader's vehicle broke down. The bump plan was simply an officer or SNCO transferring himself from his downed vehicle into his wingman's vehicle while the crew attempted to repair the problem. On paper it's no problem. In reality it's a pain in the ass. You know your own vehicle like the back of your hand. Your seat is adjusted to just the right height so you can stand up out of the turret. The radio and intercom controls are fine-tuned so you can operate them in the dark. All of your personal gear is neatly packed inside your vehicle. There is a temptation to stay with your ride until the mechanics can get it up and going again, but it's a bad idea. I had learned this lesson the hard way many times during our training.

In the Ar Rumaylah oilfields I couldn't afford to make such a blunder again, particularly after my debacle the previous night at the support-by-fire position. I radioed the two lead platoons. "Red-One, White-One, keep going. I'll catch up." I called for 1stSgt Guzman to come pick me up, and when he pulled alongside, his gunner jumped out to assist my crew in replacing the flat tire. I grabbed my map and hopped out of the turret, only to find the tire's tread completely shredded and hot to the touch. The vehicle had run over a piece of shrapnel somewhere along the way, and we had driven on the flat tire for so long it had torn itself apart. As my crew went to work removing the damaged tire, SSgt Monroe pulled up in his LAV to help speed the process. I climbed up into Guzman's turret, and together we sped off to catch up to the lead platoons. The entire exchange took less than two minutes. Twenty minutes later my LAV caught up to us, and I was back in action in my own turret.

As the company's lead elements approached the Southwest Rumaylah airfield, Lt Cullins called over the radio.

"Black-Six, we are in the vicinity of the airfield," he said. "Detaching now to provide security for LogPack-One." Although I was unhappy about the assignment from the battalion for 3rd Platoon to conduct escort duty for the logistics vehicles, I knew Cullins would have no problem. Every time Delta Company was tasked to provide a platoon to support another unit I always picked 3rd Platoon. There was no doubt they could get the job done.

"Roger. We'll see you at the screen. Be careful." I watched the platoon pull off to the west behind us, and we continued north. The company's radio net came to life again, only this time it was 1st Reconnaissance Battalion's CO calling.

"Dragon-Six, this is Godfather," he said. "We're attaching to your company now for escort to the cloverleaf."

Seven kilometers south of the cloverleaf we stopped so I could coordinate the release with 1st Recon's staff. I backtracked in my vehicle to the center of 1st Recon's column and linked up with their command staff. Before I climbed down from the turret Lt Schwartz called me from his position far ahead of us. He reported that there was a building in his zone he wanted to check out and clear. I thought for a moment and then authorized it after telling him to proceed with caution. I walked over to the battalion commander and his staff, and together we all huddled around a map he had placed across the hood of his humvee. After sketching out a plan for his companies, he told me he was ready for his battalion to split away from us immediately instead of going farther north to the cloverleaf. As we finished the coordination, LCpl Davis called down to me from our turret.

"Hey sir, Black-Five is calling for you," he said, handing down the handset to me. I answered.

"Six, this is Five," Capt Portiss radioed. "White-One found some triple-A [anti-aircraft artillery] and a suspected chemical munitions laboratory." *What?!* I tensed up.

"Are you kidding me?" I replied. "Where?"

"He's at a building just south of Highway Eight."

"Tell him to hold fast," I said, jumping into my turret. "I'm on my way right now." We sped northeast past 1st Recon's humvees and trucks to Lt Schwartz's position, where I found his platoon on-line and pointed toward a two-story building two kilometers away in the distance. Schwartz stood by the back of his vehicle, and I pulled up alongside him and climbed down.

"Sergeant Dewitt went in with his team and found all this shit," Schwartz began, holding a pile of tattered documents. "He also found some gas masks." I turned to Sergeant Will Dewitt, 2nd Platoon's senior scout.

"What else is in there?" I asked.

"Sir, there are three anti-aircraft guns dug in around the building," Dewitt told me, pointing back toward it. "A couple of bunkers also."

"What about the chemicals?" I asked. A chemical factory was really the last thing in the world I wanted to deal with, but I couldn't ignore such a report. Dewitt continued.

"There's a whole bunch of wires and batteries and shit in a room," he went on. "A shitload of white powder around and mixing bowls and just a bunch of weird shit." I thought about it for a minute.

"All right," I said to no one in particular. "Let's go check it out. Lieutenant Schwartz, your section and my vehicle." We turned to mount our vehicles, and suddenly a bunch of Marines began shouting warnings of "Truck!" and "Stop that fucker!" A small tanker truck with two Iraqis in the cab slowly approached our position, and both men inside began waving their red and white-checkered shemaghs frantically to keep us from shooting them. They hopped out of the truck's cab and ambled over toward us, smiling maniacally and voluntarily raising their hands in the air. Each man waved his identification card at us and shouted "Salaam" *Peace*. The scouts around me leveled their rifles at the men.

"Down!" yelled Corporal Raney Boulton, a team leader from 2nd Platoon. He pointed to the ground with one hand and shouted again. "Get down, motherfucker!" His other hand was wrapped tightly around his M-16's pistol grip, his finger against the trigger. More scouts ran over to put the two Iraqis on the ground and search them, but it quickly became evident that the men were compliant. I walked over to one of them and knelt down next to him.

"Are you a soldier?" I asked, pointing at him. *"Jundi?"* He shook his head. I held out my arms and, looking around like I was searching for something, asked him where the Iraqi army was. "Where jundi?" Shaking their heads, both men pointed to the east and west and adamantly gestured that they weren't soldiers. The stark contrast between the sleek brown skin covering their thin bodies and the pale, white flesh of my own, visible only above the neck because of my MOPP suit, was peculiar. Suddenly I understood the gravity of their plight, and I realized they were no threat to us.

"Give them a bottle of water and let's get out of here," I said to the scouts. "They aren't soldiers. They don't know anything." Two Marines walked up to the men and handed each a liter of the bottled water we had hoarded weeks earlier. The two men smiled again and continued to wave as they returned to their truck and drove away.

Our three vehicles cautiously closed the distance to the abandoned building. There were still anti-aircraft guns, and for all we knew someone had remanned them while we were gone. The haze from the day before had burned off, and there wasn't a cloud in the sky. On the horizon to the east the burning pillars of two oil wells set ablaze by the Iraqis in the night glowed faintly. Ahead of us, Highway 8 was empty, save for an occasional carload of people dressed in civilian clothes passing by. Several small groups of men walked along the highway from the east. Some were dressed in tattered green army uniforms, others in civilian attire. They looked forlorn and defeated. Some carried white strips of cloth indicating their surrender, or at least their submission. Each time an LAV pointed its turret at them they would raise their hands in the air until the gun was taken off them, and then they would continue walking toward wherever it was they were going.

The building and the fighting positions around it appeared to still be unoccupied, and as I prepared to dismount with 2nd Platoon's scouts to check out the area, SSgt Kappen radioed.

"Black-Six, this is Black-Seven," he began. "Bob Woodruff is requesting to come out there to film the area." I thought for a minute. We were investigating a suspected chemical lab. The last thing I needed was for a news crew to keel over from some poisonous material we had uncovered. I wasn't comfortable having a film crew follow the scouts and me around. Not believing they were trained for that sort of thing, I just didn't feel good about it. Besides, they would be in the way.

"Negative, Black-Seven," I replied, taking off my CVC helmet and replacing it with my Kevlar one.

The building was wrecked. Holes pockmarked the cinderblock walls, and craters surrounded it. Garbage and broken furniture were strewn everywhere, as were bits of military uniforms and equipment. Moving room to room with Sgt Dewitt and his team through the shambles of the structure, we were appalled by the conditions we found; the place seemed ready to fall down upon itself. But soldiers had been there, all right. There was a room for sleeping that contained some ratty mattresses, and next to it an office space sported pictures of coalition aircraft pasted to the walls. It looked like some "expendables" had been dropped off at the compound and ordered by their superiors to shoot at anything in the sky that matched the diagrams on the wall. Farther down the passageway was a storage area filled with crates of 23mm ammunition, and adjacent to that was the room that had caused the scouts so much alarm.

"This is it," Sgt Dewitt told me. He pointed to several car batteries that had been hooked up to a hotplate and some sort of makeshift washing machine or dishwasher contraption. Various foodstuffs lay around, including piles of white flour blanketing the tabletops. Lance Corporal Roufs—we were already calling him "Kodak"—excitedly snapped pictures of the flour and batteries with his digital camera.

"Jesus Christ," I said, laughing. "This is a kitchen! Look, the car batteries are powering that washing machine and hotplate, and they were making bread in here." The Marines started laughing, and Sgt Dewitt looked a bit embarrassed.

"Sorry for the false alarm, sir," he said sheepishly.

"Don't worry about it," I said, clapping him on the shoulder. "Let's go check out those guns."

Outside we found the compound ringed by three ZU-23s (twin-barreled 23mm anti-aircraft guns) and several sandbagged survivability bunkers. The guns still had ammunition belts in them, and they were in working condition. As I examined one of the guns, LCpl Davis yelled to me from the vehicle.

"Sir! Black-Seven is asking again if the reporters can come out here." *He really wants a story, but he's not getting it right now,* I thought.

"Goddammit, tell him I said no," I yelled back. "And tell him not to ask me again!" I turned around to Sgt Dewitt. "Do you have your 'hooligan kit' out here?"

"Yes, sir, it's in our vehicle."

"Go get me your bolt cutter."

A Marine returned with a long, black bolt-cutter and handed it to me. The guns had to be disabled. Whoever had manned the site before might come back and try to use them on our aircraft. *Hell,* I thought. *We're lucky they didn't stick around and try to use them on us.* But disabling the ZU was more difficult than I had thought. With no idea which wires or cables to cut, I quickly realized that I really didn't know what the hell I was doing. There had to be a better way. We could blow them up in place with our demolitions, shoot them with our 83mm SMAW (shoulder-mounted assault weapons) rockets, or take them out with 25mm high explosive rounds. Both demolitions and SMAW rockets were in short supply throughout the battalion, so I decided to use the main guns of our LAV-25s.

Our three vehicles backed away from the gun positions and sighted in on them. After pointing out to Lt Schwartz the two guns for his section, I cleared the crews to open fire. To my left and right Schwartz's LAVs barked as each main gun released a volley of HEI-T fire (high-explosive incendiary, tracer). I keyed my headset and spoke into the intercom.

"Okay, Davis. Let her rip." He squeezed the joystick's palm switch to power up the turret and the gun, and as the turret motor whined to life the gun barrel elevated to a sixty-degree angle. It was a malfunction. Inside the turret Davis cursed, and he began manually cranking the barrel down to its original position.

"Try it again," I urged. There was the same noise: a click, a whirr, and the barrel super-elevated again.

"It's fucked, Goddammit!" Davis said into the intercom.

Shit, I muttered to myself in agreement. I clicked the headset again.

"Don't sweat it," I said, probably more to myself than to Davis. "Better it happen now than when we really need it. See what we can do about it at the screen." As Lt Schwartz and his wingman continued to pump explosive rounds into the ZUs, I radioed him.

"White-One, this is Six," I said, unable to hide the disappointment in my voice. "My gun just shit the bed. Take out my target." Immediately his turret swiveled and put five rounds into the gun in front of me, cooking off the ammunition in a bright orange plume.

Disabling ZU-23 anti-aircraft gun north of Ar Rumaylah oil fields. (L to R: Capt Folsom, Sgt Will Dewitt.) Official Marine Corps photo by LCpl Andrew P. Roufs.

"Okay," I radioed the company. "Let's get out of here. Red-One, take us to the screen so we can link up with the battalion." Lieutenant Schwartz's section and my vehicle returned to where the company had halted, and the column headed west to establish the screen. The sun would be going down soon, and the company needed to be in place before darkness fell. I didn't want a repeat of the previous night.

✦ ✧ ✦

The location for the screen was a rocky area near the cloverleaf along Highway 8. The two line platoons—1st and 2nd Platoons, reinforced with the TOW vehicles—formed a picket facing west, and I positioned the Headquarters Platoon a kilometer behind them. The area we were in appeared to have been a quarry of some sort. Deep holes and piles of rock and dirt surrounded us, making perfect hiding places for the LAVs. Once the screen was established, we had nothing to do but wait. There had been a delay in the link-up between Delta Company and the battalion, and our communications with the main and forward were spotty. To the company's front, several Hueys and Cobras patrolled the skies looking for enemy resistance, but their guns were silent. They couldn't find anyone, either. After passing the alert level to the platoons (indicating how many Marines per vehicle were required to be on watch), LCpl Davis and I found a small quarry to shield the vehicle. I climbed down from the turret to get my bearings. It had been a long day of driving and trying to stay alert, and, having had little rest over the previous three days, I was beat.

Staff Sergeant Monroe and one of his mechanics showed up a couple of minutes later, and together with LCpl Davis they went to work on our gun. The entire time a parade of obscenities issued forth from Davis's mouth as he cursed the gun and those who had manufactured it. He was understandably pissed off that he had missed his first opportunity to fire in combat, and my reassurances that there would be other opportunities did little to assuage his ire. As the mechanics continued to troubleshoot the weapon system, SSgt Monroe walked around the side of the vehicle where I sat on my campstool, my head resting against the cool metal hull of the LAV.

"So this is war, huh, sir?" he asked facetiously. Monroe was young, and often aloof. Originally from Kentucky, he had had a pretty hard life. I didn't know a lot about his background, but I often figured that his lighthearted attitude was a result of an upbringing in which few people cared about him or what he did. He had confided in me weeks earlier that when he told his parents he was shipping out for Kuwait they didn't say too much in the way of reassurance.

"Yeah," I replied wearily. "Kind of seems like a CAX so far, doesn't it?" He returned to supervise my crew on the gun repairs, and as I sat there Bob Woodruff walked over with his British film crew, a cameraman named Matt Green and a soundman with the unlikely name of James Brolan. Matt began filming me as I cut a hole in a foil MRE pouch of applesauce and sucked the contents out. I tried to ignore him.

"So, what's happening now?" Woodruff asked, trying to get an idea of the situation. I briefly described what the company had done, and beyond that I told him I had no idea what was next.

"Are you surprised that you haven't met any resistance so far?"

"Yeah, a little," I replied. "But then again, this has just been the first twenty-four hours. Who knows . . . the first guys probably just pissed their pants and ran away when the RCT barreled through last night." We made small talk for a while, and then he asked the question that I knew was coming.

"Why didn't you let me film that chemical weapons site this afternoon?"

I continued eating, irritated that less than a day into the operation he was questioning my judgment.

"Because my Marines reported to me that there was a suspected chemical site, and I didn't want to unnecessarily endanger anyone. That's why I only went over there with three vehicles."

"But there weren't any chemicals there. Why didn't you let us come after that to film you destroying those anti-aircraft guns?" He was visibly irritated that I had denied him the chance to cover the event.

"Look, I'm responsible for these guys. I made the call not to let your people on the scene, and that's that."

"Well, you have to understand," he persisted. "I'm a journalist. I have to go where the story is. Today the story was at that building. We know what kind of risks we're taking. You don't have to worry about us. I've been in Afghanistan and Kosovo."

The last thing I wanted was a lecture from a reporter. I had an ingrained mistrust of the media, and nothing I had seen so far had altered my opinion.

"Listen," I told him. "I'll repeat the same thing I told you a couple of days ago. You and your crew can ride wherever you want in the company, but I'm not gonna shift forces around to get you to the front lines. Like I told you before, I always travel with the main effort, so if you want to ride on my vehicle you're welcome to it." And in truth, had Woodruff been on my vehicle when we rode over to the suspected chemical site I probably would have taken him along despite the risks. After all, I didn't want to lose time as it was. But his persistence after my first refusal angered me so much that I dug in my heels.

"But on your vehicle the turret blocks the camera too much. Also, the transponder you have with your radios interferes with the camera's reception." His response did nothing to persuade me to give him a break.

"Well, if you want to continue to ride on Staff Sergeant Kappen's vehicle, that's fine, but just remember that his combat trains don't ride up front. That's the job of the line platoons. They're the ones who will do the fighting. I wouldn't worry too much, Bob. You're gonna get plenty of chances to get shot at."

My words didn't convince him, and he left still upset with me. True, I had prevented him from getting a story on the opening day of the ground war; but that was my prerogative. I had received very little guidance on dealing with the media embeds. As far as I was concerned—and until someone told me otherwise—the embeds were just along for the ride. It was up to me to decide what to let them cover. And besides, if Woodruff didn't want to help himself by positioning his team in a prime location, I wasn't going to feel guilty about it.

Soon after my encounter with Woodruff, the battalion forward showed up and positioned its vehicles fifty meters behind my own. I grabbed my map and walked over to meet LtCol White and brief him on the company's activities since we had split from the battalion with 1st Recon. Weapons and Charlie Companies also rolled in and set into the picket with Delta Company, but the battalion was still missing the main and most of its combat and field logistics trains. They had harbored up farther south and would not link up with us until sometime the next day. Lieutenant Colonel White and Maj Harper proceeded to brief me on the overall situation, but they had little to offer. RCT-5 was fragmented throughout our zone, with the infantry battalions still dealing with the GOSPs in the oilfields. The division was consolidating and planning for the next phase of the operation, and we were unsure what was next for us. The battalion had put an incredible amount of energy into planning for the Opening Gambit, but the operation had concluded more quickly and easily than anyone had expected. Information still trickled in, but we were uncertain what was real and what was rumor. The BBC reported that a Marine had been killed in a firefight, but Lt Childers's death was still unconfirmed. We also heard a Marine CH-46 Sea Knight helicopter had crashed the previous night, killing all twelve on board. Word had it that it was a mishap, not enemy fire, that had brought the aircraft down. First LAR Battalion was more than fifty miles inside Iraq, and we had no idea what our future held in store. Despite the clear skies all around, as the sun set before us on D-Day plus one the fog was still very thick indeed.

8

Push to the Euphrates

I slept soundly the night of 21 March. The next morning I awoke shivering in my sleeping bag, and as I stared at the desolate terrain surrounding us the same thought buzzed through my brain again and again.

Wow, I'm in Iraq.

There was no sound in the desert. The screen the company had established the previous night had been quiet, with no enemy contacts reported by the platoons. As the sun rose, burning off the chill from the cold evening, Marines huddled in small clusters. They smoked cigarettes, ate MREs, cleaned weapons, and listened intently to the BBC's periodic reports on the shortwave radios spread throughout the company. We may as well have been back in Kuwait, or even Twentynine Palms for that matter. More references to the downed CH-46 and the casualty in the oilfields were broadcast, but I soon became suspect of the BBC. Throughout our time in Kuwait as we sat in the troop tent and listened to the daily broadcasts, the BBC had reported "the facts" and then some. A decidedly antiwar, antiGeorge Bush theme permeated most of its broadcasts. Just how much truth had they been reporting and how much liberal invective were they infusing? But the BBC was our only lifeline to the world outside the company perimeter, and with no update from the regiment or the division we jumped at anything put before us.

That morning Dave Hudspeth, Gil Juarez, and I met with the battalion commander and the S-3 to receive a mission update. Lieutenant Colonel White said nothing of the SNAFU of two nights earlier, and I considered the error my one "silver bullet." I didn't figure I would get a second chance. Major Harper had tucked his LAV into a depression cut into the rocky earth that almost completely hid the vehicle from view, and as we gathered around the back Lt Manson gave us a brief intelligence update. It was brief because there was nothing significant to report. RCT-5 had captured many Iraqi soldiers at the GOSPs, but they had been stoolies who knew nothing. Members of the Iraqi Special Security Organization (SSO) or of the Ba'ath Party had held most of them at gunpoint, forcing them to defend their positions against the advancing Marines. The GOSPs had been seized intact, and only a handful of wellheads in the Ar Rumaylah oil fields had been blown. Delta Company's sighting of the oil fires burning to the east confirmed the report. RCT-7 had secured the oil pumping station at Az Zubayr—the much-prized "Crown Jewel" of the Opening Gambit—with little resistance. I would later learn that the company commander who had led the attack on the pumping station was none other than Captain Tom Lacroix, another classmate of mine from Quantico. It seemed everyone from my generation of Officer Candidates School and The Basic School was reuniting in the war.

Earlier in my career, in conversations with my father, I had frequently bemoaned the fact that I might never get the chance to prove myself in combat. Each time, my father, always serious about the job I had undertaken, said the same thing. "If you stay in long enough you will get the opportunity to serve, if it is to be."

Now my chance had come, as he had predicted over the years, but it was off to a peculiar start. As I sat there with the other company commanders, jotting down our new mission orders in my notebook, I thought very little about the war or the sheer craziness in which I had become entangled. Instead, I started to think about a conversation I had had with a fraternity brother of mine a year earlier. Ashley and I had flown to Las Vegas to see a group of our friends before I departed for WestPac, and I was up late in the evening at the bar drinking with my friend. For years he had seemed in awe of my job, and he repeated something he always told me on the rare occasions we got together.

"Man, I'm glad there are people like you out there to defend our country. I could never do it." In previous years I had considered this comment a sort of backhanded compliment, never paying it much attention. But since September 11 I had developed a more caustic attitude about my profession and the risks it entailed.

"You know, that's bullshit," I said, glaring at him through the smoke trailing off my cigarette. "You say that all the time. It's not that you could never do it. You *would* never do it. If someone was invading our country, if our country was really at risk of losing everything, you could do it. You *would* do it. As it is, you chose your path and I chose mine. I appreciate your support more than anything, but don't patronize me with patriotic appeals to my ego."

"You know what I mean," he told me apologetically. "I respect what you do." Realizing I had hurt his feelings, I turned the conversation away from what I did for a living and asked him about his job. I had been too harsh with him. It wasn't my place to criticize him for not joining the military. But there was the underlying feeling that many of my military peers and I continued to have throughout our careers: we tended to resent the people we had sworn to protect.

◆ ◇ ◆

We were on the move again, this time a reconnaissance to the west along three routes. Weapons and Charlie Companies were ordered to move along Highways 7 and 8 (from our current position to the vicinity of a city called An Nasiriyah, both Highway 7 and Highway 8 merged as one), and Delta Company was assigned a southern, more rural route. While Highway 7/8 was a paved highway, Delta's route was mostly a dirt trail that twisted its way through irrigated, plantation-like farmland. My map indicated the area we would pass through was populated with several tiny villages, but the S-2 predicted we would meet no resistance as we moved through. The RCT had begun its push toward the Euphrates River crossing west of An Nasiriyah, and 1st LAR Battalion's mission entailed locating a swath of land suitable for supporting a tactical assembly area for all two thousand vehicles of RCT-5.

We were twenty-four hours into the war, and, falling back on our SOPs, the company stepped off in a manner no different from that used in any of the training exercises we had undertaken countless times before. But I was still concerned about moving through the inhabited areas. Our training had always enforced the necessity of bypassing inhabited, built-up areas whenever possible, and our training rarely included dealing with civilians while we operated. There was, of course, the token MEU exercise where the Marines were required to deal with people rioting at an embassy or a mass-casualty drill, but for the most part we trained as if we would race head-on into the enemy. We had never planned to travel among the people of a country we had just invaded. So, on the morning of 22 March we ventured into uncharted territory, both literally and figuratively. Our "highway war" had just begun.

My concerns were alleviated as we entered the first inhabited areas. As the company's column gradually inched along its route, I looked up and down the line of vehicles to see just what I had hoped: each vehicle's turret scanned back and forth, covering the danger areas and checking out anything that seemed suspicious. Although we encountered no enemy resistance, every Marine was alert to potential danger along the route.

In fact, there was no danger whatsoever. Instead, throngs of Iraqis dressed in little more than rags ran from their mud huts and tents to gawk at our armored procession passing through their neighborhoods. Children smiled and waved energetically as the column crept past them, but we were greeted by impartial, if not hostile, stares by the majority of the adults along our route. It was a hell of a sight, and it was clear to me that it was right for us to be there, doing what we were doing. After all, those observing us were the same downtrodden Shi'ite Muslims the United States had urged to revolt against Saddam Hussein twelve years earlier. But then the irony of that fact struck me. The same Shi'ites the United States had encouraged to rebel had been systematically slaughtered by Saddam Hussein's regime. Untold thousands—hundreds of thousands even—had been annihilated in a religiously fueled pogrom of epic proportions. The United States had failed to support them during the uprising in 1991. Why should they think we would do any differently a second time around? But even as I understood their suspicious looks, I still sought their approval of our arrival. I radioed to the company.

"Guidons, this is Black-Six," I said, looking at the children with their outstretched hands. "Start tossing out the humanitarian MREs to them, but don't overdo it." Each vehicle crew had been issued two cartons of humanitarian MREs before we left camp in Kuwait. Visibly different from normal MREs (at least on the outside), the humanitarian rations were sealed in fluorescent yellow pouches that distinguished them from the light brown of our field rations. Supposedly they contained food that didn't violate any of the dietary constraints imposed by the religion of whomever it was they were intended for. I wondered just what kind of nutritious crap was in these "humanitarian" rations, but we distributed them nonetheless. It was then that I observed the first image of the war that truly disturbed me. As LCpl Davis and I intermittently tossed the yellow parcels from the vehicle to the hordes of young children loitering along our route, we watched adults pushing them out of the way to get to the MREs. I was appalled. It seemed savage, pushing a child aside to get food. Was it that bad here? Had Saddam really beat these people down to the point where they were willing to deny their children these small tokens of our amity? That picture remained in my mind as we trundled forth in search of the regimental TAA.

Meanwhile, Charlie and Weapons Companies were having a more frustrating time moving along their route parallel to us. I didn't quite understand what the problem was, but Gil and Dave seemed to be encountering difficulties coordinating their movements with the battalion headquarters. Or maybe it was just the opposite. Over the radio there were many confused reports and disagreements about the true disposition of the battalion, and I was glad Delta Company was off on its own. It was true that we did our best work when we were operating independently. Whether that was an indicator of our skill or our inability to work well with others, I didn't know. But my Marines were always happy when we got an independent mission that didn't involve the battalion breathing down our necks. I was generally just as happy as they were in times like this.

We continued forward, and I heard an unexpected report over the radio from Lt Parment in the lead with 1st Platoon.

"Black-Six, this is Red-One," he said, sounding half asleep. "Be advised: we're passing through a column of seven-tons herringboned along the side of the road. A lot of Marines are showing their asses right now." It was part of RCT-1 that had made its way ahead of us. The previous day they had pushed to the northwest while RCT-5 dealt with the oilfields. I hadn't expected them to be forward of us, much less hanging out on the side of the road as they were. There had not been enough amtracks to carry all of the infantry battalions in the division, and so RCT-1 was only partially mechanized. They had one unit, Second Battalion, Twenty-Third Marines (2/23, a reserve unit that had been activated the preceding year), riding in 7-ton trucks as a motorized infantry battalion. Two-Twenty-Three was Stefan Dirghalli's unit. He had been in my platoon in TBS and had been my roommate when I was a lieutenant in San Diego. Together we surfed the waves of southern California for two years before I received orders back to Quantico. He got out of the Marine Corps shortly after I left the West Coast to work at OCS, and I was surprised to hear he had returned to the Reserves in 2002. He had joined 2/23, and he had shipped out for Kuwait shortly after me in February. I didn't expect to see him on the Iraqi battlefield, of all places, yet there he was, sitting by the side of the road with all the other Marines. Most were in various states of undress—eating, shaving, or sleeping—and the battalion looked like one big yard sale out in the middle of no where. Unable to resist the urge to heckle my friend as we passed by, I called to him.

"Hey, asshole!" I yelled at the top of my lungs, leaning far outside of my turret so he could hear me. "Hey, you fucking reservist! Make way for the Tip of the Spear!" He saw me pointing at him, and a wide, toothy grin filled his face. He stood up and shook his fist menacingly.

"Kiss my ass!" he shouted back, adding several obscene gestures to his reply. His jovial response only encouraged my childish behavior.

"Eat my dust, asswipe! Go back to Kuwait, amateur!"

My crew laughed over the intercom, and PFC Gurganus piped up from inside the driver's compartment.

"Hey sir, I just saw a guy taking a shit out in the open!"

I rolled my eyes and looked at Davis next to me. "Awesome," I replied sarcastically. "That's the kind of report I need, Gurganus. Keep 'em coming."

The built-up, sparsely vegetated area we passed through eventually gave way to desert again, and soon we were surrounded by terrain no different from that which we had traversed the previous day. Highway 7/8 continued to parallel the company to our north, but everything else was wide-open desert punctuated by palm groves and swamp-like depressions incapable of supporting the heavy vehicles of the RCT. Major Harper relayed a rendezvous point to me over the radio, and soon the company began linking up with the battalion and other elements of RCT-5. Delta Company coiled up into a hasty assembly area, and I dismounted and walked over to the forward's location. After two days of standing in my LAV's turret it felt good to stretch my legs, and once I had met up with Dave Hudspeth and several other members of the battalion staff we started joking around like a bunch of high school idiots. Everyone told stories about the previous twenty-four hours.

"Hey man," Dave said, feigning sincerity. "I heard you got the first kill for the battalion. Did those ZUs put up a fight or what?" I pulled out a pack of cigarettes and offered him one.

"Oh, kiss my ass," I said, trying to light my cigarette. The wind had kicked up, and my Zippo wouldn't light properly. Dave leaned over, trying his Bic, but had similar results. The two of us stood there, laughing and frantically trying to light each other's smokes, while unbeknown to us Matt Green from ABC News filmed us. He had been filming Maj Harper discussing the follow-on operations with the battalion commander, and we two dickheads were in the background giggling as we tried to give each other cancer. It was one of those lighthearted moments I will never forget, one where we couldn't have cared less that there was a war on. But there was little time to enjoy the moment or reflect on just how far the battalion and the regiment had pushed in one day. It was time to move again.

With renewed orders to seek out a suitable TAA for the RCT, we planned to head back east along the route the company had just traversed. Nothing appropriate had appeared in the zone shared by Weapons and Charlie Companies. After describing to the S-3 a piece of land we had observed earlier in the morning, I sent Lt Schwartz and his platoon back out to quarter it and report its ability to support the RCT. Schwartz was on the radio immediately, giving me grid coordinates for the dimensions of the assembly area, and soon the company was occupying its sector of the battalion's new coil.

The proposed regimental assembly area was a rectangular patch of empty land overlooking Highway 7/8 to the north. The highway was a six-lane divided thoroughfare that resembled any of a half dozen highways paved through the Mojave Desert in the southwestern United States. Only now we watched in amazement as endless convoys of military vehicles moved east to west in front of us. Across the highway an artillery battery had set into a firing position, the long gun tubes pointed off to the northwest. I found myself again in a position where no clear information was available as to what was next for us.

What *was* clear to me was that 1st LAR appeared to be taking a back seat to whatever units were funneling through Highway 7/8. The vehicles passing across our frontage were too far out to identify their units. I removed my helmet and pushed myself up and out of the turret until I was free of the constricted space and sitting on the locked-open hatch. Resting on my pack strapped to the hatch, I lit a cigarette and surveyed the area again. It was empty, all right, and there were few indications that we were in the middle of an armed conflict.

Suddenly the artillery unit to our front began firing off to the northwest. The explosions caused all of us on the vehicle to snap our heads in that direction. Lance Corporal Davis and PFC Gurganus began laughing uncontrollably, and Davis turned toward me.

"Did you hear that, sir?" he asked me, still giggling. I had no idea what he found so funny.

"What?" I asked him, looking across the highway at the belching artillery.

"Blue-Two just called up," Davis said. He began imitating the voice on the other side of the radio. "Black-Six, this is Blue-Two. We got artillery and *oh . . . my . . . god.*" With that, both Davis and Gurganus laughed again at the odd-sounding transmission they had both heard. Blue-Two was commanded by Sgt Cole, the Marine who had told me weeks earlier that we would never have enough ammunition. We didn't know for sure if it was Cole or one of his crewmen on the radio, but I couldn't fault whoever it was for the excited transmission. The salvo surprised all of us, and it was the first time we had heard artillery fired since our last night on the Kuwaiti/Iraqi border. The tubes firing across the road were our first real indication of the day that the war was still raging for someone, somewhere far from our current position.

The company having completed quartering and occupying the assembly area, I found myself with some precious down time. Jumping at the opportunity to clean myself up a bit, I climbed down from the turret, set up my campstool next to one of the tires, and pulled my hygiene kit from my rucksack. I had been sweating in the confines of my MOPP suit for over forty-eight hours, and I was ripe. Nuclear, biological, and chemical (NBC) training and readiness had been a part of my preparation for as long as I had been in the Corps—my first experience with a MOPP suit had me puking outside the tear gas chamber in the woods of Quantico when I was a second lieutenant. Each year every Marine was required to go through the gas chamber and annually renew his or her training with all NBC gear: full MOPP suit, the M256 chemical detection kit, and atropine and 2-pam chloride auto injectors. But the longest period I had ever spent in a MOPP suit was about eight hours straight, and that was only because the division commander had insisted the Marines spend as much time as possible in our training suits before we left Camp Pendleton. Before that, the MOPP suit was usually just an uncomfortable thirty minutes or so as we received our NBC instruction and rotated through the gas chamber for the required torture that assaulted our eyes, nostrils, and lungs. Spending two days straight in a MOPP suit was a foreign concept for me, and I thanked the Almighty that the weather in the region had been mild thus far. The longer we had waited in Kuwait—the more the war was postponed—the more I had feared a campaign in which we would be required to fight in our MOPP suits in the blazing summer heat of Kuwait and Iraq. Those fears were based less on the possibility of an Iraqi chemical attack than on the certitude that we would experience massive heat casualties from the non-permeable material of the chemical suits.

Though we wore only shorts and T-shirts inside our MOPP suits, our efforts to reduce the amount of clothing under the chemical garb had an unintended side effect. Because the suit's material did not allow our perspiration to evaporate through it, sweat condensed against our skin and gradually trickled down our bodies, pooling in our boots. This process hadn't been lessened by the fact that we had crossed Iraq's border in MOPP-2. The thick rubber galoshes we wore not only made walking clumsy, but also increased the perspiration and pooling in our boots that much more. In the field I could normally make a pair of socks last several days—a week, even, depending on how much moving around I was doing. But now, two days into the war, mine were already matted, stinking, and gross, and I wanted to change them. I remembered the bag of dirty laundry in my rucksack and my shortage of clean clothing. With no idea when I would be able to wash my clothes, I gave myself a quick sponge bath next to the LAV. I balked at changing my T-shirt and socks, a decision I would later regret.

✦ ✧ ✦

As it grew dark I smoked my last cigarette of the day and rolled out my sleeping bag next to the vehicle. The war had been in session just over two days, and already the company was settling into a routine that resembled scores of peacetime exercises in which we had participated during the previous eighteen months. Though naturally concerned about the company, I was also tired and content to go to sleep in my warm bag. I had suffered through training exercises in which the goal seemed less to demonstrate tactical skill than to prove the ability of officers and staff to remain awake as long as possible before losing all ability to function. Before the war I had told my company staff how I felt about sleep.

"Listen," I had explained, wondering how my words would wash with them. "Whenever this thing kicks off, don't expect *me* to stay awake for the entire war." I looked around at the Desert Storm veterans among my staff—1stSgt Guzman, SSgt Bright, and SSgt Reeves—and continued. "You guys may have stayed awake the whole time when you were here before, but I don't plan on doing it. I've been through too many exercises where everyone in charge is useless after the first two days or so. My point is, you guys'll know what the alert level is; you will be in charge in your platoon sectors; you should know when to call me if I'm racked out."

I didn't need to be awake and controlling them twenty-four hours a day. The Marines of Delta Company knew what they were doing. In most cases they would be able to take charge without me, thus affording me time to get the amount of sleep I really required. But in truth, there was no doubt that within the company the Marines knew I was a sleep-hound. While we had been in Kuwait there had been many days when the Marines had walked into the troop tent more than an hour after reveille to see me curled up like a little baby in my sleeping bag. True, they knew I was often awake hours after taps, still in meetings or doing work. But the fact was that I liked to sleep, and I was a much more pleasant person to be around when I was as fully rested as possible. Sleep evades you in the field. When you are constantly moving, constantly burning calories, constantly making decisions, you expend your energy more quickly. Sleep becomes something you want and need more than anything—more than money, more than happiness, more than sex. You do anything to stay awake—you drink coffee, you dip tobacco, you figure out a way to smoke cigarettes without giving off any light. The need for sleep was, without a doubt, one of my greatest weaknesses. A slow riser and a fast crasher, I was known for getting the job done as quickly as possible, getting the sentries out on post, and getting my ass to sleep. I would be the first to admit it wasn't an admirable trait to have as a commander, but at the same time I knew the company couldn't rely on me if I tried to make major decisions when I was stumbling around in an exhausted stupor. That was the reason that I would go as long as possible in the turret and then turn over the watch to the Marines in the back —Cpl Harter and Kodak—while LCpl Davis and I got some rest. I didn't want to be so screwed up from lack of sleep that I would be unable to function at the time the company needed me most.

In the middle of the night I answered a radio call ordering Delta Company to move out along Highway 7/8 at first light with the remainder of the battalion. RCT-5 planned to continue its push to the Euphrates River, and 1st and 3rd LAR Battalions were ordered to lead the road march beyond An

Nasiriyah. Third LAR would cross the line of departure at 0100Z on 23 March, and our battalion would follow in trace along the highway. As Task Force Tarawa—the Marine unit that sailed from Camp Lejeune before the war—advanced toward An Nasiriyah (a major city notable for several critical bridges across the Euphrates and the Saddam Canal), the rest of RCT-5 would bypass them. RCT-5 would cross the Euphrates at a point several kilometers west of An Nasiriyah and then move north along Highway 1 to establish another TAA. From there, the RCT would prepare to ratchet up the assault north toward Baghdad.

The company began staging outside the battalion's lines before first light on 23 March, and as the LAVs churned up dirt and sand in the assembly area, a large dust cloud settled around all of the vehicles. The absence of any wind left the dust cloud suspended around us, and soon it was difficult to see in the darkness with our NVGs. Lieutenant Parment radioed me, a clear sense of irritation pinching his usually relaxed voice.

"Black-Six, one of my vehicles just got rear-ended by a Green Victor. I don't know what the damage is yet."

Son of a bitch, I mouthed to myself. *This is the last thing we need right now.* I radioed back to Parment.

"Roger that, Red-One. We'll look at it once we get to the staging area." I shifted my ire toward Lt Stiller over the radio.

"Green-One, this is Six," I said, trying to sound casual and hide my annoyance that this was the second time one of his vehicles had caused an easily avoidable accident. "Why do your vehicles keep bumping into my LAVs?" I wasn't prepared for his reply.

"Black-Six, it wasn't one of *my* vehicles that did it last time." His acerbic remark referred to Sgt Rocha's LAV-25 grazing the side of the LAV-AT several weeks earlier. My sarcastic comment to him over the radio aside, I couldn't believe he had the balls to smart off like that. My left hand made a move to key my headset, but before I could transmit, Capt Portiss's voice preempted my own.

"Green-One, this is Black-Five! I don't know who the fuck you think you are, but keep your smart-ass comments to yourself!" There was no doubt about it: the XO was pissed.

"Roger that, Black-Five." Contempt filled Stiller's voice over the radio, and I stepped in to head off a potential argument over the net between the two officers.

"Green-One," I said sternly. "Report to my vehicle as soon as we get to the staging area." The battalion staging area was a narrow, paved access road that led onto Highway 7/8. By the time my vehicle rolled to a stop behind 1st

Platoon, the majority of the battalion was already formed in front of us and waiting for 3rd LAR to move onto the highway. As I climbed down the side of my vehicle I was nearly run over by LAVs from 3rd LAR tearing down the access road along which Delta Company was herringboned. *Good job,* I thought. *Get yourself run over by a friendly vehicle. That will look real great back home.* But the Marines in the column behind me jumped from their vehicles and shouted "Hey! Slow the fuck down!" at the LAVs driving past.

I walked around the left side of the vehicle into the sand that still blanketed this region of the country and waited for Lt Stiller. He seemed to take forever. Staff Sergeant Monroe walked past me to inspect the damage on the LAV from 1st Platoon. He returned minutes later.

"Well," he said, trying to sound flip. "Red-Two can't swim anymore."

"What?!" I said, my voice raising.

"The AT's nose hit Red-Two's back hatch and dented it along the seal. It isn't watertight anymore. You can see light through the hatch seal."

"Goddammit." I paused and took a deep breath. "All right, we'll have to deal with it, I guess." But Staff Sergeant Monroe wasn't finished with the conversation.

"Sir, this is bullshit," he said, drawing it out so it sounded like "buuuuuull-shit." "That's twice that motherfucker has banged up one of our vehicles. We had a great fucking record before his platoon came along."

"Easy, Staff Sergeant. I'll deal with it." As much as I liked him, I had to keep Monroe's comments in check, particularly since he was talking about an officer. But at the same time I agreed with him. The company did have a good safety record—the best in the battalion, as a matter of fact. The last time two vehicles had collided in Delta Company had been in November 2001. A company making it more than sixteen months without a major mishap was nearly unheard of in the battalion. Now the company had experienced three collisions in exactly one month. Like Monroe, several members of the company staff had been quick to note that our mishaps hadn't begun until Weapons Platoon joined the company. Unlike Sgt Rocha's mishap (which had been merely a scrape), the fender benders where Lt Stiller's LAV-ATs had bumped into other vehicles had caused major damage. As Stiller approached me I tried to stay cool and remember that Sgt Rocha's vehicle had also been involved in an accident. But I was so angry that it didn't come out that way.

"Yes, sir?" Stiller asked casually, staring down at me.

"Goddammit, Lieutenant," I growled at him. "Lock up your fucking body when you're talking to me."

"Yes, *sir,*" he replied, quickly straightening his body into the position of attention.

I pointed my index finger at his face accusingly. "Listen to me, Stiller. Number one: when I tell you to report to me, you don't take your own fucking sweet time, understand?"

"Yes, sir."

"Number two: Your attitude sucks. Quit acting like your shit doesn't stink. Mouth off to me like that again, particularly over the radio with the whole company listening, and I'll break my foot off in your ass. Understand?"

"Yes, sir."

"Number three: I'm sick and fucking tired of your vehicles running into each other," I said, jerking my thumb back over my shoulder toward 1st Platoon's column. "*You* are responsible for your platoon, and that includes the way they drive. Red-Two can't swim anymore because one of your crews can't fucking drive right. Marines in LAVs get killed that way."

"Sir," he explained. "The crew couldn't see in all the dust."

"Then they're supposed to slow down and tell the vehicle behind them what they are doing. That's our SOP, and you should know that. Listen to me: unfuck yourself and unfuck your platoon. I am *this* close to firing your ass right now," I said, holding my index finger close to my thumb. "If this shit continues, you're done. Do you understand me?"

"Yes, sir." I didn't know if it was a natural mannerism or not, but he seemed incapable of hiding his disdain.

"Dismissed," I said, turning to report the incident to the battalion commander. I muttered under my breath as I walked to his vehicle, and along the way I stopped to inspect the damage to Sergeant Jerel Hofer's vehicle. Just as SSgt Monroe had described, a sizeable dent disfigured one of the scout hatches, and the watertight seal had indeed been breached. Monroe's assessment had been correct: the vehicle couldn't swim anymore. Only depot-level maintenance back at the Marine Corps' massive logistics base in Barstow, California, would be able to repair the LAV's hull and restore its amphibious capability. I found LtCol White and let him know what had happened.

"The vehicle can't swim, sir. The hull is breached."

"Goddammit," he said, shaking his head. "There's no way to bang out the dent?"

I shook my head. "No, sir. Staff Sergeant Monroe looked at it. He's pretty sure it's out of our hands."

"Well, not too much we can do about it now."

"Sir, I've about fucking had it with Lieutenant Stiller. I've gotten on his case several times now, and his attitude doesn't change. Neither does his crews' driving ability."

"Well, what do you want to do? Do you want to relieve him?" I thought for a moment. It might set a bad precedent to relieve an officer so soon into the operation. Still, the company was no stranger to that sort of thing. Since taking command, I had fired a lieutenant for lying about concealing unspent ammunition. Similarly, several sergeants and staff sergeants had lost their jobs for borderline incompetence. I had exceptionally high standards. Though I always tried to give people the benefit of the doubt, as soon as their behavior had a significant negative impact on the company I became unforgiving. But at the same time, Lt Stiller did not possess the same experience as the other officers in the company. True, he had six months as a platoon commander under his belt by the time he joined Delta Company in January, but he didn't have six months *with Delta Company.* Perhaps I expected too much from him.

"Negative, sir," I said, exhaling deeply. "Let's table it for now and I'll just keep a close eye on him. Thanks."

The other company commanders and staff showed up behind the CO's vehicle, and Maj Harper gave us a quick situation update. Third LAR had been delayed in stepping off for the march across the Euphrates, but other than that everything in the plan remained unchanged.

I returned to my vehicle and told LCpl Davis to call forward the company staff for the mission briefing. Vehicles from 3rd LAR Battalion still screamed along our access road, and once the staff arrived the first thing I told them was to keep their Marines out of the road.

"It's starting to get bad out here," I said, looking up and down the access road and up toward the highway. "Someone's gonna get run over out here if we don't watch what we're doing." I really was worried. Continuing to stare at the traffic already backing up on Highway 7/8, I was concerned Marines would get flattened. I turned back to the mission briefing.

"Not too much to say. Charlie and Weapons Companies are taking the lead behind Third LAR. It's gonna be a long road march; apparently there is little to no enemy activity ahead of us."

One of the Marines on the staff piped up. "Where the hell are they?"

"You got me. I'm as much in the dark as you are. But don't let your guard down. Order of march is SOP. First Platoon, report northings and eastings every two klicks. Any questions?" There were none, and as I turned to walk away I heard Lt Parment joking around with the other lieutenants.

"I'm not even supposed to *be* here," he said, mimicking a line from a movie. Parment had been set to make his exit from the Marine Corps at the beginning of February. His service contract was up, and he planned to move to Colorado with his wife and eventually go to law school. His wife was also a Marine who had been stationed in Okinawa nearly the entire time Parment had been with 1st LAR Battalion. The two had spent a total of about six weeks together in the previous year and a half. When the Marine Corps initiated its "stop-loss" policy, which indefinitely prevented Marines from leaving active duty even if their service contracts had expired, I half-anticipated Chad would put up a fight to get out. I knew very well he opposed the approaching war, and he could have petitioned the battalion commander to release him with a waiver. But rather than fight the orders, he accepted his extension on active duty and imminent redeployment in a very professional manner. He frequently joked about his plight, repeating the same movie line, but it was obvious how he really felt. He had Marines in his platoon—his gunner, Corporal John Baker, was one of them—who had been similarly affected by the stop-loss policy. There was no way Parment would attempt to evade his obligation while his men were stuck redeploying. Despite his very vocal, liberal leanings, I had a special affinity for Chad. Both he and his wife had been officer candidates in one of my OCS training companies back in 1999, and I had watched him mature as an officer over the previous two years. I was glad he had made the choice to stay with the company.

✦ ✧ ✦

Third LAR Battalion was far ahead of us, and it was finally our battalion's turn to join the long column on Highway 7/8. Gil Juarez's Charlie Company stepped off at 0500Z, and soon the entire battalion rumbled along the freeway at forty-five miles an hour through the middle of Iraq. It was no different than any of a dozen road marches I had made between Camp Pendleton and Twentynine Palms during my career. To our left and right the landscape continued to unfold in wide, rolling plots of desert, and gradually it turned from sand to dried marshland. We had entered the once-fertile region Saddam Hussein had unmercifully drained in the 1990s as a means to drive out and punish the Shi'a Marsh Arabs after their revolt in 1991.

Suddenly I had more time to contemplate the history of my surroundings than I had planned. The rapidly moving column unexpectedly ground to a halt, and the company found itself bumper-to-bumper with thousands of Marine and army vehicles of all types. All six lanes of the highway were jammed like rush-hour on Interstate-95, complete with truck and humvee drivers leaning out their windows and hollering obscenities at each other. No one knew who had the right-of-way, and each time the battalion's convoy broke free of the traffic jam the column would grind to a halt again. There were long periods when our column sat at a dead-halt, and each time the Marines would spill from the vehicles, move to the side of the road, and light up. Some ambled up and down the column, chatting with Marines and soldiers from other units and trading for cigarettes, dip, or anything else of value. At one point LCpl Davis keyed his intercom and pointed off to our right.

"Jesus Christ, sir," he said, disgust filling his voice. "Look at them army assholes." As we passed by a column of U.S. Army 5-ton trucks and humvees, the soldiers wandered around without their helmets or body armor. Some were clad only in T-shirts. Most noticeable, however, was the carelessness they displayed with their weapons. Many had leaned their rifles up against the tires of their halted vehicles and had walked away. On more than one occasion we saw soldiers accidentally drop or knock their rifles over onto the asphalt, and then casually lean down and pick them up as if nothing had happened. In the Marine Corps it was commonly accepted that dropping your rifle meant you followed it down to the ground and performed push-ups to atone for the infraction. Your weapon is your life; you don't mistreat it. Otherwise it may not fire when you need it the most. Apparently the army didn't follow the same creed. I didn't pay it much attention until I learned later that the army's 507th Maintenance Company had been ambushed in An Nasiriyah. We heard that many of the soldiers had been either captured or killed because their weapons had malfunctioned, a claim Private Jessica Lynch later corroborated from a hospital bed after her rescue. Months later, as I read about the route her unit's

Delta Company on Highway 7/8, moving toward the Euphrates River, 23 March 2003.
Official Marine Corps photo by LCpl Andrew P. Roufs.

convoy took I realized that Delta Company had been stuck in the traffic jam about the same time. There was every possibility we had been parked alongside part of her doomed unit. Small world.

Time dragged out in the stop-and-go traffic along the highway, and soon it became just another road march for everyone involved. No Iraqi civilians lined the route, and the wide-open terrain to our flanks showed few signs of human habitation. But as the road forked, with Highway 7 continuing north and Highway 8 extending west toward Samawah, to our right on the horizon an enormous column of black smoke climbed into the early afternoon sky. It was An Nasiriyah, and soon the word from battalion filtered down to us over the radio: Task Force Tarawa was bogged down in the city. They were taking casualties—a lot of them—and the MEF was in the process of coordinating a mass-casualty medevac. Even from a distance the spectacle was difficult to watch, knowing that Marines were fighting and dying somewhere out there.

The traffic jam along Highway 8 subsided once we veered off toward Samawah, but as we neared our crossing site on the Euphrates River it was bumper-to-bumper once again. With smoke trails hovering over An Nasiriyah still visible on the horizon, I became nervous. Our vehicles were immobile along the road—perfect targets for the enemy's artillery. Occasionally a Cobra or a Huey zoomed over our heads up and down the length of the column, as if to reinforce that they were watching over us and controlling the air. It did little to alleviate the uncomfortable sensation of being a sitting duck. Captain Portiss's voice frequently sounded over the radio to chastise the company for bunching up, but there was little anyone could do. Until we negotiated the logjam at the Euphrates, we were stuck.

Five hours after the battalion rolled onto Highway 7/8, Charlie Company began crossing the Euphrates River. A small, one-lane bridge spanned the river at the crossing sight, and one of the Marine bridging companies was in the process of completing a ribbon-bridge off to the left. As Charlie Company filed across, Weapons Company began to traverse the span. The land surrounding the crossing site had fully morphed from the desert we were accustomed to in northern Kuwait and southern Iraq into a damp, marshy region. It was reminiscent of the silted-in banks and mud-flats at the confluence of the Potomac River and Neabsco Creek near my childhood home in Virginia. Movement off-road was impossible—our LAVs would sink into the muck past their tires and to the water line midway up their hulls. For sure, the company was road-bound until we got to a point where the land was dry enough to support all fourteen tons of each LAV.

The tar pit-like nature of the marshland to our flanks wasn't the only thing about it that held my attention. As we waited on the road in the midafternoon heat, swarms of gnats assaulted us. They posed no problem while we moved, but as soon as our column halted they attacked us again. They flew up our noses and into our mouths, sinking their teeth into every inch of exposed skin. With our MOPP suits on it was too hot to hide inside the turret, and even after I slathered insect repellent onto my face the attack continued. Turning in my turret hatch, I saw that Cpl Harter and Kodak had each wrapped scarves around their faces. Lance Corporal Davis and I found that the only way to combat the onslaught was to chain-smoke each time the vehicle came to a stop. In peacetime training I would have never allowed the Marines to smoke in their vehicle turrets, but now we did it all the time. It was the only way some crews were staying awake, and now it served another function: to drive away the gnats seeking to feast on our flesh.

Sitting there, stuck in traffic and waiting our turn to cross the river, boredom set in again. I had just leaned to the side of my hatch, my chin supported by my hand, when a large bang echoed to our rear. A loud, popping noise accompanied it. Everyone jumped, their first thought *Oh shit! Artillery!* Instead, a thick, brown cloud hung momentarily suspended over the company's LAV-R, and then quickly dissipated. Each LAV is equipped with two sets of four smoke grenade "clusters," one on each side of the vehicle. The smoke grenades, which are about the size of two soda cans stacked on top of each other, are seated in the clusters. They can be fired off in salvos (either side at a time) or both clusters at once to obscure the vehicle. In the case of the recovery vehicle, an electrical malfunction had caused the right cluster to cook off on its own, launching the four grenades into the air and detonating them. Fortunately, the wind conditions were favorable enough to send the toxic brown smoke on its way without causing harm to anyone. But it scared the crap out of everyone nearby, myself included.

Delta's turn to cross finally arrived, and the company slowly approached the narrow bridge in single file. Not wanting the magnitude of this event to escape the Marines, I radioed the company.

"All Dragon Victors, this is Black-Six," I said, adopting a professor-like tone over the radio. "Be advised: you are now crossing the Euphrates River and entering the 'cradle of civilization' that everyone learned about in high school world history classes." One by one, the twenty-five vehicles of Delta Company negotiated the crossing and fell back into place with the battalion's northbound column. This time, however, we moved along a dirt trail rather than the paved asphalt we had grown accustomed to on Highway 7/8. When Lt Cullins's final LAV rolled off the bridge and onto the dirt road, he radioed to inform me that his platoon had caught up with the rest of the company.

"Black-Six, this is Blue-One," he said in his usual deadpan. "All Blue Victors have completed crossing the Euphrates River." Then he added his trademark. "That was a completely underwhelming experience." There was truth in his humor. I had always envisioned the Euphrates to be a great waterway, comparable in size to the Potomac, or even the Mississippi. Instead, what we crossed was a pitiful excuse for a river. Narrow, shallow, and slow moving, the section we had passed over was practically stagnant. Disappointed, I voiced my feelings over the vehicle's intercom.

"You know," I said to no one in particular. "Some people believe that the Tigris-Euphrates river valley was the original Garden of Eden."

Lance Corporal Davis answered my pondering. "Sure doesn't look like the Garden of Eden to me."

"Yeah," PFC Gurganus added from inside his driver's compartment. "This place looks like shit."

"That's because Saddam Hussein diverted the rivers with canals and dams," I replied. "He raped this area; bled it dry. He did it to punish the Shi'ites who live down here in the south."

The battalion column continued to inch north through the marshland, which had gradually given way to countless irrigation ditches and earthen levees. As the sun sank closer to the horizon, I began to think more and more about the greater meaning of our actions.

We're in the cradle of civilization now, I said to myself, as the column moved from its dirt path onto another, identical dirt trail listed on the map as Highway 1. I wasn't a religious person at the time. I never had been. But as the LAVs crept forward, our turrets scanning for people to kill and things to destroy, the same thought shot through my brain again and again.

We just invaded the Garden of Eden.

Is God going to be on our side now?

9
Highway 1

As the afternoon of 23 March wore on, 1st LAR Battalion slowly rumbled forward on its tedious road march along Highway 1. The term "highway" was inappropriate as applied to the dirt road under our tires. Merely punctuated as it was with intermittent stretches of asphalt, it was more of a "highway still under construction." It eventually grew from a narrow dirt trail into a broad, elevated road that had been steamrolled and flattened before a final application of asphalt. Every couple of miles, in locations where drainage tunnels had been planned for construction, the elevated road was severed by gaps as wide as 100 feet. Each time the battalion's lead element reached one of these gaps it had to move down from the elevated portion of the road to negotiate a bypass around the obstacle. It was stop and go for much of the way, and I knew the Marines would have difficulty concentrating on the potential threat around us. It would be even worse once the sun was all the way down.

As it was, three long days in the turret were having their effect on me. Twenty-four hours after its first day across the border, the division had reduced the NBC protective posture level to MOPP-1. Despite the relief of being free from the rubber over-boots, my feet ached from standing for so long. A common misperception in the Marine Corps—particularly in the "straight-leg" infantry—is that life in the LAV community is easier than constantly humping around a rucksack on the ground. Doubtlessly, there is some truth to this claim. But spending long periods of time standing in an LAV-25 turret does things to your body you could never imagine. After a while, you begin to feel in your knees and lower back every bump and pothole the vehicle hits. As a lieutenant I had always dismounted the vehicle by climbing out of the turret and jumping from the hull to the ground six feet below. Years of this idiocy had played havoc on joints, and by the time I was in Iraq I always winced whenever other Marines did the same thing. As a company commander it was more common (and less painful) for me to take the time to climb down the mounting handles on the vehicle's rear, or walk down the length of the vehicle, slowly sit on its sloped front, and gingerly hop off.

For much of the movement from the Euphrates River to Highway 1, Cobra helicopters provided convoy escort overhead. By ones and twos the Cobras glided up and down the long column, alternately buzzing the vehicles with low-flying passes and pushing out wide to the flanks and forward of the lead trace to reconnoiter ground ahead of us. Normally I enjoyed watching the Cobras flying low over our heads and pushing the limits. It was exciting, something you don't witness every day. But my childish desire to see them perform acrobatics near the vehicles quickly vanished when I heard the *whoosh-BOOM* of a rocket launch and detonation to my right, just 500 meters east of Delta Company's column. I jerked my head in the direction of the noise to see a Cobra leisurely flying parallel to the company, a willowy gray smoke-trail from the gunship's rocket pod still lingering in the air. The smoke and dust cloud on the ground from the impact was directly in front of the helicopter, indicating that the gunship had either fired at something really close to it, or else had experienced a misfire. I radioed the FAC.

"Spool, this is Black-Six. What the hell was *that* all about?"

"This is Spool," Peitz replied, clearly irritated. "They had a weapons malfunction. It was either a rocket or a Hellfire." Neither choice made me happier or less concerned than the other. A 2.75-inch rocket aimed the wrong way could be just as deadly as a laser-guided Hellfire missile. Suddenly I was no longer a big fan of flat-hatting maneuvers near the company. But the escort continued, and as time ticked by my aggravation subsided and I was just as glad as everyone else to have the helos by our side. Yet up to that point the company hadn't even come close to enemy contact. Aside from the intermittent reports the battalion had received about the ongoing situation with RCT-2 and Task Force Tarawa in An Nasiriyah, we had little to no idea what to expect. We had to remain prepared for anything. To keep the Cobras on-station and flying overhead rather than heading south to refuel, the battalion air officer, a captain named Pete "Mud Duck" McArdle, coordinated with the combat trains to replenish the helicopters with the battalion's own fuel supply. It was an option I would have never thought of, and Mud Duck's ingenuity kept our aerial escort overhead until sunset.

Several hours after darkness set in, the battalion was close to reaching its culminating point along the highway, and everyone's fatigue was evident in their strained voices over the radio. Once Maj Harper issued the plan for the remainder of the evening we prepared to refuel the vehicles and hold in place for the night. The battalion's refueling assets pushed forward to our position on the elevated dirt road, and as Charlie Company was in the midst of gassing up, Maj Harper's voice returned to the battalion radio net.

"Wolfpack is engaged ahead of us." "Wolfpack" was the call sign for 3rd LAR Battalion, which had pushed more than thirty kilometers forward of us earlier in the day after crossing the Euphrates. "They are approaching near-slingshot conditions. First LAR now has a 'be prepared to' mission to go pull them out. Expedite the fueling process and stand by for a mission frag."

"Slingshot" was a brevity code 1st Marine Division had implemented before the war began. It meant the unit calling was about to be overrun by the enemy. The division's plan stipulated that if a unit announced the word "slingshot" over the radio, all available aircraft would be diverted to provide assistance and prevent that unit's annihilation.

But 3rd LAR had announced "*near*-slingshot conditions." *What the hell does that mean?* I thought. *I* sure as hell didn't know. It sounded like being a little pregnant. But the call had gone out, and now suddenly everything flying and carrying weapons was on its way to help out our sister battalion. They had stumbled into an ambush—we didn't know how big at the time—and nearly the entire battalion was engaged. Over the horizon to the north the red glow of tracer fire ricocheted skyward, and occasional flashes of light from explosions popped like flashbulbs. But the whole thing was over before we could do anything to assist 3rd LAR. They managed to withdraw with the assistance of Third Marine Air Wing's (3rd MAW) overwhelming firepower. It seemed, at least for the time being, that they were out of danger. The excitement past, Maj Harper continued to brief the company commanders via the radio.

"Continue refueling. Warlord, be prepared to establish a blocking position to the north. Charlie and Dragon will establish defensive positions to our flanks in our current position." He was serious—there was no bullshit in his voice. He was still concerned about whatever it was out there that had caught 3rd LAR in the open.

Dave Hudspeth's "be prepared to" mission became a reality, and by 2340Z his company was moving north again along the highway. Eight or ten kilometers up the road he formed a picket to snare any of the enemy personnel who might attempt to retreat south away from 3rd LAR's ambush zone and toward 1st LAR Battalion's laager site. I wondered what was going through Dave's mind as he and his company drove out into the darkness, looking for the bad guys. I was partially jealous Delta Company hadn't received the task; but I was equally relieved. The company was exhausted. As with the voices on the battalion net, I could hear the fatigue in the radio transmissions of the company's vehicle commanders. Hazy as I was, I wondered if *I* would have been up to the task had we been required to move north where Weapons Company was headed.

But soon we had our own set of problems. The company had been in positions before where it had laagered up for the night; but throughout our training the XO and I had always insisted on well-dispersed vehicle positions, because we never wanted the company to be in a position where one well-placed artillery or mortar round would flatten the entire company. Over time the Marines knew the minimum distance to place between vehicles, and it became something I rarely thought about anymore. But that first evening on Highway 1 was also the first time Delta Company had set into a nighttime defensive position with the rest of the battalion. That fact in itself was unremarkable. Coordinating with Gil Juarez, Maj Harper, and Bob Whalen was relatively easy because of their experience and their ability to speak succinctly over the radio (a quality I tended to lack). The problem was in the confined space along the highway in which we attempted to wedge the battalion. Movement off the road was, as had been predicted earlier in the day, pretty much impossible because the earth was wet and spongy. Additionally, Third Battalion, Fifth Marines (3/5) had pushed up behind us to refuel its amtracks on the stable road surface. The result was that our battalion had very little space along Highway 1 in which to establish a defensive position. We were restricted to a sector of less than two square kilometers, and the vehicles became tightly packed together in the battalion's cigar-shaped defense. Slowly the familiar, self-induced friction materialized again in the darkness, and as 3rd Platoon occupied its vehicle positions along the road, Lt Cullins radioed. He sounded beat.

"Black-Six, this is Blue-One. Most of my platoon is stuck in the mud off the side of the road. It's gonna be a while getting them out."

"Roger that, Blue-One," I replied, looking over toward SSgt Monroe's vehicle. "Do you need Black-Nine or Black-Ten to come help you?"

"Negative, not yet. I think we've got it. It'll just take some time."

I hopped off my vehicle and walked across the road to relieve myself, and as soon as I stepped down the embankment my boots sank deep into the soft muck. *Yep,* I thought. *That's gonna take him a while.*

I climbed back up the embankment to the LAV just in time to hear the S-2 calling the company commanders. I grabbed the radio handset and answered up, and he immediately began listing enemy positions. Pulling my notebook from a cargo pocket, I hastily copied the coordinates and enemy unit designations he rattled off. The list was immense. There were multiple enemy artillery, infantry, and armored units, and I recognized many of the names that had been briefed to us before we left Kuwait: *Al Nida, Nebuchadnezzar, Medina, Hammurabi, Tawakalna.* Saddam Hussein had named his Republican Guard divisions after many of the legendary figures in Middle Eastern and Islamic history. The Republican Guard divisions were among Saddam's best-trained and most loyal forces. But their religious monikers sometimes made me wonder just how much Saddam depended on God, rather than the tactical acumen of his soldiers, to bring him victory.

Nevertheless, the unexpected enemy position update made me call forward the company's officers to give them the same "intel dump" I had just received from Lt Manson. Lieutenants Parment and Schwartz appeared, and as Capt Portiss walked over, 1stSgt Guzman and SSgt Kappen joined us. Cullins and Stiller were still busy retrieving their vehicles from the mire off the side of the road. I looked around for somewhere to muster the staff and pass the information, but unless I wanted to cycle them into the back of my LAV two at a time, there was no convenient place with a light. Remembering the tried and true poncho technique, I walked around the back of SSgt Monroe's LAV and opened the hatch.

"Hey," I said into the darkness. "Do you have a poncho handy in here?" There was a rustling in the back of the vehicle, and then Monroe's voice piped up.

"Hang on a sec." There was more movement in the darkness and the clang of equipment being thrown around. "Here you go, sir." He handed me a wadded-up poncho, and as I took it from him a stench like old, stale vomit hit me in the face.

"Ah, *JEEZ*-sus!" I exclaimed, holding it out far away from my nose. "This thing *reeks!* What the hell is that?"

"Beats the shit outta me, sir," he said, giggling. "It's Lance Corporal Blanchard's." I turned around and walked back to where the staff stood, and together we all lay down in the dirt in a circle facing each other. I pulled the poncho over our heads and turned on my red-lens flashlight.

"Holy shit!" said 1stSgt Guzman, his voice raising. "It fucking *stinks* in here!"

"I know, I know," I said apologetically. "It's Blanchard's. Let's just get it over with before it kills us in here." Everyone started laughing, and I began counting off the enemy coordinates. In the filtered red glow everyone struggled to grip his own flashlight, copy the positions as I repeated them, and hold his nose at the same time. It was comical. Several times there were gasps of "I can't take it any more!" followed by everyone yanking his head out of the suffocating gas chamber and heavily breathing-in the cold night air. We made one final attempt to power through the disgusting odor. As I was more than two-thirds down the list I compared a set of grid coordinates to our position on the chart. The battalion's position was marked near the bottom of the map, and Highway 1 ran straight north up the length of it. None of the grid coordinates I repeated to the staff was anywhere near us. I compared the coordinates and my map sheet again, and realized the closest plotted enemy position was more than four map sheets away, a distance of well over 100 kilometers. *Oh, screw this,* I thought. *Quit wasting everybody's time.*

"That's all," I said, folding my map. "Don't worry about the rest of them. Head back to your vehicles and get some rest." Everyone jumped up from the prone position beneath the poncho and breathed deeply again. There were muted curses in the darkness and whispers of "I think I'm gonna puke" as the staff dispersed and walked back to their respective platoons. I rolled out my sleeping bag on the ground next to Davis and Gurganus, but before I could get comfortable the radio beeped for me again. It was Lt Cullins, his exhaustion now sounding like anger.

"This is Blue-One. We got all vehicles unstuck, but an AT backed into one of my twenty-fives." I was too worn out to get angry, and in the darkness I was more concerned with someone getting hurt.

"Are there any casualties?"

"Negative, the AT just backed into it. I'm not sure what the damage is in the dark."

"Roger," I sighed. "Check it out in the morning and let me know." I sat in my sleeping bag and fumed for a minute, irritated that yet another of Lt Stiller's LAV-ATs had had a collision. But I couldn't think straight. My energy level approached zero. *If I don't get my head down soon I'm gonna be useless,* I thought, wrapping my shemagh tightly around my head and lying back into my bag. I didn't have to look for sleep. It found me.

I was awakened several times during the night with warning orders over the radio from the S-3, detailing potential taskings for the next day's mission. The following morning, 24 March, I awoke irritable and still fatigued. It was if I had gotten absolutely no sleep whatsoever. Outside my sleeping bag it was freezing, and even wearing my MOPP suit I was still uncomfortably cold. In any other situation I would have cursed the baggy outfit for retaining so much body heat, but now my feelings were just the opposite: I praised the suit's manufacturers for the airtight quality of their product.

Shortly after sunrise, Lt Cullins approached me with details of the previous evening's vehicle collision. It was simple, he told me. Lt Stiller had ground-guided one of his LAV-ATs right into one of 3rd Platoon's LAV-25s. Administratively moving vehicles in areas where people were walking around, particularly during nighttime, required human "ground-guides" to safely direct the LAVs where they needed to go without hitting anything or anyone. It was the only way to assist the drivers, whose already-restricted field of vision was further constricted by their night vision devices. Something had gone wrong, and apparently Lt Stiller had backed one of his vehicles into an LAV from Lt Cullins's platoon. The damage was minor, but my patience with the lieutenant had run out. Two vehicle collisions in twenty-four hours was unacceptable. At that rate he would get someone killed in his platoon before the week ended. I continued to think about it while Dave Hudspeth, Gil Juarez, and I went to work planning our mission for the morning.

Late the previous evening, 1st LAR Battalion had received a mission order directing it to conduct a moving flank screen to protect Second Battalion, Eleventh Marines (2/11, RCT-5's direct support artillery battalion) and 3/5 as they moved up Highway 1. Two-Eleven would leapfrog between its PAs (positioning areas, or firing positions for the artillery batteries) while 3/5 cleared Highway 1 in the RCT's zone and mopped up 3rd LAR Battalion's leftovers from the night before. It was exciting for the three of us. A moving flank screen is a classic reconnaissance mission ideally suited for an LAR battalion, albeit difficult to execute properly. Dave, Gil, and I were practically giddy as we knelt around our maps, which were anchored to the ground with rocks to keep them from blowing away in the morning wind. We happily chain-smoked, and at one point found ourselves both smoking and dipping at the same time. It didn't surprise me that none of the footage Matt Green took that morning ever made it onto *World News Tonight.* Together we looked like a bad endorsement for the American Tobacco Growers Association.

After weighing our options and discussing mission parameters, the three of us devised a relatively simple but workable plan. Weapons Company would move out ahead on Highway 1 to scout out future PAs for 2/11, while Delta and Charlie would proceed off-road east of the highway to conduct the moving screen. Proposed routes were outlined using the trail network listed on our maps to the east, and after reviewing the plan one more time we were ready to go. I thought *Well, if the execution goes as well as the planning this morning, this whole thing shouldn't be that bad.* Major Bodkin showed up, and after we provided him a back-brief detailing our proposed plan, Dave and Gil disappeared to prepare their companies. I turned to Bodkin and told him about Lt Stiller's mishap the previous evening.

"Jesus," he said, slowly shaking his head. "What's his problem?"

I shrugged my shoulders. "I don't know, sir. But right now I have about zero confidence in his abilities."

"Well, what do you want to do?"

"I don't know yet. How many more vehicles does he have to wreck before I can fire him?"

"Listen, it's your call. I understand what you're saying. I'll support you if you want to relieve him."

"Thanks. Let me think a little more about it." I walked around the back of my vehicle to talk the matter over with Capt Portiss and 1stSgt Guzman.

"I'm about ready to fire Lieutenant Stiller," I said flatly.

"Good," replied Portiss. "Can him." He seemed as fed up with Stiller's bullshit as I was.

"Wait a second, sir," Guzman said. "Who's gonna replace him if you do that? They ain't gonna give us another lieutenant."

"That's easy. Sergeant Paul can do it. He did fine as a VC for Second Platoon while Staff Sergeant Reeves was gone." Sergeant Leif Paul was a Marine in 2nd Platoon who had already demonstrated his ability to serve as either a scout on the ground or as an LAV vehicle commander. I had all the confidence in the world in him.

"Right, sir," countered Guzman. "Then you take away a sergeant from Second Platoon."

"Well, what about moving the lieutenant out of his platoon until he screws his head on straight?"

"Sir, if you move Lieutenant Stiller out of his platoon it has to be for good," Guzman said. "You can't take him out temporarily and then put him back in later and expect his Marines to respect him. They won't."

I thought for a moment and turned back to Portiss. "Well, XO, what do you think?"

"Why don't you permanently attach his two sections to First and Second Platoons?" he suggested. "Give Parment and Schwartz control of the sections like they normally have when the ATs are attached to other platoons and Stiller will still have administrative control over his Marines. Mortars will still tactically be attached to me and the FiST, so that's no problem there."

"Yeah," Guzman added. "If the lieutenant unfucks himself then you can detach the sections from First and Second Platoons. But if you fire him you can't take him back." I considered their proposal and couldn't argue against its merit. I tried to balance Stiller's inexperience against the safety of the Marines, and the good of the company versus making a clear point.

"Good idea," I said to both of them. Then I turned to Portiss. "Get me Stiller." I reported back to Maj Bodkin and told him my plan. He thought it was a good idea.

"Okay, good to go, Seth. But let me know if he isn't working out and you want to go the other route." Then he looked around, almost cautiously, as if someone might disapprove. "Now, give me a cigarette."

✦ ✦ ✦

At 0800Z the battalion initiated its movement north along Highway 1. Delta Company took the lead. Our mission to push east of 2/11 and 3/5 and screen their movement was still on schedule, and a decidedly enthusiastic tone had prevailed among the company staff when I had briefed the plan to them earlier. They had gathered around me next to the XO's LAV, and as Spool held up my map against the vehicle's hull I pointed out the planned artillery firing position dispersed along the length of the highway. Every five or six kilometers on the map PAs had been designated by highlighted grid squares on either side of the route. Delta's route for the moving flank screen took the company off Highway 1 and wide to the east. We would be, in effect, off-roading and looking for the enemy in the dried, barren marshlands bisected by Highway 1. The enemy situation was still almost a complete mystery to us, and we had few details about 3rd LAR Battalion's ambush the previous evening. All we knew was that "Indian territory" awaited us once we stepped off for the mission, and as far as everyone was concerned it was about blasted time.

As the company's vehicles formed up in column along Highway 1 for the movement to the release point, LCpl Davis reminded me of my promise to play Metallica's *No Leaf Clover* over the radio once the company crossed the border into Kuwait. I had never done so.

"You're right," I said over the intercom. "Corporal Harter, are you back there?"

"Yes, sir," he replied.

"Put the Metallica disc in your CD player and hand it up here." A minute later Harter's hand came through the scout compartment and up into the turret, holding a small white and gray compact disc player with a set of earphones attached to it. I took it from him, set the player to the song, and held the earphones up to the microphone on my helmet. I keyed my helmet's radio switch and held it in place, freezing open the circuit for the company's tactical radio net, and then pushed the "play" button on the device. Soon the song's lyrics filled the radio net and the ears of Delta Company's Marines:

> And it feels right this time
> On this crash course we're in the big time
> Pay no mind to the distant thunder
> Beauty fills his head with wonder, boy. . . .
> Says it feels right this time
> Turn around, found new high lights
> Good day to be alive, sir
> Good day to be alive, he said. . . .
> Then it comes to be that the soothing light
> At the end of your tunnel
> Is just a freight train coming your way

It wasn't until that moment that I finally comprehended the parallel between the song's poignant lyrics and the men of Delta Company. It was the moment for which we had trained together nearly two years. Even as knowledge of the imminent danger that lay ahead raced through our minds, we were, at that instant in time, very happy to be alive. But even with the pounding lyrics resonating in my head I didn't foresee the freight train waiting for us farther up the road. Instead, once the song ended I keyed the headset again and spoke to the company.

"All Dragon Victors, this is Black-Six," I said, alternately looking up and down the long column of vehicles. "Stay alert. Focus on the mission. Keep your eyes and ears open. Most importantly, take care of each other." I didn't know what else to say to them. The company column gradually rolled to a start, and our pace quickly increased along the by-now fully paved surface of Highway 1. For the first time ever I prayed to God to allow me to do my job the right way and take care of my men.

No sooner had the company hit cruising speed along the highway than we began passing through 3rd LAR Battalion's lines. They were strung out along the sides of the road much as we had been the previous night. The Wolfpack Marines were clustered in small groups, smoking, eating, and huddling around their tiny squad stoves. They didn't appear to be set into a defensive position at all, and I wondered what the hell was going on. My thoughts were answered by a radio call directing me to link up with Maj Harper for refinements to the battalion's mission. The platoons herringboned on the road's shoulder forward of 3rd LAR's position, and I pulled my vehicle alongside Maj Harper's LAV parked at the western edge of the asphalt. I dismounted the vehicle, and with map in hand donned my Kevlar helmet. Major Harper sat atop his vehicle, studying his own map.

"Hey, Seth," he called down. "Come on up here." I climbed up the side of his LAV and sat down across from him.

"What's the story, sir?" My temples throbbed with a developing headache, and I pulled off my helmet.

"The mission has changed. Charlie, Delta, and Weapons will be providing security for Two-Eleven in their PAs while they support Three-Five's attack north. I'll give you more details once Dave and Gil get here." I looked around, a little confused. It didn't make much sense to me.

"Where's the CO, sir?"

"He's at the regiment getting more information." I hadn't seen LtCol White since early the previous morning on Highway 7/8, nor heard his voice over the radio in quite some time. I began to wonder, but backed off. There had been plenty of times when Marines in Delta Company wondered where the hell *I* was. The cancellation of our screening mission distressed me more, and rather than broach the subject with Harper alone I waited for the backup of the other two company commanders.

Dave and Gil showed up soon after, and Maj Harper repeated the mission change to them. Their feelings on the subject echoed mine, and Gil immediately vocalized his thoughts.

"Sir, why is Three-Five moving ahead of us? Shouldn't we be pushing forward to recon the area?" He glanced sideways at Dave and me as we both nodded our agreement.

"They're wasting us as an asset," added Dave.

"Don't worry about that," Harper replied. "This is a good mission."

"But sir," I began. "Providing security? For artillery?"

"Security operations are part of LAR's mission," he said curtly. "Don't worry. There are plenty of missions to go around out here." He wasn't going to budge, and we dropped it. Then Dave looked around.

"Where's the CO, sir?" he asked.

I bent my head down and brought my hand to my mouth, attempting to suppress a grin.

The three of us hopped down and together walked around the back of my own vehicle as Maj Harper drove away to find the battalion commander. A grinding, rumbling sound from the south filled the air, and soon a long column of tanks and amtracks from 3/5 barreled north through 3rd LAR Battalion's lines and past us. I turned to Dave and Gil, a cigarette dangling out the corner of my mouth.

"Man, what the fuck?" I asked no one in particular. Dave leaned over and took my Zippo from me, firing up his own cigarette.

"Yeah, I'd say this is bullshit," answered Dave.

"Man, you guys and your nasty fucking cigarettes," Gil said, slowly shaking his head. He paused, looking momentarily at the armored convoy passing us by, and then continued. "So much for sticking with doctrine." The two of them were better than I at controlling their emotions, but they were clearly irate.

"I'm not begging to get my ass shot off," I said. "But why are we just sitting here while Three-fucking-Five is out doing our job? Did someone take away the 'reconnaissance' part of our name? We haven't done jack or shit since we left Kuwait." Dave nodded, and a few minutes later he stood up and walked back toward his own company's position. Gil and I continued talking as we each sat on the ground and leaned against the vehicle's tires.

"I guess I shouldn't be talking so much shit," I said, feeling guilty.

"Ahh, don't worry about it," he replied. "We're gonna get plenty of opportunities to get shot at. I told my Marines once it happens, we'll probably wish it hadn't. They can't wait for it to happen."

"Yeah, I guess I could do without it," I said. "But I can't stand just sitting here. Neither can the Marines."

"Well," he said, staring down the road. "We've come pretty far in three days. Something's gotta happen soon." He was right. RCT-5 had pushed more than 150 kilometers into Iraq. The only enemy contact it had encountered had been in the Rumaylah oil fields and the ambush 3rd LAR had driven through the night before.

Something's gotta happen soon.

✦ ✧ ✦

Upon LtCol White's return to the battalion's position around 1200Z, we all learned the full story of what had happened to 3rd LAR Battalion the previous night. The battalion had been driving along Highway 1 and was preparing to set in to a laager position for the night when they noticed signal flares firing to their front. Continuing forward, the vehicle commanders observed shadowy figures running around on both sides of the road and occupying fighting positions already scraped into the soft earth of the highway's shoulders. Realizing they had driven right into the teeth of a U-shaped ambush, 3rd LAR's Marines immediately initiated contact with the enemy. As the LAV's fired in all directions, the Iraqis began pouring small arms fire, RPGs, and mortar rounds into their moving column. At some point the battalion's air officer called the sling-shot code over the radio, and within thirty minutes every air support platform in the region was on top of them, firing up the enemy positions and providing cover for the battalion's escape. The battalion commander himself reportedly fired over 150 25mm rounds from his vehicle alone. Apparently it was *that* kind of struggle, one in which every vehicle crew was briefly fighting for its life. Somehow the battalion managed to break contact with the enemy and pull back with no casualties or vehicles lost. They estimated it had been between a company- and battalion-sized ambush, and during the mop-up the next morning they found textbook-perfect fighting positions and multiple caches of all types of ammunition. Hearing this from the CO, we realized that we faced not some amateur militia outfit, but instead a well-trained unit fighting from its own backyard. One officer compared it to someone trying to pick a fight with the 7th Marine Regiment in Twentynine Palms.

"Apparently the few Iraqis they found alive were from the Commando Brigade and the Fedayeen Saddam," LtCol White said. I had never heard of the Fedayeen—somehow I had missed that intel brief.

"Sir, are those the ninjas in the black pajamas?" Gil asked.

"That's right," he replied. "Same as the unit that tore up Tarawa yesterday." *Tore up Tarawa?* I was lost. I leaned over to Dave.

"Fedayeen Saddam? What the hell are they talking about?" I asked quietly.

"'Saddam's Men of Sacrifice,'" Dave told me. "They're the murder squads who run around in black outfits."

"Oh," I said flatly. "You get that on ship?"

"Yeah."

I realized the rest of the battalion must have received that information while they sailed from Camp Pendleton with ATF West. *Jesus,* I thought. *If I didn't know something that important, what the hell else have I been missing?* I felt like I'd been asleep at the wheel.

"Sir, what happened to Tarawa yesterday?" I asked, raising my hand.

"One-Two took significant casualties trying to get into An Nasiriyah yesterday morning," he began. "No one's really sure how many."

During the briefing we also learned about the ambush of the 507th Maintenance Company and the heavy casualties it sustained. It was all over the BBC, and the news was reporting that the American offensive was faltering. "Operation Iraqi Freedom," as the war had been dubbed, was, according to the media, grinding to a halt. We didn't know what to believe.

"Don't believe shit," LtCol White said. "Until you hear it from me, the XO, or the S-3." His words were familiar—it was the exact same thing I used to tell my company staff when the rumors were flying.

White continued, pointing to the S-3's situation map. "Three-Five is in contact north of our position. They only made it a couple of klicks from here before they got ambushed by what looks like the same unit that hit Third LAR last night. They're bogged down, trying to clear out the ambush right now." He then turned to Maj Harper, who continued the brief.

"The mission has changed again," Harper began. "We are no longer providing security for Two-Eleven's PAs. The Highlanders will move up east of Highway One and tie in with Three-Five, which is arrayed across the road oriented north. We'll set into a battalion-level battle position oriented to the east in order to protect Three-Five's right flank. Order of march will be Dragons, battalion Forward, Warlord, Charlie." He paused, and then pointed to a diagram he had drawn. "Once Dragon ties in with Three-Five, Warlord will occupy a battle position adjacent to Dragon. Then Charlie will occupy a battle position across the road, oriented south and tie in with Warlord's right flank. Third LAR will occupy a battle position along the western side of the road and will tie in with Charlie on their left and Three-Five on their right.

"Looks like we're gonna circle the wagons," said Dave.

"That's exactly what we're gonna do," Harper replied. "And if we don't get started now we aren't gonna make it before we lose daylight."

"How fast can everyone get moving?" LtCol White asked. The sky had been overcast all day, and with only an hour of daylight remaining no one wanted to move into another position in the dark. We agreed on ten minutes, and everyone disappeared to his respective company to brief the mission change.

I walked quickly down the line of vehicles herringboned along the highway's shoulder. When I got to Capt Portiss's vehicle I yelled to him as he sat up on his hatch.

"Hey! Get the Guidons up here ASAP!"

"Roger that," he replied, picking up his radio's handset. The staff showed up in ones and twos, and I whittled the frag order down as much as I could.

"No time for bullshit," I announced. "This is gonna be quick. You all know Third LAR got hit hard in an ambush last night. The enemy we are up against are no joke. What these guys are doing is they're hiding behind these paddy dikes out here, waiting for a vehicle or personnel to get within small arms range, and then they're opening up with RPGs and mortars. And AK-47s. Alright? So keep your heads down in your turrets. Keep your gunners scanning. It's gonna be a tight fight out there."

I pointed to my map and continued. "We're here right now. We're gonna be traveling in a tactical column, turrets pointing outboard. We're going to move off road and skirt the highway until we get to Three-Five's position. They're in a BP [battle position] across the road, oriented north. Order of march is SOP. Red, when you get to Three-Five, you'll tie in with them to your left. Blue, you'll tie in with Warlord to your right. The final position for the company should be a BP oriented to the east. Any questions?"

"Rate of march, sir?" Parment asked.

"As fast as you can. We've got less than an hour of light left. Any other questions?" There were none. "Okay, mount up. We're Oscar Mike in two minutes."

Capt Portiss immediately leaned his head back and yelled at the top of his lungs. *"Short count, one minute!"*

"Short count, one minute!" Marines repeated, passing the order down the line of vehicles. Everywhere cigarettes were stubbed out, gear was re-mounted, and men climbed aboard their vehicles. I hauled myself up into the turret, pulled on my helmet, and keyed the microphone.

"Guidons, this is Black-Six. Report when set, Red-Con One." The platoon commanders immediately began responding.

"Red set, Red-Con One."

"White set, Red-Con One."

"Blue set, Red-Con One."

"Green set, Red-Con One."

"Brown set, Red-Con One."

"Black set, Red-Con One."

I looked up and down the column one last time, a ritual for me.

"Roger," I replied. "All Victors set. Red-One, we're Oscar Mike."

Lieutenant Parment's platoon rolled to a start, turning east and away from the road. About twenty or thirty feet off the pavement a tall, dirt levee ran parallel to the road. There were occasional passage points through it, but they were randomly spaced. Once a vehicle passed through a cut to the other side there was no telling when it would get a chance to get back to the highway. Regardless, 1st Platoon passed through the levee, and one by one the company's vehicles followed suit. The column slowly moved east for several hundred meters, and then turned north to parallel Highway 1. The route we ended up taking didn't even come close to resembling the route drawn on the map by the S-3. We were in the middle of a confusing maze of ditches and paddy dikes, and the undulating, rippling ground slowed the vehicles' movement to a crawl. Zigzagging back and forth to avoid tipping the LAVs or getting them mired in the intermittent bog, we made terrible progress. I looked at my watch. Thirty minutes had passed, and the company had traveled less than a kilometer. The sun was sinking fast, and the majority of the battalion hadn't even made it off Highway 1 yet. Captain Portiss's voice came across the radio.

"Black-Six, be advised: Highlander-Six is leap-frogging through the company, headed your way."

I turned around in the turret and looked at the long, strewn-out file of vehicles behind me. Lieutenant Colonel White and the forward were indeed slowly moving up Delta Company's column, their four vehicles darting in and out between the platoons and trying to make their way to the head of the file. I looked back to the front, where Lt Parment's vehicles were attempting to negotiate a levee blocking their path. *This is taking too long,* I thought. *We aren't gonna make it before the sun sets.* The battalion couldn't be stuck out in the middle of this mess after dark. I had to make a decision, and I had to make it quickly.

Much has been written about the decision-cycle called the "OODA loop," a term coined by a U.S. Air Force colonel named John Boyd. Breaking the decision-making cycle down into *o*bservation, *o*rientation, *d*ecision, and *ac*tion, Boyd's claimed that the best way to foil the enemy was to "get inside his OODA loop," that is, to disrupt one of the four parts of the cycle in order to prevent him from making a decision or acting. Decision-making can be affected by the strange phenomenon referred to as "decision-creep." Decision-creep happens when a commander tries to determine the critical time to make an important decision. He hopes that if he waits just a little longer, new information will materialize that will allow him to make the choice he actually wants to make rather than the one he would have to make given the current variables. One example of this happened frequently during training whenever my vehicle broke down. Staff Sergeant Monroe and his mechanics would swarm around it, trying to determine the problem while I stood there deciding if I should wait out the repair or transfer myself to another vehicle. I would wait two minutes for them to tell me whether it was fixable or not. If they still didn't know after two minutes, I would wait another three minutes, hoping that if they had a little more time a more conclusive answer would arise. I would keep thinking that if I gave them just a little more time they could fix it and I could be on my way. Before I knew it, twenty or thirty minutes would have passed. Similar examples had occurred when my vehicle's radio system went on the fritz. During training I often stood there in my turret thinking to myself, *If I give Harter just a couple more minutes he'll get the radio fixed and my problems will be solved.* It was because of these errors I had made in the past that we ended up enforcing the bump-plan we had used the first day of the war when my vehicle got a flat tire.

Even with those experiences behind me, decision-creep was a tough obstacle for me to overcome at the war's beginning. It was unlike me to cut my losses and proceed if the mission hadn't been accomplished. But with darkness fast approaching and Delta Company nowhere near 3/5's position, I knew we had to get back on Highway 1. Silently cursing to myself, I radioed the battalion commander.

"Highlander-Six, this is Dragon-Six. The terrain out here is extremely slow-go. It's going to take us forever to get through this shit. I recommend we bypass the off-road route and instead return to the paved road in order to link up with Three-Five before nightfall."

"Dragon-Six, you're in the lead," LtCol White replied sourly. He was clearly pissed off at our lack of progress. *"You* make the decision."

"Roger that," I replied immediately. "We're returning to the highway now." Flipping the radio control lever to the company net, I re-keyed my helmet. "Red-One, we aren't gonna make it on time this way. Take the most direct route back to the hard-ball."

"Thank God," Lt Parment replied, the relief in his voice unmistakable. "I was hoping you'd say that." Straight away his vehicles turned west toward the paved surface of the highway. As we shifted the battalion's route back onto Highway 1, I second-guessed myself, wondering if it had indeed been the right decision to make. Just then, Dave Hudspeth's voice appeared over the net.

"Dragon-Six, that's a good call, buddy." He must have been able to sense my consternation over the radio, and I recognized his comment for what it was: vocal support for my decision that he knew everyone would hear. It made me feel a lot better.

Lieutenant Parment's platoon weaved back and forth through the maze until it found a gap in the levee that skirted Highway 1. Scout teams dismounted his lead vehicles to clear the narrow opening, making sure it was clear of any enemy on the other side and that it would support passage of an entire battalion. A minute later Parment was back on the radio.

"Black-Six, be advised: there's Iraqi equipment all over the place up here. My scouts just found a campfire by the side of the road that's still smoking." One by one the company's LAVs passed through the levee again, and we witnessed Parment's report firsthand. Equipment was strewn all around—helmets, shovels, sleeping bags, and web gear—and sure enough in the middle of it all was a blackened patch of smoldering ashes on the ground. Whoever it all belonged to had left the area in a hurry, melting into the surrounding landscape. The hair rose up on the back of my neck, and I suddenly felt as if we were being watched. The sun was setting, and spidery, purple shadows danced all around us. Everything looked alive. Each bush or rock seemed to hide behind it an Iraqi waiting to jump out and put a hole in the side of one of our vehicles with an RPG. A hundred sets of hidden eyes observed us, studying our every move. In that eerie moment we all realized this really *was* "Indian territory." They were all around us—we just couldn't see them.

Once 1st Platoon cleared the levee I ordered Lt Parment to move up the road as quickly as possible to link up with 3/5. It was imperative that we anchor in the battle position, and I was unsure how long it would take the remainder of the company and the battalion to negotiate the levee's bottleneck. My vehicle angled in alongside 1st Platoon, and I noticed that, despite being oriented to the east, they were still on the road. The levee had continued to skirt the highway only forty feet or so from it. It had become an obstacle that prevented the company from fanning out and off the road. To see and shoot over the levee we had to remain where we were on the pavement. We were, for all intents and purposes, road-bound. Lieutenant Cullins reported that his platoon was set in position, and the remainder of the battalion began to array along the company's right flank. Third LAR Battalion moved in west of the road as planned, and by the time darkness enveloped us the position ended up looking like a massive strong point. Our firepower was oriented in every direction.

Vehicle dispersion was tight—about fifty meters between each vehicle—and we all felt terribly exposed. To add to our anxiety, the night sky was moonless. Far to the east a layer of fog rolled in toward us, further reducing our visibility. *We have to get past that levee,* I thought. *We don't have any room where we are.* I directed the platoons to dismount their scouts and mark passage points in the levee to facilitate the company's movement east of the barrier, but it was of no use. It quickly became apparent that we would be stuck in our position on the road. Coordination with 3/5 had gone to shit in the darkness, and 1st Platoon was unsure of the location of the infantry battalion's right flank beyond the levee. The platoon commanders radioed, relaying their concern about the bottleneck that would ensue in the passage points if the company had to fall back to the highway in a hurry. They were right. We would stay in place along the road for the night.

The wait began, but it didn't last long. Around 1930Z, the platoons reported detecting thermal images of people lurking around several kilometers to our front. With little ambient light outside, NVGs were practically useless. I dropped down inside the turret to take a look for myself through the thermal sight. Staring into the scope, I watched the white glow of body heat generated by tiny figures walking back and forth. They were out there, all right, but what they were doing we had no idea. They would appear only in ones and twos, and then they would disappear from view behind the terrain. The company's scouts had pushed forward of the vehicles, but as they peered over the levee's embankment they, too, could see nothing. They were experiencing the same problems with their optics that I was. What we could see through our NVGs that the thermal sights could not was what appeared to be headlights moving back and forth on the horizon. It didn't make sense that our goggles could pick it up but the vehicles' thermals could not. The XO radioed with an answer.

"All Victors, be advised: that's light bleed-over," Portiss said. "Whatever it is that's making that light is behind the IV [inter-visibility] line in the distance." But that only answered part of the question. The real question was, what the hell was making that light? Whatever it was multiplied, and soon those several sets of headlights turned into more than a dozen. They roamed around in the gloom, making their way through the irrigation ditches toward us. Delta Company wasn't the only set of eyes observing the phantom lights. Charlie Company reported the same, as did Weapons Company.

Maybe they were civilian vehicles. We had been briefed that the enemy fighters were now using such means of conveyance—pickup trucks, SUVs, and motorcycles—to transport themselves. They were no dummies. The enemy knew that if they tried to move around in armored vehicles our patrolling air power would find them and smash them to bits. I stood in the turret, going back and forth on the radio between the platoon commanders and the battalion staff. No one had a clear view of exactly what it was out there, but we all agreed: *something* was out in front of us, moving around. Our concerns ramped up when suddenly all of the headlights appeared to be extinguished at once. It was the final indicator to the battalion that we faced an organized attack, or at least an organized probe of our lines. Every gunner in the battalion began actively tracking the moving shapes in the darkness as best he could, and soon LtCol White called over the radio net requesting tank support for the battalion's position. Minutes later a company of M1A1 tanks from 2nd Tank Battalion rumbled and clanked into our lines. Turning their guns eastward, they searched through their own optics for the spectral enemy driving around in the dark. The tank company commander's voice sounded over the battalion radio.

"I'm looking where you're telling me to through my thermal sights right now," he said. "And I can't see anything." There was some arguing back and forth over the radio, and then the tanker spoke again.

"Listen, I have a modified fifty-power thermal sight in front of me, and I'm telling you there's *nothing* out there." Hearing that, I wondered if we had all just convinced ourselves we were under attack when we really were not. But then Captain Andrew Bone, the battalion's fire support coordinator, radioed the companies.

"Guidons, this is Highlander-Eight. Dial in illumination missions with your eighty-ones. Two-Eleven is going to be firing DPICM for us." Captain Portiss immediately radioed me.

"Already done, Black-Six. Our mortars are fire-capped and ready to go." Mortar tubes from all three companies blooped in the darkness, and seconds later the sky to our front lit up like daytime.

Oh man, I thought. *This is some heavy shit. There must be something big out here if they're gonna use DPICM.* Dual-purpose, improved conventional munitions (DPICM) is a base-ejecting artillery round that releases eighty-eight tiny bomblets designed to detonate on impact. The distribution of bomblets is a combination of anti-armor and anti-personnel grenades, making DPICM the perfect indirect fire munition. It was a weapon I had known about since TBS but had never seen used in training. No one I knew outside of the artillery community had seen it fired. In fact, very few people I knew actually *in* the artillery community had seen it fired. The reason was that it was just too dangerous because of its high malfunction rate. Estimations of DPICM's dud-rate varied between zero-point-seven and fourteen percent. Because of that, during peacetime training it was seldom employed. When it was, safety regulations mandated that it be fired into specially designated grids in the training area where people weren't allowed to go.

The illumination mission continued to light up the drained marshes to our front, but there was still no sign of enemy vehicles. The human-looking figures we had seen through our thermal viewers had vanished, no doubt hiding from the destruction they knew was about to rain down on them. As we heard the report of artillery firing to our southeast, Capt Bone's voice came across the radio again.

"Guidons, DPICM on the way." A moment later the burst and pop of the rounds ejecting their submunitions echoed in the darkness. Suddenly hundreds of bright flashes ripped through the sky as the bomblets exploded, blanketing the ground to our southeast. From a distance we heard a *bang*, followed by a sound like deafening, rapidly popping popcorn. It reminded me of a certain type of rocket you see at Fourth of July fireworks displays; there is a popping noise followed by a massive shower of orange and yellow sparks that sizzle as they fall to earth. The artillery barrage was an awesome display, and after a fire adjustment by Capt Bone, 2/11 fired two more volleys two or three kilometers directly to our front. Hundreds of tiny explosions canvassed the marshes ahead of us. No more headlights appeared for the rest of the evening.

Two-Eleven radioed the battalion, requesting a battle damage assessment (BDA) but there was none to give. Whatever the DPICM mission had hit—if it had even hit anything—was too far out to our front to discern the munitions' effects. After the radio quieted down, 1st LAR reduced its alert level. But none of us was willing to break out his sleeping bag and sleep outside. We were still too spooked about our surroundings. Another uncomfortable evening cramped up in the turrets and in the backs of the vehicles faced us.

I finally reached my own personal limit. Turning control of the turret and radio over to Cpl Harter, I climbed into the LAV's scout compartment to sort out my feet. All day long they had felt as if they were sliding around in goo, and by the time I pulled off my boots the soles of my feet burned. When I peeled off my socks an ammonia-like stench filled the scout compartment, almost overwhelming me. Thoroughly disgusted with myself for letting it get so bad, I inventoried my gear and was horrified to find that I had only one or two pairs of clean socks left. I still didn't foresee any time soon when I would be able to do some field laundry. Oblivious to the fact that my feet were slowly beginning to rot, I leaned my head back next to the radio handset hanging down from inside the turret and drifted off to sleep.

10

Storm of the Century

As 25 March began for us along Highway 1, I awoke thinking about the previous evening. What had happened? Had there really been anything out there? Were they probing us? And if so, had we blown the shit out of them with all that DPICM? Even my crew was curious.

"Hey, sir," asked PFC Gurganus. "What do you think that was last night?"

I shrugged my shoulders. "Shit, I don't know. Ghosts, maybe." The crew laughed, but I was troubled. The DPICM mission the battalion had called in had rained down a lot of death and destruction out in front of us. Understandably it was initiated as insurance against an enemy attack, but who really knew what was out there? Could the Iraqis really have been out there in tanks? It didn't seem likely. I was more inclined to believe we had seen the civilian SUVs the S-2 had briefed us about earlier. But even that didn't seem to make much sense. We had watched the lights move back and forth, as if casually driving on the road. We knew the land to our front was nearly untrafficable. The short distance the company had covered off-road proved that there was no way anything could move across the drained marshes as effortlessly as those headlights had. The undulating terrain, with its ditches, levees, and sinkholes, would have caused the headlight beams to bounce as uncontrollably as the vehicles themselves would be doing. Yet there had been no up and down movement to the lights we observed. I just couldn't explain it. For once I was eager to head over to the COC when I received the call that morning. Maybe someone smarter than I would be able to explain what the hell had been going on.

I found Dave and Gil standing behind one of the battalion Main's LAV-C2s, joking around with Bob Whalen and Drew Bone about the events of the previous evening. Dave led the charge.

"You know, I think I figured out what those lights were last night. I think it was just a bunch of Iraqis opening their doors." He mimicked an Iraqi opening the door to his house and peeking outside. "And it was like when you look inside the refrigerator, trying to figure out if the light goes off when you open and close the door. So last night there are all these Iraqi farmers opening their doors, and then all this artillery comes down on top of them. So they close their doors and the artillery stops. Then they open up their doors again and the artillery starts again. *Boom!* Then they close them. Silence. Then they open them. *Boom!"*

Everyone was rolling. You could tell we all felt a little silly about the overwhelming response the battalion had dumped down on top of the phantom headlights. After the laughter died down I spoke up.

"So, what's the deal?" I asked no one in particular.

"Nothing to pass right now," replied Bob.

"Wait a minute," I said, irritated. "I just got a call to show up for a frag order."

"Nope, no frag. Cancelled. The next mission is in a state of flux." Whalen didn't have much guidance, but he explained that the battalion needed somehow to find a bypass around 3/5, which was mopping up the Fedayeen ambush ahead of us. We still had a long way to go to get to the Tigris River, and it appeared that the RCT would attempt to cross the waterway at a town called An Numinayah. Three-Five was preparing to push forward again, but it anticipated more enemy contact to its flanks.

In the absence of clear direction or guidance from our higher headquarters, the company commanders grew flustered at what we perceived to be the battalion's increasing inability or unwillingness to press forward to where it should be. Gil had a plan.

"Listen, instead of just sitting here doing nothing, let's plan the mission ourselves."

"Yeah, that's a good idea," Dave replied. "Otherwise I'll just stand here and smoke all of Seth's cigarettes." The three of us knelt down in a circle around Gil's map and attacked the planning problem in earnest. In minutes we had developed a simple, workable plan to bypass 3/5 to the east and press north. The idea was similar to the flank screen operation we had devised the day before, but we had a better idea this time about the treacherous conditions off-road. We agreed that, no matter what route we chose, the movement would take a significant amount of time. As we reviewed the plan and copied graphics onto the laminated surfaces of our maps, the staccato of machine-gun fire erupted to the north. Three-Five was in contact again. This increased our desire to get the mission started. With the enemy focused on 3/5, we would be able to pass unhindered around their flank and push forward as we were supposed to be doing.

BRIEFING DELTA COMPANY STAFF ON HIGHWAY 1, 25 MARCH 2003.
OFFICIAL MARINE CORPS PHOTO BY LCPL ANDREW P. ROUFS.

As we waited for the battalion commander to return, Lt Manson's intelligence section prepared the Dragon Eye for a reconnaissance flight to the north. The Dragon Eye was a small, unmanned aerial vehicle (UAV) the battalion had been experimenting with for several months prior to our arrival in Kuwait. With a four-foot wingspan and body the size of a remote-controlled model airplane, the four-pound Dragon Eye was guided by an operator on the ground wearing a visor that displayed images from the small video camera mounted in the aircraft's nose. The plane was launched with a giant bungee catapult similar to the kind used to hurl water balloons, and a small propeller motor mounted on each wing powered its flight. The intel Marines could mount either a standard or night vision camera in the craft's nose, and as it flew it generated near–real time, moving imagery. First LAR Battalion was one of the few units employing the new Dragon Eye, and with 3/5 halted up the road, the S-3 and S-2 decided it was the perfect time to get the UAV in action.

But the enemy contact with 3/5 had escalated. Mud Duck sat atop his LAV, listening intently to the heavy traffic going back and forth over the radio. Two medevac helicopters south of us had been dispatched to 3/5's position to pick up casualties, and they were preparing to head north. The helicopters' flight corridor would take them directly over our heads. Realizing this and the danger posed by launching the Dragon Eye into their path, Mud

Duck dropped his handset and yelled down to the Marines preparing the UAV for launch.

"Hey! Abort that thing! Two medevacs are on the way!" The wind had begun to pick up, and it appeared as if the intel Marines hadn't heard him.

"What?" yelled back Lt Manson.

"I said abort!" yelled Mud Duck, the pitch in his voice raising. *"Fucking abort it now!"* Too late. The Dragon Eye arced into the air, the buzzing sound of its stubby propellers whining above the howling wind. Manson relayed the order to the Marine controlling the plane, and with a quick movement he directed its path straight down. Because it was too difficult to smoothly set down the Dragon Eye, its makers had given it a modular design that supposedly allowed the craft to break apart without major damage upon landing. And break apart was exactly what it did. The UAV turned downward sharply and collided catastrophically with the ground. It shattered into five pieces, which were then promptly carried away in all directions by the wind. Scratch one Dragon Eye. As the intel Marines scrambled to retrieve the plane's components, Manson seethed with anger. But then, just as Mud Duck had predicted, two CH-46 helicopters screamed overhead toward 3/5's position.

After several hours of waiting for LtCol White to return, we gave up hope of having the opportunity to "sell" the plan to him. It was midafternoon, and even if the battalion commander *had* approved our plan to bypass 3/5, we wouldn't have had time to do it properly before sunset. Weather conditions were worsening, too. The wind had increased to gale-force levels, bringing with it blowing sand of equivalent intensity and force. But the sand wasn't just blowing hard. It was *in* the air—it was part of the air itself. There was no way to escape it. Even inside the vehicles the fine dust hung like a mist suspended all around you. Writing became next to impossible. As I attempted to record the event in my journal, the grit in the air accumulated on the pages of my notebook, clogging the tip of my pen and smearing the black ink across the paper. I watched two Marines attempting to eat MREs. They had perfected a system to counter the confounding effects of the weather on their meal. Each man systematically skimmed with his spoon the top layer of the stew he was eating, flung it aside, and quickly scooped a clean pile into his mouth. They continued to repeat the process, each time skimming off the thin film of dirt that had already accumulated on the stew's surface. Skim, fling, scoop, repeat. They appeared to be working on an assembly line.

Everyone scrambled for something to cover his nose and mouth, and no one walked about without a pair of goggles cinched down tightly over his eyes. Wrapping my shemagh snugly around my head and leaving only a tiny slit for my eyes, I reached for my goggles and pulled them on as securely as possible. Proper blood circulation came second to the ability to breathe and see. My eyes watered, and the tears mixed with the dust, caking over. The tempest worsened, literally by the minute. I was reminded of the shamal in Kuwait when we had been stuck out in the field overnight. What was developing around us along Highway 1 promised to surpass that miserable night. Soon everyone had to shout to be heard above the swirling wind. Some Marines even donned their gas masks to escape the stinging particles. The sun began to disappear, and the overcast sky had turned a moldy yellow. To the north, sporadic gunshots from 3/5 could still be heard. *I can't believe they're still fighting in this,* I thought. *Tough bastards.*

Lieutenant Colonel White returned to the battalion's position, and the company commanders rushed to brief the plan we had developed earlier. Without pausing he cancelled our proposed mission, quickly adding that the battalion already had another task. We were to repeat the previous evening's mission, securing 3/5's flank. They had advanced several kilometers up the road, and we needed to catch up to them and tie into their positions. The task itself was a simple one, but it required Dave, Gil, and me to hash out the details before we had a solid understanding of what each company really needed to do. The sour weather was fast becoming a brownout, and as I briefed

Delta Company LAV-25 during first day of sandstorm, 25 March 2003. Official Marine Corps photo by LCpl Andrew P. Roufs.

the company over the radio I marveled at the fact that I could barely see the vehicle fewer than fifty feet in front of my own.

Delta Company filed out to the east, preparing to turn north toward 3/5's flank. I couldn't believe it—we were falling into the same trap we had the previous night, only now the environment was infinitely worse. As I struggled over the radio to clarify tasks for the platoon commanders, my train of thought was interrupted by Bob Whalen's voice on the battalion frequency.

"Guidons, this is Highlander-Three Alpha," he began. "Stand by for a mission change."

Are you shitting me?

"The battalion now needs to set in a defensive perimeter around Two-Eleven's PAs for the night." He proceeded to define the dimensions of our company positions, but it quickly became clear even *that* mission wasn't going to happen. Visibility had dropped to zero. The yellow sky had turned a deep amber hue as the setting sun's rays fought vainly to penetrate the driving sand. Amber melted into orange. The landscape around us, which had taken on the aura of Tolkien's Dead Marshes, now looked at best as if we were on the surface of Mars. At worst it was a scene from the Apocalypse. It was the most peculiar, yet the most fascinating, spectacle of nature I had ever witnessed. The sun was nearly below the horizon, and my anxiety was skyrocketing. Even the thermal viewers couldn't filter the curtain of dust and sand, and it had become too dangerous to move the vehicles.

I radioed the battalion. "This is Dragon-Six. Listen, we can't see a fucking thing out here. We're going to run into each other."

Bob Whalen's voice returned to the battalion net. "Roger that, Dragon-Six. All Guidons, hold your positions. Limit movement outside your vehicles."

Dave's voice jumped into the conversation. "This is Warlord-Six. I'm stuck up here with the Forward COC at CEB's [combat engineer] position. We can't make it back, either. This is the goddamnedest thing I think I've ever seen."

"Yeah, roger," Gil added. "Charlie-Six copies. We aren't going anywhere."

"This looks like God's wrath descending down on top of us for invading the Garden of Eden," I said ponderously into the radio. I paused for a moment, and then added in a mock grave tone, "Will you pray for me, Bobby?"

"Yeah, sure Dragon-Six," Whalen replied, laughing.

My thoughts quickly shifted back to the company, and I radioed instructions to them.

"All Dragon Victors, here's the plan for the night: stay in your vehicles. I want someone up in every turret with NVGs and someone scanning on every gun with the thermals. Don't move away from the vehicles. We're gonna ride this thing out until morning. Keep your eyes open, and keep monitoring the net." Someone radioed and asked about the enemy situation.

"Listen," I said, remembering what the battalion commander had told us the previous day. "We are right in the middle of an Iraqi commando brigade's training area. This is their backyard. Think of it as taking on Seventh Marines in Twentynine Palms. Those Fedayeen shitheads are out there lurking around, looking to probe us and sneak into our lines. Like I said, keep your eyes and ears open. If they want to fuck with us, I say *bring it on.*" The atmosphere was tense—it infused the radio waves just as everyone's fatigue had two nights earlier. Another vehicle commander called.

"Black-Six, why have we just been sitting here the last two days? Why aren't we out looking for them?"

"Listen, I hear you. I hear all of you. I know everyone wants to be out front doing his job. Don't worry about it. As we get closer to An Numinayah and the Tigris River we'll get all the action we can handle. The Baghdad and Al Nida Divisions of the Republican Guard are waiting for us up there."

It was my first "fireside chat" of the war. During training I had always preferred to occasionally walk around from vehicle to vehicle to talk to the Marines. It gave me the opportunity to look them in the eyes and get an idea what was really going on in their heads. But with the pace of operations since the war's beginning and the distances the company was spread across I wasn't getting the chance to walk around much. That first night of the storm I realized the necessity of relying on the radio not only to tactically control the company, but also to intermittently talk to the men and field their questions and concerns.

With the sun gone, the otherworldly colors of our "Martian" landscape receded. We were plunged into total darkness. But the storm still had more to show us than blowing wind and stinging sand. The clouds above our heads opened up, and as the precipitation combined with the dirt suspended in the air, it rained mud. The pitter-patter of raindrops on the steel hull of our LAV suddenly turned into pinging, rattling noises. The rain had turned into hail. *There is no way this is happening,* I thought. *A hailstorm in the desert?*

The battalion reiterated its mandate that all units remain in position for the evening. Having forgotten my own words of comfort following the storm in Kuwait—that if *we* couldn't see, the enemy couldn't see either—I grew paranoid, fearing that the enemy would use this opportunity to infiltrate our shallow lines and start destroying vehicles as we hid from the weather in them. I was hesitant to leave my turret for the relative protection from the elements afforded by the scout compartment, but LCpl Davis and I soon reached the point where we couldn't keep our eyes open any longer. It was time for Cpl Harter and Kodak to earn their pay. After handing off our goggles and CVC helmets, Davis and I climbed in back to sort ourselves out.

I needed something to keep my mind off the paranoia creeping up on me, so I turned to my feet. The decision had been postponed long enough: it was high time to change my socks. The burning sensation in the soles of my feet had worsened, and I wondered just how much foot powder it would take to neutralize the pain. As I slid my feet from their slimy, grainy socks, I half-expected to see a green cloud materialize. The familiar ammonia stink wafted up and into the compartment, and it wasn't long before Davis caught a whiff of it.

"*Jay-zus Christ,* sir!" he said, disgusted. "What is that? Is that your feet?!"

"Yeah, sorry," I replied, leaning down to take a closer look at them with the red beam of my flashlight. "I think I've got a problem here."

"Sir, you got a problem alright," he offered, pinching his nose shut. "Your feet have fuckin' died!"

I tended to my feet as best I could in the darkness after retrieving a pair of the precious clean socks from my pack hanging outside the vehicle. As I pulled them over the chafed skin of my feet I felt not the welcome softness of clean cotton, but instead more grit. The dust in the air had worked its way into the socks, saturating them. I was now, in effect, wrapping sandpaper around my feet. *That's great,* I thought miserably. *That's just fucking . . . great.*

With the issue of my feet somewhat addressed, I tried to occupy myself by writing in my journal. But my mind spun with images of the worst. I knew I wouldn't sleep well that evening, if I slept at all. Visions of an Iraqi commando sneaking up on my LAV and firing an RPG into its hull while I slept inside preoccupied my thoughts. As the wind whipped across it, the vehicle swayed back and forth rhythmically. Every couple of minutes I popped up out of the scout hatch to check the visibility outside, only to see each time that it was still zero. I was, for the first time since the war had started six days earlier, genuinely nervous and uncertain of the immediate future. My silent prayers weren't for my own safety, but instead for that of my Marines. I again hoped that when the time came I would perform my job the way I was supposed to and that I wouldn't let my company down.

I lay back and began to doze, my dark deliberations slowly beginning to fade. Davis snored in the seat next to me. Kodak sat in the gunner's seat, staring intently into the green glow of the thermal scope. Corporal Harter stood in the turret, my set of NVGs pressed against his eyes. Gurganus was out cold in the driver's compartment. I began to think it would be another quiet night on the highway. Suddenly a massive *ka-RUMPH* of an explosion rocked the vehicle. The blast was followed by another. And then another. Each was accompanied by a shrieking, high-pitched pneumatic whistle. The concussion of the detonations all around us passed through the vehicle hull, amplifying the noise of the blasts and making everything inside the LAV vibrate. They kept coming, one after another. Davis and I looked at each other and together yelled, "Holy shit!"

"What the hell is that?!" he yelled to me.

"Get out!" I yelled back. "RPGs! Get out of the fucking vehicle *now!*"

We scrambled to vacate the confines of the scout compartment for fear it would become our coffin. The explosions rippled the air around us, and I thought we had been caught in either an artillery barrage or an RPG attack. My fears had come true. We had to get out of the impact area or we were done for. Scaling the side of the vehicle, I yelled to Cpl Harter to get the hell out of the turret. He was disoriented.

"Harter, get the fuck out now!" Coming to, he threw the helmet and NVGs to me and jumped into the back, followed in short order by Kodak. I keyed the intercom.

"Gurganus, fire it up."

No response.

"Gurganus, fire it up! Get us the hell out of here!"

"Roger that, sir," he finally replied. *"Fire in the hole!"*

The engine rumbled to life, and as I prepared to guide the vehicle out onto the highway and order the company to do the same I paused and looked around my position. The rain from earlier in the evening had washed away much of the dust hanging in the air, and despite the thundering of explosions it was clearly visible that nothing was impacting around us. Just as I realized what was happening, Capt Portiss's voice came across the radio net.

"All Dragon Victors," he said casually. "In case you were wondering what is going on, that racket is an artillery battery about a hundred and fifty meters from us, firing a mission over our heads."

From his position in the LAV-C2, Portiss often had better situational awareness in the field than did I. He and his crew were surrounded by a massive bank of radios, whereas Davis and I had only two available nets from which to glean information at any given time. By monitoring the battalion fire support net, Portiss had been able to determine the origin of the explosions in the darkness. True to form of a good executive officer, he let me and everyone else know the information as soon as it was available. Regardless, I still felt foolish. The sequence had lasted less than a minute, and it had almost scared the piss out of me. Once we figured out what had happened the entire vehicle crew got the giggles. I think they felt about the same way I did. Up in the turret I stared intently in the direction of the battery, allowing my eyes to adjust to the dark. When the next volley erupted several minutes later I watched in silent amazement as the glowing rounds barreled overhead, trailing concussive echoes in their wakes. Somewhere north of us someone was having a worse night than we were.

✦ ✧ ✦

The sound of LCpl Davis's voice from up in the turret woke me the following morning.

"What the hell?" he asked no one in particular. "Will you look at this fucking mess?" He had opened the ammunition feed-tray of the turret's machine-gun, only to find the weapon's insides filled to the brim with mud. I looked around. Everything outside of the vehicle was blanketed in a thick layer of drying muck. The rain had turned the sandstorm into a giant mud storm, and Marines all over the company cursed as they woke to find their personal weapons sealed shut and inoperable. We began cleaning everything as best we could, but the process took forever. Gunners pulled apart the Bushmasters, only to find that they too were filled with a thin, brown gruel. Overhead the sky had returned to the moldy yellow of the previous day, and sand still filled the atmosphere. The storm wasn't finished with us yet—it was just taking a breather.

I left the sounds of Marines cursing the weather and headed for the COC. Upon arrival I learned that the previous night had been just as miserable for everyone else as it had been for me. The battalion staff stood around in small circles, filthy and exhausted. Many of their faces were so dirt-caked that they appeared to be wearing blackface. Dave Hudspeth told me about his horrible experience in the storm. After radioing that he and the forward were stranded by the weather at the combat engineer company's position, they got stuck all evening guarding a group of thirty Iraqi prisoners taken by 3/5. As if that wasn't bad enough, in the middle of the night a tank from 2nd Tank Battalion collided with one of the forward's LAV-C2s. The damage was minimal, but it got everyone's dander up. The fatigue from the previous evening's events combined with the dust caked around his face to make Dave look ten years older. It made me wonder how the hell I looked after the artillery volley. I relayed the story of my RPG scare to everyone and they laughed. Many admitted feeling the same. I was relieved to find I wasn't the only one who had been uneasy the night before.

"Bad night for me last night," I said to Bob Whalen, inhaling deeply on a cigarette like my life depended on it.

"Yeah, I hear you," he replied. "Man, I was uncomfortable about the battalion's position all night long. I haven't been that nervous since we've been in-country."

The effects the weather had on us and our equipment wasn't the only thing upon which we all seemed to agree. Dave, Gil, and I stewed about the lack of progress on the highway. There seemed almost hesitancy on the battalion's part to act. We couldn't figure out what the problem was, and the more we discussed it the more agitated we became. While meeting with the battalion staff, the three of us voiced our concerns. We added the complaints of the Marines, who by now had begun to openly mock the battalion's inaction. By the meeting's close it was clear we had sufficiently pissed off the battalion commander, and he disappeared as soon as the meeting ended. I looked at Dave, and in what had suddenly become a routine handed him a cigarette.

"You believe this shit?" I asked. "It's like we're out here just playing in the mud."

He nodded, and behind me someone grumbled, "I'll tell you what, I'm never putting another fucking sticker on my car that says 'Tip of the Spear.'" Similar displays of overt frustration and anger permeated the atmosphere.

What *was* going on? There we were, a week into the war and well on our way to Baghdad, yet the battalion wasn't doing anything. What had been a yearning on the part of many to engage the enemy as we had been trained to do had turned into a longing to just do something—*anything,* we didn't care what. Farther south, Alpha Company, which had been left behind in Kuwait to retrieve their LAVs from the port at Ash Shubayh, had finally caught up to the division. But they had been ordered by the division commander to escort refuelers north on Highway 1. At least *they* were doing something.

As it was, a pattern had emerged. One of RCT-5's infantry battalions would run into an ambush, thus halting movement along the highway until the enemy could be cleaned out. Once that was accomplished, another infantry battalion would leapfrog forward and take the lead for the regiment, leaving us again following in trace. It was infuriating. An LAV company—with its fourteen 25mm cannons, thirty-nine M240 machine guns, eight TOW missile tubes, two 81mm mortars, and full complement of Marines—brought comparatively more firepower to the battlefield than an entire infantry battalion. Multiply that by three and you have an LAR battalion that can kick just about anyone's ass. The Iraqis ambushing the RCT along Highway 1 would be no match for 1st LAR Battalion if someone would just unleash us. But nobody would, and the only explanation we could pry from the CO or the S-3 was that our battalion didn't possess the large number of dismounted troops that the other infantry battalions had. That was what was needed to really clean out the ambushes, they emphasized. The company commanders felt differently. We preferred to be forward of the regiment, uncovering the ambushes with our firepower and then allowing the grunt battalions to clean them up. We were reconnaissance, for God's sake. But it wasn't our call to make, and we were politely directed to drop it.

There seemed nothing else to do. Because I foresaw no mission in our immediate future, I decided to take the time to clean myself up. My feet were bothering me again, and I worried that they would grow into a more serious issue farther down the road. I hadn't experienced problems with my feet in the field since I had been an officer candidate at OCS in 1992. That summer had been my first time wearing combat boots for prolonged periods. Following a measly nine-mile hike, painful, half-dollar-sized blisters developed on both of my heels. I could barely walk by the time the hike was complete. After the excruciating pain of continuing to train with my feet all torn up, I had pledged to always take care of them no matter what. And I preached to my Marines to do the same. Now there I was, a week into the war, beginning to fret over them. I had to figure out a way to make my clean socks last or else there would be trouble fast. The best way to do it was by airing out my feet and powdering them at every opportunity available.

I pulled my boots off and dumped a handful of foot powder into each in an attempt to absorb the moisture collecting inside. Then, after coating both feet with more of the chalky, white powder I pulled out my shaving gear and lathered up my face for a real razor-shave. Like many, I had taken to using a small, electric shaver in the field because it was faster than, and not as messy as, using shaving cream. But the electric shaver wasn't as thorough as an actual razor, and after several days my face tended to look like shit with random, mutant hairs sticking out here and there. Plus, the act of shaving with a razor just tended to make me feel better—civilized. I had no sooner started running the razor down the side of my face than the battalion called over the radio, directing all units to assume RedCon-1 and ordering the company commanders to the COC.

So much for personal hygiene time. I was aggravated by the interruption, but hoped that at least it meant we would be doing something useful. Wiping the lather from my face, I hastily threw on my gear and ran down the road to the COC. My face was still filthy from the previous night, but the part the shaving cream had covered was now a bright, clean patch. I looked like an idiot.

Two-Five was engaged ten kilometers to the north. It was more of the same. They had been advancing forward, approaching a major intersection near a town to the west called Ad Diwaniyah when they had taken fire from more Iraqi paramilitary types. So far as we knew, we now faced no fewer than three different kinds of enemy soldiers.

There were the Quts, local farmers and herdsmen who had been forcibly pressed into service by members of the Republican Guard and the Special Security Organization. They were supposedly the least reliable and most apt to surrender as soon as possible. It wasn't their war—the only reason they were fighting seemed to be the guns pressed at their backs.

There were the Iraqi Commandos, who we estimated had been behind the technical training of the forces in the area. Each time we moved forward we saw the perfectly-crafted fighting holes along the sides of the road that were a testament to their adherence to textbook tactics.

And, of course, there were the Fedayeen Saddam—"Saddam's Men of Sacrifice"—the suicidal fanatics in black outfits and hoods who had pledged to die for Saddam Hussein rather than allow American forces to take control. The only problem was that now that the RCT and the division were making progress up Highways 1 and 7, the Fedayeen had shed their notorious black outfits for the garb of the local Shi'ite farmers. The black pajamas had made them perfectly identifiable targets. But by wearing *dishdashas* (the traditional long, white flowing robes worn by Arab men) and shemaghs they blended into the local population. We could identify them only if they wore combat boots under their robes, or if they fired on us.

No one had seen an enemy soldier in uniform yet.

Now 2/5 was consolidating for the night, and 1st LAR Battalion had to get to their position and tie in with them for their night defense. Major Harper assigned the company commanders narrow sectors in which to array our forces, and after he drew a quick diagram of the defensive position we saw that it was the same cigar-shape we had occupied two nights earlier. The RCT's plan, too, had formed a pattern: move by day until stopped by an ambush, deal with it as quickly as possible, and hold in place for the night when it was evident we wouldn't get any farther. I was puzzled. Before the war started MajGen Mattis had announced that the division would "move by night and attack by day." Either the ambushes the RCT was encountering had changed that plan, or it had become obvious no one could sustain that sort of tempo for more than a couple of days. Either way, I wasn't exactly disappointed. Despite the sizeable advantage our forces held over the Iraqis in night vision devices, the combination of sandstorm and several moonless nights had made the nights as black as sackcloth. Our NVGs needed at least some ambient light (stars or moonlight) to get a clear picture. I had no problem with the idea of setting in for the night until the moon started to appear.

"We got to get moving *now,"* Maj Harper told us. "Hurry up and get on the road." The sun was getting ready to set again. Where had the time gone? We never seemed to have enough daylight. Our habit of picking up and moving and then trying to set into defensive positions before nightfall was one I definitely didn't like. Even with a map and a GPS, trying to establish a good defensive position after dark is a dangerous task, because what looks good on the map may in reality be terrible ground. Doing it with dismounted infantry is difficult; doing it with fourteen-ton vehicles can seem next to impossible, particularly when the light conditions are as they were those first nights of the war.

A sense of déjà vu seized me as I ran to my vehicle, climbed into the turret, and radioed the platoon commanders.

"Guidons, this is Black-Six," I said, looking at my map with the grid square circled to mark the company's planned position. "We are Oscar Mike, time: now. The battalion has to get up the road and tie in with Two-Five. We'll be oriented east, with Charlie Company to our left and Second Tanks to our right." The sandstorm had kicked up again, and as vehicles from the company peeled off the shoulder and headed north on Highway 1 the events of the previous evening repeated themselves. As with the storm twenty-four hours earlier, the weather deteriorated with each passing minute. Soon it was difficult to see the vehicles of Lt Parment's platoon just fifty meters ahead of me. I shifted around in my turret and looked back at 1stSgt Guzman in his vehicle behind us. He held up both of his arms with an expression that said *Can you believe this shit?*

We had committed ourselves. The battalion was on the road and moving, and we couldn't afford to let the foul weather trip us up again. But it got worse. Five kilometers up the road all forward movement stalled, and Highway 1 became a massive parking lot. The problem was compounded by 3/5 attempting to refuel in the middle of the road as 1st LAR and 2nd Tank Battalion rolled north through the middle of it all. The sun began to sink more quickly, and with the orange glow of the sand-engorged sky fading, visibility again dropped to near zero. Our vehicles cautiously weaved in and out in a slalom around countless tanker trucks, amtracks, and humvees, which all seemed to be vying for their load of fuel first. It was, in a word, dangerous.

As if for emphasis, Lt Parment radioed the company. "All Victors, be advised: There are people in the road everywhere."

"Someone's gonna get killed out here," I said to the crew over the intercom.

"Hey, look at that guy!" said Davis, pointing off to the side of the vehicle. A Marine from 3/5 stood by the side of the road, holding a sign for all to see. It said: "Will work for food." I laughed, but I was still worried we would run over someone in the disorder of the sandstorm and the refueling effort taking place in the road. We would learn the next morning that a tracked vehicle had run over the battalion executive officer for 3/5 and a gunnery sergeant as they slept, killing the major and crippling the gunny. With that terrible accident and the tank collision with the LAV the previous night, my fears from the days before were coming true: we presented a greater potential danger to ourselves than the enemy did.

Our surroundings were pitch black as Delta Company rolled into its positions. The occupation was incredibly stressful, and the entire time, I worried a vehicle would tip over in the dark. I worried the enemy would engage us before we were properly set into position. I worried the LAVs would set in off-kilter and end up shooting each other. Worry, worry, worry. I could practically feel my hair falling out in clumps. That the vehicle commanders were able to position their LAVs as efficiently and safely as they did in all that chaos spoke volumes about their training and proficiency. I realized I shouldn't fret so much. The Marines were big boys, and they could handle themselves in the dark. After all, hadn't that been the point of all the night training we had conducted in the previous year and a half?

✦ ✧ ✦

"Captain Folsom. Sir. Wake up."

I was curled up in the scout compartment when LCpl Davis called back to me from up inside the turret.

"Huh? What is it?" I asked groggily.

"The platoons are seeing something out there."

I hopped out of the rear hatch and climbed back up to my position in the turret. It was late—close to 0130Z—and the sun was not yet up. I pulled on my helmet and keyed the intercom.

"Who's calling it?"

"Second Platoon."

"White-One, this is Six-Actual. What'cha got?"

Lieutenant Schwartz's voice answered. "Roger, Black-Six. We've got movement forward of us." Davis leaned into his gun sight and spun the turret's traversing wheel, manually slewing the gun in 2nd Platoon's direction to get a look through his thermal sight at what they reported. The company was arrayed on-line, and with my vehicle section positioned 100 meters behind the line platoons I relied on the platoon commanders to paint an accurate picture for me.

"Talk to me," I said. "What do you see?"

"We've got thermal signatures of what looks like people walking around a couple of klicks to our front. There's a bunch of them." The other two platoons radioed that they saw them as well.

Davis keyed his helmet. "I can't see them, sir."

I leaned forward and peered into the scope. The vehicles forward of us blocked our view. I had to go with what the platoons were reporting.

"Highlander, this is Dragon-Six," I radioed to the battalion. "My platoons are reporting personnel movement several kilometers forward of our position." Weapons Company called and reported seeing the same thing. The platoons continued to track the movement of the heat signatures as they ambled back and forth. It didn't make sense. Whoever it was out there had to know we were there looking at them. Light and noise discipline or not, an LAR battalion and a tank battalion parked next to each other aren't too difficult to find in the dark. Why were the figures to our front moving about so casually? Why weren't they being more careful?

Another report came through. Someone said he had seen what looked like a truck roll up, drop off more people, and then drive away. I leaned back into the scope, but again all I saw were the glowing, fuzzy white images of the LAVs in front of me. Lieutenant Schwartz radioed again. Apparently he had the best view of the contacts.

"Six, this is White-One. It looks like they just fired a mortar or something," Schwartz radioed. "There was what looked like an explosion in the middle of the group, and they all moved away from it."

"Roger, White-One. Stand by." I reported to the battalion what he had seen, and Weapons Company called to say they were preparing to fire an illumination mission. We heard the *thump-thump* of mortars to our left, and twenty seconds later the land forward of us glowed with artificial light. But even with the illumination rounds overhead lighting up the ground we couldn't get a good look at what the thermals had detected. Our naked eyes had difficulty adjusting to the contrast between the green glow of the thermal scopes and the incandescent light of the mortar rounds suspended by parachutes above us.

"Black-Six, this is White-One," Schwartz said, this time with more urgency in his voice. "They're picking up speed. They're headed right for us."

Okay, I thought. *Time to get involved.*

"Stand by, White-One. I'm rolling up behind you now." I switched to the intercom. "Gurganus, fire it up." The vehicle's engine kicked to life and we slowly moved forward. The dried marshes from the preceding days had given way to soft, tilled farmland, and the vehicle bounced up and down gently as it negotiated the furrows dug by some farmer's plow. We pulled online with the platoons, and as Davis powered up the turret and began scanning again I leaned forward and pressed my face against the scope.

Sometimes your eyes play tricks on you. Sometimes you see what you want to see. Sometimes you are so tired that you see things that aren't really there. The power of suggestion and fatigue are a dangerous combination with which I was familiar. Awake all night with their eyes glued to the green and white electron glow of their thermal sights, the Marines were now experiencing the same problem. I took a close look and then radioed Schwartz, trying to stifle my laughter.

"White-One, this is Black-Six. That's a herd of camels out there." Davis and Gurganus, both with the same view I had, started laughing their asses off. "Look," I said over the intercom to them. As the images got closer and closer it was clear that they were walking on all fours and grouped tightly together.

"Sorry, Six," Schwartz said sheepishly. "That's not what it looked like before. And I swear, there was an explosion out there."

"Don't worry about it," I replied, laughing. "Just don't engage them. All Victors, this is Black-Six. Stand down. I say again, stand down."

Captain Portiss's voice materialized over the radio.

"Roger, Black-Six. I copy White's report: camels in the open," he said dryly.

I called back to the battalion and reported the change in the "enemy" situation. It became a source of humor for everyone, including the battalion commander. After hearing a contact report later in the day about a suspicious SUV approaching the battalion's lines, LtCol White said facetiously over the radio, "Those camels must be driving trucks now."

The first rays of sunlight spilled over the horizon to our front, and despite everyone's weariness another day dawned on us. The faded yellow of the sky from the last two days was replaced by a clear, aqua blue. The sandstorm was over.

I looked at the date displayed on my watch.

27 March.

11
Medevac

It was time to move.

Finally.

All the frustration of sitting still for three days dissipated once we heard the news: with clear skies and favorable weather forecasted ahead of us, RCT-5 was being ordered to advance north up Highway 1 to the vicinity of Hantush Airfield. The makeshift airstrip was adjacent to the intersection of Highway 1 and Route 27, a lateral route that ran all the way to the Tigris River and the town of An Numinayah. Hantush would serve as both a forward arming and refueling point (FARP) and a resupply drop-off point for 3rd MAW's C-130 Hercules transport aircraft. Perhaps more important, Hantush Airfield and the neighboring village of Ash Shumali were the point at which RCT-5 and RCT-7 would take a hard right turn and make a beeline straight for the largely undefended crossing point at An Numinayah along the Tigris River. Our current route ran straight north to Baghdad, but with the delays experienced by the division, word had no doubt filtered back to Saddam Hussein that we were making a play straight up the middle along Highway 1. Third LAR Battalion was ordered to continue its attack north beyond Hantush to make the Iraqis think the division was proceeding along its original axis of advance. With the speed possessed by 1st Marine Division, the Republican Guard divisions defending Baghdad would not be able to react in time once they discovered that 3rd LAR's attack was merely a feint.

On the morning of 27 March, 1st LAR Battalion was ordered to travel north along Highway 1 beyond Hantush Airfield to establish a tactical assembly area for the RCT. The TAA would be the jump-off point for the assault beyond the Tigris River. With 3rd LAR and 2/5 leading the attack, 1st LAR's play in the problem was minimal. *Set up an assembly area?* I thought, fuming to myself. *Are they kidding me?* But how could I complain? At least we would actually be doing something. My spirits took a further dive when, during the course of the mission briefing, the S-3 announced that Delta Company would assume the "tail-end Charlie" position during the battalion's road march north.

I had no right to be angry. After all, it was unreasonable for me to expect the company to be the main effort for every battalion mission. But that's one of the things that makes the Corps so good at what it does: Marines get hacked off if they aren't afforded the chance to lead. The war itself was a prime example of this. The U.S. Army's Fifth Corps (V Corps), with the Third Infantry Division (3rd ID) spearheading it, had been designated the main effort for the advance toward Baghdad. The MEF and 1st Marine Division were the supporting effort. Never mind the fact that the routes being taken by the Division—Highways 1 and 7—were more treacherous than those traveled by 3rd ID. The bottom line was that the Marines were the supporting effort, and that pissed them off.

But then again, by that point in the war everything pissed off the Marines. The causes were legion. If a complaining Marine was a happy Marine, then we needed straitjackets to contain our joy.

First, there was no mail coming through. Because the division's priority was getting fuel and water up Highway 1 to resupply the RCTs, no one had seen any mail since several days before crossing the border. To many it was a nonissue; clearly, mail comes second to the supplies that keep the force running. But the victim in this mail shortage was the morale of the Marines. Unbeknown to us at the time, the largest mail campaign in history was underway back home in the States. Anyone and everyone was writing letters and sending care packages to their loved ones fighting in Iraq. People who didn't even personally know servicemen searched madly for some way to send packages to the troops. Everyone wanted to contribute his or her share and demonstrate support for the boys and girls fighting it out halfway around the world. Parcels by the thousands piled up in warehouses in Kuwait. There weren't enough Marines to sort the mail, and there weren't enough trucks to get it to us. There we were, thinking our efforts were going unappreciated, and this couldn't have been further from the truth. This was no Vietnam. Despite people's personal feelings about the war, they supported the troops. The shame was that we didn't know it at the time.

Second, food was getting scarce, particularly in the infantry battalions. The division commander insisted that each Marine plan for and be able to subsist on two MREs per day. But Napoleon himself had said, "An army marches on its stomach"—nearly two hundred years old, but words of wisdom nonetheless. You take a division of Marines and you put them in suffocating, claustrophobic chemical suits, you make them fight their way 150 miles up a highway teeming with guerillas and ambushes at every turn, and then you expect them to survive on two meals a day. It was absurd. Delta Company would have been in the same boat had it not been for the foresight of SSgt Kappen. In the weeks leading up to the war he had begun squirreling away crate after crate of MREs. He packed as many as he possibly could in the cargo bays of his two LAV-Ls, and he ordered the Marines to do the same on their vehicles. By the time Delta Company had left Kuwait each LAV was practically bursting at the seams with rations. But it didn't stop there. Kappen continued to hoard MREs every chance he got. Each time the battalion's field trains showed up for a resupply he would get on the radio and demand that each and every vehicle get in line and take on as much chow as the battalion would give away. No one in Delta Company went hungry throughout the entire course of the war. It got to the point where we began handing out our own food to help feed the poor bastards from the RCT. At one point, as we drove slowly along Highway 1, we noticed a squad leader from one of the infantry battalions along the side of the road with his squad of hungry young Marines. He had torn open an MRE and was dividing the meal up piece by piece to his men. The main meal went to one Marine, the Skittles to another, the fudge brownie to another, and so on. We ended up tossing down crates of MREs to feed the grunts who had, until now, done all of the fighting and the dying. It seemed the least we could do.

Finally, there were no spare parts. The shortage, which had reared its head as soon as the division had begun arriving in Kuwait, was reaching its apex. There was, simply put, nothing out there for our vehicles. LAVs entered service sometime around 1985. They were old vehicles that needed constant maintenance to stay up and running, but repair parts on Highway 1 were nonexistent. If a vehicle was catastrophically dead-lined (broken down or deemed "out of commission"), and if there was no way it could be rigged to keep running, it was cannibalized to fix the other ailing vehicles in the battalion. By the war's end the field trains were towing skeletons of LAVs that had suffered this fate. The mechanics performed superhuman feats to keep the vehicles operational, but sometimes even their best efforts couldn't keep certain LAVs off the dead-line list. The maintenance officer, Jerry Copely, did everything in his power to keep the battalion's assets rolling, sometimes resorting to unorthodox means. One time he even managed to obtain a crucial engine component by trading a coveted British porn magazine. The spare parts situation was *that* serious. Even the MEF Commander, LtGen Conway, was witness to this maintenance miracle. He watched one time as elements of RCT-5 sped forward into battle, the mechanics from an infantry battalion sitting atop an amtrack and feverishly working on it as it was towed at forty-five miles an hour toward the front lines. He later recalled that, curiously, his first thought was *Now that's* got *to be a safety violation.* But being the kind of leader he was, he understood that the Marines were doing whatever was required to keep their equipment up and in the fight. I had observed the same incident, but my opinion, as usual, expressed itself in more colorful language. *Hard core,* I thought. *Fucking hard core, man.*

✦ ✧ ✦

The company staged along the highway shoulder, and the staff gathered around me for the mission frag. Their appearances startled me. Overnight the carefree expressions on their young faces had been marred by the strain of the sandstorm and the hasty occupation of the assembly area the previous evening. I laid out the mission to them in the simple manner that, by now, was as familiar as if we had been doing this forever.

"Okay, quick, we've only got five minutes before we have to be on the road," I said to the group clustered around me. I pointed to my map. "We're here. We're going here to establish a TAA for the RCT. Order of march is SOP. Any questions?"

"In the rear again, sir?" someone asked. Nods of agreement. Mumbled curses.

"Listen," I said, understanding their surliness. "Let's just be glad we're moving away from this fucking place. If there aren't any more questions, mount up. Report when set, RedCon-One." The staff dispersed, running back to their vehicles, and soon the battalion was slowly rolling along the pavement north toward Hantush Airfield and Ash Shumali. The road was strewn with myriad shards of shrapnel. There was no way to avoid it all. It was like passing through a parade route that had been showered with steel confetti. I radioed the platoon commanders, warning them to be wary of the steel fragments covering our route. It was redundant for me to do so—their eyes were as good as mine, but with the parts shortage going on, there would be a shortage of replacement spare tires soon. Each vehicle carried a spare tire, but with all the shrapnel lining the road our supply wouldn't last long.

We passed beneath the underpass of the highway interchange—the cloverleaf—and above us a great blue metal sign pointed north toward Hillah and Baghdad. Were it not for the slanted Arabic script it could have been a sign in Kansas. Never in my wildest dreams did I think a conflict with Iraq would be like this. But there we were, cruising along in our highway war with blue skies ahead of us and a big road sign pointing to our ultimate objective: Baghdad, the cultural center of the Islamic caliphate; the home of Ali Baba; the power center of Saddam Hussein and the Ba'ath Party. All of a sudden, despite the friction of the previous week, Iraq's capital seemed well within our grasp.

The crack of high explosives detonating to our left drew our attention away from the parking lot developing in front of us. Three-Five was engaged west of the cloverleaf, and we watched as gunships rolled in to provide support for them. Hellfire missiles dropped from beneath the Cobras' stubby wings and ripped through the air, impacting two T-55 tanks beyond the cloverleaf. Most of the tanks the division had been encountering were abandoned. The Iraqi soldiers knew they didn't stand a chance, and common sense made them desert their armored vehicles rather than face an enemy whose equipment was far superior to their own. But if the air power didn't get them, the ground forces slogging their way forward definitely would.

Over the previous few days I had gained a new respect for the air wing. While the ground forces had suffered through the forty-eight-hour sandstorm, the air wing had continued to fly sorties all around us. Undeterred by the hostile weather conditions covering the region, pilots of Marine Corps F/A-18 Hornets and AV-8B Harriers, Air Force F-15 Eagles and F-16 Falcons, Navy F-14 Tomcats and Hornets, and helicopter pilots from all four services had never left our side. They persisted because they knew we on the ground needed them. By maintaining constant pressure on the Fedayeen and the Iraqi army holdouts, by continuing to pound them throughout the storm, the aviators enabled the ground forces to charge forward like racehorses at the starting gate as soon as the storm subsided.

Bringing up the rear of the battalion, Delta Company's movement along the highway was initially stop and go. But as we rode under the overpass interchange the pace gradually picked up. Scores of Iraqi civilians watched us from the buildings and fields bordering the road. The fact that there was fighting going on nearby didn't disturb them. Rather, it seemed to attract them. They would peer out from their houses, then in small groups venture outside to watch the fighting. It was a curious trend that later resulted in the deaths of countless Iraqi noncombatants. Marines and soldiers alike would later report civilian cars carelessly approaching roadblocks. When Iraqis didn't comply with orders to stop they would be gunned down. But we weren't in a roadblock situation now, and I was concerned that the observers were Fedayeen playing civilians. I radioed the company to keep their eyes on the onlookers, and soon the traffic began to clear. We once again pressed north.

No sooner had the trail elements of the company's column cleared the shade of the overpass than Lt Parment made the radio call I expected.

"Black-Six, this is Red-One," he said in his usual emotionless tone. "My vehicle just picked up some shrapnel. I've got a flat tire. I'm cross-decking now and will catch up with the column." Passing by, I saw Parment climb from his vehicle and into his wingman's LAV while his crew scrambled to get the punctured tire removed and replaced. *How many more?* I wondered. Then a crazy thought occurred to me: *Someone ought to get a working party together out here and sweep all this shrapnel off the road.* It was a ridiculous idea, of course. There was no way we could just stop everything and send out a squad of Marines with brooms. But the majority of the vehicles in the division rode around on rubber tires, not metal tracks, and with the dearth of spare parts in Iraq, the division couldn't afford to lose any more tires than absolutely necessary.

Parment sped off in his wingman's vehicle to catch up to the front of his platoon, and I called back down the column to SSgt Monroe, directing him to assist Parment's crew.

"Roger that, Black-Six. Already on the way."

We made good time, averaging close to thirty or forty kilometers an hour. The shrapnel lining the road thinned out, and soon we were on highway unmarred by the telltale pockmarks of artillery shells and small arms fire. Far ahead of us 2/5 had run into enemy contact, and I listened intently to the radio as Maj Harper and LtCol White discussed the situation. Two-Five's lead elements had reported taking fire from their flanks by more dismounted enemy personnel. Soon they were slugging it out with nearly a full company of Iraqis, and there were reports of armored vehicles occupying the objective. Listening to the messages passing back and forth over the radio, I wondered if we would come to a screeching halt again as we had after each ambush of the RCT the previous several days. My chain of thought was abruptly broken by the company frequency beeping to life. Someone began yelling the same thing again and again.

"Black-Nine just got hit by a tank! Black-Nine just got hit by a tank!"

What?! Got hit by a tank? Black-9 was SSgt Monroe's vehicle. Everyone instantly imagined the same distressing scene: a T-55 rolling up on our flank and firing a 100mm high explosive round through the side of Monroe's vehicle.

"Say again!" I yelled back into the radio. "Calm down and send your traffic again!" I needed to calm down myself.

"This is Black-Ten," Sergeant William Lyman said breathlessly. "Staff Sergeant Monroe's LAV just got hit by a tank."

The radio was suddenly jammed with people yelling, each trying to get his transmission heard. I turned in the turret and looked south toward the direction of the cloverleaf, but aside from the columns of smoke far to the west where 3/5 was fighting there was nothing. No oily, black smoke mushrooming skyward. Nothing. The confusion continued on the radio net. I keyed my headset again.

"Break, break. Everyone clear the net. Black-Ten, are you telling me Black-Nine has been shot by an enemy tank?" There was pause, and then Lyman's voice reappeared.

"Negative, Black-Six. A friendly tank just ran into Staff Sergeant Monroe's vehicle while he was helping fix Red-One's tire." Lyman's clarification didn't help dry up the beads of nervous sweat that had formed under my helmet. A sixty-three-ton M1A1 tank outweighs an LAV by forty-nine tons. Forty-nine *tons.* Do the math and you quickly realize that a fast-moving M1A1 will barrel through just about anything almost as effortlessly as its main gun rounds will. Just as I began to imagine SSgt Monroe and his crew spread out over the highway like strawberry jam, his beleaguered voice materialized over the radio waves.

"Black-Six, this is Black-Nine," he said angrily. "Everyone's alright. Corporal Martin's a little banged up, but we're okay. I'm gonna get that fucking tank crew, though."

When pressed for details, Monroe explained how he had pulled his LAV off the road to assist 1st Platoon. Enter 2nd Tank Battalion, which came screaming up the highway toward the contact with 2/5. A tank had its long barrel traversed to the left, and the tip of it slammed into the rear hatch of the LAV. Seeing the behemoth barreling down on them, Staff Sergeant Monroe had hollered for everyone to clear out, but it was too late. As Cpl Martin tried to jump from atop the vehicle, the shock of the impact threw him into the air and sent him tumbling to the ground. The only injury was sustained by Martin, who snagged his chin on the iron front sight post of his LAV's machine gun. The laceration needed a mere two stitches to close it. It was an amazing piece of luck that no one was seriously injured or downright flattened. When I talked to Monroe later in the afternoon he was fit to be tied. A long stream of profanity gushed from his mouth, his speech and mannerisms indicating that the mishap had really spooked him. Who could blame him? I probably would have shit my pants had I been in his place.

With the excitement of the collision past, the company continued up the road with the battalion. The clamor over the battalion's frequency had died down, and it appeared 2/5 had taken care of whatever enemy it had encountered north of us. We traveled about twenty kilometers until the battalion came to a halt once again. No matter how many times it happened throughout the war, I felt the same way each time we got stuck in a traffic jam: *We are the biggest target in the world out here.* Every minute the column sat immobile I expected a volley of artillery or mortars to rain down on us. I was less worried about the Fedayeen. The LAVs had excellent fields of fire to our flanks, and there was no way the Iraqis could sneak up on us with their RPGs. But no one seemed to know what the state of the enemy's artillery was. What before the war had been described as the Iraqi army's center of gravity was now a complete mystery. We had yet to experience an artillery barrage, thanks in large part to Eleventh Marines' counter-battery radar and the constant air power that hunted overhead. But there was always that uneasy feeling in the pit of my stomach, waiting for the drone of incoming rounds.

But we were certainly more prepared to receive incoming artillery than we were to receive the radio transmission that came next. Major Harper called the company commanders.

"Guidons, this is Highlander-Three," he said flatly. "Turn around and head back to the battalion's previous position." We were incredulous. It made no sense to return forty kilometers to the south, especially since 2/5 had already defeated the resistance on the objective. But no explanation was given. We had no idea why we were turning back. Because Delta Company had been traveling at the rear of the column, we were the first element to reverse course and lead the battalion column back.

With nothing ahead of us to impede our movement, we sped south along Highway 1. The radio was silent. I could only imagine what passed through everyone's mind. It didn't make any sense. It couldn't be a retreat—2/5 had just wiped out a company. Besides, Marines *never* retreat. But that was what it looked like to the uninformed, and just the mere thought of it pissed everyone off. With no explanation offered, everyone's mind devised its own rationale for the RCT turning around. We wouldn't find out the full, official story explaining the retrograde until the following day.

As the battalion slowly caught up with us, Maj Harper radioed again. He informed me that 3/5 was engaged with an enemy force in the vicinity of 1st LAR Battalion's original position. Apparently as soon as we had cleared out that morning the Iraqis had filled in the vacuum and immediately began engaging 3/5. As the battalion headed south we prepared to break one of the oldest rules in the book: never fight twice for the same ground.

Lieutenant Colonel White's voice replaced Maj Harper's on the radio, ordering Delta Company to lead the attack into our position so the battalion could reoccupy it. Charlie and Weapons Companies would be the supporting effort. I turned to LCpl Davis.

"Roll the freq to Three-Five's net I.D.," I said. There was a chirping sound over the radio as Davis keypunched the new frequency, and then I was listening to Marines from 3/5 chatter. I jumped into the conversation. "Naktong, this is Highlander-Dragon-Six."

"Go ahead, Dragon," a voice replied.

"Roger, I'm heading south and leading Highlander back to occupy the area where you are in contact." I read him the grid coordinates of our destination.

"That's Kilo Company's fight, Dragon," the voice said. "Roll to his frequency and coordinate your attack with him." Davis leaned back down next to the radio bank behind him and typed in the frequency for Kilo Company, and soon I was talking to its commander and trying to get an idea what we were about to roll into. He described what was transpiring. Sure enough, the enemy forces had fallen in behind his company and started firing on them almost as soon as 1st LAR Battalion had left its assembly area. The Iraqis firing on Kilo Company all wore civilian clothing. I alternated between talking to Kilo's CO and my platoons, and once I had a good idea what was going on I had Davis reset the radio net back to the battalion. I gave orders for a hasty scheme of maneuver to the platoons while simultaneously coordinating the company's actions with Gil and Dave over the battalion frequency.

It was a straightforward plan: Delta Company, traveling in column along the highway, would simply make a left face and roll forward on-line across the tilled field the battalion had occupied the previous night. The land was wide open, with nowhere for the enemy to hide. If the Fedayeen were stupid enough to remain exposed, Delta Company's advancing wall of LAVs would cut them down. I wanted Charlie Company to advance alongside us on Delta's left flank to ensure full coverage of the objective area while laying down maximum firepower if necessary. But as I struggled to coordinate all of this with Gil and Dave *and* explain the plan to my platoons, I became flustered. The battalion commander, the S-3, and the fire support coordinator kept interrupting me on the radio, attempting to micromanage my efforts. Then Gil's calm voice sounded again on the radio.

"Dragon-Six, we're right behind you. Just tell us what you need." What I needed was for everyone to leave me the hell alone and let me control my company. I finally clicked off the battalion radio and concentrated on maneuvering the platoons into position.

The company slowly approached Kilo Company's position. Lieutenant Cullins's platoon had taken the lead, and I radioed him to halt while I made a quick face-to-face with Kilo's CO. He told me they were engaged with about 100 militia fighters, and since our last conversation over the radio the enemy had pulled back to the southeast and into some abandoned buildings. Kilo had bombed them with both artillery and close air support, but he didn't know if the defenders were still there or not. For emphasis, he pointed to the precise location I had been told to attack and clear. *This is it,* I thought. *It's go-time.* I climbed back into my turret and keyed my headset.

"All Victors, move out as planned. Expect resistance." Almost on cue the entire company veered left off the paved surface of the highway and continued forward to the east. I radioed Gil, and as he brought Charlie abreast of us, our two companies rolled into the assembly area looking for the enemy.

There was no one there.

Whoever Kilo Company had been fighting had melted away again. It had become a standard tactic adopted by the enemy forces the RCT was fighting. They would ambush the advancing columns of humvees and amtracks, and they would engage the infantry at close range. But as soon as tanks or LAVs arrived on-scene the Iraqi fighters tended to disappear. Even with their RPGs they were loathe to engage the heavy armored vehicles. Once we realized there would be no enemy contact, the tense atmosphere shrouding the company radio net lightened up. But everyone's disappointment was obvious. How many more times could we get keyed up like that and still have no enemy contact to show for it? I began to fear the complacency that had set in during the NBC false alarms back in Kuwait would rear its ugly head again.

With the area clear of enemy personnel, the rest of the battalion soon started rolling in to reoccupy its position. Things returned to business as usual. As soon as the company was arrayed properly and screening toward the east as we had been the previous night, SSgt Kappen radioed the platoons. Before they forgot what they were doing in all the excitement, he directed them to send back vehicles in groups of two to conduct a tactical refueling with the battalion's resupply assets. I stood up high in the turret and looked to the east with my binoculars. There was nothing out there but more of the same turned-up soil. I decided to reduce the company's alert level. With the adrenaline crash after the excitement of preparing to attack the assembly area, many of the Marines would have a difficult time really focusing on the empty ground ahead of them. One Marine in each turret scanning out in front of him would be sufficient until night fell.

✦ ✧ ✦

The radio beeped, and the battalion watch officer called up the company commanders. He announced that the battalion wanted us to conduct patrols to get a better picture of what lay to the east.

"Guidons, as far as whether you send out vehicle or foot patrols," the captain said before signing off, "that's your call." I thought about it. My first inclination was to send out a platoon for a mounted vehicle patrol forward of our perimeter, but despite the open terrain and wide fields of fire the ground was still difficult to negotiate in a wheeled vehicle. While not as rough to drive on as the drained marshes from the previous days, the farmland to our front could more easily be traversed by a foot patrol. There was also the fact that, so far, the company's scouts hadn't really done much in the war. Most of their time had been spent riding around in the back of the vehicles or sitting off to the side of Highway 1 doing nothing. They needed to stay mentally engaged, and a foot patrol was the perfect solution. True, there wasn't much to see out there, but they would be eager to get out and do something. I radioed Capt Portiss with my orders.

"Black-Five, task Blue Platoon to execute a foot-mobile security patrol forward of our lines," I said. Remembering one of the things the watch officer had said, I added, "Doesn't need to be anything big, but they need to expedite it to ensure they're back by sunset."

"Roger that, Black-Six," he replied. "I'll take a look at their patrol plan and let you know when they head out." As I sat down next to the vehicle to get something to eat, I knew exactly what Portiss would be doing. After relaying the task to Lt Cullins he would radio SSgt Peralta and the mortar section, directing them to get fire-capped to support the patrol. Then he would sit down with Spool and try to determine if there was any air support in the vicinity should the scouts need it during the conduct of their patrol. Then he would review the scouts' patrol plan. If it was satisfactory he would let me know. If not he would tell the scouts to redo it. He was thorough, and I admired him for it.

After wolfing down an MRE, I leaned back against a tire and tried to relax. Lance Corporal Davis leaned out of the turret and told me the XO was calling.

"He said Third Platoon's scouts are cleared hot and getting ready to leave our lines," Davis called down.

"Good to go. Tell him to report in with me when they return."

With the scouts preparing to head out it was difficult for me to relax. It shouldn't have been. They weren't going to run into anything, and their section leader, Corporal Jared Grewing, was a tough bastard who knew what he was doing. But even after convincing myself that there was no need to worry about the patrol, my mind raced. Each time I tried to close my eyes I thought of something else that needed to be added to my ever-growing list of things to do. First Sergeant Guzman walked over from his vehicle parked fifty meters away and dropped his campstool. The two of us began talking. Like so many others he had taken up cigarettes since the war started, and we sat there chatting and smoking for several minutes. Staff Sergeant Monroe, appearing to have recovered from his rage over the tank collision earlier in the day, wandered over toward us and sat down as well. We were tired, but at the same time perhaps a little ashamed at our fatigue. After all, despite the friction of the weather and the long distances the company had covered since D-Day, we still had yet to really do anything. It almost felt as if we had no right to be so tired because we hadn't engaged the enemy yet.

As we talked, a high-pitched, muffled explosion thudded to the east. It was close, perhaps two to three hundred meters from where we sat. Monroe instinctively took a knee and aimed his rifle in the direction of the blast. It couldn't be artillery or mortars—it had been a small blast, and no shriek or whistle or buzz of the incoming round accompanied it. As we peered in the direction of the noise a smoke cloud hovered over the ground one hundred meters forward of 3rd Platoon position. No sooner had the three of us stood up to find out what it was than we heard Marines in 3rd Platoon's direction yelling.

"Corpsman, up!" they screamed. *"Corpsman up!"*

We bolted forward, making a beeline toward their position. Marines ahead of us yelled their heads off, shouting "It's a land mine! It's a land mine!" I continued running and focused on the impact site ahead of me. Figures had already gathered and were kneeling around a body lying prone in the dirt. I had barely heard the Marines' warnings.

"Monroe, stop him!" 1stSgt Guzman hollered behind me.

"Sir! Sir! It's a fucking minefield!" SSgt Monroe shouted over to me as we ran. "Watch where you're going!" I turned to see both men running along inside a deep indentation pressed into the soil by an LAV's tires. Hopping into the set of tracks, I continued sprinting toward the crowd ahead of us. I started to overheat in the sauna of my MOPP suit, and my lungs burned. *Man,* I thought, pausing to lean down and catch my breath. *I've got to stop smoking cigarettes.*

As we closed in on the site, several scouts from 3rd Platoon's patrol stood around, unsure of what to do. One scout stared dumbly at us as we ran by him.

"Goddammit, Marine!" I yelled. "Don't just stand there! Face outboard and take cover!" He dropped down into the dirt with several others, pointing his rifle out to the east. With all the confusion building up it was a perfect opportunity for any watching Fedayeen to add just a little more to the fray. The last thing we needed was for the Marines around us to let down their guard. We reached the site, where a throng of Marines and corpsmen crowded around the casualty on the ground.

"Who is it?" I asked Cpl Grewing breathlessly. "What happened?"

"It's Suarez, sir. We just stepped off on the patrol. I think he stepped on a land mine."

Lance Corporal Jésus Suarez del Solar. Twenty years old. He had emigrated from Tijuana to the United States with his family when he was in high school. I thought back to him manning his sniper position in the old, broken-down tower along the Iraqi border that first day of the war. A lifetime seemed to have passed since then.

"Is anyone else wounded?"

"No, I don't think so," Grewing replied. He began shouting "Is anyone else hit?" Marines from the patrol checked themselves, patting their clothing down. There were replies of "No" and shakes of the head. *Thank God,* I thought. I muscled my way through the crowd, pushing bodies aside. On the ground corpsmen and Marines huddled around Suarez, attempting to stabilize him. They had already cut away most of his chemical suit, and it lay in bloody ribbons in a shapeless pile next to him. I knelt and examined him up and down. Tiny shrapnel wounds peppered the lower half of his body. My initial thought that it resembled our grenade mishap the previous October quickly vanished once my eyes locked onto a dark, gaping hole on the inside of his right thigh. Hospitalman Third Class Benjamin Hodges, 3rd Platoon's senior corpsman and a certified emergency medical technician and trauma specialist, was bent over Suarez's right leg. He had jammed several fingers down inside the wound, attempting to cut off the flow of blood that rhythmically pulsed from the severed femoral artery. The soil beneath Suarez had gone black from the blood leaking from his shredded body. Seeing that and the damage to his leg, I turned back to Hodges.

"Has anyone called for a medevac?"

"Yes, sir," he replied. "Urgent-surgical."

"They're calling it in now," added 1stSgt Guzman. "The XO and Captain Peitz are working it." With them coordinating the medevac, there was little else for me to do. I felt useless.

"What can I do, Doc?" I asked Hodges. "What can I do to help?"

"Put pressure on that head wound, sir," he said, pointing to the right side of Suarez's head. Another corpsman had been holding a dressing against a laceration just above Suarez's right temple. As he pulled his hand away to begin working on the leg wounds, the gash opened back up. A jet of bright red blood sprayed out onto me.

"Hey!" I said, alarmed. "Is this one penetrating?"

"I don't think so, sir," Hodges replied. "Head wounds just bleed like a son of a bitch. The majority of the damage is to the legs and abdomen."

"Was it a land mine?"

"Couldn't be a land mine," someone piped in. "He wouldn't have a leg left if it was."

"Well," I asked no one in particular. "What the fuck did this then?"

"Hey!" someone called out. "I think its DPICM. There's one. And there's another one over there!" *Oh my God,* I thought, looking around. Scattered in ones and twos about the area were the long, bright yellow streamers of DPICM bomblets. *They're all around us.* I turned to Guzman.

"First Sergeant, get everyone out of here who isn't needed."

"Aye-aye, sir," he replied. He turned to the Marines grouped around us and yelled, "Let's go! If you aren't doing anything here, get back to your vehicles! And use the vehicle tracks to walk in. There are cluster bombs all over the freakin' place!"

I leaned in close to Suarez. He rolled his head back and forth in the dirt, moaning. His eyes alternated between looking blankly from each of us to the next and rolling up into his head until only the whites showed. He fought us as we tried to help him. With one hand I held the dressing tightly against the side of his head, and with the other I grasped his right hand.

"Hang in there, Suarez," I told him. "We're gonna get you fixed up. Just hang in there, man." I squeezed his hand for emphasis and he groaned, trying to pull it away from mine. I looked down to see that the tip of his right thumb—about the first half-inch—had been blown away in the explosion. He was in pain, and I had just caused him more. I felt terrible.

Other Marines leaned next to him with me, talking to him. Soothing him. They had done the same thing when their comrades had stepped on the grenade in Kuwait, but back then the wounded men were more scared than anything else. Now HM3 Hodges was leading the fight to save Suarez's life. He had what we all called the "Blackhawk Down wound," a severed femoral artery that was nearly impossible to repair without trauma surgery. In the 1993 raid by the U.S. Army in Mogadishu, Somalia, a Ranger had been shot through the leg. The bullet had cut his femoral artery, and despite the efforts of his fellow soldiers to save him he bled out before they could get him to the field hospital. With a similar wound, Suarez was in the same danger of dying right there in front of us if we didn't staunch the flow of blood pumping from his leg.

The sun began to dip below the horizon. We had to get him stabilized and out of there fast before it was completely dark. With the unexploded munitions all around us, anyone could detonate one in the shadows if we weren't careful. The corpsmen continued to work as the light receded, and soon flashlights appeared. In the eerie red glow of the flashlight beams, the blood and gore that painted the others and me seemed to disappear. Over the frenzied conversation taking place between the corpsmen and the combat aid-trained Marines, I heard the familiar whine of an LAV approaching us. It was SSgt Kappen's vehicle, arriving to pick up Suarez and transport him to the highway. Spool was in the process of setting up a landing zone on the flat pavement while Capt Portiss reported the incident to the battalion.

"Did you say it was a land mine?" the voice on the other end of the radio asked.

"Negative," Portiss replied. "We don't know what it was. The initial report was that it was a land mine. Now we think it was a DPICM cluster bomb. Do you copy?"

"Affirmative, Dragon-Five," the voice replied.

Staff Sergeant Kappen jumped out of his vehicle and knelt down next to me. His crew began throwing extra equipment out of the LAV's cargo hold, converting it into an ambulance and preparing it for the stretcher to slide in back. Kappen and I continued trying to comfort Suarez, but he was so out of it I didn't think he really knew everyone was there tying to save him.

"We're ready, Staff Sergeant," yelled Kappen's driver, LCpl Schaffer. The group hoisted Suarez's limp form onto the stretcher and pushed him into the LAV's bay. Kappen climbed back into his hatch and the vehicle rumbled away, packed with Marines and corpsmen inside working on Suarez. Others clung to the outside like gorillas. I looked around in the twilight at the few of us left standing there.

"Is he gonna be alright, sir?" someone asked in the fading light.

"Yeah," I replied. "We're gonna get him out of here. He'll be okay." I turned and followed the tracks of the LAV back toward the road. Walking in the tire depressions, I started noticing more of the DPICM bomblets. They were everywhere. Suddenly I was very nervous about any of us walking around this place at night.

Instead of moving to the highway, Kappen's LAV had halted next to Capt Portiss's vehicle in the center of the battle position. The stretcher was back out on the ground again, and the corpsmen continued to stabilize Suarez. The battalion surgeon, Navy Lieutenant Gordon Zubrod, had shown up on the scene and taken charge of the lifesaving effort.

"What's going on with the medevac?" I asked Portiss. Both he and Spool sat atop their LAV with radio handsets pressed to their ears.

"We're working on it. Spool and Mud Duck are doing everything they can."

"Jesus Christ," I said angrily. "We've already been out here over thirty minutes! What the fuck's the holdup?"

"The medevac helo broke down," said Spool. "We're trying to get another one." Despite my ire at the situation, I grasped that they all knew what they were doing. As I watched, they performed every task by the book, the way we had trained to do it dozens of times before. The XO and the FAC coordinate the medevac. The Ops Chief coordinates ground transport to the landing zone (LZ). We were doing it right, but it was going all wrong.

"Why are we still down here?" I asked, pointing toward the west. "Why aren't we up on the road at the LZ?"

"We're getting ready to head out now, sir," Kappen replied, walking past me. He knelt back down on the ground next to Suarez. "Don't worry, hard-charger. We're taking you to the LZ for your helicopter ride to the hospital." They reloaded Suarez onto the LAV and sped off for the road. I climbed in the back of the XO's vehicle and rode with them as they followed in trace of the LAV-cum-ambulance. As we bounced around in the darkness on our way to the landing zone, gloomy thoughts filled my head. *This is not going well,* I said to myself. *This is not going well at all.*

The bouncing stopped as the vehicle rolled up the embankment and onto the smooth pavement. I kicked open the hatch and was greeted by complete darkness outside. We had gotten Suarez out of the blast site just in time. The wait for the medevac helicopter began. As LT Zubrod and his corpsmen continued to labor over Suarez in the cargo bay of Kappen's LAV, I walked around the back of the vehicle and peered inside. Bags of intravenous fluids hung suspended from the ceiling. Suarez had regained some awareness of his surroundings, and Lance Corporal José Vargas and SSgt Navarro sat by his side, speaking Spanish to him while the medics continued their work.

I looked around. The helicopter was supposedly on its way. There wasn't much else I could do at the scene, but I couldn't bring myself to leave until Suarez was safely aboard the medevac and heading south to the field hospital. Off to the side, Bob Woodruff intently watched the Marines and corpsmen laboring over Suarez. Since the first day of the war Woodruff and his film crew had ridden in the spacious cargo hold of SSgt Kappen's vehicle. Apparently all of their camera equipment had been tossed out in the assembly area when Kappen got the word to come pick up Suarez. Woodruff needed it there on the road more than ever.

"Man, I wish I had my camera," he kept saying aloud to himself. He walked up to Kappen. "Hey, do you still have your camcorder in your vehicle?"

"Yeah, it's in my stuff."

"Can I borrow it?"

"Yeah, sure," Kappen said. "Give me a minute." Standing off by myself, I overheard their exchange. As Woodruff moved back around the vehicle I confronted Kappen.

"Hey, I heard what he wants. There's no way in hell he's gonna film this. Don't you dare give him your camcorder. In fact, do not *under any circumstances* let him film what's going on in there. Got it?"

"Yes, sir," Kappen replied.

I returned to the rear of the vehicle. Woodruff stood there looking into the cargo bay at Suarez splayed out on the stretcher. Tubes protruded from the Marine, and he was covered in bandages. A pensive look filled Woodruff's face as he watched, and I imagined him formulating how he would narrate the story of a young Mexican immigrant at death's door awaiting a helicopter to evacuate him. I walked up next to him.

"I wish I had my camera," Woodruff said again. "But Staff Sergeant Kappen said I could use his camcorder."

"You're not going to film this," I said, staring straight ahead.

"It will just be for the documentary," he protested. I turned and looked him directly in the eyes.

"You're *not* going to film this." I said coldly. He looked at me for a moment, and then dropped it. I didn't care if he was embedded with Delta Company or not. I didn't care if he created bad press about me that would follow me around for the rest of my life. There was no way I would allow Suarez's family to watch him bleeding to death on *World News Tonight*.

Somewhere a radio crackled to life, relaying a transmission none of us wanted to hear at that instant in time.

"Lightning! Lightning! Lightning!" the voice insisted. People all over the battalion's assembly responded by yelling "Gas! Gas! Gas!" Up on the road, the Marines and sailors clustered around Kappen's LAV and the humvee ambulance ripped open satchels and slammed their faces into their gas masks. Together SSgt Navarro, SSgt Monroe, and I looked down at our hips and realized we didn't have our masks with us. I remembered taking mine off as I sat down to eat over an hour earlier.

"Fuck!" yelled Monroe. "I don't have my mask with me!" Another Marine in a gas mask ran up to him and clutched his shoulder.

"Come on Staff Sergeant!" the Marine yelled, tugging on his arm. He yanked his mask off and handed it to Monroe, and the two took off for Monroe's vehicle to find his mask. They disappeared into the darkness, running along crouched over and passing the gas mask back and forth between the two of them, buddy-breathing. Staff Sergeant Navarro and I watched them for a moment and then sheepishly looked at each other.

"Well," I said indifferently. "We're dead."

"Hey, at least we'll die together, sir" he replied, smiling. We started helping the docs as they worked on Suarez. The burden of the gas masks frustrated their efforts, and all I thought the entire time was, *This is great . . . this is all we fucking need right now.* Then in the darkness someone shouted a muffled exclamation through his mask.

"Hey!" he yelled, pointing to the west. "What the *fuck* is that?!" Everyone turned to see the glowing fireflies of several missiles rocket up from the horizon and arc over our heads. As our eyes followed their radiant orange exhaust jets to the northeast, one collided in midair with what we guessed to be a Scud missile. A shower of sparks rained down from the sky, and a moment later the Scud's warhead detonated on the ground miles away to our north. Amid shouts of "Awesome!" and "Holy shit! Did you see that?" I turned back to the LAV to see corpsmen yanking off their masks to continue their work on Suarez unhindered. The "all clear" signal hadn't been announced yet, but it was obvious they didn't care.

I looked at my watch: 1730Z. Nearly two hours had passed since the time of the explosion, and the helicopter still hadn't arrived. I stormed over to Capt Portiss's vehicle.

"Goddammit!" I yelled. "What the fuck is the hold-up?!"

"I can't get in touch with anybody," replied Spool.

"We're still working on it," Portiss replied. "We might be better off doing a ground evac to the RCT headquarters. Spool is working on getting their C2 Huey for a medevac."

I thought for a moment. He was right. Realizing I had squandered precious time waiting for a helicopter that wasn't going to come, I called back up to Portiss.

"How far away is the headquarters?"

"About eight or ten klicks south."

"Call up Third Platoon," I said. "Have them send out a section ASAP to escort you and Staff Sergeant Kappen to the RCT. We've wasted too much time as it is."

I walked back over to SSgt Kappen, who had overheard my conversation with the XO. His crew was already in the process of preparing the vehicle.

"Are you ready to go?" I asked.

"We're good to go, sir," he replied. Two LAV-25s plowed up the embankment and pulled ahead of Portiss's vehicle. I walked back to the cargo bay and leaned inside once more. The docs had stabilized Suarez, and he was talking a little.

"Hang tough, Suarez," I said, gently placing my hand on him. "We're getting you out of here right now, man." They closed the hatches, and the four vehicles rumbled away into the darkness. Once the sound of the LAVs' engines had faded, the Marines and sailors began walking in ones and twos back to their platoons. I stood there in the road by myself, thinking—wondering if I had waited too long to make the call for the ground medevac. The question continued to replay in my mind.

Had I had waited too long?

✦ ✧ ✦

I threw open the flap at the entrance of the COC tent and stormed in. It was crowded inside, and the interior was illuminated by low-visibility, blue light that gave it an underwater look. I stood at the entryway and glared at everyone. No helmet, no gas mask. My hair stood up in matted tufts, and my face was streaked with dirt and blood. Everyone stared at me.

"What the fuck," I said flatly.

I stormed over to Mud Duck, who was still working the radios.

"What the *fuck,* man?" I demanded. *"Two hours for a medevac?!"* I glowered at him, the anger in my eyes obvious even in the soft blue light. He looked like a beaten man.

"I'm sorry," he said, exhausted. "The medevac helo broke down. They never got the word to us. Man, I've been doing everything I possibly can in here to get a bird out for you."

"It's true," someone added from the shadows. "He's been working four or five different radio nets to get a medevac. He finally got the RCT's C2 bird for us."

"Yeah," I replied angrily. "Which we had to drive ten klicks to get to. This is *bull*shit. How are the Marines gonna trust us to take care of them if we can't get a simple fucking medevac when *we aren't even in contact with the enemy!"* I looked around at everyone, waiting for someone to tell me to calm down. I would have decked him right there.

"I'm sorry, Seth," LtCol White said. "We were doing everything we could in here."

I stared at him for a moment. "Aye-aye, sir," I replied. I didn't know what else to say. I didn't believe him, or anybody, at that point. But there was no use in continuing to vent my spleen, so I walked back out into the cold night air. The contrast between the light inside the tent and the darkness outside blinded me, and I had to stand still for a moment to allow my night vision to return. As my eyes slowly readjusted to the surroundings I noticed two shadowy figures standing near the tent's entrance.

"Who's that?" I asked.

"It's the XO and Bob Woodruff," Maj Bodkin replied.

"Oh," I said. I thought about the unexploded ordnance lying around us in the dark. "Hey sir, think I can get a ride back to my position?"

"Yeah, no problem," he said, turning to find a humvee for me. Woodruff pulled out a cell phone, made a quick call, and then pocketed it.

"Hey, is that a satellite phone?" I asked.

"Yeah," he replied. "You want to make a call?"

"Uh-huh. That'd be great."

He handed it to me just as Maj Bodkin returned with a gunnery sergeant from H&S Company.

"Seth, the gunny will get you a ride when you're ready," Bodkin told me. I thanked him as the phone began ringing on the other end. It was close to 1830Z, which made it some time in the early afternoon back home in the states. Ashley answered the phone.

"Hey Sweetheart," I said. "How are you doing?" Hearing my voice shocked her.

"Oh my God, oh my God," she said rapidly. "I can't believe I'm hearing from you! How are you doing?"

Suddenly I didn't know what to say. Just what was I supposed to tell her, anyway? *Hi, honey. You wouldn't believe what just happened! One of my Marines just got blown to smithereens and we had to wait over two hours for a helicopter that never came! A Scud missile just blew up near us, and now I'm petrified to walk around in the dark because our assembly area is covered in unexploded cluster bombs!*

"I'm tired. We've been moving a lot," I finally managed. I looked off to my right to see Maj Bodkin still standing there. More than anything I wanted to tell her what had happened with LCpl Suarez del Solar, but I couldn't with the XO right next to me. The rules precluded me from passing that kind of information over the phone. It was killing me. She would know something was wrong—every time I had called her from the field in the past I had always told her before signing off that everyone was doing okay. Unable to bring myself to openly lie to her about it, I said nothing. The conversation was brief, and after saying good-bye I handed the phone back to Woodruff.

"Thanks," I told him. "I really needed that."

"No problem. Just let me know if you need it again."

"I appreciate it. Come on, let's get the hell back to the company."

A humvee sat idling twenty meters away, and we climbed inside for the ride back to the company area. I hopped out and walked along in a tire track in the darkness until I got to the LAV-C2. Opening the back hatch and pulling myself in, I took the handset from the Marine monitoring the radio. I transmitted to the company.

"All Dragons, this is Black-Six." The events of the night were catching up with me, and whatever I was going to say I had to do it fast before I passed out. "Get as many people on the net as you can for a quick fireside chat." One by one each vehicle crew in the company reported in. The majority of the company listened intently to their radios for news about their wounded brother.

"Lance Corporal Suarez del Solar has been transported by ground medevac to the regimental headquarters. They're going to fly him out on the RCT CO's helicopter from there. We don't know exactly what the delay in getting the medevac was, but it looks like he's going to be all right."

"Black-Six, is he going to make it back to the company?" someone radioed.

"Negative," I replied, remembering what HM3 Hodges had told me earlier. "I doubt it. There's a chance he might lose his leg, but that's it." That was followed by silence. Then someone else radioed.

"Black-Six, why did we turn around today?"

"I don't have the full details on that yet, but the word I got was that it was ordered by the army. I heard some scuttlebutt [unconfirmed rumors] that we were outrunning the army and they needed to catch up. I'll let you all know as soon as I find out more details in the morning. Any other questions?" There were none.

"I want to say 'Bravo Zulu' to all the corpsmen and Marines who worked on Suarez this evening. You did an outstanding job, and I know he would say the same thing to you if he were here. Keep him and his family in your prayers. Stay focused on our job out here and don't let tonight get to you. Keep your eyes and ears open. You all are doing a great job out here. I am proud to serve with all of you."

I signed off. With my head hanging down, I slowly trudged back to my vehicle in the moonlight. I wearily sat on the sleeping bag rolled out in the dirt and pulled off my boots. Attempting to wipe off my mouth with the back of my gloved hand, I tasted the metallic flavor of blood.

I pulled off my gloves and put my face in my hands, pressing them tightly against my eyes to ward off the approaching headache. Lifting my head, I looked back down at my palms in the moonlight.

I had blood on my hands.

12
Dark Days

I awoke on 28 March wondering if I had dreamt it all, if the episode the previous evening had been simply a figment of my imagination. I surveyed the assembly area. Everything seemed normal enough.

Then I noticed the stack of bloody clothing and equipment piled next to my vehicle.

With the light of day all around me, I inspected the damage to LCpl Suarez del Solar's gear. Where his MOPP suit hadn't been cut with the corpsmen's shears or ripped by hand, dozens of tiny holes perforated it. Everything—his clothing, his web gear, his boots—was shredded and soaked through with gobs of coagulating blood and tissue that were slowly turning a deep shade of brown. I lifted up his splintered desert boot, the entire front of which had been blown off. The tan suede material near the toes was jagged and scorched, and upon examining it closely I suddenly realized just how much of his blood covered me. My gloves, my MOPP suit, and my face were streaked with it. I was a mess. I could only imagine what HM3 Hodges and the other corpsmen looked like by the time the rescue effort was over. First Sergeant Guzman wandered over from his vehicle.

"Sir, we found another one of those DPICMs over next to my vehicle," he told me.

I continued to stare at the equipment. Leaning down and picking up Suarez's carbine, I ran my finger over the blast damage that marred the weapon's lower receiver. A piece of shrapnel had hit just above the safety catch, denting the metal and scraping away the bluish-gray protective coating. That explained the wound to his right thumb. The Marines had been trained to carry their weapons with their thumbs ready to click off the safety. I handed Guzman the rifle and lit a cigarette.

"It's my fault, First Sergeant."

"What are you talking about, sir?"

"I ordered a foot patrol instead of a vehicle patrol," I explained. "And I waited too long to get him out on the ground."

"That's bullshit, sir," he said, a hint of anger coloring his voice. "You didn't know there was DPICM out there. And you thought a helo was coming. Everyone did."

"None of that matters. It's my responsibility. It will always be my responsibility."

We heard the whine of an LAV approaching, and SSgt Kappen's vehicle pulled alongside mine. He climbed out.

"Here to collect Suarez's gear, sir," he said, eyeing the pile at our feet. "Gotta take it over to battalion supply to be inventoried." Together we placed the damp equipment in a garbage bag piece by piece until we got to the rifle.

"What should we do with this?" Kappen asked.

"Give it to Lance Corporal Ramirez and have him op-check it," I said, referring to the company's armorer. "I don't think it's gonna work anymore after the hit it took."

Staff Sergeant Kappen drove away toward the battalion's supply section, and as the rumble of his engine faded 1stSgt Guzman and I walked back to his vehicle.

"It's right over there," he said, pointing to a spot five feet in front of his vehicle. I walked up and knelt down in the dirt next to it. It was a DPICM munition, all right. It looked like a blackened can of condensed milk with a long yellow streamer hanging from its top. The streamer stabilized the bomblet in the air and slowed its descent to earth after the artillery casing ejected the munitions. The soft, tilled farmland must have caused the bomblets to fail to detonate when they hit the ground. I looked over toward 3rd Platoon. Marines were marking off the area forward of their position with white cloth engineer tape. We would need EOD at our position if the battalion planned to stay there any longer. I turned back to Guzman.

"I know this is stating the obvious, but tell everyone to watch where the hell they step out here."

"Yeah, no shit, sir" he replied, nodding his head. "You got that right."

"I'll go find out from battalion how long we're gonna be here," I added. "Let's get to work on getting EOD to mark and blow these fucking things."

✦ ✧ ✦

I returned to my vehicle and tried to clean myself up. It felt good to shed my MOPP suit and scrub off all the dirt from the previous week and the gore from the last twelve hours. After a while I began to feel halfway human again. A meeting for the company commanders had been scheduled for an hour later, so I decided to take the time to record what had happened before the sequence of events was forgotten. It would no doubt be needed for an investigation later.

Sitting there furiously scribbling notes, I looked up to see Captain Brian Smalley—the commander for H&S Company—and the battalion's navy chaplain, Lieutenant Mike Moreno, walking slowly toward me. I expected an update on Suarez del Solar. I got one, but it wasn't what I was expecting.

"I'm sorry, man," Smalley said. "Your boy didn't make it."

"What?" I asked. "What are you talking about?"

"Suarez died during the flight back to Camp Doha. He was DOA when he got there."

I stared dumbly at him, and then at the chaplain.

"God . . . damn," I managed. I couldn't believe it. Lance Corporal Suarez del Solar was dead. The two-hour delay in getting the medevac helicopter had killed him.

"You alright?" Smalley asked.

"Yeah," I mumbled. "Yeah, I guess. *Fuck.*"

"Do you want me to tell his platoon?" LT Moreno asked.

"No. I'll tell his platoon commander. He'll want to tell his Marines." I turned my head and yelled to LCpl Davis in the turret. "Call up Blue-One and Black-Eight. Tell them to come over here." I looked back at Smalley.

"They killed him," I said. "The medevac never came. They fucking killed him."

"I know, man," he said, trying to console me. "It's fucked up."

Lieutenant Cullins and 1stSgt Guzman both walked up to where I stood with Smalley and Moreno. The tightened features on Cullins's face told me he already knew what was coming down the line.

"Lance Corporal Suarez del Solar died last night en route to the hospital," I said.

"What?!" asked Guzman.

"I had a feeling that was why you called me over here," replied Cullins glumly.

"I'm sorry," I said, leaning over and placing my hand on his shoulder. Guzman stood silently next to me, slowly shaking his head. He seemed unwilling to say anything for fear he might break down. I knew how he felt.

"Well," said Cullins, looking back hesitantly toward his Marines. "Guess I need to go tell everybody." The chaplain spoke up.

"Do you want me to go with you?" Moreno asked.

"Yeah," replied Cullins. "Probably a good idea."

Together the two of them slowly walked back to 3rd Platoon's position to pass on the horrible news. It was the first time a Marine under my command had died. I didn't know what to think, or how to feel, or how to react. I thought back to LtCol White's words before leaving Kuwait:

How you react will set the tone for the rest of your men for the remainder of the war. If you collapse, they will collapse.

As terrible as I suddenly felt inside, I realized I had to keep my shit together or else things could go downhill really fast. I sat down and leaned my head back against the tire, attempting to collect my thoughts. The notion dawned on me that I now had to write the infamous letter home every officer hears about from day one of his training. How would I do it? How would I explain to Suarez del Solar's family that their son—himself a husband and father—had stepped on a friendly artillery round in a place littered with them, and that no one had told us the munitions were there?

Or that I had given the order for a dismounted patrol?

Or that he waited for a helicopter that never arrived?

Or that my decision to evacuate him by ground came only after two hours?

Then, more than ever, I understood the meaning behind the phrase "burden of command." Sitting there alone, I felt a weight settle upon my shoulders heavier than anything I had ever experienced in my life.

✦ ✧ ✦

The men of Delta Company were in a daze. The looks of bewilderment and rage that painted their faces betrayed their emotions—they didn't understand why Suarez had had to die, but they knew it could have been prevented. The battalion's static position and absence of activity did nothing to ameliorate the tension. It only gave the Marines more time to dwell on the situation.

I sought an official explanation for the previous day's turnaround on Highway 1. The answer surprised me as much as the order to return itself. As RCT-5 had approached Hantush, the commander of Coalition Forces, Land Component Command (CFLCC) had decided to initiate an "operational pause" for the land forces pushing their way north toward Baghdad. The reasons for the pause, true or not, varied. We heard them all. The combat forces had overextended themselves and were running out of fuel, water, and food. The Marine Corps was outrunning the army, who demanded a pause to catch up. The supply lines along Highways 1, 7, and 8 were being riddled by enemy ambushes. The real reason for the pause didn't matter because the ultimate reason for our turnaround was the same in any case: Although 1st Marine Division had been ready to proceed north without the army, to remain at Hantush might have alerted the Iraqis to the deception plan to the north. Our pulling back to RCT-5's jump-off point near Ad Diwaniyah would keep the Iraqis guessing.

No matter what the explanation, the fact remained that 1st LAR Battalion had been ordered to occupy a piece of land that had been heavily shelled earlier in the day. DPICM is a dud-producing munition. Regulations dictate that all units be provided grid coordinates detailing where DPICM has been employed. First LAR Battalion—Delta Company—had received no such information, and we had paid for it with the life of one of our Marines. The enemy hadn't killed Jésus Suarez del Solar. *We* had. Failures in information dissemination, communications, and the human decision-making process had proved just as deadly as Iraqi bullets. I began to realize fully the unacceptable cost of fratricide, but at the same time, the sad inevitability of such incidents.

Knowing of the numerous cluster bombs planted inside the company's sector compelled me to pull the platoons back west toward the pavement. Explosive Ordnance Disposal was scheduled to come out and blow up the bomblets in place, and I didn't want the platoons wandering around out there before the task was complete. Unfortunately, Delta Company wasn't the only unit within the RCT to suffer a casualty from the unexploded ordnance. Word filtered over to us that another infantry battalion had likewise endured an injury from one of the errant bomblets. Perhaps the only good thing that came out of the entire episode was that everyone began paying more attention to the ground they occupied—they no longer wandered around without scrutinizing the ground in front of them with a careful eye.

Walking up and down the line of vehicles, I attempted to engage the Marines in conversation. Some were willing to talk, others were not. Many of their hostile expressions implied I was to blame for Suarez's death. It was understandable. I was an officer, therefore I symbolized *all* officers. I represented the same nameless, faceless officer who had neglected to report the DPICM in our location. I represented the person somewhere south of us who never relayed the battalion's urgent call for a medevac. The Marines didn't need or want me to comfort them as they grieved. They had each other for that. I felt more distant from them than ever.

I made my way to the COC for the company commanders meeting. Several people approached me to offer condolences, the sympathetic look on their faces genuine and communicating the same thought: *It could have been one of* my *men.* Though I sought no displays of sorrow or kindness by anyone at the COC, I couldn't believe the conspicuous lack of either on the part of certain members of the battalion staff. The entire time I was there, several officers never personally said they were sorry for Suarez's death, nor did they offer me condolences. I deserved both. Suarez del Solar deserved both. But I decided not to get on my high horse about it and complain. The last thing I wanted was someone lecturing me about the sacrifices that are made during war.

But after stewing for an hour I finally unloaded during a meeting among the senior officers of the battalion. As the six of us sat facing each other around the lip of a shallow sleep trench, a discussion about the operational pause began. When the subject of mail came up, we were told there were more important things going on than getting mail to the front lines.

"You know," I said, trying unsuccessfully to subdue my anger. "The Marines out here think no one gives a shit about them. They have zero confidence that we're gonna take care of them if they get hit. We can't get a simple medevac when it's needed. No one tells us we're occupying a field covered in unexploded ordnance." They all stared silently at me. My mouth was about to get me in big trouble, but I continued anyway.

"There's no mail. There's no spare parts," I continued. "We're sitting around here rotting while the rest of the Marine Corps is passing us by."

Say something, I thought angrily. *Anything.* I didn't care if the battalion commander told me to shut my cake-hole. I just needed someone to either acknowledge the fact that we were in a shitty position or else tell me to get over it. I got neither. Instead, the conversation shifted to how the battalion's time would be spent during the course of the operational pause. At one point, Maj Harper proposed that the companies begin creating "training packages" for the urban operations we would be likely to experience closer to Baghdad. I couldn't believe it—training packages? That set me off again.

"Wait," I protested. "I think it's a little late to be training out here. The war has already started. If we aren't ready by now, we'll never be."

"I disagree with you," replied Harper. "Training is continuous. There's always time for more."

"Seth, you forget that your company has been together as a cohesive unit longer than ours have," added Gil. "Your guys probably *are* ready."

"Well, just how long is this operational pause going to be, anyway?" Dave asked.

"We don't know yet," replied Harper. "It could be as little as three days or as long as three weeks."

Three weeks?! I thought, incredulous. *There's no way in hell we can stay in this position for that long without losing our minds.*

"However long we're stuck in place we're going to spend a lot of that time conducting active patrolling in the RCT's sector," Harper added. "We're starting to look at potential zones for reconnaissance right now."

I collected my equipment and headed back toward the company's position. Along the way I shook my head, talking to myself in mumbled curses. In my frustration I kept returning to an earlier thought, which repeated itself in my head: *We have become more dangerous to ourselves than the enemy is to us.* Since the push up Highway 1 had begun, the artillery batteries had been firing DPICM all over the place with impunity. Such careless application of firepower had created multiple "minefields" everywhere. With the operational pause in effect and all forward movement halted, we stood a greater chance of dying from stepping on our own unexploded ordinance than from the enemy. Iraq had suddenly become a much more lethal place to be.

✦ ✧ ✦

Sometime in the middle of the night on 28 March, the S-3 radioed a frag order to the company commanders. Two companies would conduct a zone reconnaissance to the north, while the third company expanded the boundaries of the battalion's defensive position. At first light I made my way over to the COC. The Marines from the operations section had laid out a series of maps alongside a small terrain model in the dirt. I looked around and found Gil.

"Hey, listen," I said. "I'd prefer it if my company got the chance to participate in the zone recon this morning. I need to get my guys back in the saddle."

"You got it, man," he replied. "No problem." A moment later the battalion commander walked up to me.

"Seth, we haven't doled out who's doing what this morning," LtCol White began. "I wanted to give you a chance to decide what you want to do. If you want to give your men a break it's up to you."

I didn't hesitate. "Give my Marines a mission, sir. Let me get them back in action."

"All right then," he said. Major Harper gathered the company commanders around the terrain model as Bob Whalen distributed copies of the battalion's op-order. Delta Company became the main effort for a zone reconnaissance that would extend ten kilometers north of the RCT along Highway 1. We planned the operation with the battalion staff, discussing the boundaries of our respective company zones and the information requirements for the reconnaissance. After a while I looked down at my watch. It was 0515Z. The chaplain had asked me the previous day if I wanted him to arrange a memorial service for LCpl Suarez del Solar, and I had told him 0530Z would be a good time. I cut out from the planning session and quickly walked back to where the company had gathered to pay their respects.

As I walked, I struggled with what to say during the memorial. I had to say something. It was my duty. But I had no idea what the hell it would be. I had never done anything like this before, and while I attempted to piece together some sort of coherent address I suddenly realized the date. It was 29 March, my birthday. *How ironic,* I thought. *God sure does have a sense of humor.*

At the center of the company's position, LT Moreno and his assistant had erected the traditional memorial to signify a fallen Marine. A rifle had been thrust into the ground by its bayonet, a helmet resting atop the buttstock. Hanging down from the pistol grip, a small crucifix and Suarez del Solar's dog tags chimed faintly against each other in the morning breeze. The men gathered in a semicircle around the memorial, their dirty faces stony and expressionless. Chaplain Moreno stepped in front of them.

"Marines and sailors, we are gathered here today to honor the memory of Lance Corporal Jésus Suarez del Solar," he told everyone present. "He will not be forgotten by his family. He will not be forgotten by you, and he will not be forgotten by God." He then sang the first verse of "Eternal Father," and the passion he expressed caused a tightness to form in my chest. Looking around at the Marines and sailors assembled, I realized the service would be a lot more difficult on everyone than I had previously imagined. Lieutenant Colonel White stepped forward and spoke briefly, his words sincere. A pained expression filled his face, and it was the first time I had ever seen him exhibit a real degree of emotion.

"We can't turn our eyes away from our mission," White said in closing.

LtCol Duffy White addresses Delta Company during memorial service for LCpl Jésus Suarez del Solar, 29 March 2003. Official Marine Corps photo by LCpl Andrew P. Roufs.

"*He* never did." I knew then that, despite my disagreement with some of White's ways, there was a common denominator among commanders after all.

The sergeant major ambled forward and spoke next. "Marines die with honor. Lance Corporal Suarez died with honor. Here, on enemy soil," he mumbled to everyone. Reaching down, he scooped up a handful of dirt and held it up for all to see. Tears streamed down his face. "He died a long way from home, but he will be remembered. We got to let his honor live on. We got to hold our heads up high, we got to continue to march, continue to fight."

The chaplain called my name. I cleared my throat and looked around again at the company of Marines and sailors staring at me. I was petrified.

Keep it together, man.

I spoke.

"When I was commissioned as a second lieutenant almost nine years ago, I understood the risks I was about to undertake. I knew the risks that my men might one day face. But back then I never would have guessed that I would spend my thirty-first birthday mourning the loss of one of my Marines.

"We're here to mourn the loss of Lance Corporal Suarez del Solar. He was a motivator. He was always willing to do whatever he had to do to get the job done. He loved his fellow Marines and sailors and they loved him. During the past two years, I've spent more time with you men than I have with my own family. As such, losing Lance Corporal Suarez is like losing someone in my family." I paused momentarily, swallowing hard and fighting to keep my composure.

"Sometimes I question my faith, but I know one thing. Suarez is in a better place than we are now. I know he's up there looking down at us and he's thinking, 'Don't worry about me. Get off your own asses and go kick the enemy's ass.'"

They continued to stare at me, their eyes glazed over. I didn't know what else to say. It had been all I could muster. As I returned to my place in the crowd, Lt Cullins replaced me. After him, several other Marines stepped forward to say their piece. Sergeant Rocha, a Marine of few words, had grown up in the same city as Suarez del Solar. He noted the bond he shared with Suarez.

"Whenever I saw him I knew there was a little piece of home here," he said. "In a sense, that is gone now."

Corporal David Medici, who had been in 3rd Platoon before becoming the first sergeant's gunner, spoke of Suarez's family and the commitment we should make to them long after the war was over. "One thing I would urge you all to do is to send your condolences to his wife and to his son, so that

1stLt Doug Cullins addresses Delta Company during memorial service for LCpl Jésus Suarez del Solar, 29 March 2003. Official Marine Corps photo by LCpl Andrew P. Roufs.

when his son grows up, he has something to refer to—to look back on—to see what kind of man, what kind of Marine his father was."

Lance Corporal Randy Ranoa, who had endured boot camp and the School of Infantry with Suarez, described how their friendship had changed his life.

"He knew a lot of what we did was bullshit, but he never complained about it," Ranoa said. "He was unselfish. What was his was yours. I'm a better Marine because of him."

I glanced over at Cullins, who was taking it pretty hard. For once I knew how he felt. During the service many Marines were close to breaking down in their collective sorrow. Suarez had been well respected by everyone in the company. He had been proud of his Latino heritage, but he had never used it as an excuse or a crutch. He had been a loving father with a young wife and a sixteen-month-old child waiting for him at home. Now they would be waiting forever.

The service ended and the company gradually dissipated. One by one the Marines and sailors approached the memorial to pay their respects. They alternately knelt or stood by it, bowing their heads. Lieutenant Cullins walked over to me with tears welling in his eyes.

"Are you going to be all right?" I asked, gently resting my hand on his shoulder.

"Man," he said, slowly shaking his head. "This really burns."

"Yeah," I replied simply. "Yeah it does, man."

I turned to walk away and was instead met by Lt Schwartz, who looked down at me with a beaten expression whittled into his face.

"Sir, can I talk to you for a minute?"

"Sure," I said. "What's up?"

"Listen, sir, with all this that's going on, I want to bury the hatchet between the two of us." His offering of the olive branch puzzled me. Despite my angry exchange of words with him just days before leaving Kuwait, I had moved on and not thought about it since. My only guess was that, in light of the tragedy that had just unfolded in front of all of us, he sought some measure of internal peace.

"I wasn't aware there was one that needed burying," I replied.

"Sir, it's always seemed like you've had some sort of problem with me. Whether you've known it or not, you've always had my complete support. When you found all that graffiti written about you in the Port-a-shitters, I was the one who went in and cleaned it all off . . ."

"And I appreciate that," I said, cutting him off. "But I don't need anyone taking care of my image. Schwartz, the reason I've always been hard on everyone—you in particular—is because I want you to do your job the right way." I paused.

"And I want to bring everyone else home."

"Yes, sir," he replied. "So do I. So, can we bury the hatchet?"

"Consider it buried. Come on, let's get to work."

✦ ✧ ✦

The memorial service complete, it was time to execute the zone reconnaissance. I told Capt Portiss to assemble the company staff so I could brief them on the details before returning to the COC for the final planning. As he turned to rally everyone, LT Moreno walked up to my side.

"Hey, Chaplain," I said. "Thanks. I appreciate you taking the time to do the service. I know it meant a lot to the men."

"You're welcome," he replied. What he said next caught me totally unprepared. "Do you still want me to baptize you?"

I had not been baptized as an infant. My parents chose to raise me in the church until I was old enough to decide what path I wanted to take. As a young teenager I promptly chose to forgo church and had continued to do so in the decades that followed. It never materialized as an important part of my life. When I deployed for the first time as a lieutenant in 1997, my mother had told me of her wish for me to get baptized. I postponed it, and she brought the issue to the forefront again before I deployed in 2002. Again I demurred, and the issue remained dormant until I discussed it with the chaplain at the LSA. The week before the division left camp and crossed into Iraq, I had approached Moreno about getting myself baptized. His answer had surprised me.

"Well, I don't believe in mass-baptisms," he had told me matter-of-factly. "I believe a person must learn about the church and commit himself before he is baptized." He had been willing to hold a crash-course, one-afternoon session for all interested personnel in the battalion, but our premature departure from camp had cancelled his plans. Since then I had forgotten about it. Now there he was, suddenly offering to perform the ritual.

"What, here?" I asked, taken aback. *"Now?"*

"Sure. Do you have any water?"

"Um, yeah," I said, a little confused. I walked over to my vehicle and called up to LCpl Davis. "Hey, toss me down a bottle of water." He reached into the turret and threw out a liter of the bottled water we had hoarded since before the war. I handed it to Moreno. Davis and Gurganus sat perched atop the turret and looked down at us, wondering what the hell was going on.

"Go ahead and take a knee," he told me. I knelt at his feet, my head bowed and my eyes closed. He recited a series of passages from the rite of baptism, many of which I had to repeat after him. Then he poured water from the bottle into his hands, and after blessing it he doused my head with it. As the water ran through my hair and down my face in tiny rivulets, my shoulders slackened. The great weight that had bore down upon me began to lessen. I felt rejuvenated.

When the ceremony was complete I stood.

"Thank you for doing that, Chaplain."

"Well, like I told you before, I don't normally believe in field baptisms," he replied. "But something told me that it was your time, that it was right to do it for you."

"Well, it means a lot. More than you'll ever know."

"You're welcome," he said. "Now get back to your men. You have a job to do."

I turned and walked back around the vehicle toward my company staff, which by now was assembled in a circle waiting for me. I suddenly felt at peace as I pulled out my map and began briefing them.

Their anger and grief over what had happened to LCpl Suarez del Solar aside, the staff was charged with excitement about the mission that lay before us. It was in their eyes; but something darker was there, too. The entire company had been champing at the bit to get into the action since day one of the war. Whether it had been an internal need to prove ourselves in combat or just a craving for excitement, the naïve desire to confront death had suddenly been answered, but not in the way we had expected. With Suarez's pointless demise I sensed in them a longing for retribution, a desire to kill something—anything—to wreak vengeance for losing someone so close to all of us. I felt it, too. It had to be controlled.

"We're gonna do this thing like professionals," I said to the staff, locking eyes with each Marine. "We aren't out here to get payback for Suarez. Make sure you pass that on to every man in your platoons. Am I clear on this?" I looked around.

"Yes, sir," they all replied in unison.

"All right then. Let's do it."

There were grunts of "Ooh-rah" and "Fuck, yeah," and with that I returned to the COC for the final mission back-brief. We conducted a rock drill to demonstrate our companies' movements through our respective zones, and we coordinated handoff requirements of the air and artillery assets that had been allocated for the mission. Gil's company was assigned the stretch of land east of Highway 1, and Delta would be responsible for the area west of it. It was a basic plan, and the only difficulty we predicted was the tricky terrain our companies would encounter. Once the rock drill concluded, the battalion commander gave his final approval for the mission. We departed the COC for final briefings to our company staffs.

Upon returning to the company I found the vehicles lined up in column and prepared to step off on the mission. The staff already stood by my LAV, and after giving them the last-minute changes to the plan I passed the order for everyone to mount up. Then we got the rug pulled out from beneath us. Captain Portiss radioed, informing me that our helicopter escorts were nowhere to be found, and the company wound up remaining in place for over an hour until the situation could be worked out. By that time I had become convinced that such delays, while an unavoidable part of any operation, were detrimental to the long-term effectiveness of the company. The emotional strain on the Marines worried me. There were only so many times I would be able to turn the company on and off before they broke. It was like repeatedly heating and cooling a piece of metal. Over time the process weakens the material until it suddenly ruptures from the strain. They were riding a rollercoaster of alert levels. Each time they experienced a period of high alert that yielded no enemy contact their senses were dulled, and I feared the unavoidable complacency that resulted from it would eventually bite us in the ass.

The helicopters arrived, and we initiated the reconnaissance. One by one the vehicles from the company approached the cloverleaf, but instead of passing under it they veered west onto the southbound on-ramp from the east-west Highway 17. Even in the seemingly lawless environment that surrounded us it still felt peculiar to drive the wrong way on the highway interchange's ramp. We passed over Highway 17, our designated line of departure, and the company slowly fanned out into the platoons' respective zones. We immediately became bogged down in terrain that was in its own way worse than anything we had yet seen. Rather than the soft, unstable drained marshes and the tilled land south of us, we instead encountered a maze of levees, ditches, and irrigation canals that supported overgrown farmland. I couldn't tell what was being grown—most of it just looked like extremely tall marsh grass—but it was everywhere, and it was so thick that *anything* could be hiding in it. The platoons radioed, reporting that they were getting separated, and soon vehicles became mired in the muddy trails. Before long I looked around and realized that 1stSgt Guzman's vehicle was the only one around. We were on our own, attempting to navigate the labyrinth of canals and levees. Several times I turned around and was able to read the stressed-out expression on Guzman's face as he stood in his turret. It surely mirrored my own. Anxiety gripped me. There seemed to be an ambush waiting around every corner, and we, like the other platoons, would have no mutual support if the enemy were to open up on us.

But it wasn't just the familiar, creepy feeling of the enemy being all around us that made me sweat. Steering the vehicle through the perilous landscape monopolized every last bit of my attention. In most cases the trails and levees we traversed were no wider than the width of the LAV's wheelbase. Being just a couple of inches off track would result in the vehicle losing its traction and toppling over into one of the myriad canals surrounding us. Finally accepting that I couldn't maneuver my vehicle and the company at the same time, I radioed the XO.

"Black-Five, this is Black-Six. I'm mired down here. Are you in a position to control the company?"

"That's affirmative, Black-Six. We've got an open trail ahead of us."

"Roger that. I need time to unfuck myself and get caught back up with the company. You have the broadsword." In 1st LAR Battalion, "handing over the broadsword" meant passing tactical control from one element to another. It was a means of ensuring that whoever had the best vantage point and situational awareness was able to control the fight. At that moment in the trail network I certainly had neither.

"That's a solid copy, Black-Six," Portiss replied. "I have the monkey wrench."

I turned to LCpl Davis next to me in the turret and keyed the intercom.

"Let's get the hell out of this mess." The vehicle was perched atop a steep levee bordered by deep canals on each side. After a moment or two the LAV still had not moved.

"Come on Gurganus," I said impatiently. "Let's go."

"Sir, it's a drop-off in front of me," said Gurganus.

"What?"

"He's right, sir," added Davis, leaning far out of the turret until his knees rested against the lip of the hatch. "The berm drops right down into the water."

"Shit," I said into the intercom. "Hang on a moment." I keyed my headset again. "Black-Eight, this is Six. Back up. We're at a dead-end up here."

"Roger, Six," replied Guzman. His vehicle's driveshaft dropped down into reverse and they slowly rolled backward. I leaned out of the turret and looked down to the hard-packed dirt of the levee. It seemed solid enough, but fewer than six inches stood between the LAV's right tires and the sharp drop into the water. I rekeyed the intercom.

"What's it like on the left side, Davis?" I asked.

"We've got about a foot over here, sir," he replied.

"Okay, hang on." I said. "Get Harter and Kodak out of their hole and scanning." Hearing this, Davis dropped down inside the turret to relay my message. A moment later, the two Marines popped up out of the scout hatches, their rifles at the ready, and began searching for targets. I leaned back over the turret and shouted over the vehicle's noise to both of them.

"Hey!" I yelled, pointing my index and middle fingers to my eyes. "Keep your eyes open while we get unstuck!" Both nodded and returned their gazes to the sodden, green fields enveloping us.

"Okay, Gurganus," I said, taking a deep breath. "No problem. We've done this a million times. Just listen to me. Davis, let me know if we get too far to the left over there."

"Roger that," both answered. An outsider listening to just the sounds of our voices on the intercom would have had no idea what we were doing, yet all three of us understood perfectly.

"Okay, Gurganus, back up, right hand down."

"Steady, steady."

"Good on the left, sir."

"Steady, left hand down."

"Good, slow down, good."

"Left good, sir."

"Right hand down, hard."

"Left hand down, one o'clock."

"Stop, forward, one o'clock."

In situations like this, the only thing preventing us from tumbling off the precipice and into water was trust. Davis and I had to trust Gurganus to crank the steering wheel the correct amount left or right and apply the appropriate degree of pressure against the accelerator. Gurganus, in turn, had to trust me to make the right adjustments to get us down off the levee. One wrong move by either of us and the vehicle would topple into the canal. The chances of escaping a submerged, overturned LAV would be slim. Some time after the war I learned that many Marines and soldiers had drowned when their vehicles rolled over into canals. As many times as Delta Company was forced to negotiate narrow trails and levees bordered by canals, I was glad not to hear about that until much later. I might have lost my nerve. Later, after the combat had ended for us, Lt Parment confided in me that his greatest fear had not been enemy bullets or RPGs, but that one of his vehicles would roll over as we navigated the ubiquitous canal networks. It wasn't an unfounded fear.

The danger of the levee past us, 1stSgt Guzman and I backtracked our route and caught up with 3rd Platoon in the east. Lieutenant Cullins's section became stuck in the thick mud of the trail, and as they held back to free themselves Guzman and I pushed forward with SSgt Navarro's two vehicles. Movement continued slowly, but at least we were actually moving. It was, after all, a reconnaissance. Small groups of Shi'a farmers emerged from their mud and thatch huts to watch us roll past. Few smiled. Most glared. After the amount of artillery the RCT had dropped in the area, it was hard to condemn them. We attempted to placate them with more humanitarian rations, but it didn't seem to matter. Bob Woodruff, in a broadcast earlier in the war, had wondered whether the Iraqis were welcoming us or whether we were "simply a curiosity, maybe a source of food." As we reconnoitered our zone, it was difficult to admonish Woodruff for raising that particular question. His words had been appropriate. *So much for liberating the oppressed Shi'ites,* I thought, avoiding their emotionless stares.

Exhausted and frustrated, we reached the limit of advance in our company's zone. The enemy had done it again. He had melted into the landscape, unwilling to challenge the firepower posed by our LAVs and escorting helicopter gunships. I had been taught that a reconnaissance that yielded no enemy contact was a successful one. I had also always been told that if a reconnaissance unit becomes engaged with the enemy, it has failed its mission. Whatever. We were hungry for action, eager to report an advancing force, ready to destroy it once the authorization was given. But it wasn't to be.

We reversed course and headed south to meet our 1500Z deadline. Yet while Delta Company encountered no enemy, we did locate several prepared ambush positions oriented east onto Highway 1. As the platoons egressed to the company linkup point, Capt Portiss called forward an armored combat excavator (ACE) that had traveled with us for the operation. The crew manning the tank-like bulldozer required nothing more than a point and a nod, and soon the fighting positions no longer existed. The ACE made quick work of all of them.

Daylight began fading from the sky as the company pulled off Highway 1 and re-entered friendly lines. I walked to the COC to debrief the S-2 on the details of the reconnaissance, and as I neared the tent I ran into Gil and Dave.

"Hey, man," Gil said. "Find anything?"

"Nah," I said, disappointed. "Nothing but empty fighting positions and pissed-off farmers."

"Yeah, same here."

"Looks like the Iraqis picked up their toys and went home," added Dave. "Nothing out to the east, either."

The three of us sat around a folding table and recounted the events of the day to Maj Harper and Capt Whalen while Lt Manson and his clerks scribbled notes about the mission. There was interest in the canals and the fighting positions.

"Any tire tracks along the trails?" Manson asked.

"Negative," I replied. "Some sheep tracks, but that was about it. We're the only ones stupid enough to drive vehicles out there. It's too dangerous to move around on those paddy dikes."

"What about the fighting positions?" asked Maj Harper.

"Same thing you described a couple of days ago, sir," I said. "Well-dug, reinforced with sandbags made of old flour sacks. All were oriented on the road. All empty. Some were right next to farm huts where people lived."

"Same thing in my zone," added Gil. "Whoever was out there before wasn't there today. They heard us coming and left. I think we need to expand out to the east and flush them out."

Major Harper looked around at all of us. We could barely keep our eyes open.

"Get some sleep," he said. "I'll call you later with a warning order for tomorrow's operation." He turned to Bob, who was already nodding off. "Let's go, we got work to do." Bob groaned and moved over to the map board to begin planning. Harper was a machine—he never slept.

I returned to the company's lines and crawled into my sleeping bag. It was filthy, caked in mud and filled with gritty sand and dust, but I didn't care. Sleep had become an important commodity to all of us. I was spent, and while I continued to be disappointed that our reconnaissance had been uneventful, I was nevertheless satisfied. The company had performed well given the challenges it faced with the unforgiving terrain. We were a reconnaissance unit, and we had just provided the battalion and the RCT an accurate picture of what lay to the north. If the division ever got moving again it would have an idea what it was getting into. Hopefully someone would see the light and continue to employ 1st LAR Battalion the way it was designed.

I nodded off to sleep, only to be awakened in the middle of the night by an NBC alert. I wearily donned my mask and lay on my back, waiting for the "all clear" message. Instead of hearing it, I fell asleep again and woke up some time later. Looking around and seeing no one wearing his mask, I peeled mine off and rolled over. I was a bag of shit—sleep was more important to me than finding out if it had indeed been a false alarm.

Gil's proposal had been a success. On the morning of 30 March, Delta and Charlie Companies pushed out to the east in our own attempt to flush out and ambush the enemy. Much to everyone's disappointment, however, we still found no prey. After several hours of huddling in our ambush positions, the battalion radioed to cancel the mission and ordered both companies back to friendly lines. The mission had not been a complete washout, however. We had seen numerous piles of old ordnance strewn everywhere, and a series of observation towers that looked out over the range. This indicated that the area we had occupied was an Iraqi military live-fire training range. The reports of our being in the enemy's back yard had been accurate.

As Delta Company returned to friendly lines, I stared wordlessly at the DMZ that the land surrounding the cloverleaf had become. With shell holes and shrapnel marring the countryside and small fires burning everywhere, it resembled Europe's western front of 1917. A peculiar odor filled the air. It was the putrid smell of burning garbage and human excrement, gasoline and diesel fuel. It was the stench of occupation, the smell of a unit that had been in one place too long. I wanted out of that nightmare landscape punctuated by cat holes half-filled with shit, MRE wrappings, and errant cluster bombs. I wanted to get back on the move, north toward Baghdad. To pass the time, I repacked my gear and took a moment to air out my feet. I also tried to rest, but I couldn't get any sleep. What was next? Were we really moving? Where were we going? My mind swam.

Around 1530Z I returned to the COC. It looked like a party, and I was the last to arrive. The entire staff gathered around outside the operations tent, waiting for the word. The same thing was on everyone's mind. Twenty different conversations carried on at once.

"Are we moving?"

"I don't know."

"I heard we're making a push all the way to Baghdad."

"You're full of shit."

"Who's got a cigarette?"

"My feet are fucked up."

"I haven't changed my underwear since before we left Kuwait."

We sat around, shooting the shit until the battalion commander and S-3 showed up. The rumors were true: the following day the RCT was scheduled to move north again. We would be leaving our ordnance-strewn hellhole forever.

"Be back here at 2100Z for the mission order," Maj Harper told everyone as he led his staff into the tent for their planning session. We looked around at each other. There were nearly four hours to kill.

I curled up next to the vehicle's tires and quickly fell asleep. When I awoke at 2100Z the moon was out, and Marines slowly moved about in the soft lunar glow. I gathered my gear and returned to the COC, and together with the rest of the staff we huddled in a circle around the briefing table inside the operations tent. The orders briefing was largely a rehash of our original plan of 27 March, and despite the fact that everyone stood, many sets of heavy-lidded eyes filled the tent. Fatigue was gradually wrapping its hands around everybody, not just the Marines in the line companies. I particularly felt sorry for Bob Whalen. He never seemed to get any sleep.

I had to pinch myself to stay awake. Even putting a plug of tobacco in my lower lip failed to keep me alert, and I found myself nodding off for moments at a time. Then a muted noise far off in the distance caused my eyes to snap open.

Whumpf.

Then another.

Whumpf.

Then suddenly a rapid series all at once.

Whumpf-whumpf-whumpf-whumpf-whumpf-whumpf.

Everyone in the tent looked at each other.

I turned to Dave. "That doesn't sound like outgoing."

Almost immediately the ground shook as we heard and felt the throaty concussion of rocket-artillery rounds thundering down around us. We had no idea where they came from or where they were impacting, but inside the tent it felt like the rounds would land on top of us. Everyone scrambled in all directions. Shouts of "Fuck!" and "Get outside!" filled the air as Marines clawed for helmets and pushed their way to the tent's opening. Watching the pile-up at the exit, I was strangely reminded of infamous disco fires I had read about where firemen had found stacks of dead bodies at the exits. I suddenly understood why movie theaters always said, "In case of a fire, walk, do not run, to the nearest exit." Then again, whatever genius came up with that phrase had probably never experienced an artillery barrage. The Marines who did make it out of the tent tried to pile into a sleeping trench, which they quickly realized had been filled back in hours earlier in anticipation of the next morning's early departure. Even above the din, muffled yells of "Get the fuck off me!" could be heard from outside.

Inside the tent, with its vinyl walls rattling and the earthquake-shudder of the impacting artillery rounds, I searched frantically for my own helmet. I had set it down during the briefing and in the confusion couldn't remember where the hell I had placed it. One rolled around on the ground by itself. Thinking it was mine, I leaned down and picked it up. As I threw the helmet on and felt my skull bounce around loosely inside it, I realized it was too big. *This isn't my Kevlar,* I thought stupidly. *Some bastard took mine!* Next to me Dave knelt down, one hand covering the top of his naked head. He couldn't find his helmet either. A quizzical expression filled his face. It said *Yep, looks like it's gonna be one of those days.* He appeared to have simply accepted his fate much as I had several nights earlier during the Scud alert when I had forgotten my gas mask.

"Here!" I yelled, yanking off the too-big helmet and slamming it down on Dave's head. It turned out to be his. Looking around again in a panic, I spotted my Kevlar in the corner. No one had stolen it after all. I leaped over and snatched it up, and as I secured the strap around my chin I looked down to see two Marines hiding under the flimsy briefing table. My first thought was *Fat lot of good that's gonna do them,* but then I realized my own exposed position. I knelt down next to Dave, and together we waited it out.

Time slowed to a crawl, yet the entire episode lasted maybe thirty seconds. Once the echoes from the falling rounds faded and everyone realized the barrage had ended, Marines filed back into the tent. Nervous jokes passed back and forth between officers of all ranks. After all, we had just survived our first artillery barrage. But where the hell had the rounds landed? As we stood there, the companies reported their status. None reported any impacts in its sector. Captain Bone sat at the radio bank, trying to get a status from 2/11 on the counter-battery radar search for the barrage's point of origin. We still didn't know if the rounds raining down on our heads had been friendly or enemy. Bone spoke up and cleared the air for us.

"The impacts were less than a klick north of us. Two-Eleven thinks it was a BM-twenty-one. They're dialing in a counter-battery mission right now." Fifteen minutes after the first 122mm rockets from the Iraqi BM-21 were launched at us, 2/11 fired rocket-assisted projectiles (RAP) in retaliation. Fifteen minutes, man. It was hardly impressive. The BM-21—basically a big truck with forty launch tubes mounted on the back—was no doubt long gone.

In the middle of all of this someone in the operations tent wondered aloud, "Hey, shouldn't we be masked up?" In all the confusion we had forgotten. Masks were donned, and everyone stood around looking at each other again. Major Harper, realizing we had all had enough excitement for one night, announced the time for departure the following morning and dismissed us.

Walking back to the vehicle in my gas mask, I heard the rumble of 2/11 to the south firing its counter-battery mission. In midflight the rocket motors of the RAP projectiles ignited, and suddenly the heavens filled with a dozen glowing orange beacons arcing toward their final destination. The flashes of the impacts illuminated the horizon far to the west, and moments later the soft thuds rolled across the farmlands and filled my ears. We didn't hear anything else from the BM-21 for the rest of the night. Whoever had been responsible for firing the rockets at us probably figured he wasn't getting paid enough to risk his ass twice in one night.

I crawled into my sleeping bag—my gas mask still securely strapped to my face—and promptly fell asleep. Major Harper had been right: I had experienced enough excitement for onc night.

Enough to last a lifetime.

PART III

Closing in: Tigris, Nahr Diyala, and Baghdad

31 March–12 April 2003

13

The Red Zone

Dreams of suffocation plagued me. When LCpl Davis woke me for the final shift of radio watch an hour before reveille, I was more than ready to get up and move around. Hearing his voice and opening my eyes, I realized I was still wearing my gas mask. Whoever had been on radio watch earlier in the evening hadn't told me when the NBC alert ended. Most people would think it's impossible, but when you are tired enough you can in fact sleep in a gas mask. My face throbbed, and all around it a deep, painful crease marked where the mask's rubber seal had clung to the skin all night.

As daylight approached on that morning of 31 March, the men of 1st LAR Battalion quietly milled around, preparing themselves and their vehicles for the drive north to Ash Shumali. The long column of vehicles collectively fired up its engines and lined up in march formation, awaiting the order to move out. As Delta Company slowly pulled away from the fetid, corrupt farmland that had been our home for the better part of a week, the place where we had lost LCpl Suarez del Solar gradually receded from view. His death overshadowed the other significant episode that had occurred there: my baptism. But my baptism had been a personal event that would always be with me. It needed no physical monument. That wasn't the case with the location of Suarez del Solar's death. His comrades had felt compelled to mark with a small American flag the spot where he fell. On it someone had written "Suarez del Solar—Never Forgotten."

⁂

The trip north along Highway 1 was uneventful for the battalion. We pulled off the main highway onto an exit south of Hantush Airfield, where a narrow, paved road led from the highway east to the small town of Ash Shumali. That morning, to the south, the terrain around us had been mostly dry, dirt farmland with the pervasive canal and levee networks. But as we travelled, the terrain had transformed before our eyes; everything was lush and green, and palm groves dotted the landscape forward of our location. I ordered the company into a battle position just south of the road, and as the platoons arranged themselves a familiar call came across the radio.

"Black-Six, this is White-One," called Lt Schwartz. "We can't push too much farther forward or we'll sink." His radio transmission was followed by one from Lt Parment.

"Same here, Six. We may be stuck right now as it is." From my position along the road's shoulder, I peered through my binoculars toward the area where 1st and 2nd Platoons had situated themselves. Schwartz and Parment were correct. Their vehicles bordered a large irrigated field with more infernal ditches and canals. The mud their tires rested in threatened to swallow them up if it started raining. But, as had been the case in our previous position, the company's fields of fire were adequate. So long as the Marines remained alert no one would be able to sneak up on the company. As the XO radioed the platoons for their grid coordinates and fire-plan sketches, I walked up the road to where the COC had been established. Major Harper met me outside his vehicle as I approached.

"Send out a patrol to recon an alternate battle position here," he said, pointing to a spot on the map to our southeast. "It's gonna get crowded out here real quick."

"Roger that," I replied, turning to head back to my vehicle. I radioed Schwartz and relayed the order for his platoon, and by 1030Z they were leaving the company's lines for the patrol. The tone in his voice said that he and his Marines were happy to be out doing a mission on their own, and I envied them. I briefly considered jumping into my vehicle and going with them. With Suarez's death still fresh in my mind I wanted to be there if Schwartz and his platoon got into any trouble, but common sense quickly prevailed. *Asshole. They can handle themselves,* I thought. *Got to cut the apron strings sometime.*

Minutes later Schwartz's voice sounded over the radio.

"Black-Six, this is White-One," he said, a tinge of excitement in his words. "We just captured an Iraqi soldier trying to get away from us. We're on our way back right now."

The two LAV-25s from Schwartz's section rumbled down the road toward us, and I motioned for them to move to the COC. Schwartz climbed down from his turret and walked over to me.

"Well," I asked, smiling. "What happened?"

"Dewitt can probably tell you better than I can, sir," he replied, casually jerking his thumb over his shoulder toward the sergeant, who had just climbed from the scout compartment. Schwartz motioned for the Marine to join us.

"Tell the CO what happened, Sergeant," Schwartz said.

Dewitt energetically puffed on a cigarette and pointed back over his shoulder to the southeast. "We were out on foot over there past this field in front of us, sir," he began. "We saw this dude walking along in a green field jacket, and when he saw us coming he ditched his bag and his jacket and bolted."

"We took off after him and tackled him," he concluded. "You shoulda seen his fucking face, sir." A grin started to form across Dewitt's visage.

"Where is he?" I asked.

"In the back of the vehicle," he replied, handing me a dirty, plastic garbage bag. "Here's his shit." Lieutenant Manson had joined us, and together we sifted through the contents of the bag. Inside was an olive drab military uniform with no rank, a black beret, a worn-out pair of shoes, cigarettes, and a crumpled wad of cash that amounted to thousands of Iraqi *dinars*.

"That's a shit-load of money," I said, staring at the stack of bills.

"Not really," said Manson. "Their money isn't worth shit. That's probably about a hundred bucks or so. Maybe less."

Manson departed to locate the human exploitation team (HET) and Sgt Dewitt brought me around the back of the vehicle that contained the prisoner. Several scouts crowded around the hatches, their rifles steadily trained on a pathetic looking man sitting inside on the bench with his hands zip-cuffed around his back. The guy looked miserable. Clad only in a filthy T-shirt, baggy pants, and socks, he sat there silent and unmoving with his head hanging down. Gazing into the scout compartment, my heart filled with pity for the wretched soul in front of me. He was clearly no threat to us. I turned to the team leader in charge of the scouts guarding the prisoner.

"Give him a cigarette. This guy's probably scared shitless." A Marine pulled out a cigarette, placed it between the Iraqi's lips, and lit it. He sat there, silently smoking, his eyes downcast the entire time. He didn't make a sound.

A few minutes later Lt Manson reappeared.

"Bring him over here," he said to the Marines, motioning toward a shallow hole. "Put him in there, face down. The HET team will be here soon."

The scouts escorted the prisoner from the vehicle toward the hole, and as they laid him facedown in the dirt he started struggling and violently shaking. It dawned on me that he must have thought we were going to put a bullet in the back of his head and bury him.

"Jesus, man," I said to Manson. "What are you guys doing?"

"He needs to think we're the bad guys so that HET can come and be the good guys to get him to talk."

"Oh, come on," I said incredulously, walking around the side of the hole. I knelt down next to the Iraqi and tapped him on the shoulder. He slowly turned his head and looked at me.

"*Jundi?*" I asked. He slowly shook his head.

"Jundi Awal?" He shook his head again.

"Arif?" I asked. *"Waqeel Raqeeb?"* Another shake of the head. Either he wasn't a private, lance corporal, corporal, or sergeant, or else my Arabic was so unintelligible that he had no idea what the hell I was trying to say. I called over to the watching scouts.

"Hey, someone go get me a Phraselator." About the size of our military-issued GPS unit, the Phraselator was an experimental electronic device with prerecorded messages in multiple languages. It also had the ability to record spoken words or phrases, which it would then attempt to translate. That particular function was less reliable, so we tended to stick with the prerecorded messages. The S-3 shop had issued Delta Company several Phraselators just weeks before we left Camp Pendleton, but we were still skeptical about the device's capabilities.

A scout handed me the Phraselator, and once I finally got it working properly I scrolled down to the line that said, "We will not harm you." I pressed the "play" button and held the device next to the Iraqi for him to hear. A phrase sputtered out in Arabic, and after hearing it the man gently nodded his head. Then I scrolled the cursor down to the word "soldier" and played it for him.

"Jundi," a digitized voice said. The soldier slowly nodded his head.

"Well, shit," I said to him. "I guess my Arabic just sucks, huh?" I stood up and handed the Phraselator back to the scouts. Two Marines from HET arrived, and as they began grilling the Iraqi a Marine appeared next to me with a disposable camera. As he aimed it at the Iraqi soldier I turned to him.

"Hey, what are you doing?" I asked. "You can't do that."

"Why not, sir?"

"You're not supposed to take personal pictures of POWs," I explained. "It's against the rules. It 'exploits' them." A dejected look filled the Marine's face.

"Come on," I said to the scouts, motioning toward their vehicle. "Let's let the HET team do their job." By now the HET gunnery sergeant was sitting on the lip of the hole with the Iraqi next to him. Once he had realized we weren't planning to execute him the soldier had begun jabbering his head off to the translator. I walked back to where Lt Schwartz and Sgt Dewitt stood.

"Good job, gents," I said. Then I turned to Schwartz. "What about the recon of the battle position?"

"It's no good, sir. The land is all like this shit in front of us. We'll get stuck if we try to put LAVs out there."

"All right. Go ahead and reman your position." As he returned to his vehicle I noticed the HET gunnery sergeant was taking a break from talking with the prisoner. I approached him.

"Hey, Gunny," I said. "What's this guy's story?"

"Nothing. He's a security guard who deserted once the war started. He's just trying to get home."

"Yeah," I said, pausing to look at the emaciated figure sitting alone in the muddy hole. "Aren't we all."

✦ ✧ ✦

Just a security guard, I thought to myself as I walked back toward my vehicle. *How anticlimatic.* True, it was a bit of a disappointment, but it had been great to watch the scouts do their job. The looks of satisfaction on their faces after they netted the company's first POW had been worth it. With the movement north that morning and the subsequent capture of the security guard, I sensed the morale within the company had begun to climb.

I stopped back by the COC and ran into Maj Bodkin.

"What's the story with the POW?" he asked.

"Just a security guard who deserted, sir. HET's still working on him."

"Good to go," he replied. Then he changed the subject. "Have you checked out those buildings in front of your company?" I looked out across the field to a small hamlet with two sets of buildings that stood forward of 3rd Platoon.

"That's a negative, sir."

"Roger. Go check it out and let us know what's in there."

"You got it, sir," I replied, walking away to get on the radio. I called Lt Cullins and directed him to check out the area with his platoon. The four LAVs immediately rolled forward from their positions along the road's shoulder and vectored toward the buildings partially hidden in a palm grove. From my position, I could soon see the tiny figures of 3rd Platoon's scouts dismounting and fanning out to clear the structures. Cullins's voice sounded on the radio.

"Black-Six, this is Blue-One. We have multiple occupants within the buildings, but no hostile actions yet."

"Roger that," I replied. "Do you need back-up?"

"That's affirmative. We have a couple of vehicles stuck up here. We could use some more people on the ground, too." I sent Lt Schwartz and his platoon to assist the scouts of 3rd Platoon, who were uncovering garbage bags of cash, discarded military uniforms, rifle magazines, and an AK-47. But nearly all of Lt Cullins's vehicles had mired down in the thick mud that surrounded the hamlet. Soon Lt Schwartz's LAVs became lodged in the earth as well.

"What's the situation out there?" I asked into the radio.

"We need Black-Seven to come over here to shuttle out these detainees," radioed Cullins. Out of the corner of my eye I saw SSgt Kappen's crew closing up and mounting their vehicle to head to the hamlet, followed by their wingman.

In the palm grove the scouts from 2nd and 3rd Platoons had lined up close to a dozen detainees, all clothed in ragged dishdashas and wearing shemaghs around their heads or necks. After flex-cuffing their hands behind their backs and making them sit cross-legged on the ground, the scouts examined each detainee's identification cards. One by one they loaded the prisoners into SSgt Kappen's waiting LAV, and he began shuttling the compliant Iraqis back to the COC and the waiting HET team.

Almost as soon as Kappen had dropped off the Iraqis at the COC, we watched as they walked unescorted back down the road toward the buildings from which they had come. I inquired as to what was going on and was told the HET team had determined that our detainees posed no threat. According to the HET team, the Iraqis had looted the local military barracks after the soldiers left, taking all the cash and equipment. But our dealings with the now former detainees were not quite over. I received a call from Lt Cullins.

"Black-Six, this is Blue-One," he said, sounding irritated. "These Iraqis are all pissed off out here. They want to know where their cash went."

"Well," I asked. "Where is it?"

"I don't know."

"Are you sure none of your men still have it?"

"I'm positive. These assholes think we stole their money."

"Oh, you mean the money *they* stole from the army?" I said sarcastically. I looked at the sun sinking below the tree line on the horizon. "Don't worry about it. Just get your vehicles unstuck and come home."

"We also need Black-Nine to get us unstuck," he added. "We're all in pretty deep out here." Staff Sergeant Monroe must have been eavesdropping on our conversation, because his voice quickly followed on the radio.

"I'm on my way," he said. "Hang on."

Several minutes later I received another call from Monroe.

"I'm stuck out here, Black-Six," he said sheepishly. "We're not getting out until morning. I'll get battalion maintenance to come out here and get us out then."

"Roger that," I said. "Blue-One, go to ground. You're gonna have to wait it out tonight."

The XO's voice came up on the net. "Blue-One, this is Black-Five. Send me the grids of all your vehicles. I'll lay the mortars around you if you need them tonight." The two of them began passing coordinates and azimuths across the radio.

"White-One, detach your scouts to Blue Platoon for the night," I said to Schwartz. "Return your vehicles to your battle position. You can pick them up in the morning."

"Roger that, Black-Six," he replied. One by one his vehicles took their place back on the line as the light faded from the sky. Far out in front of us the sounds of Marines digging in a perimeter around the immobile vehicles filled the darkness. I worried about Lt Cullins and his Marines being isolated for the night, but then I remembered my thoughts from earlier in the day.

They're big boys now.

At first light on 1 April a small column of recovery vehicles cautiously inched its way across the unstable ground forward of our position toward 3rd Platoon's perimeter. Soon 3rd Platoon's vehicles were freed from the muck and back on line with the rest of the company. April Fools' Day had begun for Delta Company in a big way.

Later that morning, the company commanders received a warning order that the regiment planned to cross the Saddam Canal and the Tigris River that evening. One-Five would secure the near side of the canal, 3/5 would secure the far side, and 2/5 would secure a military compound east of the canal. Once these missions were complete, 1st LAR Battalion would follow 2nd Tanks across the canal, push to the town of An Numinayah, and cross the Tigris River there.

After relaying the warning order to the company, I sat down next to my vehicle to review the route on my map. One-Five had begun moving its amtracks down the road toward Ash Shumali and Route 27 in preparation for its attack to the Saddam Canal. Amid the noise of the tracked vehicles slowly rumbling past the company I heard a Marine shout from atop an amtrack.

"Yep!" he hollered contemptuously. "There's First LAR Battalion, 'providing security' again!"

I shook my head in disbelief. *Jeez,* I thought bitterly. *Even the grunts realize we aren't doing jack shit out here.* As I sat there fuming beside my LAV, SSgt Kappen walked up next to me.

"You believe this shit, sir?"

"No," I replied. "I really do not."

"Hey sir, something's wrong with the KVN back home," he said, suddenly changing the subject. "You need to call your wife."

"What? What do you mean?"

"I don't know. I just talked to Melissa and she said Ashley needs to talk to you about some KVN issues."

Something had to be up. Ashley wouldn't be expecting me to call her if something was not terribly wrong. Even in the past, when Delta Company had been out training, she had refrained from contacting me in the field. She took her job as the head of the company's family support network seriously, and she just wasn't the type of person to panic. Now there I was in the middle of a combat zone with her wanting me to call. It must be serious. I sought out Bob Woodruff and asked to use his satellite cell phone. Soon the line was ringing in California.

"It's a nightmare here," she told me. "The Marine Corps told Lance Corporal Suarez's family that he was shot in the head, but the TV news said he stepped on an artillery round. His dad is causing all sorts of problems about the insurance money, and I don't know what the official story is on how his son died. No one seems to know."

"Jesus *Christ,*" I growled. "They said he was shot in the head?"

"Yes."

"Listen," I told her slowly. "I was there. This is the official word: he stepped on a cluster bomb from an artillery round. He was *not* shot in the head. He had a head wound, but it wasn't from a bullet and I don't think it was what killed him. He bled to death on a helicopter on the way to the hospital."

"Okay," she said after writing down what I had said word for word. "But I don't think it will matter with his father. He has really gone off the deep end." She went on to explain how the Marine casualty assistance calls officer (CACO) had arrived on the doorstep of Suarez del Solar's father's home, only to find out that Suarez's wife, Sayne, whom he had named as his next of kin, no longer lived there. Because the CACO was only authorized to notify the next of kin of the death, he could not tell Mr. Suarez del Solar what had happened, and instead asked how to get in touch with the wife. Knowing something was wrong, Suarez's father made two calls. One was to his daughter-in-law, telling her to come quick, something had happened to her husband. The other call was to the media. He said he "wanted his son's story told." When Sayne showed up at her in-laws' home she was greeted by reporters, journalists, photographers, and a houseful of Suarez del Solar's relatives. She had not yet been told of her husband's death. It was a zoo.

After being notified about the tragedy, Suarez's father had begun pressing Sayne for information about his son's insurance money, insisting that the Marine Corps had not provided enough money for a burial. He had set up a fund in his own name asking the community to contribute to paying for proper burials for the fallen Marines. He had also published an email he claimed to have sent his son shortly before he was killed in action. I thought for a moment. That didn't sound right.

"Wait a minute," I said. "That's bullshit! We don't have email out here.

We never even had it while we were in Kuwait!"

"I know," she said. "Seth, that's my point. He's doing all this for the attention. The media is eating it up, and nothing the man is saying is true."

"What can I do?" I asked.

"I just needed the official story. I'm handling everything here with the KVN and Gunny Senn. It's just hard." I imagined her trying to tackle such an emotional situation with Gunnery Sergeant James Senn, the battalion's remain-behind SNCO. He was an outstanding Marine, but not exactly the most sensitive guy I had ever met. Ashley continued.

"I saw you on TV two nights ago. The memorial service was on the news."

"What, are you kidding? Great. Fucking *great,*" I said sarcastically.

"Everyone said you looked terrific," she began. "But I thought you looked very tired and small. Are you okay?"

"Yeah, I'm fine. We'll be all right."

"Be careful," she said as we prepared to sign off.

"Don't worry about me," I replied, watching the remainders of 1/5 pass us by in the dust. "It's more dangerous where you are than where I am right now."

◆ ◇ ◆

Suddenly I was petrified. "Get ready to swim." The S-3's words from the previous December came back to haunt me that morning when the battalion commander informed us of our impending mission. The condition of the bridge and the enemy situation at An Numinayah was unknown. Another crossing site was required, and it might be necessary for 1st LAR Battalion to swim its vehicles across the Tigris River. I was particularly worried.

"Sir, my vehicles all came from MPF," I protested to the CO. "None of them have been float tested in God knows when." It was true. We had had numerous seal and gasket problems from the equipment moldering on the ships. I doubted the LAVs were capable of swimming without ending up at the bottom of the fast moving Tigris River.

"The RCT CO said we have to be prepared to cross the river no matter what," LtCol White said. "He said, 'Duffy, if I give you the word you have to get across somehow,' so start getting your vehicles ready."

I walked back to the company's lines, shaking my head and cursing to myself. While it was true the LAV—equipped with propellers, rudder vanes, and an internal bilge pump—was designed to swim across slow moving bodies of water, it was a capability I didn't trust. The vehicle had to be properly ballasted to prevent it from rolling over and sinking in the water. As loaded down as we were with ammunition, food, and personal equipment, there was no way to accurately ballast the LAVs. Although the battalion had conducted extensive swim training while Delta Company had been deployed to WestPac, we hadn't been able to do the same. We had no way of knowing how watertight our hulls were. The prospect of losing maybe half of my vehicles and crews in the Tigris unnerved me. I called for SSgt Monroe and told him the news.

"Are you shitting me, sir?" he asked. "These things haven't been float tested! I have no idea if they'll sink or not!"

"Well, we've got our marching orders. What can we do to fix the situation?"

"I'll get the mechs on it, sir," he replied. "We'll start checking all the seals, greasing the hatch seams, you know . . . the whole preswim checklist thing."

"All right. Get me an update as soon as you can. I owe the CO a report on how many definitely cannot swim." Monroe disappeared, and soon the company's mechanics moved from vehicle to vehicle, inspecting drain plugs, greasing hinges and hatch seals, and assessing hull integrities. A team of mechanics appeared at my vehicle, and together with my crew they applied a thick layer of grease across every crevice where water could potentially leak in and flood the hull. As I stood there watching the effort, 1stSgt Guzman came up behind me.

"Are they really expecting us to swim these things?" he asked.

"Yeah, it sure looks that way."

"There's no way," he said, shaking his head. "No way."

It was the first time since the confusion of the sandstorm that I was genuinely afraid. My fears were exacerbated by the battalion's stagnant position and lack of activity—it gave me too much time to consider the possibilities. But I cursed myself, too. I had complained the entire time that our battalion wasn't getting its fair share of the workload, yet there I was, saying my company couldn't accomplish the swim mission that had just been assigned to us. Staff Sergeant Monroe sidled up to me as I brooded next to my vehicle.

"Okay, here's the deal, sir," he began. "We've got five vehicles that definitely can't swim."

"Jesus, *five?*"

"Well, it would be less if the crews would stop running into each other out here," he replied. "I can turn that five into two by switching some parts and plugs around, but two are definitely out of the game. The collisions they were in breached their hulls."

"Okay," I said, jotting it down in my notebook. "Go on."

"We're greasing the fuck out of the rest of them. We'll just have to cross our fingers and see what happens."

"Alright," I said. "Good job. I'll let the CO know."

✦ ✧ ✦

My concerns about swimming the company turned out to be baseless. The battalion learned that 1/5 had penetrated across the Saddam Canal after destroying an Iraqi company that had been defending the site. Bridging assets had been pushed forward to improve the crossing site while 1/5 prepared to pass the rest of the RCT through its position. The heavy fighting delayed our departure until late in the evening, and the call to move out came at 0100Z on 2 April. By 0200Z Delta Company was leaving Ash Shumali and heading toward the Saddam Canal and the waiting Tigris River.

That time, however, we got underway in MOPP-2. The RCT had breached the "red zone," the area where the Republican Guard was most likely to employ chemical weapons as a last-ditch effort to defend Baghdad. While we had grown somewhat accustomed to our hot, baggy chemical suits, we dreaded donning the heavy rubber over-boots again. Even standing still in them felt like someone had lit a fire under your feet. It was like baking a potato in aluminum foil. I considered removing my combat boots and simply wearing the over-boots on my bare feet. Common sense didn't prevail. Misery did. My feet continued to deteriorate.

Shortly after crossing the canal, the company encountered some shot-up military trucks and dead Iraqi soldiers lying by the side of the road. My LAV slowed to a crawl in the heavy traffic, and to our right an Iraqi corpse clad in olive drab lay sprawled out in the dirt. A burlap sack had been draped across its face. As I stood in the turret staring at it, LCpl Davis broke the silence on our intercom.

"Jay-zus," he said. "Will you look at that poor bastard? At least his head wasn't run over by a tank like that one we saw a couple days ago."

"Hey sir," called Gurganus from his compartment. "How come his face is covered up?"

"Respect for the dead," I replied, looking at the graying, exposed flesh of the corpse's hands. "And because no one wants to look at it."

"Who's gonna bury these fuckers?" Davis asked.

"Not us," I answered. "Muslims are supposed to bury Muslims. It's part of their religion."

We continued forward, and the early morning sun soon began heating up the day. As had happened so many times during the previous week, the highway quickly became a parking lot of military vehicles.

The heat of midday bore down on us, and little by little information trickled down to the companies. Second Tank Battalion had thrust ahead on Route 27 to seize the bridgehead at An Numinayah and had encountered formidable resistance in the city. During the fighting the battalion had lost an M1A1 to an RPG—a "mobility kill" to the tank resulting in no friendly casualties. Three-Five was sent ahead of 1st LAR Battalion to support 2nd Tanks and deal with the threat in the town, and they too encountered significant enemy resistance within An Numinayah.

Hearing all this take place over the battalion radio net as we sat baking in the sun was maddening. Our long column sat immobile along the road, moving forward in fits and starts. With our turrets facing outboard, scanning for any enemy activity to our flanks, we quickly realized that the fight wasn't where we were. It was forward of us. It was someone else's war—again. Off in the distance a tall pillar of thick, black smoke within the town climbed high into the cobalt skies. I shared a cigarette in the turret with Davis and thought about what must be going on with 3/5 inside An Numinayah. Again and again I asked myself the same crucial question: why wasn't the RCT employing 1st LAR Battalion in these engagements?

No matter how hard the company commanders tried, we could get no answer from the battalion commander or the operations officer. With no explanation to satisfy us we did the natural thing: we guessed. Was it that they didn't trust us? Did the RCT think our battalion was incompetent? Did they think we lacked courage? Were we simply being held in reserve?

One thing was for sure: we were mightily pissed off. The anger festered within the company like a virus silently incubating inside its host. And there was nothing I could do about it. After I had voiced my objection to the battalion's lack of employment, the S-3 had shut me down for good outside of Ash Shumali. Perhaps my complaining was how Delta Company had ended up with the inglorious mission of guarding the battalion combat trains that miserably hot day along Route 27.

Then I heard something on the radio different from the routine administrative chatter we were used to. The battalion commander and the Forward were engaged far ahead of us at the front of the battalion's column. Weapons Company had been the lead element in the battalion formation, but somehow the four vehicles from the Forward had come in contact with a group of Iraqis setting up an ambush. Lieutenant Colonel White and the other vehicle commanders let loose with a hail of machine-gun and 25mm fire from their LAVs. Around the same time, two of Weapons Company's platoons became engaged with Iraqis dressed in civilian attire and armed with AK-47s and RPGs.

I couldn't believe it. The *battalion commander* was up there fighting it out with the Fedayeen while we sat around sweating in our MOPP suits. *Okay, calm down,* I thought to myself. *You can't expect to be the main effort for every mission.* But it was beyond frustrating to listen to the CO in contact over the radio while Delta Company did nothing. With 3/5's fight inside An Numinayah still going strong, it soon became clear that we wouldn't cross the Tigris that day.

Instead, a warning order was issued for the battalion to turn north along a road that paralleled the Tigris. Our maps indicated that the road skirted a string of cabled electrical pylons west of the river, and the route became known as "Powerline Road." As I examined the line on my map that curved along the banks of the river, Spool's voice popped into my ear over the radio.

"Black-Six, this is Spool. I'm talking with a Huey pilot right now. Do you want to go on a recon flight of our route?" It was just what I needed to hear to get me out of the funk I had sunk into.

"Oh *shit yeah!*" I exclaimed. "Hook me up."

"Roger that. He'll be landing off to our south in one minute."

"That's a solid copy," I said, gathering my map and Kevlar from the turret. "Black-Five, you've got the broadsword."

"Roger," answered Capt Portiss facetiously. "I've got the monkey wrench."

I turned to LCpl Davis in the turret. "Stick with Black-Eight and Red Platoon in front of us," I told him. "I'll see you in a bit." Grabbing my map, I climbed down from the turret as a Huey circled the company column and gently set down in a field to our right. As I ran up to the idling aircraft I was met with a blast of hot exhaust and stinging dust from its spinning rotor blades. But soon after pulling myself aboard we lifted off and up into the sky, and the cabin filled with cool, fresh air. The pilot banked the helicopter to the northeast toward An Numinayah, then northwest along the trace of the Tigris. He continued zigzagging along the river, alternating the aircraft's altitude and air speed, flying what the aviators called "nap of the earth." The helicopter's crew chief crouched behind a .50-caliber machine gun mounted in the doorway, and stacked around me on the deckplates were hundreds of rounds of ammunition. It was my first taste of what a combat reconnaissance flight was like, and I was having the time of my life.

After circling the trails of smoke rising from An Numinayah, we pushed ahead of the serpentine column of 1st LAR's tiny vehicles arrayed along our route. The cool breeze blowing through the open bay doors of the Huey was intoxicating, and I had to concentrate on my map and the terrain ahead of us to keep from nodding off. It was a pleasant change from always operating on the ground. From the turret of an LAV the terrain looks very different from what you see if you are standing on the ground. From the cargo bay of a helicopter flying at five hundred feet the difference is even more striking. From my vantage point high above Powerline Road it was clear that the battalion had an open route ahead of it. The land was the same: wide open fields irrigated by a series of major canals that branched out and drew water from the Tigris. There seemed few places for the enemy to hide in the fields, but along the banks of the river was a near continuous outcropping of lush palm groves. Thick and plentiful as they were, the palm groves made for perfect ambush positions.

We circled back toward the battalion, and as the helo drew closer to the column I could see that they were already underway along Powerline Road. I pointed to a spot on the ground about halfway down the length of the convoy, and the helicopter eased down to the ground to let me out. After passing my thanks to the pilot and his crew for the flight, I jumped off and sat by the side of the road to wait for Delta Company at tail-end Charlie to pick me up. Sitting in the dust by the side of the road and smoking a cigarette, I felt like a hitchhiker thumbing a ride. As the battalion's vehicles passed me by, shouts and waves came from the Marines manning their turrets. I returned their heckles with an occasional flip of the middle finger. Eventually Delta Company approached, and after heaving myself back inside my place in the turret I called Portiss to reassume tactical command of the company. The slow movement north along Powerline Road continued.

Sunset approached, and the battalion began setting into a defensive posture for the night. By the time Delta Company arrived at the battalion's position we were the last element to fill in the gaps of the defense. I looked around, and for the life of me I had no clue how we would do it. The laager site was located along Powerline Road, and vehicles were arrayed haphazardly around the headquarters. Making my way over to the COC, I found Maj Harper and asked for clarification on how he wanted me to position my company.

"Take this sector here," he said, pointing to his map, and then pointing out to the south. "Fill it in as best you can. We'll be on the move again first thing in the morning." I called the platoon commanders and directed them to come to my position. As tired as I was, it would have been difficult to give them decent directions over the radio. In the fading light I pointed out sectors, and as they departed to situate their platoons I returned to the COC for a staff meeting. The long day on the road in the hot sun had emptied me, and at the meeting with the battalion staff I felt drugged. Concentrating on what everyone was saying became difficult, and looking around the tent I saw the same emptiness in everyone's faces. The soft blue lighting accentuated the deep circles around each man's eyes, and the ghoulish faces that filled the room were startling. As LtCol White recounted the story of his engagement earlier in the day, I noticed that he looked more worn down than I had ever seen him. Exhaustion, it seemed, respected no rank. As the same mounting fatigue that was visible among the battalion staff continued to stalk me and wear me down, a thought repeated itself in my head like a record with a skip in the middle of it.

How soon until I am so tired I can't make decisions anymore?

◆ ◇ ◆

On the morning of 3 April, 1st LAR Battalion received a frag order to continue its reconnaissance along Powerline Road. Two-Eleven needed a series of artillery position areas along the route to support the RCT's attack along Highway 6, the major route paralleling the Tigris to the north. With orders in hand, the company commanders returned to their units, and soon the battalion was on the road again.

Kilometer by kilometer we inched along, scouting out potential position areas along Powerline Road (which had been designated Route Blue). It was a relatively uneventful, even painfully boring, process, and at times it seemed like just another training evolution. But as I stood in the turret daydreaming, my thoughts were interrupted by the battalion commander's voice screaming over the radio.

"Break, break, break!" he yelled, signaling everyone to clear the battalion net. "Charlie-Six, this is Highlander-Six! If I see one more Marine from your company throw MRE trash out of your vehicles I'm going to make you personally police up Route Blue!"

"Roger that, Highlander-Six," replied Gil casually.

Lance Corporal Davis and I turned and looked at each other, our eyebrows raised.

"What was that all about, sir?" he asked.

"I don't know, but that's the last thing we need," I said, clicking my headset over to the company net. "Guidons, this is Black-Six. If you haven't been listening to the battalion net, make sure your vehicles aren't tossing their garbage out of the vehicles. I don't want to have clean up after the company."

It was hard to believe, but, of all things, garbage had become an issue. In peacetime training you bag up your garbage and carry it with you out of the training area to a dumpster in the rear. It was one of those things everyone had accepted as the norm over the years. At the war's beginning all units had been instructed to do the same, to bag up their garbage and carry it with them. It had lasted about a day or so. MREs produce a lot of trash. An LAR company has 130 men in it. Each man ate between two and three MREs a day. That's a minimum of 260 MREs' packaging material produced by a company *per day.* There was no way we could haul it all. Soon companies all over the regiment and the division were doing the only thing possible: we were burning our trash. Any time a unit was stopped along the side of the road for a significant period of time Marines would dig deep holes and start fires within them. Then they would begin tossing in crate after crate of MRE waste and stand around the flames like bums warming their hands. Any assembly area, defensive position, or laager site we passed was dotted with the orange glow of trash fires. The sickeningly sweet aroma of roasting food, foil pouches, and cardboard constantly filled our noses. It was an odd smell, one I will always associate with the war.

While it was true that garbage had suddenly become a major logistical affair, the battalion commander's public chiding of Capt Juarez over the battalion radio net hadn't been appropriate. I thought of all the times I had made similar errors in chastising my platoon commanders over the radio for trivial things. The list was long. But to hear the same thing done to a company commander by the battalion commander seemed a bad leadership example, and I vowed never to do the same thing again to my platoon commanders. It was one thing to make an immediate correction over the radio if the tactical situation warranted it. But for something as benign as Marines tossing garbage out of their LAVs to incur the commander's public wrath was not what we needed at the moment. I knew we would hear about it again as soon as we stopped.

The call came for a mission shift, and together the company commanders linked up with the Battalion Forward for another frag order. With the logjam that had developed at the An Numinayah bridgehead, the RCT needed to know if any other crossing sites over the Tigris River existed. Taking the lead as the battalion's main effort, Delta Company was directed to lead the reconnaissance along Powerline Road, while Weapons and Charlie Companies were assigned additional missions to locate lateral routes parallel to our own. It was a simple and to the point frag order, and as the three of us stood to return to our vehicles the battalion commander stopped us.

"Hey," he said, referring to the garbage issue. There was discernable anger in his voice. "Listen, I don't get pissed off like that very often, but I don't want to see that kind of unprofessional shit again. Does everyone understand me?"

"Yes, sir," we all replied in unison. I wondered if LtCol White was just as frustrated as we were at how things were shaping up for the battalion. We had been promised front row seats for the "Big Show." But now it felt like someone had pulled the old "bait and switch" trick on us, and we were going to have to settle on the nosebleed seats. As we walked back toward our vehicles, I turned to Dave.

"One day we're gonna look back on this," I said vapidly, lighting a cigarette "and just laaaaaaaaugh." I figured that was the best way to look at the situation, given that we all had our *own* shoes to fill.

As I approached my vehicle, I yelled to LCpl Davis to radio for the platoon commanders. A minute later their LAVs pulled up alongside us.

"Okay," I said, pointing to my map. "We've only got about a minute before we have to be back on the road. You know the drill: we're here." I pointed to a circle on Powerline Road. "We're taking the lead and continuing the recon along Route Blue. Weapons and Charlie will look for lateral routes. Our order of march will be SOP. Questions?"

"How far are we going?" asked Capt Portiss.

"Don't know yet," I replied. "We'll just keep going until we either find another place to cross the Tigris or the battalion tells us to stop."

"Is it true the battalion commander got a contact yesterday?" someone asked.

"Yeah, he did," I answered.

"I feel like I'm taking crazy pills," Lt Cullins said dryly, quoting an appropriate line from a movie. There were mumblings of "Yeah, no shit" among the other officers.

"Don't worry about it," I said. "Just keep your eyes open. Let's get going."

Our movement northwest along Powerline Road began once again, and several kilometers up the road I realized the strain I might be putting on 1st Platoon. Our company's SOP had always called for 1st Platoon to be the vanguard echelon during movements like the one we were conducting, but since the war's beginning Lt Parment's men had been on point the entire time. Despite the Marines' public desire to continuously be the lead element for the company, it was a position that was both dangerous and tiring. Although a traditional ambush will allow the lead unit to pass and focus its firepower on a column's main body, the Fedayeen had in the previous week proven their tactic to be to hit the lead units first. Being out on our own as the tip of the battalion's spear along Powerline Road, it was important to keep a fresh set of eyes on point.

I radioed Lieutenants Schwartz and Parment and directed Schwartz to bound his platoon forward and relieve 1st Platoon on point. Despite understanding my reasoning for the switch, Parment acknowledged the order with noticeable disappointment in his voice. I couldn't fault him. No self-respecting Marine ever wants to be put back in the rear of the column.

With 2nd Platoon in the lead, Delta Company proceeded forward along Powerline Road in our fruitless quest for another crossing site over the Tigris River. Ahead of us, a canal branched off south from the river and ran right to left across our front. Flanked by steep levees with a well-worn trail running along each embankment, the canal was a formidable obstacle, crossable only by a narrow bridge connected to the paved road on which we traveled. The canal's depth was unknown, and with its steep banks it was unlikely any vehicle that eased down into it would be able to climb back out. It was also a perfect ambush site. Anyone waiting on the other side of the canal would have a clear shot at the first vehicle to appear over the crest of the canal's embankment. As the vehicles from 2nd Platoon slowly approached the canal's crossing point, Lt Schwartz's voice suddenly filled the radio net.

"Contact! Contact!" he yelled. "One technical! Stand by!" The company's slow moving column jerked to a halt, and a moment later a thick cloud of black smoke climbed into the sky to our front.

"White-One," I radioed urgently. "Give me a sit-rep. What's going on up there?"

"Roger that, Black-Six," Schwartz replied, excitement rimming his voice. "We just blew the shit out of a technical coming at us." He giddily described how his lead vehicle, commanded by Sergeant Matthew Rea, had spotted a yellow pickup truck speeding down the road toward them. When the truck's driver saw the LAVs ahead of him, he swerved his vehicle south along the canal's embankment in a futile attempt to escape. A tarpaulin covering the truck's flatbed blew backward, revealing what appeared to be either a heavy machine gun or a recoilless rifle mounted behind the cab. Schwartz's section responded by opening fire on the fleeing technical with their main guns. As the 25mm HEI-T rounds slammed into the truck's side in a shower of sparks, it burst into bright orange flames and careened headfirst into the canal.

I sped forward to check it out, and by the time I pulled alongside Schwartz's section a team of scouts was already on the ground cautiously approaching the crash site. One thing was certain: whoever had been inside the truck's cab wouldn't bother anyone else again. I peered through my binoculars from my position, but there wasn't much left to see of the technical's occupants. Schwartz would later recall how the approaching vehicle had been so close that he could see the look of fear frozen into the truck driver's face as he drove to beat the devil. Schwartz added that the impact of the 25mm rounds exploding into the left door had thrown the driver into the passenger's lap. The mangled hulk burned and smoked for quite a while, and soon the ammunition stored in it began cooking off in violent, secondary explosions.

"Good job, White-One," I said into the radio, pleased.

"Thank-you, sir," Schwartz replied.

"Hey, Black-Six," radioed Sgt Rea, sounding hurt. "We hit him, also."

"Okay," I replied jovially. "Good on you, too."

We resumed movement up the road, and as the company passed beyond the canal I learned that tanks and amtracks from the RCT would be passing

Scout team from 2nd Platoon advances toward destroyed technical near the Tigris River, 3 April 2003. Official Marine Corps photo by LCpl Andrew P. Roufs.

through our battalion. Their destination was a small town along the banks of the Tigris called Al Aziziyah. The information was passed to me as more of a "heads up" message—Delta Company would be well forward when the RCT vehicles passed through Weapons Company's position. I wondered what was going on in Al Aziziyah. We learned that 2nd Tanks and 3/5 assaulted across Highway 6 right into the teeth of an enemy mechanized battalion in Al Aziziyah. It would end up being the most significant engagement by the RCT of conventional Iraqi army forces during the course of the war. I would later surmise that the technical destroyed by Lt Schwartz's platoon had been fleeing the town and had run right into us. Talk about it not being your day.

Several kilometers up the road our column came to a halt again.

"Black-Six, this is White-One," called Schwartz. "One of my ATs has spotted something a couple of klicks up the road that looks like an armored vehicle."

"Can you tell what it is?" I asked, looking at my map.

"Negative. I don't have eyes-on. I'm talking to the AT crew about it right now." From our position, the phantom vehicle was little more than a small black smudge far ahead of us. Even the thermal viewers in our LAV-25s couldn't make out what it was facing us. We had to rely on the LAV-AT crew with its more powerful sights. After staring intently at it for a while, I realized this Mexican standoff would get us nowhere. Suddenly, a boom reverberated up ahead of me. I looked to see the signature white smoke cloud of a TOW missile launch from one of the ATs. All eyes focused on the wire guided tank killer as it rocketed forward to its final destination. Twenty seconds later the missile found its target. An orange fireball enveloped it, and a moment later the report of the impact echoed back toward us.

"Black-Six," radioed the TOW vehicle commander. "My crew saw a turret and a gun barrel before we fired."

"Roger that, Green-Two," I replied, some hesitation in my voice. "Stand by." I flipped the radio to the battalion's frequency.

"Break, break!" I called, interrupting Capt Bone's transmission. "This is Dragon-Six. I need the Three or the Six, over."

"Dragon-Six, this is Highlander-Eight," Bone answered. "Send your traffic."

"Negative," I responded stubbornly. "I need the *Three or the Six!*"

"Stand by, Dragon-Six," he replied. I was nervous. Friendly tanks were supposed to be coming up behind us. I didn't expect any to be forward of us, but I rechecked my map to make sure we were where we needed to be.

"Dragon-Six, this is Highlander-Three," radioed Maj Harper. "Send your traffic."

"We just took out what looks like an armored vehicle up here," I said a bit hesitantly. "But we can't get a positive ID on it yet. We're inching up on it now."

"Stand by, Dragon-Six," Harper replied. As Schwartz's platoon gradually advanced, I waited on the radio for what seemed like an eternity while Maj Harper conferred with his operations and fire support officers. They were no doubt trying to determine if any friendly tanks had gotten around them and forward of Delta Company. Lieutenant Schwartz radioed first.

"Black-Six, it looks like an anti-aircraft piece. We've got a pretty clear view of it now." I initially felt a stab of anger that the missile crew had launched without radioing first. But then I thought *Well, if they identified it as a threat, then good to go.* It was unreasonable to demand that the platoons report to me every time they had an enemy vehicle in their sights. Their quick reaction could end up meaning the difference between life and death for them. I just had to trust that they knew where they were on the map and, perhaps more important, where everyone else was.

I still couldn't see exactly what the target was, and my vehicle pushed forward with Lt Schwartz's section to investigate it. I reported my intentions to 1stSgt Guzman, and the tone in his voice signaled that he was getting irritated with me for constantly leaving him behind while I checked things out with the lead platoon. I couldn't help it. Never satisfied with a mere verbal report, I always had to see something for myself.

Ahead of us a long file of Iraqi refugees migrated down the road toward our column. It was a mixture of young and old men, women, and children. The men wore mostly western clothing—trousers and shirts. Several wore dishdashas. Most of the women were clad in flowing black robes. As they made their way south in their slow hegira, all of them waved. But as in our zone reconnaissance near Ad Diwaniyah, few smiled. For whatever reason, they had left their homes somewhere far up ahead of us. No doubt they blamed us and our advancing armored column. Although we had encountered Iraqi refugees in small groups before then, this was the first major exodus we saw. They didn't seem to care about us as we drove past.

We approached the missile's impact site. Rather than finding an armored vehicle as the AT crew had thought it to be, we instead found an S-60 anti-aircraft gun. It had been aimed down the road away from us, and all around the burned-out wreckage were strewn dozens of 57mm projectiles. They had been blown sky-high when the TOW hit it. I thought for a moment that the Iraqis had simply dumped the S-60 off on the side of the road and forgotten about it. But after finding a stack of rounds seated in the gun's breach, I realized it hadn't been abandoned by the side of the road after all. It appeared as if the Iraqi army had positioned the piece down the long axis of the road with the intention of using it in direct-fire mode against our advancing forces. Palm fronds—what was left of someone's attempt at camouflage—still clung to the gun's tube. Unfortunately for them, whoever had manned it had oriented the S-60 the wrong way, and our gunners had caught it from the rear. I scanned the immediate area for any sign of the enemy gun crew, but there was nothing. No blood, no clothing. Once again, the enemy had vanished.

The four vehicles that comprised the Forward pulled up, enabling the battalion leadership to survey the scene for themselves. Staff members gathered around the S-60 in small groups, examining the wreckage. After briefing the battalion commander and the S-3 on what had happened, I expected to be chastised because my TOW crew had engaged it before it had positive identification of the AAA piece. Instead, Maj Harper pointed to a position on the map five kilometers ahead of us.

"We're going to set into a screen for the night," he said. "Position your company along the right flank. We'll be moving again in the morning."

"What's next?" I asked.

"Not sure yet," he replied. "We'll probably continue to look for another way across the river."

Whatever you say, I thought, returning to my LAV. *As long as we don't have to swim it.*

14

The Elbow

No sooner had Delta Company arranged itself in a tightly formed screen anchored into Powerline Road and near a small village called Az Zubadayah than I received a radio call from the S-3.

"Move out. Time: now," Maj Harper said. "We need to continue the recon along Route Blue and continue the search for another fording site across the Tigris."

"Roger that," I said, trying in vain to conceal my weariness. It had already been a long day, and I had looked forward to being stationary, if only for a couple of hours. "We're Oscar Mike." I handed the radio handset back to LCpl Davis and yelled to everyone around me, "Mount up!" The Marines knew that meant "Drop what you're doing, we're leaving immediately." Echoes of "mount up!" rang out up and down the line of vehicles, and after a quick radio brief we were on the move again along Powerline Road.

The speed with which my Marines responded to my orders constantly amazed me. We had always bragged about our ability to move fast, and in Iraq the Marines were proving it when it mattered the most. We could displace at a moment's notice, and the Marines knew that the quicker we moved, the more likely we were to keep getting missions. We were eager. We were naïve.

But we had also become complacent. The war had been waging for two weeks. Despite the tragedy of losing one of our own only seven days earlier and the close call with the rocket attack in Ad Diwaniyah, a sense of skepticism still existed deep in our hearts. Every battalion within RCT-5 had been involved in a major engagement—every battalion, that is, except 1st LAR Battalion. As RCT-5 began to fight its way up Highway 6 closer and closer toward Baghdad, we resigned ourselves to being sidelined. The battalion had been directed to go out and "do some of that reconnaissance stuff" on the periphery while the RCT's infantry battalions and tank battalion duked it out with the Republican Guard ahead of us. There seemed little chance we would run into any enemy activity in our assigned zone. But, as usual, it always happens when you least expect it.

That's why it's called an ambush.

Lieutenant Cullins and 3rd Platoon had leaped forward and taken the lead as the point unit in Delta Company's column. To the left and right of the paved road the usual scenery greeted us: wet scrubland benefiting from the irrigation provided by the Tigris River. Spacious farmland surrounded us in all directions. One look at the ground told me there was no way we could go off-road without the vehicles sinking deep into the mud. The earth in this region would be about as solid as Play-Doh. The closer we got to the river, the greener the vegetation was. The number of tiny villages and hamlets likewise increased, and as we passed each habitation few people waved or even bothered to look at us. We were, after all, approaching Baghdad and its Sunni Muslim population. Although we hadn't exactly received a hero's welcome by the Shi'as in the south as had been expected, we knew we were unlikely to get any support from the Sunnis. As the minority group ruling in Iraq, the Sunnis knew they had everything to lose by the Americans' coming. No one likes being booted off when he's king of the hill.

As Powerline Road neared the river, it turned north into a straight line, which then curved abruptly to the northwest just before hitting the water. From this "elbow" in the road the banks of the river were barely visible through a thick copse of palm trees and tall river grass. Farther down the road, beyond the elbow, another village peeked out from behind a date palm grove and a small berm that seemed to act as a wall surrounding the community. Straddling a narrow canal fed by the Tigris, the village included a number of small buildings, several of which were two or three stories in height. The rationale for the village's location was obvious. Being situated next to the river enabled the inhabitants to not only irrigate their crops, but also to be near a constant source of water for drinking, cooking, and laundry. They were the same reasons people have lived by the water for thousands of years. Perhaps in another time and another war the village would have been defended simply to protect its position near the river. But not now. In the words of the main character from the movie *Platoon,* if they had known we were coming that day they would have fled.

Tailing 3rd Platoon and its two attached LAV-ATs, my vehicle began to slow down as Lt Cullins's lead section rounded the bend of the elbow. I looked down at my map board to confirm our position along Route Blue. Since the start of our highway war we had taken to reporting the leading trace of our positions—within both the company and the battalion—by northings and eastings (the east-west and north-south grid lines on a map). As fast as we had been moving, and because we were largely restricted to the roads, it was simply easier to report a two- or three-digit northing or easting rather than a six- or eight-digit grid coordinate. If the lead unit reported it was at the 20 northing, finding its position was merely a matter of looking at your map and running a finger up the route until you hit that particular grid line.

Although riding in the turret of an LAV provides a better view of the surrounding terrain, there is one downside: you can't hear a thing. The constant radio and intercom traffic from the earpieces of your CVC helmet combines with the whine and rumbling of the LAV's diesel engine to block out nearly all outside noises. It's easy to get wrapped up in your own little world and lose track of what is going on around you. Staring at my map and eavesdropping on the battalion radio net, I felt LCpl Davis beating his fist against my flak jacket. He shouted into the intercom.

"Holy *shee*-it! Look!"

I lifted my head from where it had been buried in the map, only to see tiny puffs of dirt shooting up around the vehicles of 3rd Platoon like steam vents opening and closing. The tiny puffs suddenly became tall jets of brown earth kicking up around the vehicles. An RPG exploded in a white flash on the ground alongside an LAV. Then another. Then another.

✦ ✧ ✦

There is a technique in film editing where the action of a scene is depicted normally, slows down for a moment, then suddenly speeds up to normal again as if to catch up to real time. This effect is created by the camera using different shutter speeds and running the film at varying rates. Directors have employed the technique to convey the confusion, fast pace, and fog of war. I would later learn that this shuttered, slow-motion sensation is actually a common experience in firefights. The slow, crisp picture one sees during such a situation is produced by the human brain rapidly processing sensory information to allow a person to make decisions and act in a timely manner. But I didn't know that then. I experienced it for the first time at "the Elbow" on 3 April.

✦ ✧ ✦

There was a moment—a brief moment, perhaps five seconds, maybe longer—when I stood there in my turret staring dumbly at the ground erupting around 3rd Platoon. It didn't make sense. I couldn't see anybody shooting at them, but suddenly 3rd Platoon began firing back into the tree line that partially obscured my view of them. The concussion from the firing cannons blew the caked dust off the vehicle hulls in sheets, and even through the barrier of my helmet I heard the deep bass thudding of the 25mm rounds exiting the barrels. It was the sound of what many Marines in the battalion called "the big dogs barking." Lieutenant Cullins's shouts over the company radio net interrupted my momentary daze.

"Contact! Contact! L-shaped ambush!"

I reached down and flipped the radio control lever to the battalion frequency. The chatter on which I had eavesdropped seconds earlier continued unabated on the battalion net, those transmitting oblivious to what transpired in front of my vehicle. I doublekeyed the headset to clear the voice traffic from the net, and then shouted into my microphone.

"Break, break, break! This is Dragon-Six! Contact! Contact! My lead platoon is caught in an L-shaped ambush at the three-seven northing, over!"

"Roger that, Dragon-Six," a voice replied. "Stand by."

Trying to keep my cool, I called back to Cullins.

"Blue-One, this is Six. Tell me what you got out there."

"Roger, Six." As he transmitted, in the background I could hear the pinging noise of bullets ricocheting off his LAV's steel hull and the sharp *ka-chunk, ka-chunk, ka-chunk* of his main gun cycling and belching out rounds. "A platoon, maybe more. Small arms, RPGs. Fighting positions across the road at the canal bridge and next to us in the tree line."

"Roger, I copy." From his report and what I could see from my vantage point, 3rd Platoon was practically on top of the enemy positions. They were too close for artillery or close air support. *Belt buckle tactics,* I said to myself, thinking about the Viet Cong's method of avoiding American artillery. *They waited until the company was right next to them.* We needed maneuver space between them and us if we wanted to employ combined arms. I keyed my headset again.

"Pull back, Blue-One. Pull your platoon back so we can hammer them." I redirected my attention to Capt Portiss and his FiST team, knowing they would already be hard at work looking for a fire-support solution. "Black-Five, this is Six. What do you have for us?" I spun my head to see Portiss's vehicle halted along the road's shoulder next to 1stSgt Guzman, the FiST team already huddled together on top of the LAV-C2 like a football team planning its next play. Portiss answered immediately.

"Black-Six, roger. Fox-Two-Eleven is reorienting to support. Spool is working with Mud Duck right now to bring in a section of F/A-18s and a division of Cobras. Mortars are fire-capped right now."

Ahead of me Lt Cullins had begun directing his vehicles backward one by one to the Elbow's beginning. The LAVs fired in all directions. Gunners traversed the turrets one way, firing the main guns, while the vehicle com-

Delta Company fire support team (FiST) coordinates air, artillery, and mortar fires in support of 3rd Platoon in the ambush at the Elbow, 3 April 2003. (L to R: Cpl Calvin Byrd, Capt Christian Portiss, Capt Mike "Spool" Peitz, LCpl José Vargas.) Photo by Sgt Isaac McCorkle.

manders aimed bursts of fire in the opposite direction with their scissor-mounted machine guns. Scouts popped up and down in the vehicles' rear hatches in ones and twos, blazing away into the enemy's fighting positions. Through all of this the LAVs gradually eased backward in short bounds, away from the ambush's killing zone.

"Solid copy," I replied, acknowledging Portiss's report. "Blue-One is engaged; give him terminal control to spot for the mortars and arty. Blue-One, did you copy that?"

"Black-Six, this is Blue-One-Golf," responded Lance Corporal William Senn, Cullins's gunner. "One-Actual's talking to the platoon. I'll relay." Senn, who had been with the company as long as I had, was a consummate joker and skilled storyteller. Once, while the company had gathered for a brew-up after a week of training in the Mojave Desert, he made me laugh so hard I sprayed Guinness out of my nose. Senn had practically been a boy then. Now the intense voice on the other end of the radio sounded like a completely different person—older, wiser, more serious. There was nothing to laugh about now.

"Roger," Portiss replied. "Blue-One, go to mortar conduct of fire net to talk to the FDC [fire direction center]."

"One-Golf copies."

Then someone's voice spoke up on the company frequency. I couldn't tell whose it was.

"We're taking fire!" it shouted. "We're taking fire from the buildings!"

Another voice jumped into the fray. "I can see them moving into the buildings!"

Too much traffic crowded the company net. Portiss and I needed to be able to talk to Cullins, and I worried that all the clutter jamming the radio would cause a panic. I keyed my headset.

"Break, break, this is Black-Six. Clear the net. Blue-One, tell me what's going on. Paint me a picture."

"Six, this is Blue-One," Cullins had returned to the radio. "They're falling back from their positions into the tree line and the village ahead of us. We're taking fire from the built-up area."

"Roger, One. You have control where you are. Just tell me what you need to support you."

The concussion of a nearby vehicle blasting away with its main gun snared my attention. Turning in the turret, I saw 1stSgt Guzman's main gun letting loose a stream of high explosive rounds across the field and over the berm toward the village. Davis's voice appeared on the intercom.

"Sir, I can't see anything out there," he said, the turret slowly scanning back and forth in the direction of the village to our west.

"Don't shoot if you don't have a target." I looked off to my left. On the road behind Guzman's LAV the vehicles of 1st and 2nd Platoons screamed toward our position. Their desire to support 3rd Platoon was understandable. The three lieutenants had been together for over two years. They had practically lived on top of each other for six months on ship. The mere fact that they had survived that without strangling each other guaranteed that they would be close for life. Despite very different leadership styles and outlooks on life, they would walk through fire for each other. But as I assessed how crowded the entrance to the Elbow had become, I grew concerned that we would get logjammed quickly along the road. I radioed Lt Parment, whose platoon led the cavalry charge.

"Red-One, orient your fires outboard, west toward the buildings," I said. "White-One, stay to Red Platoon's left in the attack-by-fire position. Orient your fires in the same direction." Both lieutenants acknowledged their orders, and one by one their LAVs herringboned left of the road to face the village. As each vehicle rolled to a stop its main gun opened fire, the overpressure of the exiting rounds sending up the same towers of shuddering dust from the hull.

"All Dragon Victors, shot, over," called Portiss, signaling that our mortars were in the air. Twenty seconds later high explosive rounds impacted forward of 3rd Platoon. Portiss spoke again. "Black-Six, Blue-One, be advised: Cobras are inbound right now. Arty is ready to fire."

"Dragon-Six, this is Highlander-Three," called Maj Harper. "What's your situation?"

"Three, this is Dragon-Six. My lead platoon is pulling out of the kill zone. We've got a base of fire going along with our eighty-ones. We're waiting for the air and arty, over."

"Roger, we're pushing Warlord up behind you to secure your rear. Let us know what you need."

"Roger that, I copy. But it looks like we're good right now. We're killing these fuckers out here."

Lieutenant Cullins's voice returned to the company net with a warning.

"Stand by. This arty mission is gonna be danger-close." Still with the best view of the ambush zone, he had begun calling in artillery onto the fleeing enemy around him.

Sixty seconds later the first volley of 155mm high explosive rounds impacted north of his position. They landed in the Tigris River, sending great geysers of muddy water high into the air. Cullins radioed a correction, and soon rounds plummeted fewer than 200 meters from his vehicles. *Jesus,* I thought, shaking my head. *That's close.* Another adjustment from Cullins, and shells began landing around the buildings to our front. From the east another sound filled my ears. The *whup-whup-whup* of rotor blades from four Cobras sliced through the late afternoon air, and in groups of two the gunships circled over our heads like giant, metallic dragonflies. Spool's voice materialized over the radio net.

"They're all ours, Black-Six. All Victors, make sure you have your air panels mounted with the orange side out." Crewmen and scouts up and down the line of vehicles hastily shook and beat the flimsy vinyl VS-17 panels strapped to the rear of their turrets. Used to identify friendly vehicles from the air, the air panels were like magnets for the dust kicked up by the vehicles. The Marines frequently had to shake the dirt from the panel markers to make them visible.

"Roger," I replied to Spool. "Turn them over to Blue-One."

"One copies," Cullins said. "I'm off the net to talk to the birds. One-Golf will relay for me."

His voice went silent as he switched frequencies to direct the fires of the helicopters. Moments later the four Cobras passed low over the company's heads, spraying thundering volleys of cannon-fire and rockets into the tree line and the building facades. Pass after pass, the helicopters punished the built-up area in front of us, the bricks twinkling like Christmas tree lights from the impact of the high explosive rounds. Returning for another run, the gunships took turns launching TOW missiles, which snaked back and forth wildly before entering the buildings' windows and detonating inside. Magnificent clouds of black, white, and gray smoke billowed up from within the village. Glancing back in the turret, I caught a glimpse of LCpl Roufs hanging off the side of the vehicle. As he snapped pictures of the unfolding destruction a wide grin filled his face. *Oh, I can't wait to get a copy of those,* I thought.

Spool's voice buzzed once again in my earphones.

"Stand by. I just got a hold of a section of Hornets to drop some thousand-pounders." Almost immediately, an F/A-18 high above us released a Mk-83 bomb into the palm grove next to the canal bridge. The shiny aircraft veered away from the target, leaving a trail of shimmering red flares in its wake to fool any inbound surface-to-air missiles searching for the glow of its afterburner. With a deafening *crrr-ack* the ground ahead of us shook as an enormous cloud of black smoke shot into the air.

"Jesus!" I said. "What the hell was *that?!*"

"The pilot just told me he saw a vehicle in the tree line," Spool replied.

"Good to go." I quickly turned my attention to my gunner in the bowels of the turret. "Come on Davis, man, find us a target."

"God-*dammit!*" he shouted in frustration. "There's too much dust and smoke and shit, sir! I can't see a fucking thing!"

"Don't worry about it. But don't shoot unless you see something." As those words left my lips, I looked back at the column. It seemed as if every LAV-25 in the company was pouring rounds into the buildings and the surrounding tree line. The earth in the palm grove ahead of us rippled and exploded with such force that a wall of dust, smoke, and debris began to block our view of the buildings. *So much for "proportionality of return fires,"* I thought. Keying my headset, I repeated what I had just told Davis.

"All Victors, this is Black-Six. Everybody calm down. If you don't have the enemy in your sights you shouldn't be firing. Don't pull that trigger unless you have eyes on a target." Turning around inside the turret, I also realized that the company had oriented the majority of its firepower to the west. As a result, our collective derrière was exposed to the open farmland east of our position. Not knowing if the order had been passed by the platoon commanders yet, I radioed the company again.

"All Victors not directly engaged to the west need to orient to our east. I don't want anyone sneaking up on us and blowing our asses off."

"Roger, Six, we're oriented out-board," added Parment quickly.

A small car filled with an Iraqi family sped up the length of the company's column from behind. Somehow they had bypassed the bulk of the battalion, and with a fragment of white fabric tied to the vehicle's side view mirror to indicate their peaceful intentions they must have thought they would be allowed safe passage ahead of us. Marines frantically waved and shouted, desperately trying to stop the family before it drove into the middle of the company's onslaught. For whatever reason, they saw no danger in driving through the middle of our firefight. As they approached 1stSgt Guzman's vehicle, Lt Cullins radioed me.

"Black-Six, this is Blue-One. Be advised, I've got a visual on some enemy personnel trying to escape along the river. They just went inside a building behind us. I've got the Cobras inbound on them right now."

"Roger that," I replied. Fifty feet above, a helicopter rocketed down the length of the company, lining up its sights on the small mud hovel behind 3rd Platoon's vehicles. I craned my neck up to watch, and as the aircraft passed overhead it released a sustained volley of cannon and rocket-fire. A wave of heat hit me in the face as the rockets spewed from their pods and ripped through the air only meters above us. They were *that* close. The rocket fusillade careened into the hut, smoldering it in a fiery paroxysm of smoking clay bricks and wooden splinters.

Oh my God, I thought repeatedly. *Shit this close to vehicles would never be authorized in peacetime.*

"Well, Blue-One, you've made quite a mess out here today," I said sarcastically, staring at the flaming wreck of the mud hut. "Did that do the trick?"

"Yeah, Six," he replied dryly. "They're dead, all right."

The annihilation of the hut in front of them convinced the Iraqi family in the car to turn around suddenly and head south. The Cobras continued to loiter in wide circles above us, occasionally angling in to fire again. Spool called me again.

"Black-Six, do we have any more work for these guys?"

A heavy haze of acrid smoke and dust blanketed the ground and buildings in front of us. No one was shooting back at us anymore. The engagement appeared to be over. I glanced around again, and then keyed my headset.

"Negative," I said, pulling out a cigarette. "Send them home. Tell them I said thanks."

"They're asking for a BDA, Six."

I clicked the headset. "Blue-One, what's the BDA up there?"

"I'd say about forty enemy KIA, Black-Six. Give or take. There isn't much left of anything up here."

Cobra gunships in support of Delta Company during the ambush at the Elbow, 3 April 2003. Official Marine Corps photo by LCpl Andrew P. Roufs.

"That's it for the arty, too, Black-Six," added Portiss. "They have to pull trails."

The departing helicopters sped east over the company's battle position one last time, leaving the destruction at the Elbow in their wake. I dragged heavily on my cigarette and continued to stare at what was left of the ambush zone in front of us. A fire had begun in the tree line, and a spiraling tongue of flame licked up from the vegetation. The village was silent. Davis popped up next to me and unleashed a flurry of profanity, enraged that he had never gotten a shot off during the entire engagement.

"Jesus, calm down, man," I said. "You'll get your chance. Relax." Looking around again, I realized I owed the battalion a situation report.

"Highlander, this is Dragon-Six. Engagement complete. We're ready to continue forward with the recon."

"Negative, Dragon-Six. Prepare to fall back and rally with the battalion. We'll be crossing the river back at An Numinayah tonight."

"Roger, copy all."

The sun sank in front of us, silhouetting the smashed buildings of the village. The firefight had lasted perhaps twenty minutes, maybe thirty. I didn't know. As I prepared to relay the change of plans to the platoons, Lt Cullins radioed again.

"Black-Six, we've got a minivan coming toward us. Looks like the people in it are getting out with their hands up and coming toward us." Eight Iraqis, including a woman clad from head to toe in a black robe, spilled out of the van and walked cautiously down the road away from the direction of the village. Waving scraps of white material above their heads, they looked like they might have been fleeing the death and destruction that had rained down upon them earlier. We couldn't be sure, though. For all we knew, they had been part of the ambush and were now trying to escape by playing the scared civilian role.

"Roger that," I replied. "Search them. Hold them in place."

Two scout teams jumped from LAVs in front of me and ran toward the Iraqis. Their rifles at the ready and aimed at the refugees, they shouted for the Iraqis to continue forward. As the Marines frisked each man and woman, looking for weapons, I studied the scene through my binoculars. Several of the men were older, and all of them looked like locals. As one of the scouts patted down the old woman and methodically sifted through the folds of her flowing *abayah,* part of me remembered our training from the MEU. We had learned to always try to get another woman to search female suspects. *Idiot!* I chided myself. *Who cares about that shit right now! You just got your ass ambushed. Forget that textbook shit and concentrate on the matter at hand!* It was just one more of those times where rote training in certain areas interfered with common sense on the ground. After a minute or two it was clear that the Iraqis being searched weren't a threat to us. Then Lt Cullins radioed again.

"Black-Six, we've got movement out in front of us. It looks like they're trying to reoccupy their fighting positions." *Christ,* I thought. *Don't these people ever give up?* I weighed the risks. Was it necessary to go in and clear them out? After all, the battalion was waiting for us. But I saw no alternative—I didn't want the company to have to fight the same guys closer to Baghdad. Besides, I was pissed off that these bastards had had the balls to shoot at us in the first place. I keyed the radio once more.

"Roger that, Blue-One. Let's go in there and get those fuckers. Leave your ATs back where they are. Everyone else stay put. We'll be back shortly." Switching over to the vehicle's intercom, I spoke to the crew.

"Okay, Gurganus, move out slowly behind Third Platoon. Davis, yell back to Harter and Kodak to pop up and cover our ass." Davis leaned back in his seat and relayed my orders to the Marines in the scout compartment; then he pushed his eye up to the main gun's optical sight. Squeezing the palm trigger and powering up the turret, he slowly traversed the turret back and forth, alternating his visual scanning between the right and left sides of the LAV. Tucking the M240 firmly in the crook of my right shoulder, I radioed Cullins.

"Move out, Blue-One. We're right behind you."

"Roger, Blue Victors are Oscar Mike."

Rolling at a snail's pace one after the other, the five LAV-25s slowly rounded the bend of the Elbow. My heart raced, and my index finger tightened around the M240's trigger. With every main gun, machine gun, and rifle facing steadily outboard, I knew the Marines of 3rd Platoon would be on a hair trigger. Because they had been the ones most fully caught in the ambush in the first place, they were no doubt more pissed off than I was. It wouldn't take much to get them firing into the tree line. Fifty meters beyond the Elbow, flanked on our left by the palm grove and on our right by the banks of the Tigris, Cullins's lead section opened fire again.

Thump, thump, thump. The luminescent red tracers of HEI-T rounds exploded into radiant showers of orange sparks in the shadows of the palm grove.

A pause. We continued to scan. Another LAV ahead of us fired.

Thump, thump, thump.

Visibility along the road and in the tree line deteriorated. The smoke and dust from the firefight earlier had settled around us into a thick ground fog that clung to the earth, unmoving. The sun was below the horizon. With the buildings and palm grove blocking most of what remained of the direct sunlight, we would soon be fighting in the dark. We could be in a very bad spot rather quickly. For some stupid reason I thought back to one of Bill Cosby's old lines: "It's getting dark. Almost time for the monsters to come out."

"Do you have a visual on anything else up there, Blue-One?"

"Negative, Six."

"I think our job is done here. It's time to go," I said. "We're burning daylight. I don't want to get trapped out here in the dark. Fall back to the company's battle positions."

"Roger. Copy all, Black-Six."

Inside his driver's compartment, Gurganus shifted the LAV into reverse. As we inched backward along the Elbow to our original starting position I radioed the company.

"Guidons, prepare to fall back and link up with the battalion. Execute an 'Australian peel' from this position. Blue Platoon will peel first and the rest will go from there. By the time we're on the road the company needs to be back in our SOP march order."

Cullins's lead LAV pulled off the line and bounded behind the other vehicles until it was at the rear of the formation. This leapfrogging action continued one vehicle at a time until the company was reoriented farther down the road. The "Australian peel" was a relatively straightforward maneuver in theory, but not always so in practice. Yet the Marines executed it flawlessly, one vehicle after another speeding away behind the protection of the rest of the company. All it had taken from me was to say I wanted them to peel.

Simple moments like that, particularly in the face of what the company had just accomplished, made me proud of their abilities. But it also saddened me, as I began to realize they needed me less and less. I didn't know if they had ever really needed me. But in that brief firefight against the enemy, where each platoon of Marines and sailors had known exactly what to do and when to do it, little had been required of me. I would later be commended for my part in controlling the action of the engagement at the Elbow, but I and the Marines of Delta Company knew the truth: they had defeated the enemy on their own. I realized that Delta Company had just demonstrated action in combat indicative of good training and discipline, and I was just happy to have had the opportunity to play a role in their preparation for war.

The company formed up in a staggered column five kilometers to the south on Powerline Road. Each platoon reported in: no casualties, no loss of equipment. Ammunition replenishment requirements were forwarded to SSgt Kappen. It was difficult to contain my excitement. Then I remembered my bet with Lt Cullins. A year earlier, as we had prepared to depart for our WestPac, many had thought we would see action, perhaps in Somalia, perhaps in Yemen—we didn't know. The post-9/11 world was an uncertain place, and Cullins had been convinced Delta Company would execute a real-world operation. He had been sure we would see combat together. I had scoffed at the idea.

"Bullshit," I had said. "It'll never happen. Everywhere I go, peace breaks out."

"Care to make it interesting, sir?" he had replied.

The bet was placed: if the company was involved in an operation that resulted in the Marines being awarded the coveted Combat Action Ribbon, I would owe him a fifth of Jack Daniels. When the deployment ended with no joy, I tried to collect on the bet.

"How about double or nothing for Iraq, sir?" he had proposed. The bet was raised to a half-gallon. A half gallon of Jack. Not cheap, but it wouldn't exactly break the bank. Remembering all of this, I keyed my headset as the company resumed its march south to rendezvous with the battalion.

"Well, Blue-One, I guess I owe you a half gallon now, don't I?"

"Affirmative, Black-Six." The grin on his face penetrated the radio waves. Chuckling, I turned my attention back to the company.

"All Dragon Victors, this is Black-Six. Everybody did an outstanding job today. I'm proud of all of you." I thought for a moment, and then retransmitted. "I think you all just earned your Combat Action Ribbons."

The radio waves jammed with shouts of "Ooh-rah!" and *"Kill!"* We drove on into the night, laughing and yelling our heads off into our microphones. We were alive and loving every minute of it.

◆ ◇ ◆

Eventually the playful jabs back and forth over the radio net died down, and Delta Company got back to the business of linking up with 1st LAR Battalion. Far ahead of us along Powerline Road they waited. As we approached the long column, the battalion once again got underway for the bridge at An Numinayah. But as the exhilaration of the firefight ebbed and the realization of what we had done slowly sank in, I wondered if the company's reaction to the ambush had been overkill. In all, we had responded with thousands of rounds of cannon and machine-gun fire. Additionally, we had expended dozens of rockets and TOW missiles, several volleys of artillery and mortar fire, and a 1,000-pound bomb. We had swatted a fly with a sledgehammer. *Don't second-guess yourself,* I thought angrily. *They were trying to waste you. They would have, if they'd gotten the chance.*

And the village? We had taken fire from it—that much I knew. But had we gone overboard? Perhaps, but I couldn't afford to let myself think so. By ambushing our lead platoon and then cowardly using a village to fight from, the Fedayeen had unknowingly invoked the full wrath of Delta Company. Had there been civilians within the village when we opened up on it? Probably. But after hearing about what had happened to First Battalion, Second Marines (1/2) along "ambush alley" in An Nasiriyah on 23 March, I hadn't wanted to take any chances. The decision to direct the engagement toward the hamlet had been mine and mine alone. I didn't want to think about how many civilians inside the village might be dead or dying because of me, and I blocked the question from my mind. But I willingly accepted full responsibility for what happened that day. And it had happened for one, simple reason.

The enemy had been trying to kill my Marines.

15

Beyond the Tigris

Rolling along in the darkness and scanning the countryside through the soft green filter of my NVGs, I became aware of the new peril that faced the company: everyone was in danger of falling asleep at the wheel. I remembered back to stories of the 1991 Gulf War, where Marines in 1st LAI Battalion had been killed after participating in an artillery raid. The raid had been executed flawlessly, but as the LAV company returned from the mission the crews began to suffer from adrenaline crash. One LAV rear-ended another, killing the Marines asleep in the scout compartment.

With a long night-drive to the Tigris bridgehead ahead of us, I worried that someone would fall asleep at the wheel. My thoughts shifted to 1997 and a particularly grueling training exercise in which my company had participated. I recalled how, during a long, nighttime road march, my company commander had practically pleaded with the vehicle commanders over the radio to keep their drivers awake. Now I was doing the same.

"All Victors, this is Black-Six. It's been a long day, and now we're at the most dangerous part. We've got a long drive back to An Numinayah. Start talking to your drivers to keep them awake. Blue Platoon, you need to be especially aware. You've had a big adrenaline rush; you might come down hard. Everyone needs to do whatever you have to in order to keep your drivers awake. If you have to switch them out, then do it. I don't want anyone getting killed out here tonight after what we've just been through. Acknowledge."

Each vehicle commander spoke up, assuring me both he and his crew were good to go. For the moment I was satisfied, but this was no training exercise. The excitement I had often felt in the past after exercises paled in comparison to the electricity that coursed through Delta Company's bloodstream after our withdrawal from the Elbow. Soon my vehicle slowly veered to the right, and as it hit the gravel shoulder I shouted into the intercom.

"*Gurganus!* Wake the fuck up, man!"

"I'm awake, sir."

"Not a second ago you weren't. Do you need to switch out?"

"No sir, I'm good now."

"Yeah, I'll make sure of that." Feeling heavy-lidded myself, I stuffed a plug of tobacco in my bottom lip to revive my system. I considered breaking my own rules and lighting a cigarette in the darkened confines of the turret, but the crates of ammunition surrounding me persuaded me otherwise. I keyed the intercom again.

"Okay, Gurganus, listen up . . ." Six years after that demanding evening road march in southern California, history was repeating itself. Rolling along through the night, I began telling my life story to my driver to keep him awake.

✦ ✧ ✦

Kilometer after kilometer faded behind us as we traveled along through the evening, but the constant starting and stopping, the slowing down and then hurriedly speeding to catch up transformed the battalion into a massive Slinky. Known to Marines as the "accordion effect," it stretched us out into a column that reached for miles and miles into the night. Once Delta Company finally began moving again toward An Numinayah the clock approached midnight, local time. The town, which two days before had been visible for miles because of the burning hulks of armored vehicles destroyed by 2nd Tanks and 3/5, was silent and barely discernable from the surrounding landscape in the darkness. Rolling slowly through the empty streets, the company's vehicles cautiously rounded each corner. An Numinayah was the largest town we had entered since the war's beginning, and despite knowing it had been secured two days earlier I was still uneasy. But passing through it at night was far better in my opinion than doing so during the day, and as we approached the black waters of the Tigris I was relieved to be one town and one river closer to Baghdad. Perhaps more important to me, I wouldn't be ordered to swim the company across the river.

As the company filed across the bridge that spanned the Tigris, I listened to the conversations passing over the battalion radio net. They talked about continuing on with the road march. I was so tired my eyes were crossing, and each time Lt Parment radioed to report his platoon's lead trace the exhaustion in his voice echoed my own. Lt Cullins, his platoon bringing up the rear, was in worse shape. As he reported in a gravelly, strained croak that the company was all the way across the bridge, I looked at my watch. It was 2330Z, and there was no relief in sight. Knowing I had to act, I radioed Maj Bodkin, who was far ahead of us.

"Highlander-Five, this is Dragon-Six. My company just now crossed the Tigris. We're in pretty bad shape back here."

"Roger, I copy, Dragon-Six."

"Highlander-Five, the longer we stay on the road out here the more we're gonna increase our chances of killing a Marine in a wreck. The battalion's already wrecked one vehicle tonight."

"Roger, Dragon-Six, I hear you. Stand by."

He's gonna tell me to quit being a pussy and suck it up, I thought to myself angrily. My judgment clouded by stress and fatigue, I wanted to yell into my microphone, *Don't fucking tell me to stand by!* The radio crackled back to life.

"Dragon-Six, link your company up with the battalion. We're going to pull off the side of the road for a couple of hours."

I couldn't believe my ears. In my exhaustion, just the thought of an hour of sleep practically brought tears to my eyes. A few minutes later we pulled up to the battalion's rear and herringboned off to the sides of the road. It was midnight (Zulu time), and we'd been awake nearly twenty-four hours straight. Word was passed along that we would be stationary for approximately ninety minutes. Knowing that we couldn't just all go to sleep without security positioned around us, I quickly weighed my options. Ninety minutes of sleep would mean the difference between an LAV crew being able to continue the long road march into the next day and driving off the side of the road. As much as I hated to screw the company's scouts, it was time once again for them to earn their pay. I passed orders for them to establish local security around the company to allow the drivers, gunners, and vehicle commanders time to recharge their batteries. Then, falling all over myself and babbling like a mental patient on Thorazine, I collapsed in a heap on the asphalt next to my vehicle. I slept like a rock.

✦ ✧ ✦

Someone shook me awake at 0130Z.

"Come on, sir, get up. We're getting ready to roll."

I staggered to my feet, feeling as if I'd been run over in the night. Ninety minutes on the asphalt hadn't been all it was cracked up to be, and as I picked tiny pebbles and debris from the creases in my face I squeezed my eyes tightly against the pounding racket in my head. *Jesus,* I thought through a thick, gummy haze. *I feel like shit.*

Movement in the battalion resumed, and soon we were at the intersection of Route 27 and Highway 6. RCT-7 had stopped there, and as our LAVs made their way through the crowd of armored vehicles and personnel lining the road I scanned the area for signs of several Marines I knew within the regiment. Watching scores of men sit by the side of the road with their boots off made me think of my own crumbling feet. They had been encased within my desert boots and thick rubber over-shoes for over two days, and the pain and discomfort was magnified by the fact that I had been standing for the majority of that period. The fact that my feet were rotting off in such arid surroundings confounded me. I had always figured I would have to worry about my feet only in the snow and slush of winter or the rain and mud of the jungle. It was one of the greatest miscalculations of my decade in the Marine Corps.

Ahead of Delta Company on Highway 6, 1st LAR Battalion had halted and established a refuel and resupply point. Stationed along the sides of the road was an assembly line of seven-ton flatbed trucks, each with two massive fuel pods positioned atop it. Marines from the battalion's Field Trains stood by each refueler, waving in vehicle after vehicle. As with their training in Kuwait, they did it with the smooth efficiency of a well-trained team. As Delta Company waited its turn, I hopped down from my turret and moved up and down the line, searching for the battalion commander. Meeting several members of the battalion staff along the way, I received a running commentary of the previous day's events.

"Hey Folsom! Nice CAX yesterday!"

"We need to go back . . . I don't think Delta Company killed enough Iraqis yesterday."

"Sorry, you used up your ammunition allotment for the war yesterday. No more for you."

They continued on and on, curious to hear the story of the ambush at the Elbow. Remembering how frustrated I had been at the rear of the column listening to the battalion commander in contact ahead of us, I understood their thirst for details. But at the same time I didn't want to gloat, particularly in light of the fact that we had dropped so much ordnance on the village. To brag would seem tactless, a gross abuse of the power I wielded as a company commander.

I was more interested in what lay in store for the battalion. With the events of the previous twenty-four hours under our belts, I had convinced myself that the battalion would finally get a chance to really prove itself. Perhaps Highway 6—the final road that led straight into Baghdad—was where it would happen. *Don't count on it,* I thought, bringing myself back to reality. RCT-5 was already far ahead of us. Pushing so far up Powerline Road the previous day and then having to backtrack to An Numinayah had set 1st LAR Battalion back in its progress. We still had quite a ways to go to catch up to the regiment. The only information I got regarding the battalion's future was,

"We're refueling and continuing to push." A mission-type order if I ever heard one. It would have to do.

Walking from vehicle to vehicle, I surveyed the condition of the company. Despite the emptiness the men felt, the morning sunshine appeared to have brought with it a second wind for all of them. High spirits filled the air up and down the line as Marines stood in small groups by their vehicles, waiting for the gas line to move. They laughed together, sharing cigarettes and passing canteens of water back and forth. Next to SSgt Kappen's vehicle Bob Woodruff chatted with several Marines. I walked up to him and smiled.

"So, you finally get what you wanted yesterday?"

"Well, we were back too far in the column. I didn't see much from the rear."

"Well, like I told you before, nothing's stopping you from riding with me or one of the line platoons."

"But there's not enough room in those vehicles. And their transponders interfere with the camera's reception."

"Listen, I told you I'm not going to put Staff Sergeant Kappen's LAV out in front of the company. Ride with him if you want, Bob, but don't expect to get an accurate picture of the war from the back of the supply vehicle."

My words probably chafed him, and I moved on down the line, shaking my head. He had been handed a golden opportunity the previous day, and in my opinion he had blown it. Ironically in January 2006, as co-anchor for ABC News, Woodruff was in the lead vehicle of a convoy of Iraqi security forces when it was ambushed near Taji, about 12 miles north of Baghdad. Standing up in the back hatch of the vehicle and taping video of the patrol at the time of the attack, he suffered severe shrapnel wounds to his head and upper body. Doctors later claimed that the immediate treatment Woodruff received in Iraq, and the fact that he had been wearing body armor, saved his life. After hearing this unfortunate news, I reflected upon my conversations with Woodruff during our time together in Iraq in 2003. I recalled that, as we traveled together in Delta Company for that brief period between the beginning of the war and early April, he certainly was dedicated to his profession in reporting on the events we experienced. Though I never personally got to know Bob, I was extremely saddened for him and his family, and could only hope for him a speedy and complete recovery from his wounds.

I looked up to see 3rd Platoon's vehicles pulling forward to the pumps. I walked past their vehicles and shouted up to them.

"You guys kicked ass yesterday!" They replied with shouts of "Ooh-rah!" and "Kill!" I saw Lt Cullins standing next to his vehicle and approached him.

"Hey, great job yesterday, Doug."

"Thanks, sir. That was something else, wasn't it?"

"Yeah, it sure was. Are you okay?"

"Uh-huh, no problem. You should see my vehicle, though, sir. There are ricochet dents all over it. It's fucking crazy." He pointed to the side of his LAV. Sure enough, tiny dimples and chips in the dark green paint pockmarked the vehicle's hull and turret. It was something else, all right.

"Jeez-us, you weren't kidding, were you?"

"Sergeant Cole's vehicle looks the same. It was pretty hairy there for a moment yesterday, sir." He paused. "And pretty intense when you went back into it with us at the end."

"Yeah, well . . . you did good yesterday. All of you guys. Give me a cigarette and we'll call it even."

✦ ✧ ✦

Several kilometers east of Al Aziziyah, our rolling convoy came to a grinding halt once again. However, in contrast to days before, when our frequent stops had generally been along deserted stretches of highway, we now found ourselves smack in the middle of a small but heavily populated town. I had no idea how far ahead of us the traffic jam stretched, and rather than have the crews continue to idle their engines and waste fuel, I directed everyone to shut down their vehicles. All around us hundreds, perhaps thousands, of Iraqis lined the streets. Most walked or drove slowly through the formation of military vehicles lined up alongside the road, and many carried white flags fashioned from whatever material they could find lying around. This peculiar action, which I had first observed the day we crossed into Iraq, had begun to concern me. A white flag means nothing more than whoever is waving it wants a truce with the enemy. Waving it doesn't compel the other side to refrain from opening fire. But the Iraqis seemed to think that if they waved a white flag they could do anything they wanted because they knew we wouldn't shoot them. Some of the Marines even reported seeing an Iraqi man walking down the street naked and waving his white underwear over his head. Such dark humor aside, it concerned me because I feared acts of treachery by the Fedayeen, whom I expected would attempt to exploit this measure of our good will. That, in turn, could lead to the Marines firing on innocent civilians driving around with bed linens flying from their car antennas. Relaying my concerns over the radio to the company, I again felt like the master of the obvious.

"Watch these people. Don't let your guard down."

But it was understandably difficult not to do so. The apprehension demonstrated by the white flags notwithstanding, the locals surrounded us with cheers, jovial shouts, and scores of "thumbs-up" signs. Somewhere along the way we had been taught that the thumbs-up had offensive connotations in the Arabic culture. You never would have known it on 4 April. Iraqis of all ages flashed the sign to us as they strolled past our stationary vehicles. Someone within the company soberly pondered over the radio, "These people must have been heavily influenced by the Fonz."

One thing was certain: the Iraqis were welcoming us, giving us their support. It was evident in their eyes. Many approached our vehicles smiling, yelling "Saddam!" and then running their index fingers along the base of their throats. It puzzled me. I couldn't tell if they were saying, "Kill Saddam" or "Saddam is dead." We had heard that he had been targeted with Tomahawk missile strikes the first night of the war, but other than that his status was unknown. Regardless, their show of enthusiasm encouraged me. They were, after all, the reason I believed we were there fighting. One old man happily walked down the length of our column, handing out Iraqi dinars emblazoned with images of a youthful, smiling Saddam Hussein. The money was worthless now, and the man soon began tearing up the bills as we looked on. He smiled, handing me a piece of currency with Saddam's picture on it, and walked away. Sitting atop the turret surveying the scene unfolding around us, I turned to LCpl Davis next to me.

"How about this shit, huh? Ever think you'd see something like this?"

"It's amazing, sir."

"Yeah, it really is, isn't it?" Reaching into my pocket, I suddenly realized I had smoked my last cigarette after the ambush the day before. I turned back to Davis.

"Hey, I'm all out of smokes. Let me bum one from you."

"I'm out too, sir."

We hadn't counted on that. Even as stupid as it seemed at the time, smoking had become one of the most important things in life for many of us. I frequently thought back to Garry Trudeau's *Doonesbury* and his satire that often railed against the tobacco industry. In 1990, during Desert Shield, as a show of support for the troops, several tobacco firms had shipped complimentary cigarettes to Saudi Arabia. Trudeau had mocked it in his comic strip as he portrayed Mr. Butts—a giant talking cigarette—handing out smokes to the soldiers in the desert. In one strip a soldier, wary of Mr. Butts's offer of free cigarettes, declined for fear of dying of cancer.

"Lung cancer?!" Mr. Butts said. "Hey, I hate to tell you this, but you're a soldier. You might not be alive twenty *minutes* from now! Why worry about twenty years from now? Besides, you can always quit."

Believe it or not, those words accurately expressed the thoughts of everyone in the field who took up smoking or chewing tobacco. Life had shifted into increments of one day at a time. The future no longer existed. No one would die from cancer or heart disease. No one would drink too much and then drive into a tree on the way home from the bar. We were living life according to the next frag order that blared across the radio. We were living life "time: now."

"Hey, sir," said Gurganus, pointing. "Looks like that guy is selling cigarettes."

"Flag him down," I replied. "Get him over here."

Davis waved to an older man making his way down the column. I called down to him.

"Hey! Cigarettes. How much?"

He looked up at me, holding up two aqua-blue packs of cigarettes.

"Two. Five dollar."

"Yeah, fine, whatever," I replied, handing him a five-dollar bill. He walked farther down the line, pawning cigarettes and pocketing wads of American cash. "How about that shit. They're already making money off us." I fired up one of the cigarettes and inhaled deeply as I looked at the name emblazoned on the pack: "Sumer." The stale, bitter smoke burned my lungs, forcing me into a rasping, coughing fit.

"Oh, Christ, these things are *horrible.*"

"You ain't kidding, sir," Davis added, joining in my coughing attack. The shitty Iraqi Sumers would later earn a more appropriate name from all of us who smoked them in the absence of American cigarettes: "Blue Death."

As we sat atop the LAV fighting the urge to vomit, SSgt Monroe approached the vehicle.

"Hey, sir . . . be okay if I take a couple of Marines in that warehouse over there?" The company column had parked next to an old factory and adjoining warehouse, both of which were littered with vehicles and machinery of all types. The gates to the factory hung ajar, but no one seemed to be entering or exiting them.

"What for?"

"There may be some spare parts in there we can scavenge for the vehicles."

"Are you serious?"

"Sir, with our spare parts situation right now I'll take anything I can get my hands on." That much, at least, he was not kidding about. The spare parts shortage in the division had gone from bad to worse. With no repair items getting forward to us, we had reached the point where cannibalization of broken down or destroyed vehicles had become the norm instead of the exception to the rule. Any vehicle that had taken a hit from enemy fire and had been abandoned for later recovery was quickly consumed by the follow-on echelons, which picked it clean in a matter of hours. Throughout the long push to Baghdad, skeletons of damaged humvees could be found along the sides of the road. Many had been reduced to mere shells, barely recognizable as military vehicles. Earlier in the morning, as the company rounded the intersection of Route 27 and Highway 6, we had passed by the burnt-out hull of an M1A1 Abrams tank that had been hit during the fighting in An Numinayah on 2 April. It, too, appeared to have been ravaged by mechanics seeking spare tank parts.

Staff Sergeant Monroe wasn't the only one with a peculiar request. Staff Sergeant Stephen Bright, 1st Platoon's tall, red-headed platoon sergeant, walked over to my vehicle.

"Hey sir, we're going over there to bury that dog."

I looked to our left to see two Marines from 1st Platoon walk up to a wrought iron gate attached to the factory wall. A stray dog had become caught between the gate and the wall, and the animal was crushed up against the concrete corner.

"Why?" I asked.

"They're not gonna to do it," he replied irately, pointing to a small huddle of Iraqi men standing nearby. I walked over with Bright to check it out. Once I got an eyeful of the maggots writhing in the dead canine's fur and a nosefull of the sickeningly sweet stench of decay, I stopped.

"Gross. Yeah, go ahead. Knock yourself out." As I turned to head back to my vehicle the Marines engaged in a desperate tug-of-war to extract the dog's corpse from where it lay trapped between the gate and the wall. Staff Sergeant Bright had been correct: the Iraqis continued to look on in a mixture of amazement and contempt as the Marines struggled to pull the dog free and deposit its remains into the shallow grave they had excavated. I was touched by the humanity of the Marines stopping what they were doing to inter the animal, and just as angered by the Iraqis' idleness. They wouldn't stoop to bury a dead dog, even when it had become a health hazard. Instead they waited for the Marines to take charge and do it for them. Was their apathy a portent of things to come?

✦ ✧ ✦

The dizzying effect of the cheering crowds in the town east of Al Aziziyah quickly wore off, and once our chance to move came I took it. The Marines piled into the vehicles, their pockets stuffed with dozens of packs of Blue Death, and our column sped up Highway 6. But traffic continued to be stop-and-go for much of the way, and it was several hours before Delta Company finally caught up to 1st LAR Battalion's main body far ahead of us. The sheer magnitude of the traffic jams we experienced in our drive to Baghdad never ceased to amaze me. The division was restricted to only one or two routes at a time, but in all my years of training I never would have guessed that such a large part of the advance on Baghdad would involve sitting in rush hour traffic day after day. The pattern was the same on every occasion: as kickoff time approached, every unit would race to be the first element on the road, thus clogging the narrow Iraqi routes with bumper-to-bumper traffic. Frantic calls would fill the radio, directing all units to move aside as another unit from the rear pushed through the long column. Far ahead in the distance the rumble of artillery and air support filled our ears as each one of us wondered what the hell was going on. It was exasperating.

As we moved through Al Aziziyah, things were much the same. The difference was that we were forced to spend a longer period driving slowly through the carnage left in the wake of 2nd Tanks and 3/5. Burned-out Iraqi tanks and armored personnel carriers smoldered silently along the sides of the road and hidden in palm groves. Our tanks and airpower had really done a number on them, particularly those that had attempted to hide in the palm groves. The natural camouflage afforded by the canopies of wide palm fronds had been negated by the thermal imaging sights used by the aircraft high above, which had placed missiles and bombs precisely on top of the vehicles. It was easy to identify each Iraqi vehicle's killer, too. A blackened turret smashed from the top indicated a hit from a Cobra's Hellfire missile or a Hornet's satellite-guided joint direct attack munition (JDAM). A jagged hole in the vehicle's front or side pointed to a hit from the 120mm main gun of an M1A1 or a TOW missile. Secondary explosions from detonating ammunition within had torn apart many of the armored vehicles, but what surprised me was the conspicuous lack of dead enemy soldiers. The few that were visible lay strewn out along the road here and there, their gray flesh slowly waxing over in the midmorning heat. By the time we passed, most had had their faces covered by previous units. What was left for us to gaze upon looked like little more than bloated scarecrows dressed in ill-fitting green uniforms. But the number of Iraqi corpses didn't seem to match that of the destroyed vehicles along Highway 6. How many had actually fought and how many had fled?

As we inched our way along the road, I received a call from the battalion's operations section.

"Dragon-Six, we are co-located with the RCT headquarters right now. Link up with us for the next frag order." With the link-up point in sight, the company held its position on the road's shoulder while I pushed forward to get the mission order. I arrived just in time to hear Maj Harper's brief. Weapons Company had been ordered to clear Sarabadi Airfield several kilometers forward of our current position. Harper turned to me.

"Delta, attack to clear the storage facility adjacent to the airfield. Pay close attention to the boundary you and Weapons are going to share."

Dave and I looked at each other and nodded, and after a quick review of the location on my map I headed back to my waiting vehicle. I grimaced with pain as I climbed aboard the LAV, each foot on fire with every step. Pulling on my helmet, I radioed the company.

"Guidons, this is Black-Six. Move out and form up in column just beyond the COC. I'll brief you once we're set." The long line of twenty-five LAVs pulled into their tactical column once again, and after an abbreviated frag order from me, the company got underway. If anyone had told me years before in TBS—when I had botched my first detailed operations order to my platoon of fellow student lieutenants—that my frag orders in Iraq would merely consist of current location, destination, and company mission tasking, I would have thought he was nuts. Yet that was how every mission went down after our first day in Iraq and all the way until the end. As a staff, the officers and SNCOs of Delta Company had reached their apex. I could read their minds, and they could read mine. Our years of working together as a team had paid off. I also knew they could perform with little to no preparation, as could their Marines. On that day, as on so many others by that point, my words were simple.

"Weapons Company is attacking to clear the Sarabadi Airfield at Mike Bravo eight-four-three, five-seven-seven. We're conducting an area reconnaissance of the storage facility adjacent to the airfield. Any questions?"

There were none. We were on the move again.

◆ ◇ ◆

"Black-Six, watch out for that BMP tucked off the right side of the road, over," called Lt Parment. The company was almost at its objective, and as I looked off to the right I noticed a narrow road branching off and leading to an alley cul-de-sac. At the dead-end a BMP-1 sat in the shadows, waiting silently for us. It didn't appear to be damaged; instead, its occupants had abandoned it, perhaps to fight another day. That didn't really matter, though. Had it been manned it would have had a clear shot at all of us. If it hadn't hit someone from Parment's platoon, it would have gotten someone else in the company—maybe me. Staring at the abandoned infantry fighting vehicle pointed at my LAV, I understood the old saying about someone "walking over my grave." To make myself feel better I radioed the company.

"That's affirmative, Red-One. All Dragon Victors, keep your eyes open. That one just snuck up on me."

The long, narrow road leading into the storage compound was flanked by fields of tall grass and bordered by a high fence on either side of the asphalt. The choice of entry into the objective was clear—we *had* no choice. It was one way in, one way out. The road itself extended for nearly a kilometer before we would even enter the facility. That fact alone made the hair on the back of my neck rise. We would be terribly exposed in the run up to the compound. I didn't like it, but I had my orders. Dave's company was already moving on Sarabadi Airfield, and we had to catch up. Parment's platoon turned right up the narrow road, slowly trundling toward the cluster of buildings. I followed, with 1stSgt Guzman's vehicle close behind.

One vehicle at a time, the company filed through the compound's threshold, where we were met by a towering fresco of Saddam painted on a thirty-foot high slab of bricked concrete. Adorned in a military dress uniform and brandishing a sheathed saber, he welcomed us into the facility. It was the first of many portraits we would see in our final push to Baghdad. While each depiction of Iraq's leader had him dressed for different roles—soldier, *imam,* statesman, equestrian—all had one thing in common: a smile. But it wasn't that fact alone that unnerved me. What was unsettling about his omnipresent, toothy grin was the knowledge that behind that charming façade hid a personality whose pathology was so twisted that few could imagine the atrocities he had ordered and, in many cases, had himself committed. I gave the picture the finger as my vehicle rolled past it, and concentrated on the company again.

The access road gave way to an open camp with numerous rectangular barracks buildings and the humps of half-buried ammunition storage bunkers positioned throughout. It was no storage facility, but rather a military training complex. There were physical training areas and obstacle courses situated along each set of barracks, and abandoned jeeps and flatbed trucks sat rusting in heaps. The three platoons spread out and away from the column forced by the narrow entry road and glided into a skirmish line that ran the length of the camp. Slowly we rolled forward, turrets scanning back and forth for any sign of resistance. There was none. Damage to the facility was slight, and most of the structures appeared to be intact. The few people we did see standing around were unarmed and appeared to be waiting for us to leave so they could loot the camp. Like packs of mangy, stray dogs, they ran when we approached, occasionally peeking out from behind buildings or the levees that surrounded the compound to observe our run through the camp.

Although there were no Iraqi soldiers to challenge our intrusion into their home, there was plenty of ammunition. Soldiers had been there recently. Ordnance of all types had been stacked in neat piles everywhere, even spilling out the doorways of several of the structures: 82mm mortar shells, 122mm artillery shells, RPG rounds—you name it, it was there. So much, in fact, that I wondered what we would do with it all. The platoons had reached the far end of the compound, and all that remained was a trail leading through the levee that served as a barrier wall for the camp. I followed Lt Schwartz and his section through the narrow pass that opened up into a wide field. Bordered on both sides by a deep canal, the field looked like tilled farmland. I wondered if it was used to feed the soldiers who resided in the barracks. As Schwartz led his section along the dirt trail that split off to the left, I told PFC Gurganus to continue forward along our own trail that paralleled the steep dirt levee and canal to our right. Shallow holes had been carved into the bank of the levee. Each extended back into the earth about six or eight feet and was equipped with a small cot and a curtain at the entrance. Many were filled with ragged clothing and personal items like mattresses and small hibachi grills. Most were similarly equipped with plastic chairs and tiny tables, several of which still had kettles of tea, dishes, and utensils arranged on them. The tiny hovels reminded me of Tolkien's hobbit holes, and then it hit me: they were survivability bunkers for the troops. Each soldier had come out at some point and dug himself his own personal bomb shelter to avoid the approaching storm of coalition aircraft. Each hovel had become home for its occupant, and for a moment I felt a stab of pity for the soldiers who had been uprooted from their abodes and forced underground. My daydreaming was interrupted by Lt Schwartz's voice over the radio.

"Black-Six, this is White-One. We've got what looks like three MTLBs out in the field in front of us."

Lance Corporal Davis traversed the turret slightly to our left, and then spoke calmly into the intercom.

"Identified."

Straining to pick up the MTLBs—Russian-designed armored personnel carriers—through my binoculars, I finally noticed the low profile of their silhouettes camouflaged beneath netting and stacks of dried grass. Suddenly we were in the same position we had been in less than an hour earlier with the hidden BMP-1 in the alley cul-de-sac. *Son of bitch!* I cursed to myself. *If you don't keep your fucking eyes open you're as good as dead.*

"What does it look like through the thermals, Davis?"

"It's cold, sir."

I leaned down into the turret and peered through the circular scope of the thermal sight. He was correct. The vehicle was barely visible in the green glow of the screen, indicating that it was the same temperature as its surroundings.

"Can I take him out, sir?" Davis asked.

I quickly compared our position against Schwartz's across the field. Schwartz had moved farther forward than we had, and now our vehicle's geometry of fire didn't add up. Then, glancing back at my map, I realized Schwartz was right on the boundary with Weapons Company. If we fired at the MTLBs, we risked both hitting Schwartz's vehicle and shooting into Weapons Company's zone. No one was shooting at us, so I decided not to take the risk.

"Negative. Our angle of fire doesn't work with White-One out in front of us. Besides, we'd be shooting into Weapons' zone." Then I keyed my headset to the radio. "White-One, this is Six. Roger, I tally those MTLBs. You are clear to engage. Watch your left boundary."

"Roger that, Six." A moment later the *thump-thump-thump* of 25mm fire echoed across the field as Schwartz's section unloaded a volley of armor-piercing rounds into the derelict vehicles. Above the racket of the LAVs firing in the distance, I heard LCpl Davis cursing and muttering to himself down in the turret. He was pissed off that Schwartz's gunner, Lance Corporal Alex Stratton, was getting to engage targets again. I got the impression that at his first opportunity Stratton, who was good friends with Davis, had boasted about his kills with the main gun during the ambush at the Elbow the previous day. *Just relax, Davis. Quit being so anxious to kill somebody,* I thought. *This thing isn't over yet. You'll get your chance.*

Ahead of my LAV on the dirt trail sat a tan Iraqi military cargo truck under camouflage netting. Someone had parked it next to the levee, and with the net draped over both the truck and the embankment, it almost appeared part of the earthworks. Several of Schwartz's scouts prowled up to it and checked it out, then one waved to me and gave the thumb's up signal. A scout's excited voice appeared on the radio.

"This thing is full of AK-47s and ammo!"

Rolling forward to see for myself, I had Gurganus stop the vehicle next to the hidden truck. Climbing down from the turret, I could see hundreds of AK-47 assault rifles and Makarov 9mm pistols stacked inside. A scout handed me a rifle from within.

"They're all in perfect condition, sir," he said. It was a gangbanger's dream come true. As I stuck my head inside the cargo bay of the truck and peered at all the ordnance, I shook my head in disbelief. Not only were the weapons clean and serviceable, but most of them were also fully loaded. Those that didn't have a long, banana-shaped magazine inserted into the receiver sat atop stacks of preloaded magazines. The truck appeared ready to pull up to a formation of troops and hand out rifles and pistols to everyone. Grabbing a magazine of ammunition and the AK-47 handed to me by the Marine, I climbed to the top of the levee. I hadn't handled a loaded AK-47 since the very first day of the Infantry Officers Course when I was still a second lieutenant, but that didn't matter. Mikhail Kalashnikov had designed the rifle so that any moron could use it, and sure enough I quickly got it in action to test-fire it. Placing the weapon in full-auto mode, I aimed it down into the water of the canal and blew through the magazine in seconds. I would be lying if I said I didn't enjoy it. But the impish joy of unloading the AK-47 into the canal quickly subsided, as I knew we had to figure out a way to dispose of the massive weapons cache. As it was, anyone could make off with the truckload of rifles and ammunition and use it against us later. I disassembled the weapon and tossed the pieces into the deep, green water of the canal and walked back to the LAV. Davis and the rest of the crew met me at the bottom of the levee, hopeful grins filling their faces.

"Can we test-fire some too, sir?" they asked.

"Yeah, go ahead," I replied. "Hey. Fire *into* the water, and just one magazine each. No fucking around." As the vehicle crew began popping off rounds from the rifles into the canal, I radioed the battalion with our findings. After reporting the three MTLBs, I mentioned the truck filled with ordnance.

"Roger that, Dragon-Six. Continue to disassemble the weapons and throw them into the canal."

Bullshit, I thought. *That'll take forever.* I already knew the solution. I yelled to my crew up on the levee.

"Hey, mount up! Bring me a couple of empty rifles." I keyed my radio. "White-One, this is Six. I'm heading back to the company. Blow the truck in place after I leave."

As the LAV backed out of the field and began its return to the company waiting inside the compound, a sharp *crack* split the air behind us. I turned to see a thick column of smoke climbing into the sky. Schwartz had made quick work of the truck. I was ready to consolidate the company and get some rest, but the battalion radioed again for me to report back to the COC for the next frag. Dodging giant chunks of shrapnel strewn across the ground in front of us, Gurganus steered us back down the constricted access road toward where the headquarters had positioned itself. Behind us in the camp the rumblings of the platoons systematically destroying every bunker containing ammunition echoed across the fields that bordered the road.

By the time I made it back to the battalion forward I was running on empty. I was dehydrated and sweating profusely inside my MOPP suit, and my head spun. I grabbed my Camelbak and sucked down water in gulps as I walked to the patch of shade where the COC had set up. But what I was doing could hardly be called walking. "Hobbling" was more like it. My feet pounded inside their galoshes, and with each step they felt like the skin would split open. I was afraid to take my boots off for fear I would leave my flesh inside them. What had begun as a slight burning feeling in my soles more than a week earlier had graduated to the sensation of a blowtorch being held beneath each foot. I ambled up next to Dave Hudspeth. He greeted me with a cigarette.

"Hey buddy. How's it going?"

"Dude, my feet are fucking killing me," I replied, wincing.

"I hear you, man. Mine feel like two boiled chickens inside these MOPP boots." Similar gripes resonated around the COC from Marines standing in their over-boots, but as I looked around I noticed many individuals weren't wearing theirs. Most of the Marines wearing only their combat boots were officers. That pissed me off. Here I had been, feeling my feet rot off day by day while the Marines in the COC were walking around with no MOPP boots on. I spoke up.

"Hey, what's the deal? Are we in MOPP-One or Two?"

"We're still in MOPP-Two," Maj Harper replied matter-of-factly.

"Well, someone better tell them that, sir," I said, pointing to the perpetrators. Harper corrected the officers, and they disappeared to find their boots, grumbling. If I was miserable I wanted everyone to be miserable with me.

The battalion commander walked up to me. "What did you find in there, Seth?"

"Well, sir, one thing's for sure. That's no 'storage facility' like it says on the map. It's a military compound."

"It's more than just that," interjected Maj Harper. "Apparently it's a Republican Guard barracks."

"No shit?" I asked. "That explains all that fucking ammunition and ordnance." I handed two AK-47s to LtCol White. "There are hundreds of these in there, sir. They're all in perfect condition. My platoons have been blowing as much of it in place as possible, but we're not gonna get all of it."

Major Harper rallied everyone around him to pass the new mission frag for the battalion. In its assault along Highway 6, 2nd Tank Battalion had bypassed numerous enemy units in the RCT's axis of advance. According to the S-3, there were still plenty of bad guys hanging around in our zone, and our job was to continue the reconnaissance south of Highway 6. As Harper doled out the routes for each company, I looked at Dave and Gil. Together we rolled our eyes at each other. Our feelings were mutual—we were sick and tired of the battalion getting sidelined for every mission. We were emotionally beat. Now that 2nd Tanks and 3/5 were pushing ahead again, 1st LAR was left to clean up their trash on the periphery. It was insulting, and I asked myself again and again why our significant combat power was being marginalized day in and day out.

I limped back to my vehicle, grimacing each time my soles touched the ground. I seriously wondered if amputation would be a better alternative to the pain in my feet. I found LCpl Davis leading an effort to patch a hole in one of the tires.

"Look at this shit, sir," he said, handing me a jagged sliver of shrapnel six inches long. "That fucker was buried up to the last inch in our tire. Look at the plug we put in there."

Bending down, I stared at the wad of thick rubber, finger-like tubes protruding from the tire's sidewall. It was enough to choke a horse.

"Is that gonna hold?" I asked warily.

"It'll hold, sir." He was proud of his work.

"Good. Radio the Guidons, tell them to meet me here."

As Davis relayed my order to the company's leaders, I returned to the analysis of my map. Highway 6 stretched to the northwest toward Baghdad, and a series of smaller roads branching south from the highway had been highlighted. These were the routes 1st LAR had been told to reconnoiter, and the first one assigned to Delta Company had been designated as Phase Line Butler. On the map Butler wound for five or ten kilometers through several small but heavily inhabited areas until it stopped in a dead-end at the banks of the Tigris. I looked up from my map study to see the platoon commanders' LAVs rolling to a stop next to mine. Behind them pillars of black smoke rose out of the military compound. The lieutenants exited their vehicles with smiles on their faces, obviously having enjoyed the destruction of the ammunition bunkers. But their smiles quickly turned to grimaces as they climbed from their turrets and shuffled over to where I stood. They apparently shared the same pain in their feet as I did. As I briefed the company leadership on our next mission, I looked off to my left to the entrance of the access road and the towering fresco of Saddam Hussein. Beneath it a cluster of Marines from the battalion had formed for a group photograph. Next to them several Marines had gathered around a parked humvee. Someone had torn the bust from an enormous statue of Saddam and strapped it to the rear bumper. In place of his head on a platter, we would have to accept a plastic replica mounted on the back of a humvee.

With no time to rest or regroup, Delta Company stepped off at sunset and began its road march up Highway 6 to the turnoff for Phase Line Butler. As our maps had warned, the route along Butler passed through a heavily populated neighborhood, and the narrow street's tight curves restricted the vehicles to a single file. Movement was slow and dangerous. As darkness descended, civilian cars darted in and out of our column, the bright glow of their headlights blinding us through our night vision devices. We inched our way forward to the end of the route, the entire time expecting an ambush to erupt on our flanks. By the time we hit the turnaround point and began our slow egress back up the route, the Marines needed a break. Together we had been running on full steam for nearly thirty-six hours straight, and everyone was getting sloppy. Squinting through my NVGs in between the white-outs caused by passing headlights, I could see LAVs veering off the road. They wove back and forth drunkenly, narrowly avoiding cars and each other. It was only a matter of time until someone had a collision, or worse, rolled unprepared into another ambush. In our current state I didn't give us the same chances we had had at the Elbow. I radioed the S-3 and announced that the company had completed its reconnaissance of Butler. Having hoped for the battalion to tell me to hold in place, I was crushed by Maj Harper's response.

"Roger that, Dragon-Six. Proceed to the next phase line and continue your recon."

Oh God, is he shitting me? I asked myself. The same dilemma faced me that had when we crossed the Tigris the previous night. Did I call back and say I couldn't take it any longer? My own personal hell of fatigue aside, I was genuinely concerned for the men. Had we been engaged with the enemy with rounds coming in, I would like to think we would have managed to push through the exhaustion and continue on. But we weren't engaged, rounds were not coming in at us, and the next phase line was likely to produce the same negative results that Butler had. I swallowed hard and radioed Maj Harper.

"Highlander-Three, this is Dragon-Six. We're in a bad way out here, and we're becoming more of a danger to ourselves than anything else. I need to go to ground for the night, or at least for a couple of hours." As on the previous evening, I fully expected Harper to call and tell me to get my ass on the road and back in the game. His answer surprised me.

"Roger that, Dragon-Six. Hold your current position. All Guidons, report your company locations and hold in place for the night." I never learned what caused him to make that call on our behalf, but I was grateful nonetheless. The company found an unoccupied field along Butler, and after circling up the wagons into a tactical assembly the vehicle crews deployed their scouts around the area. With the plan to move at first light, we set in for the evening. By the time all platoons reported their final status in the laager point I could barely function. My feet were in such agony that it was difficult to walk properly. I hopped gingerly over to Capt Portiss's vehicle parked next to mine.

"Hey, XO, I'm crashing next to your vehicle. If battalion radios, I'm right here."

"Roger that," he replied. But I was already in a heap on the ground, out cold.

✦ ✧ ✦

What seemed like mere minutes of sleep for me was actually two and a half hours. I awoke to Portiss shaking me back and forth.

"CO, get up, man."

"Uhhhn. What's going on?"

"We're on the move again."

"Jeez," I lamented out loud. "What's a guy gotta do to get some sleep around here? What's the deal?"

"Battalion's getting ready to do an FPOL with Three-Five." Earlier in the evening we had watched an artillery battery firing long volleys to our northwest, and once Delta Company filed out of its laager site I got the details of what was going on. That day, 2nd Tanks had blasted its way up Highway 6 and run into determined enemy opposition around the 61 easting. The enemy outfit was composed of several hundred foreign fighters from countries that included Syria, Jordan, and Egypt. This influx of *jihadis* (holy warriors) was something new in the war. We hadn't expected soldiers from other countries to travel all the way to Iraq to fight us, but they had. Hiding in buildings, vegetation, and trenches along the side of the road, they had ambushed 2nd Tanks with machine guns and hundreds of RPG rounds. The barrage peppered many vehicles with small arms rounds, and we got word that two M1A1 tanks had been disabled by RPG fire. By the time 2nd Tanks was reinforced by 3/5 the RCT had sustained numerous casualties, and as 3/5 dismounted from its amtracks and attacked up the sides of the road they too began taking casualties. As 2nd Tanks pushed forward, 2/11 initiated indirect fire support for the RCT's attack west. Eventually the word went out for 1st LAR Battalion to conduct a forward passage of lines through 3/5.

Armed with that knowledge, I directed the platoons to form back up into column on Highway 6. It was hard to imagine—2nd Tanks and 3/5 had been engaged all night. I tried to imagine those tough bastards fighting it out in the dark for close to eight hours. Now we were preparing to pass forward of them. I repeated the worn-out phrase to the company.

"All Victors, keep your eyes open." Then I added, "We're heading into bad-guy country." We slowly rolled through a traffic jam of RCT vehicles that had accumulated in the dark, all waiting to push forward to where 3/5 waited. Weaving in and out through the morass of vehicles, the vehicle commanders slowly steered their LAVs around groups of Marines sleeping by the side of the road. I realized then what I had only guessed before: when it was someone else's war, it was easier to sleep. The traffic jam thinned out, and the pace of the company column picked up. So too did the chatter filling the radio waves, and soon it was difficult to discern who was saying what. As I relayed instructions to the platoons, the commander from 1st LAR's attached Alpha Company (who had joined us from 4th LAR earlier in Kuwait) jumped on to the battalion radio net, asking for information from anyone who could give it. After playing "catch-up" for weeks, Alpha Company had finally found its way back to its parent unit.

"Dragon-Six, this is Apache-Six. We just linked up with the battalion. What's going on?"

"Apache-Six, we're conducting an FPOL with Three-Five. Listen, I'm a little busy right now. Dragon-Six, *out*." Continuing my conversation with the company, I heard Alpha's CO calling on the battalion net again, frantically searching for someone who had the answers. I hated to snub him like that, but Alpha was way behind us, and I had a company to run.

Far ahead of us and off to our right, the ground rumbled and shook with the impact of 2/11's artillery. High above, salvo after salvo of rocket-assisted artillery rounds arced over our column, illuminating the sky with hundreds of glowing beacons. They sailed north in graceful waves, and as the roar of their rocket motors cascaded to earth I marveled at what was one of the most truly awesome spectacles of technology I had ever witnessed. I keyed the intercom.

"Davis, pop up and look out here." He climbed out from inside the turret and craned his neck skyward, his mouth hanging open.

"*Jay*-zus-age-Christ," he said slowly into his microphone.

The company's radio net, which only moments before had been abuzz with excited voices speaking back and forth, was suddenly silent. The Marines in the company were experiencing the same sense of awe for our surroundings and the events taking place around us. As we passed through the gauntlet paved by 2nd Tanks and 3/5, my jaw clenched and the muscles in my shoulders and back tightened at the sights that filled my eyes. Great walls of orange flame and thick black smoke towered up from oil trenches that lined the road, casting shadows that danced crazily around us. Shot-up and battle-ravaged humvees lined the asphalt, and I swallowed hard as my vehicle passed by the burned-out hulk of an Abrams tank. Parts of its blackened hull glowed orange from the fire that had consumed it, and its long barrel drooped down lazily from the turret, nearly resting on the ground. *My God,* I thought. *What the hell happened here?*

But the battle was over. With the sun rising to our east and 3/5 cleaning out the enemy far to our right, Delta Company turned north into a town called

Hatif Haiyawi. We slowly eased our LAVs through the scattered detritus of the previous evening's firefight, carefully trying to avoid the razor-sharp shards of shrapnel that blanketed the road. All the while, we gawked incredulously at the still-smoldering skeletons of enemy tanks and armored personnel carriers (APCs) lining the road. Second Tank Battalion had done its job well. To the west a gargantuan cloud of smoke billowed across the sky.

Baghdad was only thirteen miles ahead.

16
Nahr Diyala

From our position in the town of Hatif Haiyawi, one final obstacle lay between us and the gateway to Baghdad: the river called Nahr Diyala. A winding tributary from the north that flowed south into the Tigris, the Diyala posed a significant problem for RCT-5 and the 1st Marine Division. Few bridges spanned the river, and those that did had been either damaged or completely destroyed by the Iraqis themselves in a last ditch effort to stave off the invasion of their capital city. It shouldn't have been a problem for the RCT. Already the attached bridge-building units had constructed pontoon crossings for the Euphrates River and the Saddam Canal. They knew how to do their jobs quickly and efficiently. The predicament lay in finding a site suitable for the bridge units to use their skills. Locating such a site was supposed to be 1st LAR Battalion's bread and butter. But we were about to discover that locating a crossing site for an entire regimental combat team was infinitely more difficult than the textbooks claim.

With the company herringboned along the side of the road in Hatif Haiyawi, I spooned the remnants of an MRE into my mouth as I watched Baghdad burn in the distance. Whatever had been hit had created a monstrous cloud of thick black smoke that had drifted far into the sky.

Weapons and Charlie Companies had pushed farther to the north and set into a screen across the RCT's frontage, and just when I thought Delta Company had been forgotten I received orders to report to the COC several kilometers forward of our herringbone. The crew piled back inside our light armored homes and drove up the road to an intersection. Nearby the battalion headquarters had set up its command post along the road's shoulder, and Marines milled about the area. After finding Maj Harper sitting in the back of his LAV-C2, I broached the subject of the previous night.

"Hey sir, sorry I pussed out last night. We were practically dead on our feet."

"Don't worry about it," he replied casually. "You want a mission?"

"You got it, sir. What's up?"

He leaned forward with his map and pointed to a block of grid squares along the Nahr Diyala. "Here's your company's zone. Conduct an area reconnaissance to assess trafficability and possible bridging or fording sites." He looked at his watch. It was 0715Z "Can you be Oscar Mike by zero-seven-thirty?"

"No problem, sir. We'll make it happen." I raced back to my vehicle. Fifteen minutes. Compared to what I had come to expect it was all the time in the world. Radioing the company, I called the platoons forward and briefed the mission frag order over the radio as we headed to our start point. As I waited for the platoons to rendezvous with my vehicle, I looked down from the turret to a canal that ran perpendicular to the road. A small bridge covered the twenty-foot-wide waterway. Some time the previous evening an Iraqi tank had been fleeing the approaching destruction, and as it attempted to speed across the narrow bridge something caused it to run off the road. It now lay upside down in the canal, with only its treads protruding from the cloudy green water. From the vehicle's position I could only guess that the doomed crew was still inside. It reminded me of the story of an Abrams tank from First Tank Battalion earlier in the war.

Immediately following the two-day sandstorm, we had heard that 1st Tanks was missing one of its M1A1s. It seemed preposterous—how could you lose a seventy-ton main battle tank? But we soon learned the answer. During its long road march north to Highway 1, 1st Tanks crossed the same bridge over the Euphrates River that we had earlier on 23 March. At some point during the blinding sandstorm an M1A1 crew veered the tank off the side of the bridge and plunged into the water below. It remained there for several days until it was finally recovered. The story of that tank crew's watery demise sent chills down my spine every time I thought about it. Apparently the Iraqis in the canal below us had met the same horrible fate.

My map displayed a partially-improved road that ran parallel to the Nahr Diyala. It quickly became known as "River Road," and judging from the map I thought it would make our job of finding an appropriate crossing site much easier. What the map didn't indicate, however, was the difficulty we would encounter just trying to get to the river in the first place. Immediately upon leaving the paved road and heading west toward the river the company became trapped in a confused network of canals, levees, and untrafficable paddy farmland. Vehicle movement was once again restricted to the unpredictable and unstable trails created by generations of herders and their flocks. The trails shared one similarity: most seemed to lead to the canals that drew water from the Diyala, but they tended to dead-end there. After an hour the company had traveled less than a kilometer, moving back and forth, starting and stopping, backtracking and cutting across-country. At that rate it would be sundown by the time the entire company got to the river. Time had priority; the RCT had to get across the river, and soon. The army, racing toward Baghdad from the west, faced no obstacle to entering the city as we currently did. It was Delta Company's job to make up for that handicap.

Before I knew it, the terrain had split the company into two columns. There was no use trying to reunite the two halves, and I decided that perhaps two separate elements would have a better chance of successfully reaching the river than would the long circus parade we had been. I radioed Lieutenants Parment and Schwartz.

"Keep heading west. My section will split off here with Blue Platoon. We'll meet you at the river." Together with 3rd Platoon, our six vehicles negotiated our way across several more kilometers of broken farmland. We encountered a number of abandoned artillery pieces and trucks along the route, and as our formation slowly passed a series of date-palm groves we could see a variety of military vehicles hidden inside. They included APCs, bulldozers, and bridge-building equipment, all quietly sitting in the concealment of the palm fronds. I marked the location of each site in our GPS receiver, knowing that someone would have to police all of it up at some point.

Our small caravan rolled to a stop at the banks of the river. The waterway varied in width, as did the height and angle of its banks. In some places the land gradually eased down to the water's edge, but in others the embankment made a sharp drop of twenty or thirty feet. With the maze of canals and levees behind us, two challenges presented themselves to the company. Not only did we have to find a suitable crossing site, but we also had to find an appropriate route from the paved road to the water. The second task was potentially more difficult than locating a site for the bridgelaying crews. As I prepared to move north along River Road with 3rd Platoon, Lt Parment's voice broke the airwaves.

"This is Red-One, we're in contact at the nine-zero northing." As Parment spoke, his voice competed with the clanking of his LAV's main gun inside the turret. Excited chatter picked up on the company net, and I broke in.

"Break, break, this is Black-Six. Clear the net. Red-One, what's going on down there?" Six or eight kilometers to the south, echoes of 25mm fire reverberated up the riverbed to our position.

"Roger, Six. We're taking pretty heavy fire from what looks like an ammo dump on the river's eastern bank."

"I copy, One. We're Oscar Mike." I keyed the intercom. "Punch it,

Chewie!" Howling into the intercom like Chewbacca from the movie *Star Wars,* Gurganus stepped on the LAV's accelerator, sending the vehicle forward down the road in a shower of gravel and dust. Turning my head to the rear, I noticed with satisfaction 1stSgt Guzman and 3rd Platoon hot on my trail as we raced south along the bank of the river. The LAV spun around a corner, and unexpectedly a small white car containing an Iraqi family blocked our path to the firefight. They sat in the car, stunned at our presence and unmoving. Davis and I hung out of the turret, yelling at them.

"Move, Goddammit!" Davis shouted.

"Yeh-lah!" I yelled, ordering them in Arabic to hurry up. "Get the fuck out of our way!" But our shouts didn't seem to convey our sense of urgency. Davis dropped back inside the vehicle, and suddenly I felt the grinding and heard the high-pitched whine of the turret's hydraulics powering up. The main gun's long barrel traversed left and depressed until it aimed directly at the car and its occupants. They got the message and quickly moved from our path. *Well,* I thought indifferently. *We just lost* their *hearts and minds.*

The LAV rounded another corner, where we nearly ran into a column of LAV-ATs from Weapons Company. Like the Iraqis in the car before them, the Weapons crews didn't understand our need to get past them. They sat motionless in their vehicles, staring blankly at me as I wildly gesticulated at them.

"Hey!" I shouted over the engine's idle. "Get out of our way! We have to get south!" The vehicle commander of the LAV closest to us and blocking our path pretended to ignore me. I pointed my finger directly at him and made eye contact.

"MOVE . . . YOUR . . . FUCKING . . . ASS! I slowly mouthed to him.

The LAV pulled forward, allowing a passage point for us, and we sped through. As our convoy raced down the bends of River Road to reinforce 1st Platoon, I formulated a better picture of what was happening. Lieutenant Parment's LAV had become mired down in the mud alongside the road. As his second vehicle section pulled forward to provide security, the entire platoon came under fire from a compound hidden in a palm grove on the river's eastern bank less than a kilometer away. Staff Sergeant Bright's section immediately returned fire into the compound, which turned out to be an ammunition storage facility. The impacts of the 25mm HEI-T rounds detonated the ammunition stockpiled inside, and when 3rd Platoon and I arrived on scene the compound had become the wildest Fourth of July display I had ever seen. Colossal, fiery explosions rocked the compound, sending orange globes of flame and dirty gray billows of smoke skyward. Rockets of spinning ordnance and white-hot shrapnel buzzed in all directions. Never before had we seen anything of that magnitude except on the silver screen. On the road ahead of me, 1st and 2nd Platoons continued to pump cannon and machine-gun fire into the area surrounding the storage facility. My unnatural admiration for the events playing out in front of me was interrupted by Lt Cullins's voice breaking through the radio.

"This is Blue-One. Contact! We're taking fire from enemy personnel across the river." Behind me the *thump-thump-thump* of Bushmaster fire sounded as 3rd Platoon opened up on the enemy fighters entrenched on the river's far banks. I radioed Capt Portiss.

"Black-Five, are we fire-capped?"

"Affirmative, Six. We have arty standing by also."

"Roger, fire these fuckers up. Blue Platoon will spot the rounds."

"I can't see anything down here, sir," Davis said angrily into the intercom.

"Then don't shoot!" I snapped back. Rekeying my helmet, I radioed the battalion. "Highlander, this is Dragon-Six. Contact, enemy ambush, nine-zero northing."

"Roger, Dragon-Six, what do you need?" It sounded like Bob Whalen on the radio.

"We're getting ready to work eighty-ones and arty right now. Will report, out."

1st and 2nd Platoons engaged with enemy personnel at exploding ammunition dump on the Nahr Diyala River, 5 April 2003. Official Marine Corps photo by LCpl Andrew P. Roufs.

I turned my attention back to the company. The bursts of 25mm fire from 1st and 2nd Platoon had become sporadic. From the looks of it, the devastation caused by the detonating ammunition dump had pretty much taken care of whoever occupied the immediate vicinity. Out to our west across the river, however, the enemy continued to fire on Lt Cullins and 3rd Platoon. Moments later Portiss's voice was back on the net.

"Eighty-ones, shot, over."

The impact of the high explosive rounds across the river sent towers of earth upward around the defending enemy irregulars. Almost on top of that landed artillery rounds from 2/11, their concussive overpressure flattening the palm trees that surrounded the ambush site.

Meanwhile, ordnance from the storage compound continued to cook off on the near side of the Nahr Diyala. As the company returned fire into the tree line, I caught a slight movement out of the corner of my eye. Glancing down in front of my vehicle, I saw tiny splashes of water jumping out of a ditch that ran alongside the road. *What the hell is that?* I thought. Then I heard it. It began as a slight chirp, then after a few moments it turned into a brief, sharp whistle barely audible through the earpieces of my helmet. I lifted the thin Kevlar shell off my head, straining to hear whatever was causing the peculiar sounds. They grew louder, even more so now that I had removed my helmet. The chirping, whistling sound was shrapnel spinning through the air past me and my vehicle. The heavier ordnance—artillery rounds and rockets—had finally started detonating inside the inferno of the ammunition dump, and the accompanying shrapnel was reaching all the way out to my vehicle. I radioed Lt Parment, who himself was much closer to the ongoing carnage.

"Red-One, this is Six. Report your status, over."

"Roger, Six." As he spoke, his microphone picked up the same chirp in the background. "There isn't too much left out here." Another zing split the air behind him. "We're pretty good to go." Another whistle. Throughout it all, Parment, ever the deadpan, remained as cool as an ice cube even as deadly shards of flying metal rended the air around him. As far as I was concerned, that was my cue for us to beat feet and get the hell out of there.

"Guidons, this is Black-Six. That's enough. It's getting too dangerous out here with all this shit flying around. Get your men inside your vehicles and egress back to the hardball road." Small arms fire from across the river continued to impact around us as the company pulled out of its position and began its retrograde back toward the battalion. Another voice sounded on the radio.

"Break, break! We've got incoming, over!" A volley of Iraqi 82mm mortars from across the river began raining down near the company's vehicles, impacting harmlessly in the undulating farmland around us.

"Let's go, people," I called into the radio. "Hurry up and get the hell out of here."

"Black-Six, this is Five. Blue-One has eyes-on across the river. Request to remain back with Blue to finish prosecuting this fire mission and get a BDA, over."

I quickly considered Portiss's appeal. They were out of the immediate danger posed by the exploding ordnance from the ammunition compound, and their vehicles had taken some measure of cover behind an elevated portion of River Road. I looked around. The company was strewn all around the farmland, each platoon separated from the next by zigzagging canals and levees. We needed to consolidate and reorganize ourselves. First and 2nd Platoons would also need a reload of ammunition after the hell they had just delivered to the ambush zone on the river bank. All that aside, I knew Cullins and Portiss could handle themselves where they were.

"Roger that, Black-Five. Prosecute the mission and get the hell back to the hardball ASAP. Everyone else, make your way back to the link-up point. Report when set." Bit by bit, the fragmented company navigated its way through the labyrinthine terrain until we hit the paved road where the COC had established itself. I owed the battalion commander a report on the crossing site reconnaissance and an explanation for the giant smoke cloud that had filled the sky to the south.

Had I made the right decision in directing the company to fall back to the road? Months later I would learn that a first sergeant from 2/5 had been killed by flying shrapnel from a similar ammunition dump along the road to Baghdad. But I didn't know that at the time, and I wondered if I should have held the company in place and continued to duke it out with the enemy dug in across the river. But there was already confusion about Delta Company's position along the river. Earlier I had heard Dave Hudspeth on the radio trying to explain to the battalion that my company wasn't where it was supposed to be. That part I could explain: the difficulty in negotiating the canals and levees had channeled the company farther south along the river than we had planned. But I would have to explain something else. We had uncovered neither a suitable crossing site across the Nahr Diyala nor a workable route to the river for the RCT's heavy vehicles.

In other words, Delta Company had failed to accomplish the mission, which meant I as the commander had failed to accomplish the mission.

◆ ◇ ◆

Our LAV rolled to a stop fifty feet from an abandoned Iraqi BMP-2 parked on the road's gravel shoulder by the COC. The fighting vehicle's rear troop hatches were ajar, and from the looks of it the vehicle had been picked clean by Marines. A group of officers were clustered around the battalion commander behind one of the command vehicles. I joined them.

"Sorry that took so long, sir. The terrain in that farmland is murder."

"So, what happened out there?" LtCol White asked, interested. It was a good sign.

"The company got split up in that trail network. I ended up to the north with Third Platoon in Weapons Company's sector. First and Second Platoons ended up down south on the river. First Platoon got ambushed from a huge ammo dump on the riverbank. When they returned fire the whole place cooked off."

"You got some pretty big explosions going on out there."

"You can say that again, sir. It was like fucking Hollywood."

"Did you get a BDA?"

"Last I heard was about thirty or forty of them, between the guys at the ammo dump and the ones shooting at us from across the river."

Lieutenant Colonel White paused for a moment. "Okay, what else?"

"Bad news, sir. We didn't find any fording sites while we were out there. But it took so long just to get to the river going through that maze that we didn't have much time to look really hard. Then there was the whole ambush thing." What he said next lifted my spirits a bit.

"That's not really an issue. It looks like Dave found something suitable in his sector around the nine-five northing."

"Roger that, sir," I said, still disappointed with myself.

The staff continued to pass administrative information back and forth, including a directive from 1st Marine Division that the MOPP level had been reduced a notch. As we wrapped up the meeting Dave spoke one last time.

"There's one more thing, sir. That general was out there when we engaged those Iraqis on the other side of the river. He flipped out and started calling Warrant Officer Day a 'murdering cocksucker' and shit like that. He also said he was going to make sure Joe got a court-martial."

White paused and thought for a minute. "Okay, check. I'll bring it up with Colonel Dunford." The battalion staff members went their separate ways. Not knowing what the hell Dave was talking about, I pulled him aside.

"What was that all about?"

"Ah, that general and his writer buddy decided to go swimming in the river right about the time Joe Day's vehicle got engaged by some Iraqis in a truck across the river. His 'coax' jammed, so he hit the guy with twenty-five mike-mike. Blew the guy apart like spaghetti. Anyway, the general freaked out when he saw it. Called Joe a murderer in front of his Marines and shit like that. He wants an investigation."

I was perplexed, not at Day's engagement, but instead at the fact that a retired general officer who had been following the division around to write a book would put himself in such a compromising position. I was also angered that he would second-guess our foreign exchange officer like that. Joe Day had proven himself a capable officer and leader. No one had any reason to doubt him or his abilities. I walked away from the COC feeling disturbed over the episode. Months later I was thankful to hear Joe Day had been exonerated of any wrongdoing in the incident.

A half-mile up the road the last vehicles from 3rd Platoon pulled out of the trail network and linked up with the rest of the company herringboned on the shoulder. I walked up to Capt Portiss.

"Any more problems out there?"

"Negative. We got a pretty decent BDA after we finished up with the arty and mortars."

"Check. Listen, we're in a temporary holding status right now. Circle up the wagons by the road, get some local security out, and let's get everyone's heads down."

"Roger, sounds good to me."

"Oh, one more thing," I added. "Division dropped the MOPP level back down to MOPP-One. Tell everyone to get their rubber booties off."

"Thank God," he replied heavily.

Portiss turned and directed vehicles to cover the road that bisected the company. The order went out for the scouts to cover the area around the vehicles, and after I was satisfied that all was going well I sat down in the dirt next to my vehicle. My feet throbbed heavily, and after gingerly pulling off the thick rubber over-boots and sweat-soaked combat boots I leaned in close to examine the damage. It was the first time I had seen my bare feet in three or four days, and what I saw startled me. The chafed flesh was red and painful to the touch, and both ankles had swelled to twice their normal size. The skin felt paper-thin and ready to burst at the slightest pressure, and faint red streaks appeared to be crawling up my ankles from the soles. *Uh-oh,* I thought, grimly. *This doesn't look good. Time to stop being a tough guy.* I yelled for the Headquarters Platoon corpsman, Hospitalman Third Class Nathan Sprinkman.

"Doc, my feet are fucked up," I said, lying on my back with my feet elevated on my campstool. Just acknowledging the fact made me feel like a non-hacker. He leaned in close and poked the soles of both feet. I yelled.

"Ow! Jeez-us that hurts."

"Yeah, you've got a lot of swelling down there. I've been seeing a lot of this. You really need to stay off your feet for a while, sir."

"Yeah, right, Doc."

"Well, try to keep them clean and keep clean socks on, then."

"Well, I'm fresh out of clean socks. I'll figure something out."

"If those red streaks get any worse I'll give you some antibiotics. . . ." But his words fell on deaf ears. I was out cold in the dirt.

◆ ◇ ◆

"CO, wake up. We're moving."

I snapped awake and sat up. "Huh? What's going on?"

Portiss was next to me again. "Battalion just called and told us to move out to the river."

Delta Company's mission had changed from locating a fording site to establishing a screen along the river's banks. Weapons Company would be on our southern flank and Alpha Company would situate itself to our north. Delta's LAVs slowly filed back into the canal/levee maze toward the river, this time taking a different route to avoid the confusion experienced earlier. Halfway to the river bank we approached a tiny village on the outskirts of a large palm grove. As our column eased its way through the winding trail it was like an encounter between the twenty-first century and the middle ages. Old men and women and their families tended livestock and miniature gardens around their simple mud huts, yet our passage through their homesteads elicited little visible reaction. At the village's periphery the copse of date-palm trees thickened, but not enough to conceal a large ammunition dump hidden within. Although not guarded or defended like the storage facility from which 1st Platoon had taken fire earlier that morning, this makeshift ammunition dump had clearly been placed next to the village for one reason and one reason only: the Republican Guard knew that if we found it and attempted to detonate it, the resulting explosions would level the village and kill most, if not all, of the inhabitants. There was nothing we could do. We marked and reported its position and continued our measured patrol to the screen.

The column wound its way back into the open. But before we knew it the narrow earthen levee upon which our vehicle tires precariously clung suddenly had run out, trapping the first half of the company's column. Lieutenant Parment radioed the bad news.

"Black-Six, we're at a dead-end here. We need to back up."

Shit, I thought. *Shit, shit, shit. This is getting old.* I radioed back.

"Roger, copy. All Victors, hold in place. I say again, hold in place. Don't pull up on this paddy-dike, over." I looked behind me to see another three or four LAVs already committed to the confines of the levee. Now there were no fewer than ten vehicles poised nearly bumper-to-bumper on the elevated and terribly exposed embankment. I looked to my left and right and realized the company was in a prime position for another ambush.

"Back up," I radioed. *"Slowly."* To our left the wide-open, muddy field greeted us. To our right a deep swamp extended out to a tree line one hundred meters away. It was a perfect place for the enemy to hide, and as the LAV commanders methodically directed their drivers to reverse direction I expected the shadows in the trees to light up with the muzzle-flashes of another ambush. But when the tree line remained silent, another, more pressing fear gripped me: we were once again in danger of rolling our vehicles off the steep sides of the levee and into the stagnant water below. With each steering correction made by the vehicle commanders to their drivers, the knobby tires of the fourteen-ton LAVs ground the brittle surface of the embankment apart until less and less of it remained stable. The crumbling levee quickly deteriorated to the point where in some places both right and left sets of the LAVs' tires hung off the edges.

It was nerve-wracking. As we worked our way out of our current predicament, the villagers behind us signaled the rest of the company and pointed to a bypass that provided safe transit through the paddy and forward to the banks of the river. By taking pity on us, the villagers had saved the company from an evening of driving around in circles for God knows how long.

The sector along the river delineated for Delta Company stretched only a few kilometers, and the platoons packed tightly into vehicle positions right off River Road's shoulder. As the platoon commanders began reporting their boundaries, Lt Schwartz's voice sounded on the radio.

"This is White-One—Contact! Enemy personnel across the river!" The *thump-thump-thump* of 25mm fire from 2nd Platoon resonated along the banks, and as day turned to dusk the tracers arcing across the river's expanse glowed a brilliant neon red. Several bursts of fire from 2nd Platoon's main guns sent the enemy personnel on the opposite bank to ground, and Schwartz called to request mortar support. Once the rounds crashed into the trees hiding the irritants across the river, the engagement was over almost as soon as it began. The brief game of cat and mouse between 2nd Platoon and the shadowy figures across the water defined how the enemy would engage us—and how we would respond—for the entire four days Delta Company operated along the Nahr Diyala.

Swift movement across the sky in front of the company caught my eye. Silhouetted in the fading dusk, a Navy F-14 Tomcat swooped across Delta Company's frontage, and then climbed sharply. A moment later the crack of high explosives sounded off to the company's flank. I radioed Spool.

"What the hell's going on? Where did that F-14 come from?"

"I don't know," he replied. "We're trying to get him out of here right now."

But the damage had already been done. Or almost. Thinking an LAV-AT platoon from Weapons Company was an enemy armored vehicle formation, the Tomcat had dived in on it and dropped a five-hundred-pound bomb in their midst. It was a close call, and it rightfully got the Weapons Marines' dander up. The F-14 incident—like the strafing of Marines and amtracks in An Nasiriyah on 23 March by an air force A-10 Warthog—proved once more that the Marine Corps' sister services were still not yet capable of providing effective close air support (CAS) of Marines on the ground. The F-14 had seen a target of opportunity along the Diyala's banks and engaged without terminal control from anyone on the ground. The A-10 pilot in An Nasiriyah, although dispatched by a forward air controller in an adjacent company, later acknowledged that he had never received adequate training in armored vehicle identification. The experience of watching an aircraft execute a bombing run on a friendly unit made me resolve never to employ CAS unless it was Marine aircraft, or at least until the navy and air force improved their track record. The mutual trust that existed between Marine Corps infantry officers and aviators—a trust developed as a result of shared training and hardships at The Basic School early in our careers—was what had allowed us to call in the Cobras practically right on top of us during the ambush at the Elbow on 3 April. We would continue to do the same thing throughout the war, each time relying on people we had never met to push the envelope in the air above us as far as it would go. You couldn't expect the same from the other services.

As the engagement across the river subsided, I received a radio call from the battalion to report to the COC for a commanders meeting. Leaving the company in the capable hands of the XO, I directed Gurganus to turn around and head back to the paved road five kilometers away. With the light outside fading, the trail network assumed a new look. Our previous route seemed to have been swallowed by the landscape, and our vehicle was soon lost in the confusing canal/levee/trail warren. Every promising trail led to a dead-end or drop-off every time. Cutting across-country was out of the question. The areas that weren't broken and soggy were filled with thick, impenetrable vegetation that would stop anything short of a bulldozer. It didn't take long for me to call the battalion and report my lack of progress.

"Highlander, this is Dragon-Six. I'm stuck out here in this maze. There's no way I'm gonna make it on time."

Bob Whalen's voice answered. "Roger that, Dragon-Six. Don't bother. We'll pass the information to you tomorrow."

We backtracked our circuitous route and finally, more than an hour later, located the company command post. Captain Portiss had set Headquarters Platoon into a 360-degree formation within a dried-up paddy bordered on all sides by another raised levee. In the dark the vehicles were silent, and Marines roamed the perimeter in pairs. The only noises were the murmur of radios and hushed conversations within the LAV-C2. Staff Sergeant Kappen and 1stSgt Guzman met me on the ground as I climbed down from the turret.

"How goes everything out here?" I asked. "Is everyone set in?"

"Good to go, sir," replied Kappen. "Local security is out, radio watches are set up, and the platoons are reporting in to the XO."

I looked around for a moment. "Roger that. I'll go see what the XO is up to."

"Go to sleep, sir," said Guzman, the tone in his voice stern.

"Yeah, we got it right now, sir," added Kappen.

There was little use arguing, and it was difficult for me to make a case to stay awake anyway. My voice was hoarse and raspy, my eyes drooped, and I swayed back and forth drunkenly from the throbbing in my feet.

"All right, you don't have to tell me twice," I managed. "You know when to wake me." I lay down on the rock hard paddy-bed beneath my feet and stared up at the stars. Before sleep caught up with me I thought about how far Delta Company had come. There had been a time when I would have tried to stay awake all night to monitor radio traffic, a time when the Marines had not yet earned my trust and confidence. But that was in the past now. In my heart I knew the men were doing their jobs in the manner that they were trained. They had graduated, and although I felt satisfaction and security in the fact that they no longer required close supervision, the same sense of disappointment that had surfaced days before remained closeted in my mind. I dozed off and slept heavily, oblivious to the sporadic mortar volleys that punished the enemy soldiers across the river throughout the night.

I awoke on the morning of 6 April reborn, ready to take on the world. Guzman and Kappen had been correct: I had needed the rest. Had they not practically forced me to get some sleep I might actually have physically shut down. I would later hear about a regimental commander within the division who had fallen asleep right in front of his battalion commanders during a staff meeting. It was an egregious error on his part, yet it reminded me how close I had come to doing the very same thing. Fatigue makes you say and do weird things, and sometimes you just can't go on. But it's easier to deal with when you are surrounded by men whom you can trust.

The sun rose at our backs, illuminating the tree line on the far side of the river. Schwartz's voice sounded again on the radio.

"Black-Six, we've spotted two tanks in the trees on the other side of the river. Request permission to take them out with TOWs."

"Are they hot?" I asked, referring to the heat plume that would be picked up by his LAV's thermal sights.

"Negative."

I thought for a moment. Most likely the tanks had been abandoned, but I wasn't willing to take that chance. We had been lucky so far, and with the short range across the river I doubted an enemy gunner would miss one of our LAVs.

"Roger. Take them out, over."

Seconds later, the hissing *whoosh* of two TOW missiles shrieked across the river's calm waters. The thud of their impacts immediately followed.

"Targets destroyed," reported Schwartz.

I relayed the engagement to the battalion's watch officer. He responded by directing me to shift the company's screen to the north in order to cover a broader swath of the river. Drawing the new boundaries of our sector on the acetate of my map, I divided the territory along the river's bank into three platoon sectors and relayed the information to the platoon commanders. The company's vehicles backed out of their observation positions and onto River Road, and once again we were on the move. Our progress was hindered at one point by a herd of filthy sheep sauntering down the dusty road. *Great. Yet another way to get ambushed out here.* In another time and another war I might have simply given the order for the lead platoon to plow through the herd, regardless of the number of animals crushed beneath our tires. But with no one shooting at us yet, such an order would no doubt result in unpleasant consequences. We could do nothing but orient our turrets outboard and look for the enemy trying to sight in on us.

As each element within the company reached its designated sector, the vehicles cut left sharply off the dirt and gravel of River Road and into the vegetated slope overlooking the water. Our arrival surprised several armed Iraqis across the waterway from 2nd Platoon.

"Black-Six, this is White-One. My section has a visual on about a squad of Iraqis with weapons."

"What are they doing?"

"Not much, just staring at us. They're wearing web gear also. Request permission to fire a warning shot at them."

"Roger, White-One." I realized immediately the mistake I had made by granting Lieutenant Schwartz's request. He really didn't need to do anything but just let them be. But before I could override him I heard a burst of machine-gun fire from his vehicle. His excited voice jumped back on the net.

"They're engaging us, Black-Six. We're returning fire." The Bushmaster's *thump-thump-thump* cycled once again, and I radioed Schwartz.

“I’m Oscar Mike to your position, White-One.”

Captain Portiss jumped on the radio. “Six, Spool’s got a section of Hueys standing by, over.”

“Roger, Five. Turn them over to White-One.” I keyed my intercom. “Step on it, Gurganus.” The LAV lurched forward, and the hydraulics powered up within the turret as Davis squeezed the palm trigger. Ahead of us two gunships rolled in above Lt Schwartz’s vehicle and began strafing the vegetation on the river’s far bank with minigun and .50-caliber machine-gun fire. On their second pass both helicopters fired volleys of flechette rockets into the tree line, the hundreds of tiny nail-like darts shredding the vegetation and kicking up clouds of earth and undergrowth. And then it was over. Schwartz radioed.

“This is White-One. Engagement complete.” Second Platoon once again had more kills under their belts.

This engagement troubled me. I was reminded of the ambush at the Elbow and my concern about overkill. Analyzing the contact report made by Lt Schwartz, I realized there had been little point in calling in the gunships. I didn’t want to second-guess the lieutenant, particularly since I hadn’t been on the scene at the moment of first contact. But surely his vehicles and their organic weapon systems could have handled an enemy squad, if it had in fact been an enemy squad in the first place. Everyone and his brother in that part of the world carried an AK-47. It was as much a part of the culture as squatting to urinate. Had the Iraqis’ intent been hostile? I continued to think about it throughout the day.

After positioning the command post on a rise overlooking the river and the majority of the screen, I climbed from my space in the turret and sat in the shade created by the vehicle’s hull. The weather, which only weeks before had been chilly, had heated up to the point where wearing MOPP suits was barely tolerable. I sat next to the vehicle, sweating my ass off and squirming at the uncomfortable sensation of perspiration running down my back and pooling in my shorts. Swarms of gnats and flies buzzed around my head, seeking the moisture of my eyes and mouth. My earlier desire to attack the day was replaced by a yearning to go home. Hell, to go *anywhere* away from that place. As I sat cursing and swatting the air around me, Staff Sergeant Kappen walked up and took a knee.

“Bad news, sir. Got a water shortage in the battalion.”

“How is the company doing?”

“Almost out.”

Just hearing the words made me suddenly crave a tall, cool glass of water. But I figured it would be bad form to start pulling on my drinking tube while Kappen told me we were running out. I sighed.

"All right. Pass the word. Keep physical activity to a minimum until battalion gets this resolved." In my discomfort I suddenly questioned why I was doing what I was doing. Feeling sorry for myself, I had to constantly remember that I had volunteered for the kind of job I held. It was also necessary to remind myself that I had begged to remain in command of the company for the war. There was no one to blame but me. The same phrase repeated itself inside my now-pounding head. *One day I'll look back on this and be glad I experienced it.* But an even louder thought quickly drowned it out.

This sucks.

✦ ✧ ✦

That night as I slept in the hole dug alongside our vehicle, the distant thumping of 25mm fire to our north awakened me. I called up to Gurganus, who sat in the turret manning the radios.

"What's going on?"

"Charlie Company's engaged, sir."

I sat up in my sleeping bag. "How are they doing?"

"They sound like they're all right, sir."

I lay back down and fell asleep. Gil Juarez was one of the most capable officers I had ever met. The shit would really have to hit the fan for him to need our assistance.

Several times in the night I was roused from my slumber by the radio watch, telling me the XO needed me to approve a mortar mission. Earlier that day at the battalion staff meeting several officers from the operations section had made it clear that all indirect fire missions had to be approved by company commanders. I understood the intent of the regulation, but my confidence in Capt Portiss was so high that I considered the order a nuisance. *He's smart, he won't screw it up.* But I heeded the order. I slept curled up next to the vehicle tires, my map board next to me and the radio handset hanging down from inside the turret. Each time the Marine on radio watch called down to me, I would pop my head out from inside my sleeping bag and press the handset against my ear. The XO would read off an eight-digit grid coordinate somewhere across the river and a description of the target, and after proofing it on my map I would authorize the fire mission. It was most certainly not the way I had learned to approve indirect fire missions. Contact with the enemy, the mystery and intrigue of which had fascinated Delta Company for so long, already seemed routine. Although earlier in the war the Marines had griped continuously about the company's lack of action, even with only three major engagements under their belts everyone was quickly growing tired of it.

✦ ✧ ✦

The morning of 7 April represented a milestone of a different sort for all of us. At 0100Z the battalion executive officer announced over the radio that we would assume MOPP-0 that morning. *MOPP-Zero?* I said to myself, incredulous. *No more chemical suit?* When I woke up again ninety minutes later I thought I had been dreaming. But as I looked around the company CP, Marines moved about the area clad only in their desert patterned utility uniforms. With American forces completely encircling Baghdad, the division had made the assessment that we no longer faced a credible NBC threat. All that was required was that we continue to wear our gas masks strapped to our persons. Compared to the suffocating hell of living in our MOPP suits, the order to retain our gas masks didn't bother us at all. Like a child tearing open his presents on Christmas morning, I ripped the chemical suit from my body and cast it aside in the dirt. For eighteen days straight I had been trapped inside it, and suddenly my body felt liberated. The suit itself was filthy and covered with tiny rips and tears, which I had attempted to repair along the way with green duct tape. Having been sweated through countless times since 20 March, the material was crusted with crystallized salt stains and the clotted brown scabs of LCpl Suarez del Solar's blood. Despite the fact that the uniform I quickly donned was dirty, the soft, cool cotton material against my chafed skin felt like a silk suit compared to the MOPP ensemble. Like a rubber exercise outfit, the greenhouse of the chemical suit had caused me to shed weight by burning fat. When my body had run low on fat it had begun consuming muscle for energy. My camouflage utility uniform hung loosely from my emaciated body. Before departing Camp Pendleton I had weighed 200 pounds. Now I was nearly down to 175. *At this rate I'm gonna melt away into nothing by the time this thing's over,* I thought. The dramatic weight loss frustrated me.

As I sat next to my vehicle lamenting my body's deterioration, Bob Woodruff walked over with a drawn, sullen look on his face. I stood up to meet him.

"What's up?" I asked.

"I just found out that my best friend, David Bloom, died yesterday."

"Jesus, I'm sorry to hear that. How did it happen?"

"They think it was DVT, deep veinous thrombosis."

"What's that?" I asked, confused.

"It's a blood clot that stops your heart. A lot of people think it's caused by sitting with your knees bent for a long time. Anyway, he died of a pulmonary embolism."

I had never heard of DVT before then. Supposedly the condition occurs frequently in crewmen sitting inside cramped armored vehicles and obese people on airlines sitting for long periods. Hearing this from Woodruff alarmed me. I thought back to the countless hours my Marines had spent contorting themselves inside their turrets and scout compartments. If it was indeed a legitimate condition, then I could expect men to start dropping like flies at anytime. Hell, *I* could keel over after all the time I had spent hunched in my turret seat behind the thermal sight.

Woodruff hesitated for a moment, and then spoke again.

"I need to get home for his funeral. My wife and his wife are best friends, too. They're both taking it pretty hard, so I need to go be with them. Can you get me on a helicopter to the rear?"

"That's not up to me, Bob. I'll have to ask my CO. He's the only one who'll be able to approve or disapprove it. But I'll try."

Woodruff rode with me to the COC, where he was quickly whisked away on a nearby Huey. It was the last I heard from him. The news of his best friend's death was tragic, and I felt for him. But Woodruff's request also filled me with a furious resentment. In his position as an embedded reporter he was free to come and go as he pleased. After all, covering the war was just a job to him. No paycheck, no headline story, was worth missing his friend's funeral. The Marines weren't so lucky. With the war in full swing and the capital of Iraq in sight, no such request would be honored if best friends or even family members of my men passed away back in the United States. We were all in it for the long haul. In the parlance of the times, the Marines knew that the only way home was through Baghdad.

17

The Strip

The sky above our screen along the Nahr Diyala had turned overcast, and I expected rain to begin falling any minute. Back at the company command post, SSgt Reeves stopped by our position. His slow, ambling gait almost resembled a waddle, and I could always recognize him from a mile away. As he approached my LAV I called out a greeting to him.

"Hey, Staff Sergeant. How're you doing?"

"Not bad, sir. Yourself?"

"Can't complain. I'm not wearing my MOPP suit anymore." We talked for several minutes, and after a while it was clear that something troubled him.

"So, what's really on your mind?"

"You think the company might be getting carried away in all this, sir?"

"How so?"

"It's just some things I've been hearing the Marines say. I wonder if they're heads aren't totally screwed on." I knew exactly what he was talking about. My concerns mirrored his, and on the ride back to the company's position that afternoon I had decided to speak to the company about them. Staff Sergeant Reeves's musings reminded me of that plan, and as he got up to leave I told him.

"Just so you know, I'm gonna radio the company and talk to them about all that. I'll be including what you and I just talked about."

"Thanks, sir." He paused for a moment and then spoke again. "Hey, how's your Copenhagen supply doing?"

I grumbled. "Shit, it's been empty for a long time. I've been living off Blue Death for the last couple of days." With that, Reeves reached into his trouser pocket and tossed an unopened tin of tobacco to me.

"Here you go, sir."

"Hey, no way Staff Sergeant. I can't take a can from you."

"Sure you can, sir. I've got plenty."

"Well, gee. Thanks." I was practically speechless at his act of kindness. When there's a tobacco shortage in the field you can never expect anyone to just give away his stash. But that was the kind of selfless guy Reeves was. He winked and turned to leave.

It was indeed high time for me to have a fireside chat with the company. But perhaps more importantly, I needed to have a private talk with Lt Schwartz as well. He had gained a reputation within the company for being too quick to engage suspected enemy personnel. I first heard it materialize within my crew as they discussed the engagements the company had fought with the enemy. Schwartz's name came up often. But as soon as I heard a Marine say, "Boy, Lieutenant Schwartz sure likes to kill everything, doesn't he?" I knew I had to get involved. The situation had come to a head the previous night when I heard his voice on the company net.

"There are a bunch of wild dogs near my position," he had said. "They're foaming at the mouth; I think they're rabid. If they come any closer to my position I'm going to shoot them with my pistol."

His posturing over the radio had alarmed me, and I jumped on the net. "Negative, White-One. Stand down."

Remembering that and the events of the last five days, I radioed the company.

"Here's the deal. It's been a long two weeks for everybody. But the company has now had three engagements: the Elbow, the ammo dump, and the contacts across the Diyala. Every platoon has now been in combat.

"Now that that's out of the way, it's time for everyone to step back, take a deep, cleansing breath, and start thinking more about who or what we're supposed to engage out here. Up to this point, our guidance from higher-up has been that if anyone has a weapon, he's to be considered hostile and can be killed on sight.

"But remember, we're in a country where *everybody* has an AK-47. It's a status symbol out here, but it's also a form of self-protection. Remember, just because we *can* shoot everyone holding a weapon doesn't mean we *have* to do so. Let me be clear: Positive identification of enemy personnel is required prior to engaging, and no one is to fire his weapon unless the enemy is in your crosshairs."

It felt as if I was preaching to them, but their judgment out on the line would be the only thing that prevented needless killing. Although I didn't want to doubt decisions made by Lt Schwartz after the fact, his behavior had to be addressed. After giving it much thought, I directed the platoons to shrink the coverage of the screen, and I pulled 2nd Platoon off the line and back to the rear of the company's position. They had been involved in the most fighting so far, and the Marines needed to cool down some. By serving as the company's reserve they could also rest and ease off the trigger. As 2nd Platoon collapsed its position on the screen, I radioed Lt Schwartz to report to my position. I didn't look forward to the conversation we were about to have.

Earlier in the day one of the company's SNCOs had confided in me some news about Schwartz that had further distressed me. Just before 1st Platoon was engaged at the ammunition dump, one of the LAV-ATs had become stuck in the mud and required another vehicle to retrieve it. Schwartz and his wingman had attached their winches to the trapped vehicle and were attempting to free the TOW crew when Parment's platoon was ambushed. Hearing the report of enemy contact over the radio, Schwartz and his wingman disconnected their cables from the mired vehicle and sped off to the battle, leaving the AT crew stuck in the mud. The fact that he had handed over the recovery effort to his platoon sergeant did little to change my assessment of the situation. Schwartz's decision reflected poor judgment, and when he showed up at my vehicle I challenged him on the story's authenticity.

"Is that true? Did you really leave that AT crew stuck in the mud?"

"Yes, sir. I thought Lieutenant Parment's platoon needed reinforcement."

I looked him right in the eyes. "That was a bad call."

"But I left Staff Sergeant Reeves's section behind to get the vehicle unstuck."

"Irrelevant," I countered. "You ditched that crew so you could go get into the fight. What kind of example does that set for those Marines who were left behind?"

He stared blankly at me, not sure what to say. I continued.

"Listen to me: you need to cool your jets. You've quickly developed a bad reputation for yourself in the company. The Marines think you're kill-crazy."

He looked shocked. "What makes them say that?"

"Well Jesus, man, what do you think? Your platoon has had the most enemy contact and the most engagements. You're always the first on the scene. That by itself isn't necessarily a bad thing. But when the Marines hear you on the radio saying you're gonna kill a bunch of dogs with your nine-millimeter, or they hear you keep asking to fire warning shots at people across the river, or they see you leave a stuck vehicle behind so you can go jump into a firefight, they develop their own opinions. It doesn't matter if they're true or not." My words had hurt him.

"Sir, have I ever fired any of my weapons without your permission in any of these instances?" he asked heavily.

"No, but you need to watch yourself. You're looking like you're trigger happy." I paused momentarily.

"Listen, Brandon," I continued. "You're doing a good job out here, but your Marines don't need you to be a trigger-puller. They need you to be their leader right now. They're looking to you to be the mature one, the rational one. The one who will make the right decisions over the radio. You understand what I'm saying?"

"Yes, sir."

"All right, then. Take your platoon off the line, assume the company reserve, and get some rest."

✦ ✧ ✦

I sat mulling over a letter I had just received from Ashley. Earlier at the COC, someone had handed me a package she had sent via the new adjutant who had flown out to join the battalion in Iraq. I tore open the thick manila envelope to find handfuls of candy, beef jerky, and a stack of computer printouts. Sitting down to read the letters, I discovered that Ashley had emailed my family and friends and told them she was sending a package that would reach me faster than the conventional mail (which was still not reaching us at all). Everyone had responded with emails, which she then printed out and included in her care package. Their words reminded me how lucky I was to have the wife, family, and friends that I did.

I saved Ashley's letter for last, but I was startled by the sentences that jumped off the page at me. Angry, upset words described the pain, anguish, and frustration she had gone through dealing with the aftermath of LCpl Suarez del Solar's death; anger at me for not telling her the truth over the phone the night it happened; frustration in dealing with Suarez del Solar's father, who had launched his own political crusade to protest the Marine Corps and the war that had taken his only son from him; anguish at the exposure to the constant stream of graphic images that filled the television, yet never knowing my location or whether I was even alive. But I couldn't identify with her pain, nor could I allow myself to dwell on the greater meaning of her words. I needed a clear mind, one free from the emotional obstacles that would cloud my ability to make proper decisions. I didn't experience the same apprehensions that usually filled Marines' minds—fear that she would leave me, or that she would spend all of our money or screw my best friend. I wasn't afraid she would drop her support for me and what I was doing. What concerned me was how much the damage that was being inflicted upon her would affect her later, after my return home. Only time would tell.

I was in a black mood, half wishing I had never received mail in the first place, when Second Lieutenant Russell Obar, the new battalion adjutant, showed up at my vehicle. The investigation into LCpl Suarez's death was underway, and I was first on the list to be interviewed. As he began questioning me, I interrupted him.

"Wait a minute, Lieutenant. Aren't you going to read me my rights?"

"Well, I wasn't planning on it, sir. I'm just trying to get some background facts."

"Am I suspected of responsibility for his death? Because if I am, you better read me my rights."

"Negative, sir. The investigation is focused on higher headquarters' complicity in the Marine's death."

I stared at him. "Good. Okay, let's get it over with, then."

Drawing from my journal notes, I rehashed the details surrounding the evening of 27 March. I was glad I'd been quick to record the event. Without what I had written down on paper, my memory wouldn't have provided an accurate accounting of that horrible evening. After Obar finished questioning me he asked to speak with Lt Cullins, who was already making his way to the command post.

Cullins walked up next to my vehicle and sat down on a dirt ledge next to the tires. He pulled out an unopened pack of Marlboros and displayed it for me to see, the cellophane glistening brightly.

"Mmm, care for a fresh, stateside cigarette, sir?"

"Holy cow!" I exclaimed, leaning over and snatching the pack from him. "Where did you get these?"

"Sandy sent them to me. Can't complain about a woman who sends you tobacco." He tore into the pack and offered me one. "So, what's going on, sir?"

"This is Lieutenant Obar, the new adj. He needs to talk to you about Suarez."

As the two lieutenants discussed the investigation, I turned back to the other side of the LAV where the crew was trying to carry on a conversation with three young Iraqi boys. They had watched us from afar for close to an hour, and the three of them had finally summoned enough courage to approach the Marines. One made a motion with his hands that looked like opening a book, and then he pointed to his eyes and the pages.

"Looks like they want magazines," said Gurganus. He reached in the back of the vehicle and returned with a handful of rumpled hotrod magazines. "Hey, this what you want?"

The boldest Iraqi child snatched the magazines from Gurganus's hand and bolted away from our position and out into the middle of the field to our front. He sat down by himself and immediately began thumbing through the pictures in each periodical, an amazed look plastered across his face. Meanwhile, small groups of local farmers and herdsmen cautiously approached the platoon positions out on the line, bringing with them offerings of *na'an* bread, lamb, and tea. Thanking the Marines profusely, they described how the enemy soldiers had retreated back across the Diyala River. Our arrival and the fireworks we had brought with us had apparently scared off the bad guys. It was the kind of news that we needed to hear, and the way we wanted to hear it. The locals' willingness to speak with us and provide us with actionable intelligence signified a victory of sorts. We now knew that even this close to Baghdad there were Iraqis who supported our efforts to topple Saddam Hussein and his henchmen. But we still had the streets and alleys of Baghdad to contend with. Would our reception be as cordial once we were inside the city?

✦ ✧ ✦

Though we had only sat on the banks of the Nahr Diyala for three days, our static posture made it seem like weeks. More aggravating than our lack of activity was the fact that no suitable crossing site for the RCT could be found. Well, that wasn't exactly accurate. Weapons Company had discovered a fording site in its sector that would be capable of supporting a crossing, but everyone soon realized the banks of the Diyala weren't the problem. The obstacle preventing RCT-5 from crossing the Nahr Diyala in its sector was the terrain itself leading up to the river. The crisscrossing network of deep canals, treacherous levees, and unstable ground made passage by the RCT's heavy equipment next to impossible. Regimental Combat Team 5, which had fought as 1st Marine Division's main effort for the majority of the drive to Baghdad, now had to take a back seat as RCT-7 pushed across the Nahr Diyala farther to the south. The knowledge that the terrain didn't support a crossing in our sector did nothing to alleviate the sense of failure I felt for myself, the company, and the battalion as a whole. We were a reconnaissance unit, yet our reconnaissance and analysis of the river and its approaches had yielded nothing tangible for the regimental commander. After bitching and complaining for so long about the battalion not getting to play, we had finally been given a doctrinal mission and had come up short.

The long-awaited push into Baghdad was set for the morning of 8 April. Delta Company received a frag order to displace south along the Nahr Diyala and establish a support-by-fire position to support 1/5 and 3/5 as they crossed the river into Baghdad proper. We arrived and set into position along an elevated portion of River Road that overlooked the slow-running waters of the Diyala twenty feet below. Almost immediately I heard a report over the radio from Lt Stiller.

"Black-Six, this is Green-One. We've got a visual on two tanks to our front, across the river. One's a T-55 and the other's a T-62."

"Are they hot?"

"Negative. They don't appear to be manned right now, but we can see rucksacks strapped to them." The packs hanging from the sides of the tanks indicated they were still in working order. If their original occupants weren't around to operate them, someone else could. That answered the question for me.

"Roger, Green-One. Take them out."

The *whoosh* of two TOWs hissed up the riverbed, and we all watched intently as the missiles screamed toward their targets. One after another they found their marks, each exploding with a visible flash and delayed *bang*. Thin tendrils of smoke leaked from the holes in the tanks' armor, and they smoldered for fifteen minutes. The heat from the missile impacts finally reached the ammunition stores deep within the turrets, which cooked off into great plumes of fiery plasma that shot fifty feet into the air. From our vantage point more than two kilometers away, the intense burning of each tank resembled the flare produced when an entire book of matches is lit—brief, powerful, and over in seconds. Blackened shells replaced what had once been formidable fighting machines.

Sadly, destroying the two tanks would prove to be the highlight of our support for the RCT's river crossing. The company spent most of that long day watching someone else's battle rage across the river as Cobra helicopters buzzed low over the palm groves, rocketing and shooting up derelict tanks and APCs left and right. Our greatest enemy turned out to be squadrons of flies swarming around us. They attacked in black clouds, seeking all the moisture our bodies could provide. It didn't make sense. Why couldn't these bastards seek moisture down at the water right below us? As I struggled to eat an MRE, the flies decided they wanted to sample that as well. I sat next to the vehicle, the foil pouch of the MRE tucked between my knees. With one hand I spooned the stew quickly into my mouth while the other hand vigorously waved back and forth in an effort to swat away the legions of flies attacking my food. In all the moving and squirming about I managed to spill a dime-sized drop of stew on the front of my utility blouse. From nowhere a troop of the hungry insects closed in on the stain, consuming it. Together their teeming mass seemed to boil on my uniform, and my stomach churned. I felt like puking. But my shouts of disgust and efforts to swipe them away were in vain—this was clearly the flies' turf. I was merely a nuisance to them.

The afternoon burned away, and from our support-by-fire position we could no longer see elements of RCT-5 slowly advancing into the outskirts of Baghdad. I felt useless. It had become a familiar emotion. My silent fuming at the situation was interrupted by Maj Harper radioing with new instructions.

"Collapse your position. Link up with Weapons Company to the south and rendezvous with the battalion at the RCT's crossing site."

The bridge that led from Highway 6 across the Diyala had been damaged and could no longer support vehicle traffic. But that didn't seem to matter for us. The bridgehead had been secured by elements of RCT-7 the previous day, and another crossing had been forced by a unit from RCT-1. Getting into Baghdad was apparently old news.

Delta Company wound its way down the final stretch of River Road to the intersection that led to the RCT's crossing site. A clog of armored vehicles extending back more than a mile greeted us, and I radioed Dave Hudspeth to ask him for a guide to his position. We found his company parked in an empty lot on the southern side of the access road leading to the crossing site. Vacant stares and bored looks filled his Marines' faces. They had been there for a while, and from the looks of it the traffic jam in front of them hadn't moved an inch. I split the company into two columns parked on either side of the road in similarly vacant lots, and with Weapons Company we awaited the arrival of the battalion forward. Iraqis of all ages swarmed our stationary vehicles, alternately begging for food and attempting to separate us from our money with offers of Blue Death cigarettes. The price of tobacco had climbed to five dollars per pack—twice as much as I'd paid less than a week earlier. We needed cigarettes and the Iraqis knew it. Capitalism had found its way to a nation of people most of whom had no running water. I shook my head in disbelief. *Is this what we're here for?* I thought bitterly as I sat atop my turret. *So they can rip us off?*

Light began to fade from the sky. I suspected we were about to be in for a long night, and as the drivers within the company disappeared into their compartments to install their night-driving devices we finally heard from the battalion commander.

"Warlord-Six, Dragon-Six, this is Highlander-Six. We won't be crossing the Diyala tonight. Turn around, head back, and link up with the battalion at its assembly area at the following coordinates."

I relayed the location of the battalion's position to the platoons, and together we made a U-turn and headed back east toward Highway 6 and the battalion. Our effort to beat the sunset failed, and as the company column approached the battalion's assembly area in the darkness a Marine from the operations section described where we needed to situate our vehicles within the formation. The battalion had formed itself into a tight coil, and as Delta Company occupied its position we soon realized our vehicles had taken up too much room on the battalion's perimeter. The vehicle commanders had been accustomed to dispersing their vehicles in the dark, but the battalion wanted us to park our LAVs practically on top of each other. I climbed down from my turret and walked over to Capt Portiss's vehicle.

"We're too spread out for the battalion. Take care of this for me, will you?"

"Too spread out? Are you fucking kidding me?"

"Nope. They want us in tight. Make it happen."

"Roger. I hope no one drops an artillery round in the middle of this clusterfuck."

The rearranging of the companies in the battalion coil began to dissolve into chaos, and I left it for Portiss to deal with. I was ready to blast off, but I needed to go see the battalion commander.

Earlier, just as the company turned around and headed back toward the battalion's assembly area, the radio had exploded with LtCol White's angry voice.

"Break, break, break! Dragon-Six, this is Highlander-Six. I want to see you and your Weapons Platoon commander as soon as we get back to the assembly area!"

But as I approached the forward looking for LtCol White, I realized I had forgotten to bring along Lt Stiller. I found the CO standing by his vehicle.

"Sir, you wanted to see me?"

"Yeah, where's Lieutenant Stiller?"

"He's back trying to get his platoon into position. What happened, sir?"

"Well, back there at the traffic jam when your company turned around to head back here I sat there and watched one of his vehicles cut a high-speed U-turn and miss another LAV by inches."

I slowly shook my head. "Goddamn. Well, sir, I apologize. But it's no surprise to me. That's just the tip of the iceberg. He has the most consistently unsafe platoon in the company. I can't even remember any more how many collisions his vehicles have had. They also keep getting stuck in places they shouldn't be."

White shook his head, and then nodded as if in agreement. I continued to rant.

"I'll tell you, sir. I'm sick of his shit. I have been for a while. If you give me the word now I'll shit-can him in a heartbeat."

"No. Go get him and bring him to me. I want to talk to him one last time. I'm going to make it clear to him that if he screws up one more time, he's through."

"Roger that, sir. Sounds good to me."

I disappeared and returned five minutes later with Stiller. Lieutenant Colonel White immediately launched into him.

"Lieutenant Stiller, I have to tell you . . . I am not impressed at all by your performance out here. I sat and watched one of your LAVs almost smash into another one, and it didn't so much as slow down afterward. Personally, I'm sick of your shit. You are the worst lieutenant in this battalion. You seem to think you don't have to listen to anyone else but yourself. You seem to think you know a lot more than you actually do. Well, you don't, and I'm going to tell you this: if I don't see immediate improvement, you are facing an adverse fitness report. Or an outright relief for cause. I've already spoken with your company commander. He's going to tell you what you need to do to improve, and you better listen to him. Do you understand me?"

Stiller nodded slowly. "Yes, sir."

"Roger. You two are dismissed."

I walked back to the company position with the lieutenant in tow. As we made our way through the darkness, I outlined for him how to correct the problems in his platoon.

"Listen, you need to pull all of your NCOs and vehicle commanders aside and tell them what's up. You're the one who's in charge. Let them know that. They may be the ones that run the platoon on a day-to-day basis, but you're the one who's responsible at the end of the day. If they aren't doing what you want them to do you need to deal with it, and I mean immediately. You can't keep hazarding your platoon like this. Someone's gonna get killed, particularly with all these traffic jams out here."

I rambled on for close to an hour, pointing out basic actions the lieutenant needed to do in order to be successful at his job. They were rudimentary things he should have learned in the six months before he reported to Delta Company, but none of that mattered now. The battalion commander had laid down the law himself: Stiller had one more chance.

✦ ✧ ✦

The wind picked up and blew hard that night, and upon opening my eyes the morning of 9 April I found my sleeping bag covered in the now-familiar film of sand and dust. It had invaded my sleeping bag, and I was covered in grit from head to toe. The fact that I had spent the night sleeping on a rock worsened my mood. Sore and irritated, I called for the company staff to assemble around my vehicle for the latest frag order.

"We're moving out first in the order of march to cross the Diyala into Baghdad this morning. Once we get across we'll head north to screen the RCT in sector."

The staff members returned to their platoons to prepare for the company's departure, and as I walked around my LAV I noticed an orange glow flickering inside the cargo bay of one of the mortar vehicles. Huddled around the tiny flame of a squad stove and trying to heat coffee, the crew was oblivious to the danger posed by the ninety-odd mortar rounds and highly flammable propellant surrounding them. Momentarily speechless, my mouth hung open until finally a booming roar emanated from deep within my body.

"Is that a fire *in there?!"*

Realizing they had been caught, the Marines quickly tried to extinguish the stove's flames as I yelled for SSgt Peralta. Already angry with Weapons Platoon and its leadership because of the antics of the previous night, I leaned in close to Peralta and yelled at the top of my lungs.

"Are your Marines out of their fucking *minds?!* What the fuck are they thinking, Staff Sergeant?!"

"I don't know, sir. I'll fix it."

"You goddamn better! Unfuck them, or I'll unfuck you!"

He turned and immediately laid into the offending Marines. His shouts and curses echoed far beyond the company's position as I stormed back to my vehicle. Seconds later the quick *rat-tat-tat* of a machine-gun burst filled the quiet morning air. *Please don't let that be what I think it is,* I said to myself. The sound was close by, and as I stormed around the side of SSgt Peralta's LAV I saw a Marine standing on the engine grill cover of the second mortar vehicle. His M249 machine gun, its bipod legs open and extended, was pointed down into the radiator cover. A thin wisp of steam curled up from the radiator, and a look of total astonishment had melted across the Marine's colorless face. He had been attempting a functions-check of the weapon, but had forgotten to remove the ammunition belt from the feed tray. As he pulled the charging handle to the rear to examine the chamber, the charging handle slipped from his grip and sent the bolt home against the ammunition. It was a stupid mistake of negligence—an amateur's error.

"Is everyone okay?" I asked the nearest Marine.

"Yes, sir. It went off into the radiator." I would later discover that shards of metal from the radiator casing had embedded themselves in the shoulder of one of the mortar men. Had I known about that when it actually happened I probably would have come completely unglued. Instead, I closed my eyes tightly for a second, and then turned around in the direction of the COC and the battalion commander. I was halfway there when LtCol White met me.

"That sounded like . . ."

"It was, sir," I said angrily. "Nothing we said to Stiller last night sank in. I found one of his mortar crews sitting around a fire inside their vehicle a few minutes ago. A Marine from his other mortar crew just fired a burst of 'five-five-six' from his SAW into the radiator."

White gritted his teeth. "Goddammit."

"I'm ready to fire him right now, sir. Just give me the word."

He didn't hesitate. "That's it. Can him. Ask the battalion XO where he wants to put him."

I called for Stiller, who ran over to where I stood. He glared down at me.

"Lieutenant Stiller, I'm relieving you of your duties. I no longer have confidence in your ability to control your men. Pack your bags and report to the combat trains."

Pausing for a moment, he finally replied, "Aye-aye, sir." He stormed off.

Even as the words came out of my mouth I wondered if my decision had been one based on solid evidence or simply blind rage over Stiller's stupidity. I stood there silently and quickly took stock of everything he had done—or failed to do—in the previous two months. Staff Sergeant Monroe, his face pinched into an angry caricature of itself, stomped up to me as Stiller walked away.

"Well, that fucker just dead-lined his vehicle."

"What?" I asked. "You're shitting me."

"Nope. The radiator has three holes in it. It's done."

I felt vindicated. Lieutenant Stiller's days as a platoon commander in Delta Company were over. He had been given every chance in the world, and he had blown it. I had never wanted to relieve an officer, particularly in combat, but I couldn't afford to divert any more energy thinking about it. There was too much left to do. There was also the question of who would replace him. With no other lieutenants around to fill the void he had left, command of the platoon automatically went to his platoon sergeant, Staff Sergeant Jorgé Molina-Bautista. Hopefully he wouldn't make the same mistakes his lieutenant had.

✦ ✧ ✦

By 0330Z the battalion was back on the road to the ribbon bridge spanning the Nahr Diyala. Morning traffic was light; few American vehicles filled the approach to the bridge, and there were no Iraqi vehicles to be found. The recent spate of Marines and soldiers unknowingly firing on civilian vehicles at checkpoints seemed to have scared the locals into staying foot mobile rather than cruising around town in their cars. That was fine with me. Reports of suicide car-bombers had increased, including a detonation next to an M1A1 several days earlier. In our own battalion, Marines from Alpha Company had thwarted a grenade attack from a vehicle at a checkpoint east of the Nahr Diyala. Everyone was on edge. As we prepared to cross the river into Baghdad, that sense of anxiety only increased.

The ribbon bridge spanning the Diyala, which was nothing more than a series of connected pontoon segments barely wide enough for a tank, was shaky even beneath the weight of our fourteen-ton LAVs. I wondered how well it fared under a seventy-ton Abrams. As it was, the Marine directing traffic across the span only allowed one vehicle at a time to cross. As a result, it took a substantial chunk of time to get the company, and then the rest of the battalion, across the waterway. Once Delta Company was on the other side, movement slowed to a crawl as the battalion gradually made its way across in the same fashion we had. We turned north along the western river road, which, unlike its counterpart on the opposite bank, was merely a narrow dirt trail that wove in and out of the palm groves bordering the approaches to the city.

As the vehicles continued their deliberate creep north along the trail, Lt Parment radioed me from his platoon's position on point.

"Black-Six, this is Red-One. We're at the nine-zero northing where we shot up that ammo dump. Check it out."

I turned my gaze eastward across the water toward the palm grove that had concealed the ambushing enemy four days earlier. All that remained were blackened, shredded stumps of trees and the debris of battle. Artillery tubes hidden within the grove, twisted by the searing heat and explosions, curled and drooped. Skeletons of trucks and jeeps sat half-melted in the ashes. Charred splinters of ammunition crates littered the landscape. Staring at the scorched swath of ground, I thought one thing was certain: whoever had been hiding out in there had picked the wrong company of Marines to screw with that day.

Charred remains of date-palm grove that hid ambushers on 5 April, as seen from the opposite bank of the Nahr Diyala on 9 April 2003.

The river trail took us through tiny hamlets that bordered the river, and every couple of kilometers we passed abandoned Iraqi tanks and APCs. Many still appeared to be operational. I wondered if anyone would do anything to remedy that—spike the guns, tear up the transmissions, anything. Rounding one sharp bend in the trail, the company happened upon a scene reminiscent of the overturned Iraqi tank it had seen in the canal days earlier. A T-72 tank, the crew of which was clearly eager to depart the area, had collided with a BMP-2 infantry fighting vehicle along the trail. The collision, which merely dented the corner of the BMP's hull, had forced the tank off the trail and onto the steep embankment. It remained there unsteadily, ready to tip over. But, unlike the crew of the tank in the canal, the crews of these two vehicles appeared to have escaped with their lives.

First LAR Battalion's previous mission to screen north of RCT-5 dissolved once we crossed the Nahr Diyala. With the Marine Corps and the army flooding into the city, Saddam Hussein's regime had completely fallen apart. Later accounts claimed that Saddam had watched American troops taking over the city, and as he was shuffled into a car to escape he muttered, "Even my clothes have betrayed me." It was a fitting phrase; Hussein was identifiable whether he was in a business suit, a dishdasha, or a military uniform. He himself had seen to that. But at the time we had no idea he was even still alive. What we did know was that Baghdad—the administrative heart of the caliphate and the birthplace of algebra—had collapsed. As Marines toppled statues of Hussein, the city split at the seams. Looters roamed the streets, ravaging every government office in sight. Iraqis of all ages filled the streets, searching for treasures hidden within Ba'ath Party headquarters buildings. Unfortunately, as we would later learn, they searched for treasures in the local museums, too.

We pushed forward and crossed an abandoned canal that ran to the northwest and paralleled a crosshatched, gridded urban slum on Baghdad's periphery. A dilapidated Shi'ite ghetto, it ironically had been named Saddam City. The cookie-cutter, contrived shape on maps and satellite imagery made it apparent that Saddam City had been planned for one reason only: maximizing the use of space to cram as many Iraqi Shi'ites as possible into its constricted boundaries. RCT-5 had established its headquarters in an empty government building east of Saddam City, across the defunct canal and adjacent to Highway 5. With our previous mission overcome by the events transpiring around us, the battalion crossed the canal and staged its vehicles in a vacant lot overlooking Saddam City. Seeking a mission update, the battalion Forward departed the lot while the companies remained stationary. It had already been a long day, and the mind-numbingly slow pace of the battalion's movement up the western bank of the Nahr Diyala had exhausted us. Many Marines used the downtime to catch quick catnaps. Most, however, sat in awe as the widespread looting unfolded in front of us. The Iraqis giddily carried away anything not nailed down. Sheet metal, appliances, wood, metal and plastic tubing, furniture, tires—all of it belonged to them now, and they were happy to let everyone know it. But they were no longer looting just government and military structures. They were going after everything. Someone would have to put a stop to it sooner or later. I wondered who that someone would be.

◆ ◇ ◆

"I want you to plan a mounted patrol in our zone, north of Saddam City and up Highway Five."

Major Harper's words caused my eyes to light up as we stood together inside the empty pool hall that had become 1st LAR Battalion's new headquarters. Portraits of Saddam Hussein lined the concrete walls of the room, which itself was filled with a long row of green-felted billiard tables. Creased, sweat-stained maps marked with various colored lines and symbols had been laid out on the pool tables, and Marines from the battalion staff stood around in small groups planning the next operation.

"It doesn't need to be long," he added. "Ten klicks, max. You just need to get out there and show the flag, let them know we're here. Be back before dark." He continued by offering me bits of advice based on Marine operations in Somalia. I got the distinct feeling from listening to him that many of the lessons were ones he had personally learned the hard way. But he never said "*I* did this" or "*I* did that." He understood that I needed to learn on my own without him lording his own combat experience over me, and I respected him for it. Sitting down at one of the billiard tables, I mapped out an eight-kilometer patrol route through a stretch of Highway 5 that came to be known as "the Strip." The whole route passed through built-up urban sprawl that lined both sides of the road, and this made me noticeably edgy. If things went south the situation could deteriorate quickly. There were few places visible on the map where the company would be able to turn around if we got into trouble, and a conspicuous lack of lateral routes would make the act of reinforcing us, if we needed it, equally difficult and dangerous.

As the Marines loaded themselves for bear, I briefed the staff on the patrol. They understood the risks we were about to take, yet everyone was eager to execute the mission. Even with an indefinite enemy situation in front of them and a patrol route that screamed "ambush!" they still yearned for action—for the continuing chance to prove themselves and their ability to accomplish the mission as they had trained for it. Their dedication, their bold willingness to charge into the unknown, left a lump deep within my throat.

Delta Company was on the move at 1330Z. With less than two hours before sunset, we headed north up the Strip. Standing in the turret, I shouldered my M240 and tightly clenched its pistol grip with my right hand. With my left hand I keyed the switch to my headset. Radio traffic within the company was constant.

"This is Red-One, Phase Line Hammer."

"Lateral route to the east."

"This is Black-Five, vertical danger area."

"This is White-One, Checkpoint One."

"All Victors, keep scanning. Keep your eyes open."

"This is Blue-One, all Dragon Victors clear Checkpoint Three."

"This is Red-One, crowds coming up."

We waited for the ambush, fingers curled around triggers, turrets rhythmically scanning back and forth like ominous steel metronomes. But instead of finding a hostile crowd waiting to kill us, we discovered thousands of impoverished Iraqis yelling and screaming their heads off. They cheered us on as the company's column lumbered through their neighborhood. Our mounted patrol became a pageant of sorts. I radioed my sentiments to the company.

"I can't believe this. This is like homecoming and Mardi Gras all rolled into one."

"Yeah, minus the beer," a nameless voice replied.

Smiling and waving at us, giving us the thumbs-up and yelling "Thank-you!" and "Bush! Bush!" the Iraqis treated us like returning heroes. Traffic of all types, human and vehicular, clogged the streets as the locals pushed forward to catch a glimpse of our armored procession. The column's movement became stop-and-go, and each time LAVs halted the people held their scrawny arms out toward us, making offerings. They held in their hands packs of cigarettes, vegetables, featherless, anorexic chickens, and handfuls of eggs. I agonized at the absolute destitution in which these people lived. The neighborhoods of Al Wuedayah, Abbud al Gu'ud, Falah al Mahmud, and Abd al Husayn al Musawi were run-down—slums no different from Saddam City to the south. Garbage and debris choked every corner, run-off from the overflowing trash heaps that had sprung up behind the buildings. I struggled to understand the scene of human decay that played out before me. Here they were, amid their own misery, hailing us as their liberators, cheering us, and presenting us with what little they had to offer. I stared at it all. This was not a movie. This was not a television miniseries. This was real. I considered the stark contrast between the simple luxuries of my own life back home and the daily struggle faced by these tragic souls. On several occasions I was nearly overcome with emotion as I watched the eyes of these wraith-like figures sparkle in our presence. All ages were in attendance, and soon many women and young girls peeked out from behind their doors and curtains to steal glances at us. They grinned from ear to ear, occasionally pulling down their veils to reveal their faces to us. *You will never see anything like this again*, I thought. At that instant, as I stood in my turret and surrounded by thousands of faces filled with hope and admiration, my mind cleared. All the anguish of the long weeks and months leading up to the war, all the frustration and fatigue, all the misery of being there, faded away into the ether. Suddenly it all became worth it.

The sun began its rapid descent below the horizon, and I signaled the company to pick up the pace to meet our return deadline. The radio, which an hour earlier had been filled with voices of caution and warning, now buzzed with excited, lighthearted comments.

"They gave us food!"

"They gave us cigarettes!"

"The girls were showing us their faces!"

"These young Iraq women are hot, but the old ones are hags!"

Delta Company LAV-25 on patrol on "the Strip," north of Saddam City, 9 April 2003. Official Marine Corps photo by LCpl Andrew P. Roufs.

Lieutenant Parment's stoic reply said it all. "I guess that's what thirty years of tyranny will do to you."

✦ ✧ ✦

We returned to the new command post and assembly area 1st LAR Battalion had established in the pool hall and its surrounding lot. Vehicles lined the compound's perimeter. The noise of the city had died down with the setting sun. As the company's LAVs filed into the crowded assembly area, a long column of amtracks, tanks, and humvees from RCT-5 headed north up the Strip, going in the direction we had just patrolled. I wondered if they would receive the same cordial reception in the dark.

The billiard room had undergone a dramatic transformation since I had seen it before the patrol. The maps that had been piled up on the green felt were now taped to the walls, and banks of radios and speaker boxes lined the tables. Staff officers and enlisted Marines darted in and out of the hall, and after several minutes I located the battalion commander and the operations officer. Major Harper would want a mission debrief to give him and the CO a better idea of what lay beyond our perimeter. More important, however, would be my report on the humanitarian situation unfolding along the Strip north of Saddam City.

"How did it go out there, Seth?" asked Maj Harper.

"It was unbelievable, sir," I replied, slowly shaking my head. "Un-fucking-believable."

"Why?"

"The enemy situation is zilch. It was like a fucking parade out there for us."

Lieutenant Colonel White spoke up. "How so?"

"Sir, it was like Mardi Gras out there. Thousands of 'em, lining the streets. Smiling. Waving. Like I said, it was unbelievable."

"What about the route?" asked Maj Harper, bringing me back to the purpose of the debrief. "What's it like?"

"It's a tight road, bordered by one- and two-story buildings. Supports traffic easily, but there are next to no lateral routes. Most just lead into the landfill east of the Strip." Then I turned to LtCol White. "Sir, I've never seen poverty before in my life like that out there today. And I've been to some shitty countries before this."

"Pretty bad, huh?"

"Yes, sir. Listen, we need to get some sort of humanitarian assistance out there for them. Red Cross, Doctors Without Borders, anything. Everything has been looted around here. If the government has really dissolved, then things are gonna get bad out there real quick. They're gonna need food, water . . . hell, everything."

"All right," White replied. "I'm not sure what we can do at our level, but I'll raise the issue with the RCT. I think there's going to be a lot of that going on around here."

After finishing my debrief, I walked out of the billiard room-cum-operations center in search of some much-deserved and needed rest. A flicker of light from a darkened room across the courtyard caught my eye. Movement in the room similarly caught my attention, and when I poked my head in the door I realized about twenty or thirty persons had crammed themselves in there. The room was lit only by the dull white glow of flashlight beams, which moved about randomly in a strobe effect. The light passed quickly over Marines' faces, and the looks I saw varied between wide, toothy grins and clenched jaws. Eyes filled with humor, and others squinted with anger. No one talked. No one, that is, except one voice. I heard it immediately—loud, stern, commanding.

"Now, take off your shirt."

What the hell is going on?

I grabbed the nearest person and voiced my thoughts. "Hey, what the hell is this?"

"One-Five captured these six guys and turned them over to us for processing. They're in Al Qaeda."

"Are you shitting me?"

"Negative," he said, pointing to one terrorist in the corner. "Most of them had Syrian passports, but that fucker right there had a French passport on him."

I looked around the darkened room again. In each corner a small figure sat cross-legged, a burlap sack draped over his head and his wrists zip-cuffed tightly behind the back. None of them moved an inch—they were either ballsy as hell or scared shitless. From the looks of the gigantic Marine master sergeant manhandling them and conducting the strip search, I figured it was the latter. His voice boomed again in the darkness.

"Now, take off your pants."

Suddenly the detainee stood naked before us. A young man barely out of his teens who had traveled hundreds of miles from his home to kill Americans, he now seemed very small and very afraid.

Al Qaeda, I thought, turning to leave. *Syria. What does it all mean?* What I didn't know at the time was that foreign fighters were in the process of traveling from all over the world to fight and kill Americans. Iraq had become the new battleground in their *jihad,* or "holy struggle," against the United States. Less than a week earlier, 2nd Tanks and 3/5 had battled foreign fighters who had made their way to Iraq through Syria, Jordan, and other neighboring countries, but hearing about it didn't compare with actually seeing jihadis in custody. Watching this surreal scene pan out before my eyes, I didn't know what to think. I hadn't counted on this. I had expected to fight the infamous Republican Guard all the way to Baghdad. I had expected to deal with throngs of surrendering Iraqi soldiers. Neither had happened. In fact, not one uniformed Iraqi soldier had fired on Delta Company. Our enemy had been members of the Fedayeen, dressed in civilian clothing and ambushing us from the shadows. Could we count on the arriving jihadis to do the same? We had taken Baghdad, yes, but suddenly I realized we weren't going home yet.

18

Isolating Baghdad

With the capital of Iraq captured by the Marines and army, the course of the war took a dramatic turn on 10 April. Baghdad, which before had seemed the ultimate objective—the one that would set us free—was in chaos. The looting had persisted nonstop, and enemy action was still highly possible. Overnight the mission to penetrate Baghdad shifted to restoring order and isolating the city to prevent enemy forces from entering or leaving. The latter task fell to 1st LAR Battalion, and that morning we prepared to displace to a new command post along Baghdad's northern rim.

With Marines running everywhere, readying their vehicles for our imminent departure, the company was in good spirits. They had witnessed a historic event the previous day, and the warm reception we had received from the Iraqis along the Strip had done wonders for many who had begun to question what the hell it was we were doing there in the first place. As I strapped my gear to the side of my vehicle, Matt Green, the cameraman from Bob Woodruff's news team, approached me.

"Hey, mate. Looks like me and James are going to have to leave you all today."

His announcement caught me off guard. "Huh? What are you talking about?"

"Well, we got to get to where the story is. I just met a chap who's gonna give us a ride into downtown."

I had figured this was coming. We had all heard about Saddam Hussein's statue being pulled down by a Marine tank the previous day, and I could tell Matt and James wished they had been there to record the momentous event. It was a journalist's wet dream. Other reports had filtered in over the previous twenty-four hours that, along with the rioting and looting, Iraqis had begun executing Ba'ath Party members in the streets. The reports were unverified, of course, but Matt and James were journalists, and their job was to report. Even though Bob Woodruff had left, they were still obliged to get as much footage of Baghdad's fall as they possibly could. It was, after all, the news story about which everyone wanted to hear. The incredible feats that the Marines and soldiers had accomplished in their twenty-one day scramble to Baghdad were suddenly overshadowed by the fact that Baghdad's residents had gone berserk.

"Well," I added. "I hate to see you guys go, but I understand. You have a job just like we do."

James joined us, and I turned to him.

"So," I began. "You're leaving us, huh?"

"Yeah, afraid so," replied James. "Here, I've got something for you. I know you like these." He handed me a black and white-checkered shemagh he had obtained when he was in Afghanistan the previous year. Woven from a material finer than the soiled, ragged one wrapped around my neck, its smooth texture felt cool against my skin.

"Thanks, man. It's great." His gesture touched me. I reached down and pulled the blackened captain's insignia from the front of my flak jacket and handed it to him. "Here you go. Something you can remember *us* by. You guys be careful out there."

He pinned the rank to the breastplate of his own body armor. "Thanks, mate. This is great—now people will get the hell out of my way because they'll think *I'm* a captain."

I extended my hand and shook each of theirs, bidding them a fond farewell. In all, I hadn't enjoyed the experience of having a media team embedded within Delta Company. Although their reporting had enabled our families back home to monitor our progress, for me their presence had been an interruption of our normal routine, and my overall impression of the media hadn't improved since the war had started three weeks earlier. Woodruff and I hadn't seen eye to eye on many things during his time with the company, and his attempt to film LCpl Suarez del Solar's medevac had forever colored my impression of him. But James and Matt, with their dry, British humor and realistic approach to doing things, had proven themselves to be good guys. We would all miss them.

✦ ✧ ✦

Delta Company stepped off from the pool hall compound at 0400Z and displaced to the new 1st LAR command post several city blocks away. The new CP, though still isolated from Baghdad and Saddam City by the defunct canal, provided better protection for all of us. Several two- and three-story buildings stood within the compound, which was further bordered by a high wall that hid the LAVs from view. In general, the entire facility was a safer place in which to park the vehicles and send out patrols. The platoons manned their positions behind the walls, and no sooner had we set in than I got the word to report for a new frag order.

Major Harper had set up a map of Baghdad on the ground next to his LAV, and as Dave, LtCol White, and I stood around him he briefed the new mission.

"One-Five has been in heavy contact since zero-one-Zulu this morning. They stormed a presidential palace inside Baghdad, and they took significant casualties. Last word was about twenty-six. Two-Five was just ordered to reinforce One-Five." Harper then turned to me.

"Delta, your mission is to relieve Two-Five in place and assume their blocking positions along Highway 2 in order to control the flow of traffic in and out of the city and prevent enemy personnel from entering or exiting."

I scribbled the task in my notebook as the S-3 directed Dave to expand a blocking position to achieve the same end state: prevent the enemy from getting into or out of Baghdad. Once Delta had completed its relief-in-place and Weapons Company had established its own set of blocking positions, the battalion would end up guarding a chunk of land that covered the northern routes into and out of Baghdad from the Nahr Diyala in the east, across Highway 5, and all the way to the Tigris River in the west. It was a tall order for us with Charlie Company off working with 1st Reconnaissance Battalion, but we understood the importance of the mission.

The original war plan had called for the U.S. Army's Fourth Infantry Division to invade Iraq from Turkey. The combined push of 4th ID from the north and 3rd ID and 1st Marine Division from the south and east would effectively strangle Baghdad from three directions. But with Turkey's last-minute decision not to allow American troops use of its territory, no Coalition force had attacked Baghdad from the north. The three major routes leading north out of the capital—Highways 1, 2, and 5—had become ruptured arteries of people and traffic trying to escape the madness within Baghdad, or else attempting to return to their homes within the city. Highway 1, to our west across the Tigris River, would be covered by 3rd ID. First LAR Battalion would cover the rest—a stretch that previously had been controlled by four infantry battalions.

Delta Company filed slowly out of the compound and made its way to the first available bridge spanning the abandoned canal. With the situation inside the city still uncertain, I wanted to avoid actually entering its boundaries. I preferred to skirt the urban areas, but we quickly realized that what I wanted didn't matter. Even the large, 1:40,000-scale map of the city I refer-enced failed to present a workable route that would keep us outside Saddam City's built-up areas. The company's column soon found itself navigating a maze of routes that ran back and forth across the abandoned canal, and I was reminded of our frustrations with the canals and levees earlier in the war. Few workable routes paralleled the northern bank of the canal, and those that did either ended abruptly or turned north, away from the city.

At one point the company ended up on a route that took us back north across the canal and into a small village on Baghdad's periphery. As 1st Platoon inched its way across the bridge, a crowd of hundreds of Iraqis formed around the rest of the company's stationary vehicles. Their facial expressions were less receptive than those on the Strip, but they nevertheless appeared willing to come up to us and talk. One man called up to LCpl Davis in the turret.

"I am going to speak English to you now, yes?"

"Yeah, okay," Davis replied, leaning down and smiling. The two of them began a disjointed conversation, and as I looked around I noticed the crowd's size had begun to grow. They all stared up at me, looking like they expected me to say something. *Well, here goes nothing,* I thought. I raised my hand and ran my index finger across my throat and yelled.

"Saddam's dead!"

Fists shot above their heads and jubilant yells filled the air. I shouted again.

"Allah-u-Akbar!" (God is great!)

More shouts. More smiles. I was on a roll.

"Al-Hamdu l'Allah!" (Praise be to God!) They were in a frenzy now. Seeing that our column was rolling forward again, I keyed the intercom.

"Let's get out of here, Gurganus," I said, relieved to leave my first attempt at statesmanship behind.

The village on the northern bank of the canal was even more impoverished and uninhabitable than our patrol up the Strip the previous day, yet the residents were just as ecstatic to see us. The squalor they lived in was ungodly. Raw sewage seeped through the streets, filling the air with the pungent smell of human waste. Several hundred meters farther up, the street dead-ended into a massive landfill. It was impossible to tell exactly where the village ended and the refuse began. The villagers were quite literally living in a garbage dump. As the column made a slow U-turn to navigate its way back to the canal, I watched the Marines perched in their turrets. Their faces were drawn, filled with shock, pity, and revulsion at the suffering displayed in front of them. I knew exactly how my men all felt.

An hour had passed, and the company had traveled less than a kilometer. Time was ticking away, and 2/5 was waiting for us. The zigzagging across the canal continued, however, because no workable bypass presented itself. Farther up the canal, we reconnoitered an abandoned military compound that turned out to be a surface-to-air missile storage and launch complex. SA-2 and SA-6 missiles the size of telephone poles had been arrayed around the compound, all pointing skyward. Most were covered with camouflage netting, and few appeared to be functioning. It was evident that they hadn't been moved in quite some time. We rolled into the compound, and as the platoons circled the perimeter my vehicle pulled up next to a prominent, one-story building situated in the center. Painted on the outside was an eight-pointed star with missiles in the center and an Iraqi flag flowing across the top. A wooden cutout of an SA-2 had been mounted on an ornate wall that ran along the walkway leading inside. I keyed my intercom.

"Hold up here, Gurganus."

I pulled off my helmet and climbed out of the turret. Out of the corner of my eye I caught a glimpse of 1stSgt Guzman's vehicle coming to a sudden stop and Guzman jumping out of his own turret to catch up to me. Together we cautiously poked our heads inside the building, our pistols drawn. Wind whistled through the empty halls. As everywhere else, the occupants had vanished as soon as they heard us coming. For the most part the place had been ransacked, but maps still covered the walls and papered the floors. Diagrams of coalition aircraft similar to those we had seen in the AAA site the first day of the war were plastered on the walls. One map of Baghdad in particular caught my interest. Almost four feet in length on each side, it had been mounted in a flimsy frame and covered in heavy acetate. Thick, red circles stretched out around the city, delineating the maximum ranges of both the SA-2 and the SA-6. Upon further examination, I noticed multiple circles overlapping to form a tight ring of anti-aircraft protection around the capital's borders. It was an impressive diagram, but to my knowledge no friendly aircraft had been shot down inside the city. I wondered whether the Iraqis who had manned that site had really tried to defend the city with their missiles or had just abandoned their posts like the rest of the Iraqi army. The compound as a whole seemed mostly intact, and the majority of the damage appeared to have resulted from looting. I returned to my vehicle and radioed the XO.

"Black-Five, mark this location and report it to higher. Someone needs to take care of it after we're gone."

"Roger, Six. I'll add it to the list of UXO sites that need to be demo'd." The sarcasm in his voice was obvious. For days we had been locating and marking monstrous caches of the enemy's unexploded ordnance (UXO), yet we wondered if anyone above the battalion level planned to do anything about it. It was easy to understand the push for our forces to keep moving, but leaving all those free weapons and ammunition behind would later come back and bite American forces in the ass.

First Platoon exited the missile compound and located another back-alley road along the northern bank of the canal. But when the company suddenly found itself in the middle of a traffic jam of honking cars and loitering pedestrians, I knew our time had just about run out. As much as I wanted to bypass the city, it was unavoidable if the company was to link up with 2/5 before nightfall.

"Red-One, this is Six. Find the first available crossing that will take us south of the canal. We'll skirt the edge of the city all the way until we get to Highway Two."

"Roger, Six. We're Oscar Mike."

Lieutenant Parment and his 1st Platoon pushed forward quickly to scout out our new route. Once the company crossed the canal back to the south we began racing through a series of narrow alleys as fast as our diesel engines would take us. Parment did his best to follow a street that the map listed as paralleling the canal the entire way, but as we had discovered so many other times, the view on the map differed substantially from the reality on the ground. Rather than closely following the trace of the canal, the street twisted and cornered, at times turning sharply south and detouring multiple blocks into Saddam City and the adjacent neighborhoods of Hayy Adnan, Ash Sha'b, and Hayy Sumar. Everyone was on edge. Abandoned ordnance littered the streets. Anti-aircraft guns and long, dusty belts of 23mm ammunition sat tucked into cul-de-sacs. Stacks of mortar rounds accompanied sandbagged 82mm mortar tubes on street corners. Iraqi soldiers had been there—there was no doubt about that. But we couldn't count on them continuing "not to be there" the entire way. As we approached every corner we expected an RPG team waiting to ambush our convoy or a roadblock designed to trap us in a kill zone. Relief cascaded over me when Parment's voice returned to the radio.

"This is Red-One. I have a visual on Highway Two now. About another two or three blocks and we'll be there."

"Roger, One. Keep pushing. I want us out of the city as fast as possible."

"Roger, pushing."

One after another Delta Company's LAVs exited the built-up area and pulled onto Highway 2 and the bridge spanning the canal. The causeway led us to a roadblock facing south that had been established by a company from 2nd Tanks. East of the road, 2/5 and the regimental Main had erected their command posts in an adjacent built-up area. At first it wasn't clear whether the area had been bombed or was simply not yet fully constructed. Bare buildings without windows or doors were everywhere, and smashed rubble filled the streets and sidewalks. A Marine directed me to the command post, and after receiving a brief on Delta Company's sector and our requirements while we were there, I sat in on the tail end of a frag order being given by 2/5's battalion commander. They were going into the city to reinforce 1/5 in a firefight that had been waging all night. First LAR Battalion was going nowhere. It was like the world's biggest joke had been played on us.

Regimental Combat Team-5's main headquarters was preparing to leave as well. After searching for a location for the company command post, I finally settled on an open area shielded by a set of buildings next to the Main. It provided adequate concealment from the road, but that was about all. Plenty of danger areas still surrounded us, but we would have to make do. The bulk of the company was to establish blocking positions facing north and south along Highway 2 and along a road on the eastern bank of the Tigris River. After acknowledging their orders, the lieutenants moved the platoons into their assigned positions while I guided Headquarters Platoon and the combat trains into our new home.

"I think we're gonna be here a while," I told Capt Portiss. "Get the OE-two-fifty-four up and get a comm check with battalion."

"Roger that. How long you think we'll be here?"

"A couple of days, at least."

"Well, you think we should augment the platoons with Headquarters personnel?" he asked. "The line platoons are gonna burn out pretty fast out there."

I looked out toward the highway. A sea of Iraqis waited impatiently at both platoon positions that blocked the north and southbound lanes of Highway 2. The Marines patiently searched every person who wished to enter or exit Baghdad and denied entry or egress to all vehicles. Portiss's estimation had been correct—this was going to get old fast.

"Good call. Get with Monroe and Kappen, take all available personnel from Headquarters Platoon, and apportion them out for road guard duty. Just make sure there are enough Marines back here at the CP for radio watch and to man the vehicles if we have to make a quick getaway."

"You got it."

A commotion had developed behind me where the RCT had set up its own CP. As several staff officers sat in plastic chairs conversing with the local Iraqi *sheikh*, a team of Marines dragged two screaming prisoners past the group. The contrast between the sheikh and the enemy prisoners was striking. Freshly scrubbed and immaculately dressed in flowing robes, the sheikh casually yawned as the handcuffed prisoners fought to break free from the Marines.

Together they bawled and howled to the sheikh, their hands outstretched in gestures of mercy and anguish. It was clear that they sought his aid in releasing them from the Marines, but the sheikh's bored yawn and the roll of his eyes signaled an obvious message to the prisoners: "You dumbshits. You're not getting any help from me. I told you not to fight the Americans." Realizing their leader had abandoned them, the two prisoners wailed like widows and continued to thrash about as the Marines hauled them away. The spectacle puzzled me, but then again just about everything did in that country.

✦ ✧ ✦

Something more pressing was on my mind: my feet. They were hamburger in my boots, and with each step I walked on hot coals. My gait had become a shamble, and serious trouble would soon face me if I didn't find a remedy. The building our vehicle had parked behind was vacant, and after taking a look around I found a kitchen tucked away inside it. A trickle of running water ran from the faucet. It was all I needed. I hobbled back to the vehicle and pulled my nasty, filthy laundry from my rucksack and toted it back inside to the kitchen. Finding two large plastic tubs in the corner, I filled one with detergent and water and used the other to rinse. Soon all of my socks and T-shirts were clean—well, cleaner than they had been before I pieced together my hasty laundromat. Pleased with myself, I hung the wet clothing on a hat rack and placed it outside to dry in the sun. What I didn't take into account was the quality of my wash and the occasionally blowing sand that stuck to the wet material. Several hours later I had a full batch of moderately clean and very coarse, scratchy socks and T-shirts. I was back at square one.

The barren building piqued my interest, and as I wandered from room to room through its narrow passageways I found personal effects of the Iraqi soldiers who had occupied it before us. I felt uncomfortable rummaging through their personal mail and photographs. Pictures of young Iraqi men posing in their uniforms and brandishing AK-47s lay everywhere, as did photos of young soldiers with wives or girlfriends. These men were much the same as we were, and rifling through the mementos made me feel as though I was violating someone's privacy.

I stopped going through their belongings and instead moved to the next building, where thousands of pieces of ordnance—7.62mm rounds, 12.7mm rounds, RPG rounds, grenades, flares—awaited me. It was stacked in large piles, which in some cases extended all the way to the ceiling. In some rooms the ordnance was neatly arranged, but in others it appeared to have been dumped without concern for what went where. I picked up a rifle magazine pouch and three AK-47 magazines to go with it. It was all in perfect condition, as if it had just been dropped hours earlier. I took the items back to my vehicle and placed them on the ground next to a Republican Guard beret I had found earlier in the day. Staring at the personal equipment filled me with mixed emotions. Although hesitant to take war trophies, I was comforted by the fact that none of what was spread out before me had been pulled from a dead body.

My ambivalence worried me, and I found myself overwhelmed with feelings of guilt and despair. Life had become cheap out here. Whether because of the callous attitude I had adopted about the death and destruction surrounding me or because of my casual rifling through a private residence, I had suddenly become quite conflicted. I revisited the previous twenty-one days in my mind, and one idea stood out more than anything else: I felt as if I had accomplished little more than getting one of my men killed. I wondered what lay in store for me. Even with American forces continuing to pour into Baghdad, danger still lay around every corner. Could my time above ground be counted in weeks, days, hours, or minutes on the clock? But something else bothered me. I feared that the Iraqis would soon resent our presence just as they had at first cheered us on. Worse, I feared we would find ourselves battling not only the loyal Ba'ath Party regime holdouts, but also the impoverished, oppressed people we had come to save.

✦ ✧ ✦

The setting sun brought with it sporadic sniper fire that annoyed us for less than an hour. Whoever was doing the shooting didn't seem to possess the motivation to perform his job properly. Perhaps he thought that if he were more accurate, if he presented more of a threat, then we would come after him. The potshots were over almost as soon as they had begun. My musings on the poor quality of the sniper's work were interrupted by the voice of the Marine standing radio watch in the LAV-C2.

"Captain Folsom! The Forward and Charlie-Six are Oscar Mike to our position right now."

What's that all about? I wondered. It was dark, and skulking around the outskirts of Baghdad didn't seem like such a hot idea. But minutes later I heard the whine of LAV engines approaching our position, and soon they were filing into the open area and parking around the vehicles that comprised our company command post. I was in the midst of recleaning and powdering my feet when Gil Juarez walked up to my vehicle in the darkness.

"Hey, man," I said. "Have a seat. Where the hell have *you* been? I haven't seen you for, like, three days."

"Oh, man, we've been busy . . ." He proceeded to tell me how Charlie Company had been detached from 1st LAR Battalion several days earlier and attached to 1st Reconnaissance Battalion for a reconnaissance-in-force north to a town named Baqubah. They had planned to conduct a raid on the Iraqi Forty-first Mechanized Brigade, and throughout the drive north along Route Green, Charlie Company had been in constant enemy contact for more than twenty kilometers. During the course of the running ambush, which included sporadic 82mm mortar fire raining down on top of the company, one LAV-25 had all four of its starboard side tires blown out from the flying shrapnel. Another vehicle lost a thermal imaging screen to mortar shards, forcing the driver to steer blind throughout the course of the engagement. Gil himself had been put on the hot seat as well. Two RPGs passed just feet over his head during one engagement. At another point, when his vehicle's main gun malfunctioned, he passed off his scissor-mounted machine gun to his gunner while he engaged the ambushing Fedayeen with his own rifle. I sat there with my mouth hanging open and listened to Gil's absolutely amazing story. Expecting him to close the story with news that his company had taken heavy casualties, I was floored to hear that they had, in fact, sustained none.

The battalion commander joined us soon after Gil finished his story. I briefed him on Delta Company's activities earlier in the day. He looked exhausted, and as he explained the battalion's ongoing mission to isolate the city from the north, he mentioned something about all three LAR battalions forming up together for an operation.

"But that's just hearsay," he said. "No decision has been made yet."

Hearing that, I changed the subject. Together the three of us talked for a few more minutes until Gil and the CO decided to return to the battalion's headquarters. They had come and gone so quickly that it was as if they had never even been there. Remembering how difficult it had been to get to our location from the COC, I wondered why they had even come in the first place.

✦ ✧ ✦

The morning of 11 April found Delta Company still assigned to roadblock duty along Baghdad's northern boundary. No end to the monotonous work appeared in sight, but for the Marines actually standing guard at the checkpoints it was stressful. Soon after daylight the crowds trying to enter and exit the city reemerged, and they didn't dissipate until after nightfall. I hadn't seen the majority of the company since our time along the Nahr Diyala, and I wanted to talk to the platoon commanders to see what we could do to reduce the workload of the platoons. If we could possibly lower the manpower requirements for the blocking positions, the Marines might be able to maintain their energy levels indefinitely should the company be stuck in place for an extended period. I found 1stSgt Guzman sitting next to his LAV.

"Hey, First Sergeant, let's go troop the lines."

He quickly jumped to his feet. "Good idea, sir."

"I'll go with you," added Capt Portiss. "I'm bored off my ass."

"Wait, sir," interjected Guzman. "You want to promote Gurganus?" He reminded me that PFC Gurganus's promotion warrant had come in recently. I paused and looked around the area.

"Yeah, good idea," I replied. "Now is as good a time as any. Get everyone over here."

Guzman assembled the Marines from Headquarters Platoon, and I grabbed Gurganus.

"I think it's time to promote you Gurganus, don't you?"

He looked around at the Marines standing in a semicircle around him. "Yes, sir. I guess so."

With everyone standing at attention, 1stSgt Guzman read Gurganus's warrant authorizing his promotion to lance corporal. I leaned in and pinned the small, black insignia to Gurganus's body armor, then I shook his hand.

"I'm jealous, Lance Corporal Gurganus," I told him. "I can't think of a better place to get promoted than in a combat zone. Congratulations."

The Marines crowded around him, offering their congratulations and handshakes. After a minute of this I spoke up.

"All right, all right, enough love. Time to move out and go see the platoons."

◆ ◇ ◆

With Portiss riding in the turret next to me, my section pulled out of the CP and drove west toward 1st Platoon's position. I had assigned Lieutenant Parment and his platoon a road to the west that paralleled the Tigris River and led north out of Baghdad. Somewhere across the river was 3rd ID, but with no radio communications and the natural obstacle created by the river and the surrounding orchards, there was no way Parment could link up with them. The previous day he had simply replaced the unit from 2/5 and continued with the original mission. As my section navigated its way to Parment's position, I remembered him radioing me the previous day. He had told me his platoon was having a difficult time getting into position because of a downed power line in their path. I had told him to hurry the hell up, and when he requested to cut the line I rebuked him over the radio.

"*Negative,* Red-One," I had said. "We can't go around tearing up the city's infrastructure."

I never heard anything from him about the power line after that. As my two vehicles traveled along the southern bank of the abandoned canal, I understood why Parment had had such a hard time on the way to his checkpoint. A massive high-voltage power line suspended by a series of giant pylons drooped across the embankment at turret-level, blocking our passage to 1st Platoon's checkpoint. One of the pylons had been damaged somehow, and it bent over as if clutching its midsection. I looked at Portiss next to me.

"Is it live?" I asked.

"I don't know. I don't hear anything buzzing."

There was no way around it. To our left was dense vegetation, and to our right was the steep drop-off of the canal's embankment. I contemplated lifting the cable, but the prospect of a couple million volts surging through my system caused me to reevaluate the situation. I looked around again. The power was out everywhere—that much had been clear the previous evening. I yelled back into the scout compartment.

"Davis, hand me up the mattock handle."

He passed the heavy, wooden axe handle to me, and I cautiously moved up to the cable.

"I don't know if this is such a good idea," warned Portiss.

"Come on," I replied. "It's safe. It's wood—it won't conduct electricity." But the cable, more than an inch in diameter, was too heavy and awkward to lift with the mattock handle. Try as I might, I couldn't get the leverage I needed with the mattock. *Oh, fuck it,* I thought, defiantly. *There's no power running through this thing.* I dropped the mattock handle back into the turret, grabbed the cable with both of my gloved hands, and hoisted it above my head.

"Let's go, hurry up!" I yelled. "This thing weighs a fucking ton!"

Gurganus eased his foot on the accelerator, slowly bringing us forward while I gingerly walked along the top of the vehicle to provide clearance. As I crested the turret and prepared to drop the cable off the back of the LAV, I saw 1stSgt Guzman looking at me and slowly shaking his head. Moments later he had the cable lifted above his head and was guiding his own vehicle under the obstacle as I had.

The road leading out of the city toward Lt Parment's checkpoint was surrounded on both sides by orchards and palm groves. It provided 1st Platoon the benefit of narrowing the Iraqi foot and vehicle traffic, and the Marines at the checkpoint seemed to have cracked the code on the search procedures.

"Hey," I asked Parment. "How the hell did you end up getting around that downed cable back there?"

"We lifted it up and drove under it."

"Well, *how?*"

He looked at me sheepishly. "I lifted it up with my hands."

"How did you know it wasn't live?"

"I guess I didn't, sir."

"Yeah, that makes two of us."

"I figured I could be faster than electricity by just smacking it with my hand," he added. "I guess we were lucky."

"Yeah, no shit."

I then changed the subject and introduced the idea of reducing Lt Parment's security requirements and providing him more Marines from Headquarters Platoon.

"We really don't need them, sir," he replied. "With only two lanes going through here we're able to manage the shifts pretty well and get the Marines some rest at the same time. We can keep doing this for a while."

"All right. It just may *be* a while. I'm not sure yet."

I decided to attempt an alternate route back that wouldn't take our section by the downed power line, but the only alternative we had was to follow a narrow trail that skirted the canal's northern bank. The trail quickly ended, and we found ourselves slowly plowing the LAVs through the thick vegetation of an adjacent orchard, making our own trail. Several hundred meters later the tree line opened up and the vehicles pulled back onto another trail that ran parallel between the orchard and Highway 2. As we made our way north along the path, Portiss's voice suddenly sounded on the intercom. There was calm urgency in his tone.

"Tank."

"What?" I asked. "Where?"

He pointed to the orchard on the vehicle's left. Straining my eyes to see, I could just barely make out the light tan of an Iraqi T-72 hidden in the trees. *How the* hell *did he see that?* I thought, keying the intercom again.

"Hold up here, Gurganus." I turned to Portiss in the turret. "Let's check it out."

We both grabbed our rifles and jumped out of the turret. Moving cautiously through the tree line, our rifles at the ready, we started a close-target reconnaissance of the enemy vehicle. Behind me the sounds of twigs softly snapping caught my attention. I looked over my shoulder to see 1stSgt Guzman moving right behind us, his rifle up and ready as well. Together the three of us closed in on the T-72 from the vehicle's rear, and we heaved a collective sigh of relief to find it abandoned. From the looks of it, the vehicle's crew had probably taken their leave a day or two prior. There was still food and personal equipment lying around, and we could see where the Iraqi soldiers had munched on dates and rice while they waited in their hiding position. I was surprised the vehicle was still intact. Most of the tanks we had seen hidden in palm groves had been found by Coalition airpower and destroyed. Most, that is, but not this one—it was ready to move and shoot.

"Mark it," I told the XO. "Someone needs to come out here and blow this thing." We patrolled back to our waiting vehicles after Portiss entered a waypoint in his GPS to record the tank's location.

The section pushed on to 2nd Platoon's checkpoint, where the crowds had increased substantially since the time we had left that morning. Lieutenant Schwartz walked up to me.

"We could use some help out here, sir. We're getting mobbed."

"Yeah, I can tell. Roger. We'll get you a couple more Marines from Headquarters."

As we stood there catching up, 1stSgt Guzman appeared by my side.

"Sir, I need to talk to you over here," he said, motioning over his shoulder with his thumb. We walked away from everyone, and then he lit into me.

"What the hell was *that* all about, sir?"

"What are you talking about?"

"That shit with the tank. What were you doing?"

I became defensive. "The XO saw a tank in the tree line. I decided to check it out."

"Goddammit, sir! Going after a tank with a rifle?! You can't be doing that shit!"

"Come on, First Sergeant," I said, trying to lighten the atmosphere. I could tell he was pissed off at me. "It was derelict, anyway."

"You didn't know that. And what's with lifting up that power line back there? How did you know there wasn't any electricity going through it?"

"I didn't," I said flatly. "I took a chance. Same with the tank. Big deal."

"Listen to me, sir." His voice took on a deadly serious tone. "You can't be doing all this crazy shit. If you go down, this whole company goes down."

"Oh, for Christ's sake, give me a break. They'll be fine. They know what to do."

"That ain't the point. You're the leadership for this company. The Marines won't be able to handle it if you get yourself killed. Trust me, I know."

His words struck me. Guzman hadn't jumped knee-deep in my ass like that since the previous summer in Jordan, when the XO and I had ventured into a trench to disarm a hand grenade that hadn't detonated properly. Guzman's concern for me—his concern for the company's well-being—seemed genuine, and it was then that I realized this man would be a close friend of mine for the rest of my life. He was acting in my best interests, although I didn't understand it at the time. Reflecting on the episode later, I realized my decisions to lift the power cable with my bare hands and go after the Iraqi tank had been two of the stupidest, most dangerous calls I made in the course of the war. I could have turned the section around and searched for another route on the northern side of the canal; I could have ordered the section to hit the gas and drive away from the tank; or I could have called in artillery or air support on it. But I had needed to see them for myself. The incident was significant in another way: it exemplified how careless, how numb to danger I had become in such a short span of time. I worried that the same ambivalence I had discovered in myself the previous night could adversely affect my judgment and my ability to keep myself alive and lead my Marines.

◆ ◇ ◆

Our section returned to the company CP, and I remembered I had been directed to attend a meeting at the RCT headquarters in LtCol White's place. We hopped into our LAV and casually drove across the canal and into Baghdad, an action that only two days earlier would have spelled disaster for a lone vehicle. The streets were crowded, and despite the destruction left by the looting and the sporadic firefights, life seemed to be returning to normal for Baghdad's residents. Our route led us to a compound within the city that had been commandeered by the regiment for its command post. As I climbed down from my turret, a group of Marines standing guard pointed me toward an indoor basketball court for the commanders meeting.

I felt out of place. Because I was the only captain among a gathering of lieutenant colonels, very little I could say would carry much weight, if any at all. Scribbling notes, I was surprised to hear that 1/5 actually took about forty-five casualties during the battle that began late in the evening of 9 April. Many Marines within the battalion hadn't reported their wounds—even after the fighting was over—for fear that they would be medically evacuated and taken away from their buddies. In one particular case, hours after the shooting had ended a Marine approached a corpsman and asked for help with a wound to his arm. He told the doc that he needed more battle dressings because they kept soaking through with blood. When the corpsman asked him how many dressings he had been through, the Marine reportedly replied, "I stopped counting at nine."

There was other news, too. Colonel Dunford, the regimental commander, informed us that combat operations were coming to an end, and that stability operations were about to begin. That information didn't please me, as it would likely mean more checkpoint duty for Delta Company. Dunford concluded the meeting by mentioning the possibility of 1st LAR Battalion detaching from RCT-5 and getting attached back to 1st Marine Division. I didn't make too much of it. Danger wasn't the only thing that no longer seemed to faze me—scuttlebutt rolled off me like water off a duck's back.

I returned to the company CP, and once there decided to take a walk around the built-up area surrounding us. Until that point, my knowledge of the neighborhood had been limited to the few buildings immediately surrounding the CP. Poking my head into the crumbling structures, more of the usual greeted me in each one: thousands of 7.62mm rounds and hundreds of RPG and 82mm mortar rounds. The sight of the discarded ordnance was staggering. It was everywhere, stacked in every corner and under every staircase. Much had been made of the Iraqis' refusal to fight us as we advanced on Baghdad, and I will forever wonder what it was about the American advance that caused the majority of the enemy to abandon their uniforms and weapons and run. Was it our speed? Our firepower? Our reputation? I don't know and probably never will. But as I stared at the tons of ammunition and weapons that filled the nooks and crannies of every building, one fact was evident: if the enemy soldiers previously hiding there had even halfheartedly attempted to defend the neighborhood, we would have sustained massive casualties. Instead, they had just dropped everything and run.

Returning from my tour around the block, I found the CP in a commotion. Staff Sergeant Monroe walked up to me, a pensive look plastered across his face.

"What's going on?" I asked.

"We got two terrorists over there, sir. Second Platoon detained them at their checkpoint."

"Oh yeah?" I said, raising an eyebrow. "What's their story?"

"You gotta see it. They had a shit-load of weapons and ammo. We got it all over there by my vehicle."

"Where are they?"

The Marines had placed the two Iraqis within an empty building foundation, the concrete walls of which rose up four feet from the ground. The chambers of the foundation formed perfect holding cells for the two detainees, and the Marines had separated them and placed both under guard by the time I got there.

"Check this shit out, sir," a Marine said, pointing to the ground next to Monroe's LAV. Neatly arranged in the gravel were a cheap-looking .38 Special, a 9mm Beretta pistol, a snub-nosed commando-style AK-47, and the crown jewel: a nickel-plated AK-47. Two olive-drab chest bandoliers stuffed with loaded AK-47 magazines were laid out next to the weapons, as were several boxes of .38-caliber and 9mm rounds.

Monroe handed me two sets of identification, each of which had been assembled like a passport. I scanned each one, unable to read the Arabic script. But one thing stood out in each: the crest for the Ba'ath Party.

"Has anyone called for HET?" I asked.

"Yes, sir," answered 1stSgt Guzman. "It's been a while, but no response yet."

I walked over to the makeshift holding cells with Monroe and Guzman in tow. Monroe pointed to one of the detainees.

"That one doesn't speak English." He turned and pointed to the second Iraqi. "But that one there does."

I turned to Monroe. "Go get me that nickel-plated AK and the nine-mil." Moments later a Marine handed me the two weapons. I pulled back the rifle's charging handle and peered into the chamber, and then performed the same function with the Beretta. Both were clean and hadn't been fired recently. I leaned down against the foundation's concrete wall and stared at the Iraqi sitting inside. He looked up at me, his eyes wide with fear.

"As-Salaam-Alaikum," I said. "Peace be upon you."

"Alaikum-Salaam," he muttered back to me.

"Do you speak English?"

"Yes."

His accent was thick, but understandable. I picked up the AK-47 and held it out in front of him.

"Where did you get this?"

"My brother and I, we have it for to protect ourselves."

Interrogating detained Iraqi found with weapons at checkpoint in Baghdad, 11 April 2003. (L to R: LCpl Andrew Martin, HM2 Hector Capistrano, Capt Folsom, 1stSgt Ruben Guzman, SSgt Brian Monroe.) Official Marine Corps photo by LCpl Andrew P. Roufs.

I leaned in closer. "Bullshit. What is your job?"

"I am telling this man here," he replied, pointing to one of the Marines. "I am a dentist. I was given these weapons for to protect myself and my brother."

"Do all dentists speak English as well as you?"

"I do not know."

"Do all dentists carry around nickel-plated assault rifles?"

I held the opened identification card in front of his face and pointed to the stamped symbol. "What does this mean?"

"It is Ba'ath Party," he said, his eyes downcast.

"Do you belong to the Ba'ath Party?"

"I want to talk to you now, so I will tell you," he began. "Many, many people belong to Ba'ath Party."

I began to get frustrated. Not knowing how to speak anything but a handful of Arabic phrases was a handicap that prevented me from communicating with him, and his succinct answers in English offered me nothing. Most important, however, was that I really wasn't trained on how to interrogate a detainee. I leaned in to give it one more shot.

"Listen, my friend. I'm going to ask you one more time: where did you get these weapons?"

"I am telling you, I bought these weapons for to protect myself."

"Okay, which is it?" I demanded. "Did someone give them to you or did you buy them?"

"Yes, can I talk to you now? I will like to tell you what happened . . ."

I cut him off. "Everything you say is a crock of shit." I turned back to Monroe and Guzman. "This guy doesn't pass the 'sniff-test.' Get him out of here, go turn him over to CSSC [combat services support company] and make them deal with him. We don't have time for this bullshit."

"What about the weapons?" Monroe asked.

"Turn them over as well." I turned to leave, and then stopped and turned back toward them. "Except the nickel-plated AK. We're gonna keep that for the battalion." I leaned down and dumped the AK-47 magazines out of one of the chest bandoliers. "And I'll be taking one of these, thank you very much."

Puzzled looks filled the faces of Monroe and Guzman as I put my arms through the bandolier and tied it around the back of my flak jacket.

"Hey, if he really isn't a terrorist or Ba'ath Party official or Republican Guard, what does he need an ammo bandolier for?" I paused. "And if he is one of those, he's got bigger fucking problems than me taking his shit. Besides, this thing works better than my own, issued deuce gear." As I turned again to walk away, a team of Marines hoisted the two Iraqis from their cells and escorted them away. From the corner of my eye I saw SSgt Monroe dumping the magazines from the other bandolier and donning it over his body armor.

The radio crackled to life with the voice of Maj Harper, who told me that the regiment's counter-battery radar had picked up six enemy indirect fire sites in Delta Company's sector.

"I need you to check them out immediately, Dragon-Six. Time: now." The urgency and haste of the mission frag order no longer rattled me. Practically everything in the war had been "Time: now." Why would this change?

But, as with many other operations, the sun was setting, and I was steamed at the mission and the lack of planning time afforded us. Harper reminded me of the requirement to continue with the roadblock mission as well, and I scrambled to piece together a team to accomplish the mission. It wasn't Harper's fault. Someone in the regiment had picked up the signals on the radar screen and forwarded the information to someone who decided it needed to be checked out. It was in my sector, so I got the mission. That's the way things happen, but it didn't mean I had to like it. I just had to do it.

The six sites bordered the built-up area that shielded our CP, and to execute the mission I assembled a composite platoon comprising a section each from 2nd and 3rd Platoons. I included my section and the XO's vehicle. After a quick brief over the radio, our seven vehicles stepped off as the sun dipped below the horizon. We drove around in the dark for an hour, eventually finding three ZU-23 anti-aircraft guns—the same type we found on the first day of the war—hidden in the vegetation north of our built-up neighborhood. But finding them troubled me. I didn't think these weapons were the target the counter-battery radar had triangulated. Granted, I didn't understand the full capabilities of CB radar, but at the time I was under the impression that it could only pick up artillery or mortar fire. With that understanding, I expected to find artillery or mortar pieces.

"There's nothing out here, Black-Six," radioed Lt Schwartz from his position on point.

"This doesn't make sense," I said. "Unless we got a false report from the counter-battery folks."

"Black-Six, if they got a reading for mortars, whoever was firing them could have easily picked up and moved," offered Capt Portiss. His answer made the most sense.

"Roger. Mark these ZUs. Stand by." I switched over to the battalion net. "Highlander-Three, this is Dragon-Six."

"Go, Dragon-Six."

"Roger, no joy on those counter-battery contacts. All we found in our sector were three ZU-Twenty-Threes."

"Roger that, Dragon-Six. Go ahead and mark them for destruction." His next transmission surprised me. "Mission complete. Return to your CP, rally your company, and prepare to link up with the battalion for attachment to Task Force Tripoli."

The rumor about detaching from RCT-5 and rejoining the division had been true after all. Harper relayed the plan to rendezvous with the battalion, and as our composite platoon rolled through the darkness back toward the company CP, I radioed the platoons out on their checkpoints. In groups of twos the vehicles from the platoons slowly filed into the open area surrounding the command post, and as the last LAVs were ground-guided into our position Maj Harper radioed me once again. We were to leave our location the next morning and conduct the link-up with 1st LAR Battalion then.

I called up the company staff as Marines shuffled around in the dark. It was the first occasion we had all been together in a long time.

"Get a good security watch going around the perimeter. Then get everyone else's heads down. We leave here at zero-one-thirty-Zulu to link up with the battalion and Task Force Tripoli."

"What's 'Task Force Tripoli'?" someone asked within our huddle.

"Beats the hell out of me," I replied, shrugging my shoulders. "We'll find out soon enough."

PART IV

Vortex: Tikrit, Ad Diwaniyah, and the Return Home

13 April 2003–20 May 2003

19

The Tunnel

Delta Company departed the ammunition-laden neighborhood as planned at 0130Z on 12 April. We moved north along Highway 2 for several kilometers before turning east onto an adjacent road that bordered a large field. The platoons formed a wide circle to establish the assembly area for the battalion, and an hour later vehicles from the other companies began to file in and assume their positions within the massive coil. The battalion was joined by a long column of 7-ton trucks containing Golf Company, 2/23. Soon the assembly area expanded, and we were joined by 2nd and 3rd LAR Battalions. As far as I knew, all three battalions had never been co-located or employed together as they were then. By my estimates, together the three units amounted to more than five hundred armored vehicles, trucks, and humvees, and nearly three thousand Marines. It was an impressive sight.

Our mission, however, remained a mystery. As I sat by my vehicle watching the battalions file into the now-gargantuan assembly area, Delta Company gradually withdrew from its positions marking the TAA's boundaries and assumed its own sector to the northeast. A radio call from the battalion directed all commanders and staff to report to the COC for the mission update, and minutes later Maj Harper was briefing all of us.

Even though Baghdad had fallen, the war wasn't over yet. Active enemy forces still remained north of us in Tikrit, Saddam Hussein's birthplace. Because the U.S. Army's 4th ID had been denied access through Turkey, Tikrit was believed to be a hotbed of activity still, the last remaining enemy holdout. The MEF wanted a force in Tikrit, and it wanted that force there quickly to catch the enemy off balance. To accomplish the mission, 1st Marine Division formed Task Force Tripoli using all three LAR battalions as the centerpiece. Commanded by the assistant division commander, Brigadier General John Kelly (himself a former battalion commander of 1st LAR Battalion), Tripoli also comprised an artillery battalion, a truck-mounted infantry company, a combat engineer platoon, a Navy SEAL detachment, and various other cats and dogs. It was believed that elements of the Republican Guard's Adnan Division awaited us in Tikrit. That was all that was known, and after the initial overview Harper dismissed us back to our companies while the battalion staff turned to planning.

Tikrit was more than one hundred kilometers to our north, and with the long road march facing us I put the company into "rest and refit mode." The Marines sat around their vehicles cleaning weapons, reorganizing equipment, and napping in the shade. An hour later a couple of canary-yellow mailbags showed up. We couldn't believe it—it was the first real batch of mail the company had seen in nearly a month. Even the fact that many of the letters were postdated weeks before the war didn't dampen the mood around the assembly area as Marines stopped what they were doing to read the news from home.

We staged our vehicles to move out at 1330Z, but 3rd LAR Battalion had discovered that the bridge site across the Tigris River was untenable. The wait loomed once again, but it didn't faze the company. We were professionals at it. As the sun began dropping, the movement order came down the line. We finally stepped off on the seventy-five-plus-mile road march to Tikrit.

Getting the task force across the Tigris in the darkness took time, and we were on the road all night. Throughout the evening Davis and I took turns mixing up "frappuccinos" from our random, leftover MRE coffee, cocoa, sugar, and creamer packets. We also passed his can of Copenhagen back and forth. But even with the caffeine-sugar-nicotine high, the trip was murder. Mile after mile passed in the darkness, and as I stared through my night vision goggles the silence of the radio waves was periodically broken by Capt Portiss yelling across the company net for everyone to keep scanning their turrets across the countryside. By the time we approached Tikrit everyone was beat. The familiar slurring sound of exhausted Marines speaking into their microphones filled my ears, and for the hundredth time I was amazed by the resilience of the Marines in the company. Plenty of opportunities presented themselves for the drivers to fall asleep at the wheel and run their LAVs off the road. But as in every other operation to that point, they held fast and executed their tasks magnificently.

The surrounding landscape in the approach to Tikrit was a lush, vegetated expanse of fields, date-palm groves, and canals. It was a far cry from the deserts and drained marshes of southern Iraq. But the emerald beauty of the area was marred by dozens of long, black oil trenches snaking their way along the highway's shoulders. Luckily they hadn't been ignited, but thick, black crude oozed from them and leaked across the asphalt of the highway. It was a mess, and I remember thinking what a pain in the ass it would be for someone to clean up.

As the sun's rays crested the horizon on 13 April, the battalion herringboned along the shoulders of Highway 1 a few miles south of the city. A call echoed across the radio for the company commanders to report back to the battalion forward for the final frag order that would take us into Tikrit. Once we were all assembled behind his LAV, Maj Harper ordered Delta and Weapons Companies to establish blocking positions across Highway 1 at the southern entrance to the city. With Weapons Company situated to the west and Delta covering the highway and the land to the east, we would be able to stop any enemy personnel attempting escape from the city. It was a simple plan and a simple mission, and we returned to our vehicles for the last push toward Tikrit.

In the final stretch of road leading to the city's outskirts nothing seemed out of the ordinary, save for a splash of red graffiti scrawled across the wall of a building next to the road. Delta Company rolled into the periphery of Tikrit, the first U.S. forces there. After setting the platoons into their battle positions the strain and fatigue from the previous evening's road march took hold of me once again. I lay on the warm engine grill cover of my LAV, thinking about the graffiti we had seen and what it meant. In just two words the cryptic message communicated that not everyone in Iraq was overjoyed that we had eradicated Saddam Hussein's regime, and as I nodded off, the blazing red message we had witnessed glowed in my head like a warning beacon.

"DOWN USA."

✦ ✧ ✦

"Don't worry. We're gonna go get those motherfuckers right now."

My blood boiled.

The vision of the rocket propelled grenade slamming into the LAV-25 from Weapons Company and the feeling of AK-47 rounds cutting the air around me jump-started my system. The emotion that I had experienced during the company's first ambush on 3 April washed over me again: *I can't believe these motherfuckers are shooting at me!*

From my position in the turret I looked west across Highway 1 toward the LAV-25 that had been struck by the RPG. It was stationary now, but thick, black smoke still leaked from its splintered muffler. After radioing Dave Hudspeth I switched the control box back to the company.

"Guidons, this is Black-Six. Enough of this hit-and-run shit. Here's the plan: White-One, move your section up and abreast of my vehicle. Stay east of the tree line. Keep your second section stationary on the company's screen with Blue Platoon."

"Roger," replied Lt Schwartz. "White-One copies."

I continued. "Red-One, your Victor is with me on the road. Move your second section up on line with us and west of the road."

"Roger, Six," replied Parment. "Red-One copies."

"Red-Four copies," added SSgt Bright.

I keyed my headset again. "Everyone dismount your scouts. Our six vehicles will roll through and clear these bastards out. Anything you can't see or get to, use your scouts on the ground. Keep your vehicle movement slow and deliberate; stay abreast so we don't shoot each other up."

Captain Portiss jumped into the conversation. "Black-Six, mortars are fire-capped. Spool has helo support coming in as well."

"Roger that, Five. Red-One will spot for indirect fire and control the air."

"Roger, Five copies."

"Red-One copies."

Moments later mortar rounds exploded in the tree line forward of us and Cobra gunships buzzed overhead, making passes over the tree line. My fatigue from the long night spent driving from Baghdad had vanished, replaced by white-hot adrenaline coursing through my veins. As my composite platoon prepared to roll forward to destroy the enemy attempting to ambush us and infiltrate our position, the events of the previous twenty-four hours seemed a thousand years behind us. We began to creep up the road, toward the exploding mortars. My concentration was broken by a radio transmission buzzing in my earpiece.

"Dragon-Six, this is Highlander. Stand by for an updated frag order, over."

Oh, shit, I thought. *Not now.*

"Negative, Highlander," I radioed curtly. "We're in contact at the one-eight northing right now. I will contact you once we're done here. Dragon-Six, *out.*"

Our measured, orderly movement north continued. The turrets of the six LAVs methodically rotated left and right as the gunners and vehicle commanders strained to spot the RPG teams hiding in the tree lines that bordered the highway. Scouts cautiously advanced alongside the LAVs, their rifles and machine guns held tightly at the ready position. The undulating terrain of the tree line had created perfect defensive terrain for the ambushers, covering their displacement and concealing their actions until the last possible moment. Sporadic, blurred movement forward of us in the trees was met with the *thump-thump-thump* of 25mm fire, the staccato *rat-tat-tat* of machine guns, and the tinny *pop-pop-pop* of rifle fire. From my perch in the turret I squinted my eyes as I searched for enemy silhouettes, the butt-stock of the M240 once again tucked solidly into my shoulder. I alternated between the intercom and the company radio net.

"That's it, Gurganus. Easy, easy, good pace."

Back to the company. "This is Black-Six. Steady, stay on line. Watch your targets."

Back to the intercom. "Davis, keep your eyes open, keep scanning. Find me a target."

We proceeded north, still moving at a crawl, the thudding of mortar rounds and thumping of 25mm fires vibrating around us. Ahead of us, the enemy hid in the thickets in small teams of two and three. As we slowly closed with them, they aimed their RPG launchers into the sky and began lobbing the grenades at us like miniature artillery rounds. Overshooting us, many of the enemy's rounds began landing farther south near the site of the refueling point SSgt Kappen had established for the company. Even as RPG rounds impacted around them, Kappen continued to direct the refueling of the remainder of the company. The battalion Forward was also caught in the beaten zone, and the Marines from the headquarters jumped for cover to escape the plummeting AK-47 and RPG projectiles.

Forward of us a string of civilian cars had backed up, creating a traffic jam in the highway's southbound lane. Twenty or thirty Iraqis milled about in a group at the front of the traffic jam, probably wondering what the hell was going on around them. Just as we had seen through the entire war, rather than flee the scene of all the violence the civilians simply stood around watching the action. Lance Corporal Davis's voice came over the intercom.

"I got a guy walking across the highway."

"I see him too, sir," added Gurganus.

Ahead of us an enemy fighter moved slowly out of the western tree line, walking toward our vehicle. He waved his hands back and forth above his head, attempting to surrender, and as he made his way across the median the scouts between my vehicle and Lt Parment's began yelling at him. Even through my headset I could hear their shouts.

"Freeze!"

"Stop motherfucker!"

"Get on your face!"

The figure continued to move toward us, not heeding the Marines' commands. *If he keeps coming he's gonna get blown away,* I thought. I pulled the machine gun back into my shoulder and sighted the weapon high above him for a warning shot. *Aim high,* I thought. *Don't blow this dude's head off, just get him to stop.* As I squeezed the trigger, the machine gun rattled in my grip. A volley of 7.62mm rounds arced over the man's head, but it didn't faze him. *Man, what the hell?* I thought. We moved closer and closer toward him, and he toward us. Glancing down from the turret, I watched the scouts moving in a graceful combat glide, their rifle sights up to their eyes, their barrels steady as they advanced toward the enemy fighter. Seeing the scouts move so skillfully, it was clear that my warning shots were unnecessary—one wrong move by him and he would be dead from the Marines' bullets. He finally got the message and eased himself down to his knees, his hands still high in the air.

Suddenly the tree line behind the traffic jam erupted again with enemy rifle and machine-gun fire, placing the crowd of civilians and the surrendering soldier between the ambush and our position. Bullets bounced off the pavement and thudded into the earth around our platoon, kicking up tiny geysers of dirt and dust. The team of scouts left of my vehicle dropped to their knees and simultaneously returned fire into the tree line, sending the crowd of civilians scattering in all directions as rounds ricocheted off the blacktop. The man attempting to surrender in front of us absorbed the full brunt of the Marines' return volley. Hit in the head by either a 5.56-millimeter round or a shard of flying asphalt, he tumbled forward on his face momentarily, and then righted himself on his knees again. Shimmering red blood pumped rhythmically in sheets from the wound, and he crawled feebly toward us, alternately clutching the hole in his head and gawking in astonishment at his blood-soaked hands. Picking up our speed a notch, we rolled past him as he lay in an expanding pool of red. Two scouts ran up to his sprawled body, grabbed him, and dragged his limp body to a medevac point LT Zubrod had established in a small checkpoint shack one hundred meters to our south. The Marines dropped the wounded Iraqi in a heap next to another who was receiving treatment from Zubrod and his corpsmen. An enemy soldier 2nd Platoon had shot earlier would survive the wound to his leg. The one who had been hit in the head would not.

We continued to move forward, our senses tuned like fine instruments to the slightest movement in the tree line forward of us. A report abruptly filled the airwaves of our radio net. It sounded like SSgt Bright's voice.

"*Contact!* Truck!"

In the southbound lane a tan military flatbed truck sped toward our advancing skirmisher line and barrelled around the traffic jam. Bouncing up and down violently and occasionally leaving the asphalt, the vehicle came to a bumpy, skidding stop off the shoulder and alongside the western tree line. Figures clad in civilian clothing and carrying rifles spilled from the truck's cab. As they raised their weapons in our direction they were met by a thunderous hail of fire from Bright's vehicle section. The fighters dropped, their bodies twitching violently as they hit the ground. To my left across the road a team of scouts moved swiftly alongside Bright's vehicles, closing in on the Iraqis who had just been cut down. Wounded, the enemy soldiers from the truck struggled pathetically to level their weapons at the Marines, who simply responded with bursts from their rifles before moving forward back into the fight. *Get some,* I thought.

The three vehicle sections, still generally abreast of each other, lumbered past a concrete reinforced culvert tunnel that ran west to east beneath the road. Another report from SSgt Bright came across the radio.

"Be advised, three enemy personnel just ran into that tunnel. We have a scout team going in to clear them out."

Sergeant Isaac McCorkle, the chief scout from 1st Platoon, closed in on the western entrance of the tunnel with Lance Corporals Saul Pando and Chad Weise. Together they hurled a volley of hand grenades into the tunnel's mouth, and SSgt Bright relayed the team's warning over the radio.

"Fire in the hole!"

Three muffled thuds in rapid succession shook the ground above the culvert, and a cloud of gray concrete powder billowed from the tunnel's opening. But then the explosion of the scouts' grenades was followed by the sound of another, smaller blast—the explosion of an enemy grenade. Staff Sergeant Bright's voice filled the radio again.

"Man down!" he yelled. "Man down!"

Oh shit, I thought. *Someone's hit.*

"Red-Four, this is Six," I demanded. "Report. Who's hit?"

"Sergeant McCorkle just got hit by a grenade!"

The scout team pulled away from the tunnel's opening, and a moment later Bright's voice returned once more to the radio.

"Be advised, McCorkle and the others are okay. They're all fine. He just got stung in the ass by some shrapnel. Weise took some, too, but they're okay."

To my right, Lt Schwartz's vehicle section advanced slowly through the tree line. He hadn't yet passed the eastern entrance to the tunnel. With the enemy soldiers still hiding inside the tunnel beneath us, we couldn't afford to continue advancing until they had been eliminated. The risk was too great that they would pop out behind our formation and shoot us in the ass with an RPG.

"Red-Four, White-One, hold fast," I said quickly. "Red-Four, I'm turning the tunnel over to White-One. Stay clear of the western entrance, over." The last thing we wanted was two scout teams entering the shaft from opposite ends and shooting each other up instead of the enemy hiding within.

"Roger, Black-Six," replied Bright. His two vehicles held their position just forward of the tunnel's opening.

"White-One," I continued. "Send your scouts in and clear those bastards out of there."

"Roger that, Six. They're Oscar Mike now."

In short bursts of movement, a scout team from 2nd Platoon bounded forward through the tree line to the tunnel's entrance. Sergeant Will Dewitt and Lance Corporal Josh Nour, who together had helped me disable the anti-aircraft gun the first day of the war, advanced toward the opening with Lance Corporal Floyd Reed and Hospitalman Third Class Shaun Wistrom in tow. I briefly thought back to New Year's Eve three months earlier, when I had received a call at two o'clock in the morning from the naval base in San Diego. Reed was drunk and needed to be picked up, and I was the only one around to do it. As Ashley and I had driven him back to Camp Pendleton, I had thought, *When is this guy gonna grow up?* Now there he was, racing with his teammates toward a firefight that had already wounded two Marines. He was doing perhaps the most adult thing a person can do.

The fire team stacked itself up behind mounds of dirt that had been excavated to give the culvert tunnel the proper drainage it required, and from my position on the road above them I leaned down toward Sgt Dewitt. He had maneuvered himself up to the tunnel's mouth and was crouched into a small depression next to the culvert's concrete foundation. Our eyes met, and over the roar of my LAV's engine and the chaos unfolding all around us I yelled down to him at the top of my lungs.

"FRAG THAT FUCKER!"

A maniacal grin spread across Dewitt's face, and with our eyes still locked together he nodded. With a shout to LCpl Reed, the two Marines pulled hand grenades from their web gear. Pressing their bodies tightly against the corners of the concrete foundation, they pulled the safety pins from the grenades and with three nods of the head timed their throws together. Each man lobbed his grenade into the tunnel's mouth and jumped back behind the protection of the concrete wall. Moments later two simultaneous thuds shook the road. Almost on top of the explosions, Dewitt and Reed leaned back around the corners and emptied their rifle magazines into the tunnel's maw. It was, in a word, beautiful. I had watched these Marines train together for more than a year, practicing and rehearsing these very same moves. Now there they were, executing impeccably.

But something was wrong. Dust billowed in sheets from the tunnel's entrance, and in twos and threes the team intermittently leaned around the culvert's corners to fire their rifles and toss grenades into the darkness. Whoever was in the tunnel wasn't dead yet. I keyed the intercom.

"Back up, Gurganus."

Davis looked up at me from inside the turret. "What's going on, sir?"

"They need more firepower. We're gonna give it to them." The LAV rolled slowly in reverse, and when it was south of the tunnel I told Gurganus to stop. Leaning out of the turret again, I waved my arms at Sgt Dewitt, motioning for him to approach the vehicle.

"Hey!" I shouted. "Do you want my Two-Forty?"

He nodded. "Yeah!"

Unlocking the bolt that seated it in place, I hoisted the machine gun from its scissor-mount and handed it down to Doc Wistrom. Dewitt had already moved back to the edge of the culvert to direct his team, and Wistrom stood by the side of the road holding the machine gun and its long belt of ammunition. A look that said *What the hell do you want me to do with this?* filled the corpsman's face.

They don't have anyone to man it, I thought. *They need help.* I keyed the intercom once more.

"You guys stay put. I'll be right back." I grabbed my Kevlar, hopped down from the turret, and snatched the machine gun from Wistrom. "Come on, Doc. You're gonna be my ammo-man." Together we moved down to the tunnel's entrance, where the remainder of the team once again was stacked against the concrete slabs that shielded them from the fire coming from within the culvert. Wistrom and I moved in behind Sgt Dewitt as he wedged himself against the corner of the slab. He looked over his shoulder at me holding the machine gun, the same crazed grin stretching from ear to ear. He was having the time of his life.

"Pie it off for us," I told him. "And we'll spray it down in there." Lance Corporal Reed, weighted down with the squad's radio strapped to his back, wedged himself in tightly between Dewitt and me and Wistrom. Together with LCpl Nour on the entrance's opposite corner, the five of us nodded our cue to move. Dewitt and Nour went first, leaning quickly around their respective corners and releasing long, sustained bursts of fire into the tunnel's opening. Reed followed suit, moving just right of Dewitt and at the same time firing burst after burst from his M-4. With all three scouts firing into the culvert as fast as they could, Wistrom and I darted out in between Reed and Nour. I shouldered the machine gun, aimed hastily into the darkness, and squeezed the trigger.

Click.

Misfire.

"Fuck!" I shouted. "Get back!"

The team leapt back behind the protection of the concrete slabs, and from his kneeling position Sgt Dewitt shouted to me.

"What's the matter?"

"The fucking thing misfired!" I growled back. I knelt down beside him and popped open the weapon's feed-tray to reseat the ammunition belt. Slamming the cover back down, I looked back at the team. "Come on, let's try it again."

A guttural sound had begun to emanate from within the depths of the tunnel, and for a brief moment we traded puzzled looks with each other. The team stood up and reset itself to clear the culvert again, and we converged on the tunnel's entrance more smoothly the second time around. The procedure repeated itself: Dewitt and Nour spun around their corners and fired; Reed squared off next to Dewitt and fired; Wistrom and I jumped in between Reed and Nour. With the earsplitting *pop-pop-pop* of the team's carbines reverberating around me, I squeezed the trigger once more.

Click.

You have got to be shitting me, I thought morbidly. *There is no way this is happening.*

The team saw me jump back for the defilade provided by the concrete corner of the tunnel.

"Fuck!" I shouted in frustration. "Fuck, fuck, fuck!"

"What's the matter with it?" asked Wistrom.

"Fucking piece of *SHIT!"* I yelled, pulling the weapon's bolt back and realigning the ammunition for a second time. With the rest of the team continuing to fire into the darkness, Wistrom and I resumed our positions in the center. Breathing heavily, I cradled the cumbersome weapon by my side and pointed it into the tunnel. I held my breath in an effort to steady the weapon, but also in prayer that the goddamned hunk of junk would work properly and save my life. *Third time's the charm,* I thought, squeezing the trigger.

Click.

I threw the machine gun down in disgust and slid to my right to seek the cover of LCpl Nour's position. In unison the team spun and jumped to escape its terribly exposed position. But as they did, a grenade thrown from deep within the tunnel exploded with a booming roar and a concussive shower of dust, metal shards, and concrete fragments. A sharp stinging sensation suddenly pulsed beneath my right eye, which responded by snapping shut and welling up with tears. Something from the blast—a tiny rock or maybe a sliver of metal—had bounced off my cheek bone without even breaking the skin. It was the same stunning feeling as getting snapped in the face with a rubber band, and I pressed my hand against it to stifle the pain. To my left Sgt

SCOUT TEAM FROM 2ND PLATOON CONVERGES ON CULVERT TUNNEL CONTAINING ENEMY JIHADI SOLDIERS IN TIKRIT, 13 APRIL 2003. (L TO R: SGT WILL DEWITT, CAPT FOLSOM, LCPL JOSH NOUR, HM3 SHAUN WISTROM.) OFFICIAL MARINE CORPS PHOTO BY LCPL ANDREW P. ROUFS.

Dewitt leaned over, rubbing his shin where a small hole oozed a thin rivulet of blood.

"Son-of-a-*bitch!*" I shouted, pulling my pistol from its holster. Behind me Wistrom drew his own pistol. We moved up alongside Dewitt, Nour, and Reed, and together the team angrily charged the tunnel's entrance. I was in a rage, pissed off that whoever was cowering in this hole in the ground had summoned the balls to throw a grenade at us. My cheek throbbed, and my only thought was, *I'm gonna kill this fucker.*

As the dust and powder dissipated and began to settle inside the tunnel, the throaty human wail within turned into an angry howl. Outside, the company's firing had died down. We were left only with the shouts of the wounded enemy soldier in the darkness.

"Go away!" he shouted in heavily accented English.

We moved cautiously toward the sound, our eyes fighting to quickly adjust to the culvert's shadows. The figure inside yelled at us again in a shrill intonation that sounded as if someone was impersonating an Arab stereotype.

"I throw bomb!" he cried. "I throw bomb!" At the sound of the man's voice, Sgt Dewitt turned to me.

"Are you fucking kidding me?" he asked.

The air cleared in the tunnel, finally affording us a clear view inside. In the far left corner of the culvert's chamber, no more than ten feet away from us, three limp bodies lay twisted together in the dust. Two twitched violently as dark red stains spread across their clothing. The third sat slumped against the tunnel's wall with a small, black grenade clutched tightly in his hand. He too was bleeding from a half-dozen wounds. Yelling his head off, he repeated his ultimatum.

"Go away! I still throw bomb!"

We raised our weapons again and began yelling at him.

"Drop it!" someone commanded.

"Drop it, motherfucker!" another emphasized.

"Eer-me see la-huk!" I shouted to him in Arabic, focusing the tiny front sight of my Beretta on the center of his chest. "Drop your weapon! Now!"

"No!" he wailed, raising the hand that held the grenade. "I still throw bomb!"

I squeezed the trigger. The pistol kicked in my hands.

Inside the narrow confines of the tunnel the report was deafening. The soldier emitted a piercing, high-pitched yelp and flopped over backward in a bloody heap next to his comrades. I slowly lowered my weapon as the five of us stared at the jumble of bodies, each man alone in his thoughts. Sergeant Dewitt finally broke the silence.

"I guess he's not gonna 'throw bomb' anymore."

One of the soldiers twitched again, his sneakered foot spasming in the culvert's powdery dust. Lance Corporal Reed shouted in alarm.

"Hey, that motherfucker's still moving!"

"No," interjected Doc Wistrom. "That's just a reflex action. He's dead."

"Your contact's still moving too, sir," LCpl Nour said in the tunnel's gloom. I turned my head to see the four men staring at me.

"Well," I said indifferently. "Let's see." The men we had been fighting were fanatics, determined to fight to the last breath. That much had been evident by the jihadi clutching the grenade even in the face of a certain, violent death at our hands. I knew that to risk physically checking his twitching corpse would be to needlessly risk the lives of my men. I pointed the pistol's barrel back toward the man, aimed at his leg, and squeezed the trigger. *If he's playing dead,* I thought. *He won't sit still when I plug him in the thigh.* The 9mm round thudded loudly against his flesh. No movement.

"He's dead alright," I said matter-of-factly.

Together we cautiously approached the three corpses, our weapons lowered slightly.

"God-damn," someone muttered.

The bodies were clad in civilian clothing and green canvas chest bandoliers, now soaked through with gore. Crimson sprays of blood spackled the concrete walls and glistened in the gravel lining the culvert's floor. A sharp, sweet smell filled the air in the chamber. I stared down blankly at the man I killed, wondering what had happened to the grenade he was wielding. Had he already pulled the pin? Would it go off if we moved him? I didn't want to find out. My revulsion at the pile of cadavers lying before us hastened my decision. Suddenly I wanted out of the tunnel more than anything I had ever wanted in my life. I turned back toward the team.

"Good job. Now let's get the hell out of here."

"Do you want us to search them, sir?" one asked.

"No," I replied flatly, already walking past them and out of the tunnel. "Move out."

I leaned down and grabbed the M240 by its carrying handle and lugged it up the embankment back to my waiting vehicle. One thought resonated in my head.

I just killed a human being.

At the time I didn't think of it in terms of right or wrong—it had been an act of self-defense to protect the fire team and myself. Moreover, at the moment, all I had been able to think of was that my Marines needed help. Nonetheless, I knew the instant I pulled the trigger that my life had changed forever. For better or for worse, I didn't know. It was different from the air strikes and artillery barrages I had approved earlier in the war. I knew then that whether I killed more enemy soldiers or managed to make it home without having to do it again, I would never forget that moment for the rest of my days. The image had seared itself into my memory banks as surely as a branding iron against raw flesh.

This was no longer someone else's war.

✦ ✧ ✦

Climbing up into the turret, I angrily threw the machine gun at Davis.

"Fix this fucking thing," I snarled. "It almost got me killed down there."

"Roger that," he replied. "Highlander's been calling for you, sir."

I keyed my headset. "Highlander, this is Dragon-Six, send your traffic."

"Roger, Dragon. Report back to the Forward ASAP to brief your sit-rep and receive new mission frag."

Looking around, I realized I had ignored the battalion long enough. The fighting in the tree lines had quieted, but the engagement was far from over. Highlander was correct: they needed to know what the hell was going on up where Delta Company was. As our vehicle turned around and drove south down the highway toward the Forward, Spool's voice materialized over the radio.

"We need a medevac at our position for some wounded enemy personnel," he said. Then, with barely a pause at the end of his sentence, he spoke again. "Never mind, they're dead now. No medevac required." I would later learn that Capt Portiss and his vehicle crew had attempted to assist some wounded enemy soldiers, who responded by trying to draw their weapons on the Marines. Portiss and his team killed them instantly.

To the south, the vehicles of the battalion Forward sat in column along the right side of the road. Major Harper was already in the midst of briefing the new frag order when I walked up. He stopped when I arrived.

"You alright, man?" asked Gil. The frazzled look on my face betrayed my emotions.

"Yeah, I'm fine."

"What's going on up there?" the battalion commander demanded. Explaining what had happened after the Weapons Company LAV had been disabled by the RPG, I opined that we needed more Marines on the ground forward of Delta Company's position. Lieutenant Colonel White conferred with Maj Harper for a moment, and then the two turned to face the Golf Company commander. Together they agreed to dismount his company of grunts into the tree line to flush out the ambushers and enable the rest of the battalion to continue its movement into the city. As we stood in a small circle, BGen Kelly approached LtCol White. A moment later White turned back to me.

"Seth, tell the general what you just told me."

I turned to face Kelly. "We just engaged about a platoon or less of enemy up there, sir. They're using defilade and the vegetation in the tree line to conceal their movement and sneak up on us. They're also hazarding civilians to shoot at us. Fired right through that traffic jam up there to get to us."

"How many did you all get?" he asked.

"I think we got about fifteen or so. They're working in groups of two and three, hiding in the trees and culvert tunnels."

"Tunnels?" he asked, raising his eyebrow. "How do you know?"

"Because I just took one out myself, sir." I turned back toward LtCol White, as if to explain my actions. "Son of a bitch threw a grenade at us, sir."

"Good job, skipper," Kelly said.

"One more thing, sir," I added, remembering a report I had heard upon my return to the rear. "One of the wounded bad guys up there is Jordanian."

"Alright, Duffy," Kelly said bluntly. "What's your plan?" Together the group went over the revised scheme of maneuver once more, and I turned to remount my vehicle.

"Call the company, Davis. Tell them to form up in column on the road, and get the guidons to our vehicle."

One by one, Delta's LAVs filed in place along the road's shoulder, and the company staff appeared.

"What happened, sir?" someone asked. As with the battalion staff, they could read the tension still carved into my face.

"Nothing," I said curtly. I held up the large-scale map the S-3 had just handed me. "Here's the plan: Golf Company's gonna move north and clear out the tree line for the next klick or so until they get to this built-up area here." For emphasis I pointed to a one square–kilometer, gridded urban area on the map. I continued.

"Delta will take the northern half of the town; Charlie will take the southern half. We'll be three platoons abreast, moving west to east, hedgehog style. It's gonna be tight. Keep your eyes open, and have everyone popped up. Blow away anyone in the town with a weapon. Any questions?"

"We need maps," Capt Portiss said.

"I've got two, that's it," I told them. "The XO and the FiST get one, I get one. Everyone else, copy down what you need. We've got about ten minutes." As the three platoon commanders knelt in a tight circle and furiously scribbled hasty maps of the town, I leaned back up against the dusty hull of my LAV and lit a cigarette. Portiss walked over to me.

"Where do you want me and the trains?"

"Tuck your vehicle in between mine and the first sergeant's. Combat trains bring up the rear with security."

"Roger that." He turned to walk away and was replaced by 1stSgt Guzman.

"You alright, sir?" he asked, staring at me.

"Yeah, fine."

"What happened back there?"

"Nothing. Just blew a guy away in that tunnel up there."

"Why did you get off your vehicle?" he demanded. "What were you thinking?"

"I don't know, First Sergeant," I said apologetically. "I don't know what I was thinking. Guess I wasn't."

"You gotta stop this shit, sir. You're gonna get yourself killed."

"Don't worry about it." I dragged deeply on the cigarette and looked him in the eyes. "I'm done."

On the ground the platoon commanders were finishing up their map sketches.

"All right," I said, interrupting them. "Mount up, stage on the road."

The column inched into place on the highway, and the company awaited the order to move out. With the inevitable delay facing us, the Marines dismounted to smoke and stretch their legs. In the bushes to my vehicle's right a small group of Marines had clustered together and were pointing to the ground. Jumping down from the turret to see what the hell they were gawking at, I found a dead body lying at their feet in an enormous puddle of blood. It had soaked the underbrush around him and mixed with the dirt to make a thick, brown gruel. We stared at the corpse.

"Boy," a Marine said aloud. "Someone really wasted this fucker, didn't they?"

The body lay on its back, riddled with tiny fragmentation and shrapnel wounds. The worst was a gaping hole in his thigh, which he had futilely attempted to tie off with his belt. Eyes glazed over and blankly staring skyward, he resembled a mannequin. The ashen, jaundiced pallor of his skin guaranteed that I would never visit a wax museum again for the rest of my life.

"Yep," I added, leaning down and picking up what looked like a passport resting next to him. It appeared as if he had pulled it out at the last minute to show someone who he was. "Someone killed him deader than shit." I examined the identification. It was a Syrian passport.

"What's it say, sir?" a Marine asked.

"He's a foreigner. He's a jihadi," I said, shaking my head. "What the fuck . . . we're not even fighting Iraqis anymore."

Flies had begun landing on the body, swimming in the coagulating blood. I turned back to the Marines crowded around the remains.

"Come on, get back to your vehicles," I said. "This ain't over yet."

The battalion column stepped off and rolled into the small township south of Tikrit. Trepidation and tenseness not felt since the evening on Highway 1—when the company had pulled out of the marshes and confronted the phantom army to the east—permeated the atmosphere. Everyone's asshole was puckered tight. The Marines were advancing straight into a potential urban ambush—a fire sack—and everyone knew it. Never before had I witnessed Delta Company more alert, more ready for anything, than it was on that patrol. As our wall of steel trundled methodically through the streets, the radio was silent save for the lieutenants making periodic position location reports. Turrets rhythmically scanned left and right, up and down, the gunners' eyes glued to their sights and scrutinizing every building, every alley. Behind me, Capt Portiss's vehicle rolled slowly, bristling like a porcupine with Marines pointing rifles in all directions. Outside, no one walked the streets. No faces peeked through curtains. The town was dead.

Lieutenant Parment keyed his headset. With a new seriousness in his voice, he mused aloud, "I never thought I would say this, but it's too quiet out here."

And it was. But the operation was over before we knew it. With the exception of two abandoned anti-aircraft guns on the town's periphery destroyed by 2nd Platoon, the company reached the edge of the neighborhood before dusk without enemy contact. The word seemed to have gotten around.

Don't fuck with the Marines.

◆ ◇ ◆

We were back on Highway 1 and moving to link up with the battalion. As Delta and Charlie Companies cleared the small town, Weapons Company had likewise secured a large compound less than a kilometer to the north. With the entrance to Tikrit open for business, 2nd LAR Battalion's long column passed through 1st LAR's lines and onto the highway interchange that bypassed the city to the west. I later learned 2nd LAR went on to direct a series of devastating air strikes against an Iraqi airfield, annihilating scores of fighter aircraft and helicopters.

But 1st and 2nd LAR Battalions hadn't been the only elements of Task Force Tripoli that had been busy that day. During the long road march up Highway 1, 3rd LAR Battalion had been ordered to secure a small town called Samarra, forty kilometers south of Tikrit. Although 3rd LAR's task had been to cover the remainder of the Task Force's movement north, the mission quickly shifted when an Iraqi informed the Marines that he knew where American prisoners of war were being held inside the town. The Marines provided the Iraqi informant with a GPS, taught him how to use it to map a route, and convinced him to go to the POW site and return with directions. Knowing full well that the entire situation could be a trap, 3rd LAR's battalion commander opted to send in his Delta Company to grab the Americans. Captain Gordon Miller, a classmate of mine from the LAV Leaders Course, led his company to the site and rescued the POWs, barely firing a shot in the process. The POWs included two downed airmen and the five survivors of the Army's 507th Maintenance Company, which had been ambushed in An Nasiriyah three weeks earlier on 23 March.

That evening, 1st LAR Battalion set in around the compound Weapons Company had secured earlier, and Delta Company pushed off to the east in a battle position oriented north. The action and excitement of the day was rapidly catching up with everyone. They needed sleep, and lots of it. I weighed the options: on our western flank was Weapons Company, to our south across a narrow road was Golf Company, and to our east were the steep banks of the Tigris River. Only the company's front was open, and in my fatigue-influenced state I rationalized setting a minimum alert status. Marines roamed about inside the perimeter in various states of undress as I sat in the LAV-C2, struggling to record on paper the day's events.

Heavy-lidded, my eyes refused to stay open. The adrenaline highs and the subsequent crashes of the tunnel fight and the movement through the town had combined to reduce me to an exhausted husk. I knew I required sleep as much as the men at that point. But with an operation into the heart of the city pending for the next morning, it was important for me to remain near the radio as the frag order took shape. I compromised, deciding instead to sleep next to the LAV-C2 and its chattering radios.

On the ground next to the vehicle Capt Portiss snored in his sleeping bag. I eased the filthy suede boots from my putrid feet and rolled my bag out between the sleeping forms of Portiss and his driver, Lance Corporal Aaron Merrill. My interrupted nap on the engine grill cover that morning excepted, it was the first time I'd been in a horizontal position since late on 11 April. Time had expanded, and with each coming morning the days and weeks that had preceeded it seemed farther and farther behind us. My home and my life with Ashley became a distant dream. Little seemed to exist for me except the young men of Delta Company and the reality of war we had finally realized.

As I stared at the twinkling stars above me, sleep finally closed in. In the darkness far to my left the unexpected *pop-pop-pop* of rifle fire echoed behind the company's position. I bolted upright in my sleeping bag, blinking my eyes to adjust to the dark. A split second later the tree line to our south erupted in strobes of orange muzzle flashes. The night air ignited with rifle and machine-gun fire as the red embers of tracers sizzled through Delta Company's lines. Two rounds cracked over my head, sending me back down into the dirt. Beside me, Portiss lay on his right side, unmoving as if still asleep. Everywhere Marines and corpsmen leapt half-naked from their sleeping bags, clamoring for weapons and mounting vehicles. I rolled over, practically on top of Portiss, only to find that he was not sleeping but instead behind his rifle and scanning the tree line for a target. Someone jumped on top of me, and over my shoulder I could see it was the naked form of LCpl Merrill, crazily pointing his own rifle over me.

"Give me that fucking thing before you hurt someone!" I shouted, yanking the rifle from his hands. "Get some fucking pants on, man!"

The tracers continued briefly, followed by a massive explosion that cooked off next to the battalion command post. Bright orange sparks illuminated the night sky, and minutes later multiple secondary explosions rocked the area.

"What is that?" I asked aloud. "Mortars?"

"That was 'five-five-six.' And those tracers were red," Portiss said angrily. "That's gotta be Golf Company shooting at us."

Throwing the weapon back at Merrill, I stood up and ran to my vehicle for my own carbine stashed in the turret. Gurganus, naked except for his flak jacket, met me as I approached.

"What's going on, sir?"

"Shit if I know," I replied, grabbing my M-4. I raced back toward the LAV-C2 and mounted Spool's AN/PAS-13, a brick-sized infrared viewer, on my carbine. As I scanned the tree line back and forth for whoever or whatever had been shooting at us, the battalion radio net vibrated with excited rants about enemy personnel in the trees. Major Harper managed the chaos, attempting to locate units. The company commanders called in, again reporting their unit positions. A report filtered through that a small firefight between two Marines and two Fedayeen had begun along the road that separated Delta and Golf Companies. It quickly became evident who was doing most of the shooting. Portiss had been correct: Golf Company had lit us up.

Angry as I was at the intramural firefight and the danger in which Golf Company had placed us, I had learned my lesson. Golf Company to our rear or not, we reoriented six LAV-25s to face the tree line to our south to scan all evening with their thermal sights. The restraint Delta Company had demonstrated by not randomly firing back into the darkness during the fusillade was extraordinary. Their rucksacks peppered with bullet holes, the paint of their LAVs chipped from the impacts, the Marines held their fire. Even when Cpl Martin—the Marine who on 27 March had barely survived the tank collision on Highway 1—was grazed across the top of his foot by an incoming round, he held his fire until he knew who was shooting. *That's* discipline.

When the situation finally resolved itself I collapsed in a heap on top of my sleeping bag, my head spinning. The previous twenty-four hours replayed themselves again inside my throbbing head like a grainy splice of film. The grueling nighttime road march from Baghdad; the firefight in the tree line and the tunnel; the armored push through the town; the friendly fire from Golf Company—it had been a hell of a day. But it had been more than that.

It had been Delta Company's shining hour.

20
Stabilizing Tikrit

The full story behind the friendly fire in the night unfolded for us the morning of 14 April. Some time after the companies had all set into their positions for the evening, the battalion gunner and two sergeants walked up the road that separated Delta and Golf Companies. An old Willys jeep with a 106mm recoilless rifle and piled high with rounds sat off to the side of the trail in the tree line, and the gunner and his Marines moved in to disable it. Two shadowy forms approached them in the darkness, and when the Marines verbally challenged them the figures opened fire with AK-47s. Despite being wounded, both sergeants returned fire and killed the two jihadi soldiers. During the brief exchange of fire, Sergeant Bryan Benson took a round to the chest. Instead of killing him, the 7.62mm round penetrated the dense Kevlar material, passed through a rifle magazine, and ricocheted across his chest. Sergeant Benson escaped with barely a scratch. Considering what could have happened, *that's* luck. Like the majority of the Marines and sailors in 1st LAR Battalion (myself included), Benson had not been issued the new small arms protective inserts for his body armor. Known as "SAPI" plates, the expensive, composite armored inserts were hard to come by. Many Marines in the division had survived multiple gunshot wounds because they had been wearing SAPI plates in their flak jackets. Others who hadn't been issued the plates had to hold their breath and pray they didn't get hit.

When Benson and Sergeant Nieves Avila returned fire on the jihadis, the task force's Navy SEAL detachment opened fire to the south into Golf Company's lines. Not knowing who was shooting at them, Golf reciprocated by opening fire to the north, thereby spraying down Delta Company, the SEALs, Weapons Company, and the Battalion COC. A Marine fired an AT-4 antitank rocket into the jeep containing the recoilless rifle, and the heat from the accompanying explosion began cooking off all of the rounds into the area surrounding the COC. Unbelievably, only one Marine in the battalion took shrapnel—in the leg.

Sometime later in the evening, after the pandemonium of the intramural firefight, the battalion issued a new frag order. The order required Delta Company to clear in zone up Highway 1 through Tikrit's center while Weapons Company moved in to secure the Tigris River bridge. Golf Company received a mission to seize a palace compound in the city's east, and to assist them in accomplishing the task, the S-3 directed me to detach a platoon to them. At first light I called for Lt Cullins.

"Listen, I'm attaching you and your platoon to Golf for their palace mission this morning."

"You mean those bastards who shot us up last night, sir?"

"That's right," I replied. "Keep your eyes open out there."

"Aye-aye, sir." He shook his head contemptuously. "Jesus, I feel like I'm taking crazy pills again."

"Yeah," I sighed, lighting a cigarette. "Welcome to the club."

Hastily constructed earthen berms had been bulldozed into the streets in an attempt to obstruct our movement, but it wasn't long before 1st LAR Battalion was steamrolling through the streets of downtown Tikrit. Advancing north along the main drag, the Marines scanned back and forth for any sign of resistance. But unlike the maze of Baghdad, which had been interspersed with sandbagged machine-gun, mortar, and AAA emplacements, the streets of Tikrit were largely empty. The only threatening structures we encountered were a series of holes along the sides of the road, each lightly camouflaged with flimsy sheets of tin or plywood. It was difficult to tell whether they were survivability shelters designed to shield against bombing raids or spider holes to conceal ambushing jihadis. I wasn't willing to chance the latter. The experiences of the previous day indicated that we were still fighting a deceitful and determined enemy. As if hearing my thoughts, Lt Schwartz radioed me during a brief halt in the company's advance up the road.

"Black-Six, request permission to frag these fighting holes next to the road."

"Affirmative," I replied. "Do it."

Moments later, muffled thuds reverberated up and down the street as scouts dismounted their vehicles and lobbed grenades into the warrens. Each episode was the same. A team would cautiously approach a spider hole, the Marines' rifles at the ready. One man would lean down and lift the camouflage covering, while a second would pull the pin on a grenade and toss it into the gap. Shouts of "Fire in the hole!" would ring out, and seconds later the ground would shake momentarily, launching the camouflage covering into the air. The scouts would then move on to the next hole farther up the street.

We held fast in our blocking position at the intersection of Highway 1 and a street leading to the Tigris bridge that the battalion had labeled "Route George." Throughout the company, vehicle crews continued to scrutinize the buildings and alleys surrounding them. The city was a ghost town. No one walked the streets, and the only sound that could be heard was the idle of our engines and the periodic thump of grenades detonating underground. The battalion radio beeped for me.

"Dragon-Six, this is Highlander-Three. Warlord has secured battalion objective three. Move your company and attack to seize the new presidential palace northwest of objective three."

I keyed my helmet to answer Maj Harper. "Roger, Highlander-Three, solid copy. We're Oscar Mike, time: now." The path to the palace now open, Delta Company (still sans 3rd Platoon) veered east and darted past blocking positions established by vehicles from Weapons Company. As the company approached the bridge spanning the river, we could see to our left a massive structure sitting high above the banks of the Tigris. A long, winding road looped back and forth in narrow bends and hairpin turns up the cliff face to the palace. As we guardedly approached it, all I could think about was how much it resembled Adolf Hitler's Eagle's Nest compound high in the Bavarian Alps of Berchtesgaden. And there we were, advancing up the road to capture it. The LAV crews formed a tight perimeter around the looming palace, and as the company set into position, all were struck by a sense of awe at the structure's size and splendor.

The palace was silent. From our elevated position we could see vehicles and crews from Weapons Company setting up road blocks on the eastern side of the bridge. The center of the span had been torn open during a Coalition bombing raid, and the Marines in their LAVs had the unenviable mission of not only serving as traffic control guards but also testing the structural integrity of the damaged bridge.

Climbing down from my turret, I surveyed the area. The battalion had directed Delta Company merely to seize the compound; it would be the job of the SEALs to enter and secure the palace itself. But there was no sign of them yet. *Oh, screw this,* I said to myself. I turned to 1stSgt Guzman.

"Hey, come on. Let's go exploring." He rolled his eyes and hopped down from his vehicle. I could tell Guzman had about had it with my capriciousness, but rather than argue with me about checking out the palace interior he grabbed a weapon and followed me inside. Together we walked around the building's front and strolled right through the main doors. An enormous chandelier hung suspended above marbled floors and brilliantly frescoed walls. Ornate designs spiraled up columns of alabaster and marble, and there was gold, gold, gold everywhere. It lined the walls, the bathrooms, the staircases. But the place was empty. Not looted, just empty. We came to learn that many palaces in Iraq were similarly barren. They had been constructed by Saddam merely as a symbolic testament to his power. So far as we knew, there had never been any plan to furnish such strongholds. Regardless, none of the priceless decorations adorning the walls of this palace interior had been taken. In contrast to the mad surge of pillaging that had taken place in Baghdad, little such chaos had occurred in Tikrit. It was, after all, Saddam Hussein's home town. These people knew what side their bread was buttered on.

Guzman and I exited the building, and minutes later the SEAL team arrived on the scene. Dressed in high-speed body armor and communications rigs, they jumped from their humvees and stacked themselves tightly against the wall, preparing to enter and clear the palace. Guzman and I stood off to the side, our arms casually folded across our chests, and sniggered. Together we had beaten the SEALs to be the first ones into the palace.

The battalion Forward rumbled up the hill and into the palace courtyard, followed in short order by the task force headquarters. With its central

Capt Folsom in front of palace on Tigris River secured by Delta Company, 14 April 2003.

location, pristine condition, and commanding view of much of the city, the palace was quickly designated as the new command post for Tripoli. Soon the area bustled with Marines, and Maj Harper walked up to me.

"What are you doing now?" he asked me.

"Nothing, sir. Just standing by, I guess."

He pointed down to a sliver of an island squatting in the center of the Tigris. On it another palace compound, considerably smaller than the one in which we now stood, sat unsecured.

"You want to go check out those buildings?"

"Yeah, you got it, sir," I replied. The island and the compound together were too small for the entire company, so I grabbed Parment and Schwartz and their wingmen to join me and 1stSgt Guzman. Our six LAVs rattled across the small bridge and into the compound, which compared to the palace we had just seized seemed like a huddle of resplendent guest houses. The buildings were fully furnished, however, and loaded as they were with crystal, china, silverware, and Persian rugs, it was all Guzman and I could do to stop the men from picking the place clean. Marines ran around in excited groups, jumping on silk-sheeted beds and crapping in cool, porcelain commodes. Like the palace we had just seen before it, the compound was deserted. Now we owned it. But more than that, we owned Tikrit.

We rested on the island for a while, enjoying the cool breeze flowing over the running waters of the Tigris. From our position on the water the main palace compound looked even more brilliant and menacing than it had earlier that morning. So much had happened in the previous two days that it was difficult to assimilate and process all the information. We had quite literally swept in and taken control of Saddam Hussein's stomping grounds with barely a shot fired. Looking around at the palace complex, with its plush facilities and secure location, I thought *I would have no problem at all holding the company in place right here for a while.* Instead, my plans to take a break were put on hold once the next frag order was issued.

Major Harper rolled out a laminated map of the city and pointed to a large area outlined in black magic marker.

"This is Delta Company's sector," he said, tapping the highlighted region. All told, it covered close to six square kilometers of urban sprawl. "It's yours. Do with it as you please."

I examined the map. The sector was too large to mount a full defense. There was the option of establishing a strong-point defense, but that would spread the company too thin and make it too immobile. I pointed back to the map.

"I'll put a company patrol base right here, sir," I said, circling with my finger a symbol labeled as a military complex. "From there we'll divide the area up into platoon sectors and run mounted and dismounted patrols. That'll keep the locals on their toes."

He looked at me and grinned. "Sounds like a plan. Take off when you're ready." I finally realized I had been too harsh in my opinion of Harper earlier, in Kuwait. He was a good man, a brilliant tactician, and a strong leader. I felt as if I had earned his trust, and my basic back-brief to him was all he needed to approve my plan for the company.

We were on the move again, leaving the comforts of the palace compound behind for the task force headquarters. A quick ride downtown and the company soon arrived at its destination. As it turned out, however, the military facility I had designated had been bombed to smithereens. Crushed by a JDAM, it was dangerously uninhabitable. But one block away we found an abandoned residence surrounded by a ten-foot-high concrete wall, and after the scouts cleared it out and conducted a detailed search the platoons filed in and parked their vehicles around the perimeter. The dwelling's good physical condition and the luxuries and uniforms inside indicated that it had been occupied by a member of either the Republican Guard or the Ba'ath Party. Overflowing with comfortable furniture, china, and paintings, the house included several working bathrooms. As the Marines lined up to use the toilets and cycle through the showers, I knew we had found a home for the next little while. *At least,* I mused, *until the water runs out.*

While the Marines showered and checked out their new digs, Capt Portiss and I developed a plan for the company's sector that ensured continuous, randomly-timed vehicle and foot patrols covering a variety of routes throughout the neighborhoods. After briefing the final plan to the battalion over the radio, I looked around the compound's interior. Marines sat in small groups next to their vehicles, cleaning weapons and shooting the shit. They compared stories about the action from the previous days, arguing over who shot what and how close so-and-so had come to getting wasted. Whenever a patrol prepared to leave the base or return through the wrought iron gates, everyone would "stand-to," heightening their alert level until the patrol had either arrived or departed safely.

We set in for the night in our new accommodations. I wandered through the house, examining its furnishings. Judging from the myriad medications strewn about, the previous occupant had either been a doctor or else someone in extremely poor health. He had children as well. Two bedrooms were filled with girl's clothing and magazines. Each door I opened shed new light on the family who had lived here before we entered the city. Oddly, I was devoid of guilt. From my skewed outlook, necessity dictated that we occupy the house. It fulfilled the company's requirements, and as I examined the dark, olive fabric of a discarded military uniform I reminded myself that I was standing in the enemy's house. *He would do the same to your home,* I thought. *Or worse.*

I continued my search. I wasn't out to loot the place, but I did need socks. A few more days wearing the sand-encrusted socks around my feet and I was likely to become a medical case. However, there were no socks to be had. Either someone had already picked the place clean, or this family didn't believe in wearing anything between their feet and shoes. But then, rifling through a chest of drawers, I found what I was looking for. Well, not exactly true. What I had found were four pairs of little girl's stockings. I tried on a pair for size. They only came up past my ankles, but their smooth texture soothed my chapped, rotten feet. *Oh, to hell with it,* I said to myself, stuffing them in my trouser cargo pockets. Although they would be covered in looted girl's socks, my feet were now on the way to healing.

The line for showers thinned out, and once one of the bathrooms opened up I took the opportunity to take my first real shower in more than a month. It was a peculiar sensation, bathing to the echoes of Cobra gunships whirling in the background as they executed rocket and gun attacks just a couple of blocks away.

As I stood there taking a shower, I mulled over the fact that some events defy description. Only the truly gifted can accurately describe moments filled with terror and exhilaration, moments such as the hot, red radiance of friendly tracer fire cracking past you in the darkness.

Or the sixth sense you seem to develop as you navigate your vehicle into hostile territory teeming with rocket propelled grenades that will evaporate you.

Or the emotions that race through your mind after you kill someone from a range close enough to see the expression on his face as he breathes his last breath.

How would I ever be able to communicate these things to my wife? My family? My children? With the water from the tiny showernozzle cascading down over my head, I felt my perception of life as I knew it changing, evolving. One hope filled my heart: that I wouldn't take the burden of my experiences home with me. I wanted to resume my life with Ashley as it was meant to be before I had been thrust into this violent situation.

◆ ◇ ◆

The platoons patrolled throughout the evening of 14 April, and the following morning the Marines awoke in the compound somewhat rested and noticeably more at ease than they had been in previous days. The comforts of our new accommodations notwithstanding, it was necessary to relocate the command post elsewhere in an effort to keep whoever was observing us off balance. Spreading out the satellite map of the city on a wide, oak table in the dining room, I examined the company's sector. Fewer than five blocks away was a building designated on the map as a recreation center. Like our current location, it appeared to be surrounded by a wall, and I tentatively planned to move the company there. The patrols continued, and 1stSgt Guzman and I mounted our vehicles to report to the battalion's new command post.

With Task Force Tripoli fully occupying the presidential palace seized by Delta Company the previous day, 1st LAR Battalion had shifted its headquarters to a smaller compound on an adjacent hill that likewise overlooked the Tigris. I wandered around the COC tent, glancing at the maps taped to the situation boards. The radios buzzed with situation reports and intelligence updates, and it appeared as if the tempo of operations had already begun to subside.

Activity within the city, however, had picked up, and the ghost town of the previous two days was transformed by throngs of Iraqis making their way through the streets. Guzman and I made our way back in the direction of the company compound, and en route I decided to check out the recreation center for myself. Surrounded by a tall concrete wall depicted by the satellite imagery, the facility was perfect for our new compound. A small building equipped with showers and eastern toilets stood at the compound's center, and behind it a drained, Olympic-sized swimming pool festered with slimy, green runoff from past rainfall. There was enough room within the walls to park the company's vehicles around the perimeter, and as I surveyed the quiet neighborhood surrounding us I decided it was perfect, at least for now. We returned to the company and passed the word for the relocation to begin.

Once set up in our new home, the Marines attacked the showers again, and it wasn't long before the facility's water tanks were drained. Halfway through the day, Maj Harper and Capt Whalen showed up to check out the company's new position. As we sat on the steps of the rec center talking, the subject of the firefight in the tunnel came up. Bob Whalen, who before working in the S-3 had been a platoon commander in Delta Company, knew many of the Marines well. Sergeant Dewitt had joined us, and Whalen pressed the Marine for details about the engagement. Realizing he had an eager audience in Harper and Whalen, Dewitt excitedly replayed the story with exaggerated details about my actions.

"So then we're standing there while this guy is shouting 'I throw bomb!' and Captain Folsom rolls his head slowly like Danny Glover in *Lethal Weapon.* Then, *pow!* He blows the guy away."

Harper and Whalen were rolling. Shaking my head and attempting to play it off, I muttered, "Oh, for Christ's sake, come *on.*" An uncomfortable feeling gnawed at my stomach as they pressed me for details, and I did my best to downplay my actions. It didn't work—they were genuinely enthusiastic to hear the minutiae of the engagement.

Meanwhile, as the platoons progressed with their patrols throughout their sectors they began uncovering numerous ammunition and arms caches hidden throughout the city. Since the patrols had begun the previous afternoon, the platoons had uncovered hundreds of RPGs and mortar rounds, as well as rifle grenades, artillery ammunition, and many anti-aircraft pieces. That evening, when Lt Parment called to report that his patrol had uncovered yet another house containing dozens of ammunition crates, SSgt Bright added that he had located three S-60 AAA guns. As we decided which find was more important to guard for the night, Bright called in and reported that his section had pushed the guns into the Tigris River. Problem solved.

As we came across cache after cache, I learned Delta Company wasn't alone in this regard. The evening of 14 April, while reconnoitering a hospital in their sector, Charlie Company had discovered upwards of eighty thousand AK-47s. Still stored in their packing crates, the rifles were in mint condition. Similar caches were found in schools and public buildings, and as the reports filtered in one by one I marveled again at the sheer volumes of ammunition and weaponry that for some divine reason had not been used against us in our push north to Baghdad and beyond.

The weather turned cold and drizzly the morning of 16 April, the first rain we had seen in weeks. While the platoons continued to walk their beats around the city, the Marines not out on patrol took turns hiding from the elements inside the dry interior of the recreation center. First Sergeant Guzman and I returned to the COC, and while making my rounds I ran into the battalion commander. As we stood talking together, he informed me that the battalion would be expanding its sector of responsibility within Tikrit. The sector shift would affect the companies significantly, and once set, the battalion would begin the complicated business of rebuilding and reorganizing the police force for Tikrit. Although the Marine presence this time around prevented the sort of looting and disorder seen in Baghdad, the absence of indigenous law and order had created a vacuum that enabled locals to exact mob justice on those who had wronged them in the past. In particular, local Tikritis took out many of their frustrations on the Iraqis from across the Tigris, whom they distastefully (and probably incorrectly) dubbed "Kurds." The outsiders from across the river, the locals claimed, had come across the bridge to loot the city. The Tikriti townspeople wanted revenge, and if a police force didn't materialize soon the situation would devolve into chaos. In his capacity as the battalion commander, LtCol White became Tikrit's interim police chief, while Dave

Hudspeth, Gil Juarez, and I would likewise assume the duties as area commanders for our respective sectors. In time, he explained, we would work side by side with our counterparts in the newly formed Iraqi police force. I wasn't wild about the idea of Marines becoming policemen, but I held my tongue.

Several other officers showed up, and Bob Whalen replayed for them the story of my episode in the tunnel. For emphasis, he completed the story with the exaggerated mimicking of my actions. Everyone really got a kick out of it, but I felt that I would have rather not had the conversation. Several officers later made comments such as "I heard about your grenade battle and the guy you killed. Man, you are so lucky." Their naïveté and ignorance silenced me; they seemed actually *jealous* that they hadn't been afforded the opportunity to take a life. Amid the laughs and jabs, one captain spoke up.

"So, what's Delta Company's body count now, anyway?"

I paused, mentally recounting the company's few engagements. "I really don't know. I reckon it's between seventy-five and one hundred." They "oohed" and "ahhed," high-fiving each other and congratulating me. Had I been in their shoes, watching from the COC as the LAV companies duked it out over the course of the war, I probably would have shared their bravado and unquenchable thirst for details. Chris Portiss had aptly noted once that no one wants to sit on the sidelines and watch his team play the entire game, and so I understood the hoots of enthusiasm and words of encouragement of the officers. But my perspective had changed. To accomplish the mission, to save lives, I had been forced to make decisions that brought the wrath of God down upon the men who had opposed our advance through Iraq. It began on 3 April on the banks of the Tigris River, with what Bob Woodruff had eloquently described as Delta Company's own "mini Shock and Awe campaign." It ended on 13 April with me jumping into a fight to help my Marines and then killing a jihadi soldier at close range. Making war—taking lives—was for me no longer something to joke about with boyish words of admiration and longing. I had finally seen what I had often wondered if I would experience. Four years of college education, nine long years of professional service as an infantry officer, and in the end it came down to a firefight in a barren culvert tunnel. The trite phrase "just doing your job" had taken on real meaning for me and the Marines of Delta Company.

✦ ✧ ✦

A conversation I dreaded surfaced soon thereafter. To stabilize its manpower for the coming war, the Marine Corps had in early January enacted the "stop-loss/stop-move" order. Actually, it was probably this that had enabled me to remain a company commander for the conflict. But the war was winding down and the Marine Corps wanted to get its personnel situation back to some system of normalcy. I knew it was coming, and when the battalion commander and his XO began talking to me about the possibility of executing my orders to graduate school there was little I could do to protest. Lieutenant Colonel White informed me that the warning order from Headquarters Marine Corps had been published, and that my name was among those on the list designated to execute orders as soon as possible.

"What's your preference?" asked Maj Bodkin.

I hadn't expected that question, but my answer surprised me. "I hate to leave Delta Company, sir. They're like my family now, but . . ."

"But?"

"Well, I know how this will sound, but I'm beginning to feel like my work with the company is done. I've been their CO for a long time, and they probably don't need me as much as they once did. If they *ever* did. I've gotten very close to them, too. Sometimes I think the situation could affect my decision-making process."

Bodkin repeated his question. "So, what do you want to do?"

In my mind I reviewed the words I had just spoken. It was all true. Daily I had struggled to pass on something new to the Marines that would be consistent with my longtime efforts to make them the best company in the battalion. But more and more I realized the company was running itself. The memory of a similar revelation I had had in 1997 haunted me. I remembered being a lieutenant watching my platoon during a training exercise in Jordan. I had been a platoon commander for nearly two years, and I realized suddenly one day in the desert that the Marines no longer needed me. I had worked myself right out of a job. History was repeating itself for me. But there was more to it than that. My affection for the Marines and sailors of Delta Company had distorted my judgment. The fear of losing another one after coming so far was making me a bit paranoid in assessing risks as I assigned their missions in Tikrit. I had found myself continuously roaming the company lines, practically pleading with the Marines to take care during the course of their routine patrols. Indeed, I could now be accused of the same fault I had found in Lt Schwartz little more than a month previously: I loved my men too much. But deep down I took comfort in recalling one of the many conversations I had had with my father over the years. One of the things he impressed upon me was his view that the absolute best commanders were those who trained their troops well and constantly "worried" about their welfare and safety. And so, emitting a sigh, I turned to Bodkin and gave him my final answer.

"I won't fight the orders to Monterey when they come through." I had to get on with the next phase of my career, and I knew that this "plan" was really what LtCol White and I had agreed to in January of 2003.

Returning to the company's patrol base, I found myself talking with Capt Portiss about his own confrontation with the enemy on 13 April. He had led his Marines in the attempt to retrieve the wounded jihadi soldiers, who returned the gesture by reaching for their weapons. Relaying the story to me, he seemed to feel much as I did about my own engagement. Together we found comfort and solace in our shared anxiety. His engagement with the enemy not as close and personal as mine, Portiss admitted that his decision to pull the trigger had been based on a hunch that the wounded enemy personnel were going for weapons. More than anything, the uncertainty of it all troubled him. Hell, I had been certain when *I* pulled the trigger, yet feelings of ambivalence still weighed mightily upon me.

Together we learned several Marines within the company were pissed off that they had been denied the privilege of engaging in close quarters battles like my own, and we shared a sense of incredulity. Corporal Grewing, from 3rd Platoon, had developed an attitude problem stemming from his lack of an opportunity to kill. I pulled him aside.

"You're upset, aren't you?" I asked him.

"Yes, sir. It's fucking bullshit. I've been training for the last four years of my life to do this, and I never got the chance."

"You should be glad."

He rebuffed my gesture. "That's easy for you to say, sir. You got yours."

Slowly shaking my head, I put my hand on his shoulder. "Trust me. It's just not that cool."

But my words once again fell on deaf ears. I knew he wouldn't accept what I had to say until he had experienced it himself. I walked away, hoping he would never get his wish.

✦ ✧ ✦

Life for the Marines in Tikrit quickly settled into a routine, which would have been fine anywhere but there. Routine was dangerous, as it led to complacency and afforded the Marines time to complain about why they were there and wonder when they would be allowed to go home. It was a short-timer's attitude, and I found myself as guilty of it as anyone else.

On 17 April I linked up with the senior officers of the battalion at the task force's palace headquarters. We had been directed to meet with the local individuals who had been "selected" to re-form the police force so order could begin to be restored within the city. Minor looting and incidents of crime had persisted, and suddenly many locals had begun establishing their own road blocks and stopping cars. Automobiles suspected of containing Kurds from across the river were ransacked, and occupants were pulled out and beaten with makeshift shillelaghs. On several occasions, Delta Company's platoon checkpoints had been compelled to break up the mobs, which were armed with clubs, knives, and wrenches.

Before the meeting, the seven of us sat together in a circle, discussing the impending billet changes within the battalion. I had learned that indeed I would be turning over command of Delta Company and heading home at the beginning of May. Since I had finally accepted the inevitable, it came as somewhat less of a shock than I had imagined it would. For reasons unbeknown to me, the news provided me some measure of relief, though I was careful to hide this from everyone. To display my emotions openly would no doubt have been looked upon poorly, and the news ultimately would have made its way back to my men. The last thing I wanted was for them to think that I was anxious to leave them for the comforts of home. While discussing the upcoming billet changes, I offered up Chris Portiss's name for consideration as the new Weapons Company commander. Dave Hudspeth had been slated to take over the S-3 once Maj Harper left, and I believed Portiss to be a perfect fit for the vacancy in Weapons Company. Though another captain was slated to assume command of Delta Company, I preferred Portiss to take my place because of my unwavering confidence in his abilities. He had served faithfully as my XO and had demonstrated all the qualities necessary to fleet up to company commander. I committed myself to try to sway the battalion commander's opinion later after the meeting with the locals.

The police chief hopefuls arrived at the palace, and they couldn't have been any shadier had they come straight from a Hollywood B-movie. There were eight or nine of them, and most resembled Saddam Hussein himself. Complete with slicked-back hair, mustaches, and dark, leather coats, they looked like a bunch of gangsters as they chain-smoked foul smelling cigarettes and eyeballed us from across the room. We soon realized that gangsters were about what they were. Our interpreter, an Arabic-speaking Marine captain named Ben Connable, conversed animatedly with them for an hour. His voice periodically rose nearly to a shout as they haggled back and forth with him, but it was evident he knew what he was doing. Because of the chiefs' demeanor and tacit unwillingness to provide LtCol White with a written copy of the local laws, Connable deduced that they were Ba'ath Regime holdovers. Loyal to the hard line, they were just waiting to be placed back in charge and for the Marines to leave so they could start cracking skulls again. After the Iraqis left, Connable turned to LtCol White.

"Sir, forget about these guys. They're thugs. You don't get as high up as they are around here without having personally killed people who oppose you."

White mulled over the situation momentarily, and then spoke. "All right, tomorrow we'll start from scratch." He turned to Harper and Bodkin. "Get the interview process for the police force started tomorrow. Those assholes won't be considered, but we need to figure out some way of vetting the applicants."

The next morning, the most peculiar job fair I had ever witnessed took place in a walled-in palace compound fewer than two kilometers from the battalion headquarters. The word had gone out on the streets that the Marines would begin accepting applications for the Tikriti police force on 18 April, and before long the event resembled a "cattle call." Iraqi men of all ages showed up in droves, lining up for the chance to become a cop under the new establishment. Sitting atop my vehicle in the early morning sunshine, I surveyed the crop of hopefuls. Most were young men, though some real old-timers waited patiently alongside them as the crowd grew into a snaking line that wrapped around the side of the compound. Shaking my head, I realized just how difficult the task would be for the battalion. Lieutenant Colonel White had been correct. If we didn't figure out a way to investigate these characters' backgrounds, chances were that we'd end up placing a lot of former regime loyalists back in charge of the city. Unlike Second World War Europe, where locals could largely be counted upon to finger former Nazis and collaborators, few Tikritis had come forward to assist us in such an effort. As in Baghdad, most official paperwork identifying government personnel had been destroyed by saboteurs, making it nearly impossible to check someone's background.

As the battalion staff put the finishing touches on the screening station, Capt Portiss showed up to conduct some final coordination with me. Earlier, before leaving the recreation center I had told him my plan to relocate the command post. The company had been static for several days, and because I had conducted a turnover with two captains from 3rd LAR Battalion the previous day our sector of responsibility now included a large swath of land west of Highway 1. Pointing to the map spread out in front of us, I outlined a general area for the platoons to reconnoiter for a patrol base. As I prepared to head to the screening station, SSgt Monroe cautiously approached me carrying a small, camouflaged backpack. A dubious expression creased his face and he sighed heavily.

"Sir, the Marines got a couple of chickens while they were out on patrol. Is that all right?"

I looked at him quizzically. "What do you mean?"

He held up the backpack, unzipped it, and out popped the heads of two live chickens. Clearly expecting me to tear into his ass for the Marines' actions, Monroe was surprised by my reaction.

I laughed. "Cook 'em up!"

Back at the screening station, Portiss was irritated when I provided the update for him. The S-3 had redrawn the company boundaries, and as a result Delta's new sector shifted west of Highway 1 and south to the built-up area the company had patrolled with Charlie Company the evening of 13 April. His frustration was understandable, as he had already located a suitable compound in which to base the company. I handed him a fresh set of maps and boundaries, and then jumped on a Huey for a reconnaissance flight around the city to get a bird's eye view of our new sector. As the helicopter climbed into the sky I mentally kicked myself for forgetting to bring my camera. Tikrit was truly beautiful from the air. Absorbing the majestic architecture of the historic city along the banks of the Tigris, I wondered how such a magnificent place could have been witness to such horrors for so long.

I returned from the brief flight to find Portiss still at my vehicle, scrutinizing the company's new sector on the map. Together our two sections mounted up and departed in search of a new compound for the company, and after an hour of driving the streets, it appeared as if we wouldn't find an adequate site to laager up the company. With our vehicles parked temporarily in a rundown lot, I began weighing our options.

"What about that?" Portiss asked, pointing to a large, blue warehouse straddling Highway 1 to the south. Rolling up on the building, we found to our delight that it was nearly perfect. Surrounded by a tall concrete wall topped with barbed wire, the warehouse appeared to have once stored grain and other dry foodstuffs. We dismounted our vehicles and checked out the ransacked compound. Most of the grain had since been removed, but tiny plastic bags of wheat flour still dotted the dusty floors. The facility was large enough to house our vehicles behind the walls and within the warehouse itself, and as a patrol base it was centrally located within our sector. It was in the perfect location for a patrol base. As a bonus, the compound was isolated from the surrounding neighborhood, with good fields of fire and observation from the walls.

"Call the company forward," I yelled to Portiss as 1stSgt Guzman and I continued to explore the inside of the building. Empty as it was and sporting a smooth concrete floor and massive sliding doors, the warehouse resembled an aircraft hangar. It provided the ideal setting for conducting maintenance on the vehicles. But one of the sliding doors was secured by a heavy padlock.

"Well, that's gonna have to come off," I said, drawing my pistol. *Time to see if this thing holds up to the Master Lock test,* I thought, aiming the Beretta at the padlock.

Behind me, Guzman said, "You sure you want to do that, sir? That bullet's gonna chase us around in here." His tone was grave, disapproving. Lowering my weapon, I slowly shook my head. He was right, as he usually was. Staff Sergeant Monroe had a gargantuan boltcutter in his toolkit, and I knew it. There are many reasons why first sergeants exist. Once again Guzman had proven his value.

In the distance the whine of the company's LAV engines approached, and a small group of Iraqi teenagers curiously wandered over to see what was going on. In the warehouse's front office I stood with them, asking questions in broken Arabic from the Xeroxed phrasebook the division had distributed before the war. They caught on well as I struggled to convey that we wouldn't harm them, and to allay their biggest concern as to how long we would remain there. They appeared friendly, repeating in broken English, "America, good!" The oldest among them, a young man in his late teens, displayed for me the pockmark of a bullet wound he had suffered at the hands of an Iraqi soldier a decade earlier. As I leaned down to examine the faded scar, the youth glimpsed the red fabric of a small Iraqi flag jutting from my trouser cargo pocket. A critical look filled his face, obviously unhappy that I had pilfered his country's national symbol. In a magnanimous gesture, I pulled the standard from my pocket and presented it to him, clapping him on the shoulder and saying *"Sadeeqy,"* "My friend." The four of them waved and thanked me, walking out into the sun and away from the compound. Leaning down, I buttoned the cargo pocket still containing several more of the tiny flags. *Sorry pal,* I thought. *These are going home with me.*

By the time I walked back outside the company had arrived and was already firmly ensconced around the warehouse perimeter. Strolling around the compound, I couldn't believe my eyes. Everywhere there were chickens, fresh fruits and vegetables, and cases of bottled soft drinks. The Marines had gone wild at the market, and now they were having themselves a barbecue. Try as I might, I just couldn't be angry with them. They were so happy, sitting in small clusters around their vehicles cooking chicken and kabobs on spits over makeshift grills. To see them in such high spirits after the gloom and monotony of the previous weeks was uplifting. Meanwhile, perched in their turrets, duty Marines from each platoon continued to scan the horizon for enemy activity in the area surrounding the compound. Vehicles intermittently departed the camp in pairs and returned after patrolling the sector. Delta Company still hadn't forgotten the reason we were there.

✦ ✧ ✦

Doctor Omar appeared outside the compound's wrought iron gate. The Marines had found him at one of their checkpoints the previous day, and Capt Portiss had quickly deduced the man could assist our efforts. A small, English-speaking gentleman who had earned a Ph.D. in agricultural sciences in London, Omar reminded me of Mohandas Gandhi, but with a mass of gray hair and wearing a wrinkled black suit. I sat down with him inside the patrol base and asked if he would be willing to help us vet the police applicants for regime holdovers and other corrupt individuals. He agreed, saying he would follow me in his car to the screening station. Portiss pulled me aside.

"You might want to put him in your LAV for the ride over there," he suggested. "So no one gets a look at him."

I thought momentarily. "Yeah, you're right. He might wake up with his throat cut if someone sees him hanging out with us." I turned back to Omar. "Sir, would you mind riding in the back of my vehicle for the trip over there?" He looked perplexed.

"To protect your identity," Portiss interjected. "We don't want any of the undesirable applicants seeing you screening the paperwork."

"Yes," Omar replied pensively. "This is good idea."

We stuffed his black-suited form into the scout compartment of my LAV and sped off to the screening station. I introduced the doctor to the Marines on the screening staff, and while they prepared the paperwork we sat down and talked for about an hour. The manner in which Omar talked spoke volumes about his intelligence, and I found him very interesting. When I asked him what he thought about the Marines being in Tikrit, he told me that the residents would accept it because they considered it God's will—*insh'Allah.* I didn't bother telling him that the jihadis on Highway 1 sure didn't seem to accept our presence. But in our discussion I also learned that Saddam Hussein had not, in fact, been born in Tikrit. Instead, he hailed from a small village named Ad Dawr, more than a dozen kilometers south of Tikrit. To enhance his image, Saddam had boasted to everyone that he, like the legendary Saladin, had been born there in Tikrit. Dr. Omar also surprised me by opining that the people of Tikrit had suffered more under Saddam's hand than any other city in Iraq during his rule.

"Why's that?" I asked curiously.

Omar adopted an academic tone. "He and his security forces were like American cowboys who always returned to town and caused trouble."

It didn't add up. From the looks of it, Tikrit was the best tended city we had seen in Iraq. As a whole, the townspeople weren't overjoyed at our presence, either, and I began to wonder just how genuine this tiny man really was.

The battalion XO and the screening team finally called Omar in to have him evaluate the applications. As I contemplated my conversation with the doctor, LT Moreno climbed from a humvee and sat down beside me. Seeing the opportunity, I asked to talk with the chaplain in private about my experience in the tunnel. He stood silent as I recounted the story blow-by-blow.

"How do you feel about killing that man?" he asked bluntly.

"Man, I really don't know how I feel, Chaplain," I replied, dragging heavily on a cigarette. "I don't know, I've been going back and forth in my mind over and over again. I go from extreme highs to extreme lows sometimes."

"That's good. Your ambivalence is good."

"I don't understand," I said, confused. "What do you mean?"

"Seth, I've spoken with a lot of Marines in the battalion since we've been out here. Some of them can't get enough of the killing. They have long roads ahead of them. Your road, I think, will be a shorter one. Your struggle with what you have done is you struggling with your humanity. In His own way, God empowered you to do what you did. It was necessary in order to protect your men and to protect yourself."

I pondered what he had said. Hearing those words from a levelheaded outsider who didn't appear to envy what I had done put me at ease. I turned back to him.

"Listen, for what it's worth, I'm glad I was baptized before it happened. For some reason that makes me feel better about it. I won't forget what you did for me, Chaplain."

"You know, I told you before, I normally don't baptize anyone unless he has undergone the requisite instruction and learning." He paused. "But apparently in your case there was a higher reason neither of us knew about."

With Dr. Omar once again crammed into the rear of the LAV, we departed the screening station and returned to the company patrol base. After seeing the doctor off, I made my way back inside the compound and walked around the perimeter, talking to the Marines. Sergeants Dewitt and McCorkle, along with LCpl Weise, stood around, and with the three of them together I examined their wounds from the grenade blasts in the tunnel. The battalion commander and sergeant major had been pressing me about recommendations for awarding Purple Hearts to the three men, and before committing to it I wanted to check them out for myself. Two tiny lacerations, already healing, marred Sgt Dewitt's right shin. Lance Corporal Weise bent his head down to reveal a narrow cut across the back of his neck. I turned to Sgt McCorkle, who dropped his trousers and proudly displayed his backside. It was an experience I could have done without. He too sported a nick—on his butt-cheek—and he held up the scorched trousers he had worn at the time of the firefight. A jagged burn mark blackened the fabric, which itself had absorbed most of the grenade's blast.

I shook my head. "Looks like it almost burned your ass off."

"I thought it did at the time, sir," he replied.

There was no doubt about it. The three men had been wounded, but did they really rate Purple Hearts? The criteria for the award dictated that the individual in question had to be treated by a medical officer to receive it. None of these three Marines had done so; the corpsman had evaluated their wounds and sent them on their way. The Purple Heart was a big deal. It was the kind of personal decoration Marines want, but at the same time they don't *really* want. I didn't want to prevent these men from receiving the award, particularly after they had risked their lives alongside mine. But I thought back to LCpl Suarez del Solar. He too had received a Purple Heart, but he had paid the ultimate price for it. In a way, after Suarez's death and all we had been through since, I believed anything minor—such as the nicks and scratches those three Marines had sustained in the tunnel—degraded the award. At the same time, Cpl Martin had turned down a Purple Heart for the minor wound he had sustained during the intramural firefight with Golf Company. Similarly, Sgt Dewitt would later request that his Purple Heart paperwork be withdrawn. It was their choice, and I respected them for their decisions. But as for the other two Marines—McCorkle and Weise—I relented, and after inspecting their injuries one last time I told them the paperwork would be submitted. After that it would be up to the battalion.

As the sun slowly dipped below the horizon the Marines extinguished their cooking fires and prepared for the next round of patrols. First Sergeant Guzman informed me that SSgt Monroe's orders for school had come through, and he was waiting to hear when Monroe would ship out from Tikrit. I spoke briefly with Monroe, congratulating him on his selection to become a Marine Security Guard. He was ecstatic, babbling happily about getting back home to California and making the drive across the country to Quantico. We shared Monroe's joy—in some small way his imminent departure signaled the beginning of the end for Delta Company's deployment. If the division was prepared to fly him out of Tikrit, we reasoned, the rest of us couldn't be too far behind.

Turning my attention to Lt Parment, I listened with interest as he vented his frustrations concerning his Marines. His maturity clearly shone through as he complained to me.

"You know, sir, my Marines just don't get it sometimes. They don't seem to understand that I am going to expect them to do their jobs the right way because I'm the one who is ultimately responsible for whatever they do or fail to do."

I snickered. "Man, listen to you. A couple of months ago I was on your ass all the time. Now here you are acting, dare I say, 'responsibly'!" It was as if I was talking to a different person than the languid, skeptical young officer of a year earlier.

At that moment I realized Parment had finally come into his own as a commander. My private fears had taken root. I had no further excuse for trying to stay on as the company commander. It wasn't so much that they didn't need me—all units need a commander. Rather, Delta Company had come of age, and in more ways than one. I was proud to have been a part of it all.

21

All Good Things . . .

The morning of 19 April brought with it the realization that I had been in command of Delta Company for exactly two years. I was truly amazed at everything that had come to pass during that time and how much my life had changed since that spring day in 2001 when I took command. Mounting my vehicle and returning once more to the screening station, I met with the battalion commander, the S-3, and the battalion XO, who briefed the assembled company commanders on the details of future operations. We in turn detailed our activities in our respective sectors. Following our meeting, I approached the battalion commander and told him about my recommendation of Chris Portiss to relieve me of command *vice* having another captain take charge of Delta. The reason for my recommendation was simple: I wanted to preserve the stability of the company. The Marines had begun to smell the barn and question why they were still in Iraq, and they required a strong leader—someone whom they already knew and trusted—to bring them home safely. White wasn't very receptive, telling me that another captain had already been slated for the company after me. However, to his credit, he did tell me he would take what I had to say into consideration. In truth, I anticipated he would hand over stewardship of Delta Company to the original candidate, and I wondered if the captain in question was ready to lead the outstanding Marines of our cohesive unit.

Lance Corporals Davis and Gurganus returned in our vehicle to pick me up, and they announced news that caught me off guard.

"Hey sir," Davis said. "Staff Sergeant Monroe's leaving today." Monroe's final orders had not only come through, they had also required that he transfer immediately. He was leaving that day and had already been transported to the COC to await a ride to the airfield. I jumped in the vehicle and keyed the intercom.

"Get me to the COC, *now,* " I said, afraid we would miss him. We sped through the streets to the battalion Main, where I found Monroe on the Iridium phone talking to his parents. I stood off to the side, patiently waiting for him to finish his conversation, and when he was done he set the phone down and walked up to me. We stood there momentarily, silent and unsure what to say. I finally opened my mouth.

"Thought I was gonna miss seeing you before you left, Staff Sergeant."

He smiled. "I'm glad you made it, sir."

We stared at each other again, and I unceremoniously shook my head. Suddenly I didn't know what to say to this man who had earned so much of my respect and admiration over the years. "I swear, man. It's been a hell of a trip, hasn't it?"

"Yeah, it sure has."

"I'm gonna miss you, Staff Sergeant. I sure enjoyed the hell out of working with you. It was an honor being your company commander, and I'm proud to call you my friend. You're a hell of a Marine, and a true asset to this company. We're *all* gonna miss you."

"Sir, I've been in Delta Company seven years. It's the only thing I know about the Marine Corps. They're all my family. I don't know what I'm gonna do without them."

"I know what you mean."

He paused, and then spoke again. His response surprised me. "Sir, you know I was ready to get out of the Marine Corps. I just wanted you to know that if it wasn't for you I wouldn't have re-enlisted."

His words struck a chord in me I didn't know I had. It was obvious that he was finding difficulty saying such a thing, and he cut himself off. Neither of us was prepared for the emotions we suddenly felt, and I quickly shifted the conversation. After a moment we shook hands, and he turned to walk away. Part of me walked away with him. He had never disappointed me, he had cared for the Marines more than anything, and he had always supported every decision I made as a commander. I couldn't have asked for anything more in a Marine.

✦ ✧ ✦

After we left the COC I decided to return to the 18 northing along Highway 1—the location of the company's firefight on 13 April and my engagement in the tunnel. Earlier that morning I had learned Golf Company had been there the previous day, policing up the dead bodies. I didn't envy their gruesome task—the corpses had been there nearly a week. As I listened to the Golf Company CO debrief the battalion commander on the mop-up operation, I casually mentioned the three dead men in the tunnel.

"Did your men find the three jihadis stashed in that culvert tunnel?"

"Which tunnel?" he asked. I was surprised he hadn't heard the story.

"Three of those bastards ran into a drainage tunnel to hide from us before we killed them. They had a lot of grenades and ammo on them."

He pondered it for a moment, then said, "You know, I really don't know if the Marines cleaned them up or not."

I turned and looked at LtCol White, raising an eyebrow. He slowly nodded his head.

"Why don't you go check it out, Seth. You know exactly where it happened."

I left with no further guidance. I didn't know if White wanted me to dispose of the bodies myself or what, but his direction afforded me the opportunity to revisit the site regardless.

We drove south on Highway 1, and as we approached the location a hundred memories fired in my brain like a strobe of popping flashbulbs. The stench of death still hung like a cloud in the air along the side of the road, a smell impossible to describe if you have never experienced it. For some bizarre reason, the smell of decomposing human beings is different from the sweet, pungent odor of roadkill that has been splattered on the highway. It is a smell of rotting chicken, of eggs that have sat too long, of milk that has gone sour. It is the meat you left on the counter while you were on vacation, disintegrating and corrupted. It turns your stomach, and when you realize what's in store for the corpse lying in front of you—the bloating, the discoloration, the maggots—your stomach churns some more. As the stink assailed my nostrils, I began to wonder if returning had been such a good idea after all.

Gurganus pulled the vehicle off the road's shoulder just short of the tunnel, and I turned to Davis in the turret.

"Come on," I said, climbing out. We dismounted and walked down the slope to the washout of the culvert's entrance. Our weapons drawn, we entered the tunnel's maw once again. *If I had strolled in this carelessly six days ago,* I pondered. *I would have been killed instantly.* Entering the dimly-lit shaft, I realized it was nearly the same time of day as it had been before. The light at the tunnel's mouth was similar to how it had been then, and I recognized the fortune that had shone upon us that fateful afternoon. Had the sun been any farther east or west, it would have darkened the tunnel to the point where we wouldn't have been able to see within whatsoever. I held my breath and peered inside. To my relief, there were no moldering bodies. If there had been, I might have screamed.

Gazing around the culvert's entrance, I finally understood how the three jihadis had survived our team's grenades and rifle fire. At the mouth of the tunnel the earth had been excavated into a shallow depression and a small berm. When the scout team tossed their grenades in the tunnel's entrance, the dugout area absorbed most of the grenades' fragmentation and blast. On the other hand, the depression had more than likely saved *us* from the grenade tossed by the last man inside the tunnel. Regardless, the way the entrance had been hollowed out had required us to go in and clear out the tunnel in the manner we did. As I traversed the ditch and made my way down the tunnel, I stumbled upon one of the grenades the jihadis had wielded. Still live, the pin firmly seated in place, it was the shape of a small, dark green soup can. Turning it over in my hands, I was reminded of the DPICM round Suarez had stepped on so long ago. There was every possibility that the grenade I held in my hand was the very same bomb that final jihadi had threatened to throw. Some of the uncertainty that had plagued me in the preceding week slowly dissolved as I pocketed the grenade and continued the ten feet down the tunnel where the jihadis had lain just days earlier. Two large, coagulated puddles of brown blood stained the gravel, and dried splashes of gore painted the wall. I could clearly see where my pistol round had passed through the man and sprayed his insides on the bulkhead behind him. I stared wordlessly at the scene for a minute. Behind me, Davis inspected the scene and muttered, "God-*day*-um."

We proceeded down the length of the tunnel to the western entrance where Sgt McCorkle's team had made the first attempt to dislodge the jihadis. The blast patterns in the gravel marked where McCorkle's team and the jihadis had traded grenade volleys, and at the entrance I found a rusting AK-47 magazine. We retraced our steps through the culvert and walked north along the eastern tree line where the jihadis had sought to sneak up on our blocking position. The two of us had gone no farther than fifty feet before we found a stack of RPG rounds and more hand grenades. A green canvas bandolier similar to the ones worn by the jihadis in the tunnel lay next to the ordnance. It was a creepy feeling, holding in our hands weapons that had been intended to kill us six days earlier. We silently gathered up the ammunition and loaded it into the rear of our LAV.

As Gurganus put the vehicle in gear and directed it back north toward the patrol base, I sighed heavily and keyed the intercom.

"Man, I'm glad that's over. And I'm glad those bodies weren't still in there."

Davis turned and looked at me. "Oh, come on, sir. You aren't getting soft on us, are you?"

"Shut your suck-hole, Davis," I snapped. "Don't talk shit to me until *you've* been through something like that, got it?"

"Yes, sir," he said, his head down. "I didn't mean nothin' by it."

"Yeah, I know," I said, glancing up the road toward the city. "I just wish that whole thing never happened, is all."

But I was glad to have returned. Seeing the tunnel under different circumstances had answered several questions that still lingered in my mind. The experience was, in a way, cathartic for me, and I realized that seeing it again and understanding how the entire episode went down might help me begin to make peace with the experience.

We pulled into the company's compound and unloaded the enemy ordnance in a pile on the pavement next to the warehouse. Someone asked, "Where did all that come from?"

I held up an RPG round. "This was the shit those bastards were trying to kill us with last week."

As Marines gathered to look at the pile of ammunition, I walked off by myself. Other things had to be done. With my departure impending, I contemplated the tedious process of writing fitness reports for my staff. There were personal awards to write as well. I sat down and began composing the summary of action that described Lt Cullins's actions at the Elbow on 3 April. Scrolling down the electronic form on my computer screen, I checked the block for the award I planned to submit: the Bronze Star.

Easter Sunday, 20 April, began with orders for me to link up with my army counterpart who would assume control of Delta Company's sector of Tikrit. In the preceding days, elements from the army's 4th Infantry Division had begun rolling into Tikrit, and soon they would relieve Task Force Tripoli and resume operations throughout the city. At the palace I met a company commander for a mechanized infantry company from 1-8 Infantry. Pointing to the location of Delta's patrol base, I gave him and his assembled staff a quick orientation and recommended they follow me back to the compound for a more thorough briefing and turnover. They struck me as typical of many of the army officers I had dealt with in the past: tactically proficient and zealously dedicated to SOPs.

But they were also inexperienced and jealous of all the Marines had accomplished, a fact apparent through the barrage of questions they hurled at me. What was it like in Baghdad? How many firefights had we been in? Part of me couldn't criticize them. After all, their equipment had sat on ships for weeks waiting to get into Turkey, and by the time they off-loaded in Kuwait and pushed north through Iraq the fighting had ended. But I brushed off most of the questions except those that directly pertained to their future operations around Tikrit. I just wasn't eager to sit around and tell war stories.

CAPT FOLSOM (R) BRIEFING U.S. ARMY INFANTRY COMPANY STAFF DURING TURNOVER BETWEEN TASK FORCE TRIPOLI AND 4TH ID IN TIKRIT, 20 APRIL 2003. OFFICIAL MARINE CORPS PHOTO BY LCPL ANDREW P. ROUFS.

Captain Portiss and I agreed to participate in what the army called a "right-seat ride"—a trip around the city to afford them a detailed view of the area in which they would operate—and together with our army counterparts we jumped into their humvee and headed into town. The four of us drove the sector as Portiss and I pointed out checkpoints and major areas of interest. Once the army officers realized we weren't interested in offering details about our personal actions, they redirected their questions to more relevant issues. What was the temperament of the locals? Where were the major arms and ammunition caches being found? Who could be trusted in the area? There was no doubt about it: they were by the book. But by the end of the ride they seemed taken aback at how aloof Portiss and I were. *When you've been through what we have, you'll understand,* I thought to myself.

Upon returning to the compound, I attended the Easter Sunday services Chaplain Moreno was conducting at our position. I listened intently as he spoke to us inside the cool, breezy warehouse.

"This has been an Easter different from any other that any of us has ever experienced," he said to the Marines and sailors sitting in a circle around him. "You have all faced life and death together. It has been an Easter you had to fight for."

Moreno's sermon touched a chord among those present, and after the service many Marines and sailors wandered off on their own within the compound to be alone. I, too, took time by myself to ponder the meaning of what the chaplain had said, both during the sermon and in private two days earlier. He was correct. Easter of that year truly had been something to fight for, and I knew that I would forever associate the coming of spring with the events my men and I had experienced together.

With the army company waiting outside the compound in its tanks and Bradley fighting vehicles, I realized we had to finally give up our walled-in home and vacate the premises. Delta Company mounted its LAVs and departed the warehouse for the battalion's new assembly area in a large field in southern Tikrit.

The battalion had received a warning order that it would be retrograding south to Ad Diwaniyah to continue stabilization operations there. No one in Delta Company was jumping at the news that we were returning to the town where LCpl Suarez del Solar had perished and where we had stagnated for so long at the war's beginning. But we all recognized the upcoming mission for what it was: one step closer to going home.

The news of the retrograde elevated my disposition, and I joined Capt Portiss and his crew in a pickup game of Hacky Sack as we hung around the battalion's new assembly area. Many months later I would look at a picture of the five of us kicking around the tiny beanbag that day. Even in the graininess of the photograph the levity of our mood was palpable.

◆ ◇ ◆

The assembly area was hushed except for the occasional beeping of the radios inside the LAV-C2. It was early morning on 21 April, and I sat monitoring the radios in the final hour before sunrise. Lance Corporal Vargas, standing firewatch outside his vehicle, began talking to me. He was joined a few minutes later by LCpl Schaffer. Together the two Marines asked me questions about graduate school in Monterey and what I would be doing as a foreign area officer after I left the battalion. They were silent for a few minutes, and then LCpl Schaffer spoke.

"Man, it's gonna fucking suck when you leave, sir."

Vargas joined him, "We're really gonna miss you around here, sir."

"You've really taken care of us," added Schaffer. "We're afraid what's gonna happen after you leave."

A lump formed in my throat. Their comments had caught me unprepared, and I was touched. I swallowed hard.

"You guys have no idea how much that means to me. I didn't take this job to be liked. You know that. But it really means a lot when I hear something like that from the troops."

I excused myself, needing to be alone for a moment. Their words reminded me of a brief conversation I had had with Lance Corporal Aaron Johnson several days earlier. Johnson, who had never really said anything to me in the past, had suddenly asked about my departure and who would take over. His words and tone of voice reflected genuine concern about who the new company commander would be. I found myself choosing my words carefully so as not to sink my replacement before he even assumed command. I owed him that much at least. But keeping my mouth shut was difficult. Everyone on the staff knew who my relief was, and many had let me know they didn't want him to replace me.

The situation in which I found myself vexed me. I had to convince LtCol White to see my point of view and place Portiss in command after I left. It seemed to me that a real possibility existed that the combination of the numerous billet changes and the new commander's personality would cause the company to rapidly fall apart. All we had worked for in the preceding two years could disappear. Every commander goes through the same, irrational thought process. But that knowledge didn't make it any easier for me, and I knew I had to get over it and move on.

Later that morning, a call came through directing me to attend a commanders meeting at the palace COC. Captain Portiss accompanied me to give him the chance to make his pitch for command to Maj Bodkin. Once we arrived at the palace headquarters, Portiss and I went our separate ways—me to the mission brief, and he to find the battalion XO.

Inside a palace ballroom the S-3 had assembled dozens of map sheets that together covered the distance from Tikrit to Kuwait. Kneeling down to study the giant atlas, I traced 1st LAR Battalion's progress throughout the war. We had made a hell of a journey. As I sat there pinpointing every enemy engagement that involved Delta Company I realized just how impressive the entire campaign had been. A tidal wave of memories washed over me as each location we had occupied called to mind the events that had occurred there.

Ad Diwaniyah, where LCpl Suarez del Solar was killed and the war really began for us.

Ash Shumali, where the company captured its first enemy prisoners of war.

Az Zubadayah and the Elbow, where 3rd Platoon was ambushed and the company unleashed its firepower and aggression for the first time.

The Nahr Diyala, where even our sporadic engagements with the enemy couldn't overshadow the company's failed reconnaissance.

"The Strip" north of Saddam City, where we were met not with resistance from the enemy, but with cheers from thousands of Iraqi civilians.

Our blocking positions north of Baghdad, where for two days we isolated the city and played traffic cop.

The 18 northing, where we fought in the tree lines and in the tunnel to open up Tikrit.

Finally, Tikrit itself, Saddam Hussein's historical (if not factual) birthplace, secured and liberated by the company as part of Task Force Tripoli.

Remembering each and every episode, I struggled to concentrate on the battalion's operations order for the three hundred kilometer march south. Once in place in Ad Diwaniyah with the remainder of 1st Marine Division, the battalion planned to continue stability operations and begin the transition into retrograde operations. Despite the news of another long nighttime road march, the room buzzed with excitement at the news that we were leaving Tikrit. Deep down, all knew it was only a matter of time before the situation in town turned bad and the relative friendliness of the Iraqis wore off. And we had trained for war, not for policing and occupation duty. We were ready to go home. The trip south, even in the face of continued stability operations, was at least moving us in the right direction.

We returned to the TAA, and during the trip Portiss told me Maj Bodkin had given him the final word: the officer originally slated for command would take Delta Company, and Portiss would remain as XO until the unit's return to the States. Although unhappy about the decision, he seemed to take it well back at the assembly area. I too had resigned myself to the fact. You can disagree with a commander's call, and you can voice that difference, but at the end of the day you have to support his decision. I expected no less from my own men.

First LAR Battalion's long column escaped into the dark of night at 1900Z, with Delta Company bringing up the rear. *First in, last out,* I mused. *How fitting.* Rolling along through the inky blackness, the platoons began the first in a long string of monotonous position location reports that were to occur every two kilometers. I dreaded the protracted, boring trip we faced. My vehicle crew felt the same.

Lance Corporal Davis keyed his intercom switch. "Hey sir, how about some music?"

"You read my mind, man. Do it up."

He passed me Cpl Harter's compact disc player, and after wiring it into the vehicle's intercom system I heard the familiar lyrics of Ozzy Osbourne wailing through our headsets. The Marines crammed into the tight space of the vehicle shouted their approval, yelling for me to crank it up. As the disc shifted to the next song and the company's column began to exit Tikrit, I turned up the volume on the intercom system. The lyrics, simple and juvenile, were oddly fitting for the occasion in which we had found ourselves:

> Times have changed, and times are strange,
> Here I come, but I ain't the same.
> Mama, I'm coming home.
> I could be right, I could be wrong,
> Hurts so bad, it's been so long.
> Mama, I'm coming home.

Glancing sideways in the turret and chanting along with the music, I met Davis's grinning visage. He nodded his head, smiling, and I winked at him and clapped him on the shoulder. We drove off into the night, singing together at the top of our lungs.

✦ ✧ ✦

Strung out in the darkness, the battalion's protracted convoy stretched for miles. The distances wreaked havoc on our VHF radios, and communications between the companies and the battalion headquarters were erratic. As the battalion approached Baghdad, an LAV-25 from Charlie Company veered off the highway and rammed head-on into a concrete "Jersey barrier." The collision totaled the vehicle, but spared the crew. Glistening fuel, engine oil, and coolant leaked from a dozen fissures in the vehicle, darkening the asphalt of the highway. Bits and pieces of the LAV littered the road. Bringing up the battalion's rear, Delta Company sped past the ruined vehicle as mechanics attempted to hoist it onto a low-boy truck for the remainder of the march south. Seeing the LAV smashed all over the highway caused me to reiterate to the company over the radio to stay awake, and we continued.

Farther down the road, as the battalion's main body rolled through the southern outskirts of Baghdad, the night lit up with red tracer fire from Golf Company's trucks. Claiming they were taking fire from the right, the entire company opened up into the neighborhood as they passed through it. From our position in the column behind them we scanned back and forth, searching for the enemy shooters. But the episode was over as quickly as it had begun, and whoever it was (if ever it was) disappeared back into the city. We found nothing.

The return trip south to Ad Diwaniyah lasted all night. As we approached the city, long convoys of army vehicles from 4th ID rumbled from the opposite direction up the northbound lane. *Have fun,* I thought sardonically. *We're out of here.* With the new sunrise of 22 April taking hold in the east, Delta Company approached the cloverleaf interchange that would take us west into Ad Diwaniyah. As we rolled along the familiar cloverleaf, the atmosphere

DELTA COMPANY MET BY CROWDS OF IRAQIS UPON RETURNING TO AD DIWANIYAH, 22 APRIL 2003.

was quieter than it had been three weeks earlier. The debris of battle scattered across the road by RCT-5's onslaught had been cleared away. Few reminders of the skirmishes fought around the interchange still remained. From the looks of it, you would have never known such pitched fighting had occurred. It was as if we had never been there in the first place.

The battalion wound its way through the heart of downtown Ad Diwaniyah, where thousands of cheering Iraqis lined the streets and mobbed our vehicles. Most of the locals rushing to greet us appeared to be children. Forgetting where we were, I thought, *Aren't these kids supposed to be in school?* They shouted and waved, motioning wildly for us to give them food, candy, and money. But none of them appeared to be starving. No emaciated faces filled the crowds, and the arms that waved at us energetically weren't rail-thin with malnutrition. Looking at one smiling, overweight child, I remembered the observations Bob Woodruff had made earlier in the war about the locals seeing us only as a source of food and thought bitterly, *Do they just want a handout? Is that all they see us as?*

The division had centered its new assembly area in an abandoned military compound, and all around the area old trucks and equipment sat rusting. Ironically, the compound was believed to have been the point of origin of the enemy rocket attack made on RCT-5's position along Highway 1 the evening of 30 March. Iraqi tanks and armored vehicles in various states of repair and disassembly filled a run-down maintenance bay. An obstacle course for physical training crumbled with neglect. The place was a dump. Dust blew constantly, and the tires of our vehicles sank in the soft, sour earth. It was a far cry from the lush surroundings of Tikrit and the amenities of the different patrol bases we had occupied there. But the compound was to be our new home for an indeterminate period, so we settled in around the perimeter. Walking from vehicle to vehicle, I noticed the weariness stitched into the Marines' faces. Their slurred speech and almost drunken behavior told me the grueling road march throughout the night had taken its toll. I looked around, and with nothing else to do for the time being, I turned to 1stSgt Guzman and Capt Portiss.

"Get everyone's head down. They've earned it."

Guzman returned minutes later to drop off a stack of mail for me. I was already fast asleep.

✦ ✧ ✦

In our dusty camp in Ad Diwaniyah our daily routine soon returned to some semblance of normalcy. The morning of 23 April the Marines and sailors of 1st LAR Battalion gathered together for their first unit formation since before crossing into Iraq more than one month earlier. The warning order we had received in Tikrit came to pass, and the men were told that stability operations had indeed begun. No information was passed detailing when the battalion would begin its retrograde to Kuwait, but the battalion commander announced that "stop-loss" personnel would soon depart for home.

My change of command was planned for 1 May. Shortly after that I would leave for Kuwait with the battalion's stop-loss Marines, and from there we would head home. I returned to the company's position and continued work on fitness reports and awards, racing to complete the paperwork before the change of command. With less than a week before the turnover, I wanted my tedious administrative requirements completed as quickly as possible. But as I crafted each official summary of action and transcribed the combat history of Delta Company, I recalled once more all we had accomplished. I thought again of the memories that had been created and the bonds that had been forged. Despite the tragedy of losing Suarez del Solar, despite my episode in the tunnel, despite all the frustrations and angst and heartache, one thing was certain: being Delta Company's commanding officer had been the pinnacle of my career to date.

That night I dreamt for the first time about combat, and the man I had killed. RPGs and bullets sizzled everywhere, and the jihadi appeared in front of me, clutching a grenade. I fired my pistol at him, but he laughed diabolically and began to ridicule me. I emptied my weapon into him, and as each projectile penetrated his body he continued to cackle. My last round finally silenced him. I awoke, sweating and breathing heavily. Looking around the assembly area bathed in the half-light of early morning, I wondered how many more times that nameless man would invade my dreams once I had left that place and resumed my life.

✦ ✧ ✦

The days blended together in that last week before I left Delta Company. Little remained for me to do in preparation for the new commander taking over, and in the final days I spent many hours just killing time. Life in the assembly area moved slowly, and apart from conducting daily vehicle and weapons maintenance, the Marines had little to occupy their time. Mail deliveries, which in the preceding weeks had been few and far between, flooded the assembly area with letters and packages from home. Whereas before the Marines had by necessity hoarded such precious commodities as wet wipes, socks, and tobacco, they now passed around the goods without a second thought. Stacks of battered care packages cluttered the area around each vehicle, and Marines gorged themselves on cookies, candy, and beef jerky. Bodies that had shrunken from weeks of field rations and backbreaking operational

Crew of "No Leaf Clover" in Ad Diwaniyah the morning after a sandstorm, 24 April 2003. (L to R: Capt Folsom, LCpl Andrew Roufs, Cpl Kevin Harter, LCpl Bryce Gurganus, LCpl Josh Davis.)

tempo began to fill out once again, their chiseled features smoothing and their waistlines expanding. Color returned to their faces, and although boredom filled their days, they were happy.

The battalion began planning in earnest for an upcoming mission to the Saudi Arabian border, where jihadis were believed to be crossing the desert to infiltrate Iraq. After some discussion on the matter, it was decided that my replacement, instead of me, would participate in the operational planning. Because the mission was set to commence after my departure from command, he needed the continuity to ensure success within the company. I assisted him as much as possible, and together we conducted a turnover that would set him up for success once he took command. But I refrained from telling him too much about the Marines and the way the company ran. He would draw his own conclusions from what I had to say, and then he would do things his own way after I had left. That's just the way things are and always have been in the Marine Corps.

I awoke one morning and realized it was the last day before the change of command ceremony. Time—the previous two years—had gotten away from me. That afternoon, I dug into my map case and withdrew the escape maps distributed by the S-2 before the war. Unlike the flimsy paper stock of the standard navigational charts we had all used, the escape map was woven from a coarse material that felt like starched cloth. It had been designed to assist downed aviators in surviving and evading the enemy in a foreign country. Aside from indicating latitudes and longitudes, the map also contained pictures of edible plant life and an image of an American flag. Its purpose struck me as appropriate for the occasion—we had escaped Iraq—and I selected the chart that represented the area surrounding Tikrit. Delta Company had been the first American unit there, and because of the role we had played in securing it, it symbolized more to me than Baghdad.

I unfolded the map and moved from vehicle to vehicle, asking the Marines to sign it for me. Sitting down with each crew, I traded stories with the men as they passed the map back and forth and scrawled in black ink across the heavy material. The process took all afternoon, and I finally walked back to my own vehicle and sat down to examine the words the Marines had written. Expecting a mass of hastily scratched signatures and nothing more, I was speechless at the farewell they had given me.

"I could not have asked for a better man to work for," penned 1stSgt Guzman.

"Never doubt your leadership kept your men alive," added SSgt Kappen.

"I will always remember our commanding officer going into the tunnel with us," declared LCpl Nour.

"It's been an honor and a blessing for Delta Company having you as our CO," wrote Cpl Martin.

"Wherever you go, we're always behind you," scribbled LCpl Blanchard.

I read the messages over and over again, my heart heavy with grief at leaving behind these young men. In the course of two years I had demanded the world of them, and they had delivered it in spades. Staring at their notes of praise, thanks, and encouragement, I felt a love for them no one could ever understand. It was a gift unlike any other I had received in my life. The only words that had ever meant more to me were when my wife said "I do" on the banks of the Mississippi.

✦ ✧ ✦

The morning of 1 May dawned bright and sunny, but the warm rays of sunlight did little to lighten my dark mood as I lugged my personal gear across camp to the battalion headquarters. In an act of finality, I shaved my scraggly mustache and did my best to clean my uniform for the coming change of command ceremony.

Delta Company formed in the assembly area's center, and the battalion staff arrayed itself to the side for the ceremony. My replacement and I marched in front of the company, and the chaplain gave the benediction. As the adjutant read the orders officially relieving me of command, I was struck by the contrast between me and the man taking my place. He stood next to me dressed in an unsoiled, up-to-date Marine Corps "digital-patterned" camouflaged uniform. By contrast, I was clad in stained, rumpled old tricolor desert fatigues. The irony wasn't lost on me, and I thought cynically, *Out with the old, and in with the new.*

First Sergeant Guzman approached me with the company guidon, ceremoniously presented it to me, and saluted crisply. Turning to my left, I handed the standard to the new company commander, who then returned it to Guzman. Rendering a salute to the new CO and shaking his hand firmly, I said simply, "Take care of them." We exchanged places in front of the formation, and I turned to face the battalion staff. It was time to say my piece. I had spoken to the entire company in private the previous evening, and now I repeated my words to the officers and SNCOs assembled in front of me.

"Ernie Pyle, the famous war correspondent, once talked about the 'powerful fraternalism in the ghastly brotherhood of war.' He said the millions of people far away at home must remain forever unaware of this brotherhood. I want to talk about this brotherhood assembled before you this morning.

"I have served with these young men for over two years. During that time, they have put aside their differences and bonded together as a team. As a family. They have demonstrated the meaning of sacrifice and putting others before self. They have molded themselves into combat-hardened veterans capable of accomplishing any mission. In the words of Colonel Nathan Jessup in *A Few Good Men,* for them it has been about 'placing your life in another man's hands, and then asking him to do the same.'

"I witnessed this firsthand on March Twenty-Seventh, when Lance Corporal Suarez del Solar was mortally wounded. The Marines and sailors fell upon him like moths to a flame, fighting with everything they had to save the life of their fallen comrade.

"I saw it again on April Third, when Third Platoon was trapped in an ambush and every platoon rushed to their aid to help them escape. And again on April Fifth, when the company did the same to assist their comrades in First Platoon along the Diyala River.

"I saw it on Highway One in Tikrit, when teams of Marines rushed headlong into rifle and grenade fire to kill jihadis entrenched in a culvert tunnel.

"These things will never be forgotten, and I will never forget these men. They are my family, and the only words I can close with are those of William Manchester:

"'Men, I now know, do not fight for flag or country, for the Marine Corps or glory or any other abstraction. They fight for one another. Any man in combat who lacks comrades who will die for him, or for whom he is willing to die, is not a man at all. He is truly damned.'"

When I had finished, I turned to face the men of Delta Company assembled before me one final time; I stared into their solemn features and repeated to myself the words I had just uttered.

I will never forget you.

The mantle of command officially handed over, I turned to walk away as the new commander addressed the company for the first time. I barely heard a word he said—too many thoughts raced noisily in circles in my mind.

22
A Different War

One minute I was a company commander for a light armored reconnaissance unit, and the next minute I was not. I made the transition from the employed to the unemployed so quickly, you would have never guessed the job had been mine in the first place. Having already hauled my personal belongings to the battalion staff's living area and completed my administrative work for the company, I had nothing to do except sit around with other similarly jobless officers and revise awards that had been written within the battalion. Many billet changes had taken place around the same time as mine, and like castoffs the jobless officers congregated in adjoining rooms in the barren building that had become 1st LAR Battalion's headquarters. The battalion prepared for its upcoming mission to the Saudi border; an epidemic of gastrointestinal illness spread like wildfire through the camp; and we proofread awards. I also reviewed the awards that had been submitted by the officers of Delta Company. In all, more than twenty Marines in the company had been nominated for awards ranging from the Navy-Marine Corps Achievement Medal to the Bronze Star.

My quick relocation from the battalion to Kuwait for a flight home never materialized. For a week I sat around the dusty headquarters building, swatting flies and dodging the shits. Everyone seemed to have the illness, and some burgeoning poet had suggested we change the name of the town from Ad Diwaniyah to "Ad Diarrhea." It was easy to tell who had contracted the mysterious ailment. Those afflicted lurched around the area in a trance, clad only in T-shirts and shorts. The only time they were vertical was when they stumbled to get to the field toilet before crapping or puking all over themselves. As the battalion had raced through Iraq, few Marines had become sick like this. But now that we were stationary and able to pass germs around to each other in the overcrowded assembly area, everyone fell victim to such illnesses. Like an obsessive-compulsive, I washed my hands neurotically and refused to shake hands with others. Crapping my guts out was the last thing I wanted to do before going home, but eventually even I succumbed to the bug. It was as if Iraq had given all of us one final going away present.

Across the battalion's camp, Delta Company was busy planning and rehearsing for its new operation. Though I fought the urge to make trips over to their area, I frequently found myself making excuses to do so. *I need to return this award write-up for corrections. The company commander might need some help reconciling the inventory discrepancies. I think I left something on my vehicle.* But each time I caught myself at the last minute and mentally scolded myself. *Don't be that guy!* I thought. *Don't be the guy without a life who can't move on.*

Instead, I sat around wasting time with the other officers returning home with me. Chad Parment, Drew Bone, Tom McGee, and I intermittently passed awards paperwork back and forth among ourselves and chain-smoked each other's cigarettes. As the battalion departed for its operation, a small contingent of headquarters Marines was left behind under the charge of two warrant officers: Jerry Copely, the maintenance officer, and Ken Vice, the battalion assistant communications officer. The six of us told and retold stories from the war. We talked about good times, bad times, and how we would have done things differently if given the opportunity. In the growing heat of the Iraqi summer, our conversations invariably became giant bitch sessions. But it was something we needed, and by the time our last night together approached I felt I knew these five men on a different level than I had before the war. In particular, Chad Parment and I finally got to know each other as officers and friends rather than as senior and subordinate. Had it not been for those long summer days waiting for a ride to Kuwait, I don't believe we would have stayed in touch after the war as we have.

✦ ✧ ✦

Our number finally came up, and on 8 May we piled into a convoy of buses for the return trip south to Kuwait. The convoy drove throughout the night, and never in our month of combat operations did I feel more vulnerable than in those hours driving through the darkness of the southern Iraqi desert. Stacked in buses with nothing to protect us but our own rifles and pistols, we felt like ducks in a shooting gallery. Each busload of Marines and sailors had rehearsed immediate action drills to prepare us for ambushes, but without any heavy weapons escorts we knew the likely outcome: we would be toast. But the ambush never came, and by early morning we were offloading the buses in Camp Mathilda. Our second wait began, this time for seats on a plane to the United States.

The heat in Kuwait was even worse than it had been in Ad Diwaniyah, and we spent our days hiding from the sun in the sweltering tents erected for personnel transitioning out of the country. The combination of chow hall food, a post exchange, and exercise equipment made me realize just how far away from danger we all were. I finally began to allow myself to relax. But those last days in Kuwait were the worst. I was reminded of my childhood days when I would stay up all night on Christmas Eve. The time went by slowly, but those final hours before sunrise always felt like an eternity. As with looking at the presents within my reach, I could practically see the plane that would take us back to our families. But time dragged on, and before long my excitement at going home ebbed into contempt for the military system that held me hostage in the desert. I couldn't figure out what the delay was, and no one had an answer for me. The longer we went without a plane ride home, the angrier I became.

But then, ten days after leaving the battalion in Ad Diwaniyah, the news came to our steamy tent. We were leaving the next day. We loaded our gear and headed to the tent where the military police conducted their contraband inspections. Since before the end of the war, word had filtered down informing the Marines what they could and could not bring with them back home. So-called "amnesty boxes" filled every tent, providing the men with every opportunity to dump contraband items such as Iraqi weapons, ammunition, and alcohol. Marines angrily dumped off bayonets, 7.62mm rounds, and countless other restricted items they had collected over the course of the war, always mumbling how stupid the rules were. I frequently inventoried my own stash of war souvenirs—the beret, the gas mask, the flags—to ensure I had nothing illegal with me. Yet as I approached the inspection tent that final time, I noticed the sign on the wall describing what was and was not contraband. Among the items listed as illegal were personal pictures and identification cards that had belonged to Iraqis. In my bag I still had the passport I had taken from the dead jihadi in Tikrit. Examining it once again, I realized it fit the criteria for smuggled goods. I searched out an MP before entering the screening station.

"Hey, what about enemy passports?" I asked a sergeant standing by the tent's entrance.

"Contraband, sir," he said. "Counts as identification or pictures."

"Well, Jesus Christ," I replied bluntly. "I pulled it off a dead terrorist trying to ambush my company. Who the hell's gonna miss it?"

"Sorry, that's the rules."

I stormed away from the tent and out into the shadows of the camp's perimeter. Kneeling down in the sand, I retrieved the stained, crumpled document from my pack and flipped through it. *If I can't keep this thing,* I thought bitterly. *Then no one will.* I pulled my scratched, dented Zippo from my pocket, clinked it open, and struck it alight. The orange glow illuminated the writing stamped inside the passport, and as I touched the flame to the corner it danced eagerly up the paper. Dropping the burning identification into the sand, I watched the pages blacken and curl up into ashes. *Adios, you son of a bitch,* I thought darkly, stamping out the smoking embers. *Good riddance.*

But that wasn't the last of my frustration with the contraband inspections. I had managed to make it all the way to the boarding area at Kuwait City International Airport with a flower I had cut from the palace garden in Tikrit the morning Delta Company seized the complex on the Tigris. The beds of colorful flowers surrounding the palace had struck me as odd, but their natural beauty in the face of destruction had caused me to cut one and press it in my journal. I had thought it would make a nice gift for Ashley upon my return. But now, literally at the last minute as we prepared to board the plane, a sign warned me: "No plants or agricultural items may be brought on board."

Oh, come on! I thought. But I caved. The notion of getting caught, of getting busted for something so trivial, petrified me. Suddenly I was in a panic, and I rifled through my carry-on bag to find the dried flower. I tossed it in the final amnesty box as we were herded into the passenger holding area. Mumbling curses to myself, I boarded the plane. Infuriated at the system for its stupid rules, I was angrier at myself for following them. After all, I had just returned from a war. Why the hell couldn't I take a harmless flower home to my wife? I stewed for much of the flight home, which itself was a stark contrast to our flight into Kuwait of months earlier. The United Airlines flight crew that had carried us from March Air Reserve Base to Kuwait had treated us as heroes before we had even done anything. But our return trip was aboard an airline I had never heard of, and the flight crew was a rude coven of hags from New York City who didn't give a hoot who we were or what we had just been through. I was oblivious as our flight home angled into the skies over Kuwait and the Marines aboard cheered and hollered. Beneath the surface, the anger simmered.

✦ ✧ ✦

Our plane circled the airfield at March ARB one final time, and as it touched down on the tarmac the exhausted Marines and sailors cheered once again. We were back on American soil. As the aircraft taxied down the runway and toward the reception point, the passengers anxiously squirmed in their seats, eager to get the hell out of the tube in which they had been held hostage for hours. Unable to smoke, unable to drink (a fact made painfully clear by the vulgar flight attendants), the Marines fidgeted like caged animals poised to break free of their chains. When the plane finally came to a halt, someone boarded, and moments later a woman's voice sounded over the intercom system.

"Welcome back, Marines!" she said, the tone in her voice joyous and sincere. "We are proud of you and what you have done. Once you debark the plane, please take advantage of the food and services we have set up for you in the hangar."

From somewhere behind me, a faceless voice commented, "Unless they have whores for us, I don't want to hear it."

The woman on the intercom continued, unaware of the remark. "Also, when you get off the plane you will not have to touch your bags. We already have that taken care of."

The passengers began to exit the plane, and I walked out of the cabin and into the bright sunlight. On the edge of the tarmac, two fire engines sat blaring klaxons and firing their water cannons into the air. A hundred people stood waiting for us, cheering and waving American flags. A banner stretched across the hangar, proclaiming "Welcome Home, Heroes!" Dozens of strangers leaned out to shake my hand, and in silent contemplation I thought of my father and his service in Vietnam thirty years earlier. He and his thousands of counterparts had never received a hero's welcome such as that playing out before me, and I thought soberly, *This one's for you, Dad.*

The bus ride across the southern California countryside was filled with excited chatter, and two hours later we pulled into the battalion's camp at Las Flores. Dozens of families waited, shouting and waving at us. But instead of stopping, the bus rolled right on past them and up to the battalion armory. Despite the long months of separation and anxiety, we had to first turn in our weapons. Thirty minutes later I dragged my gear down the ramp to the parking lot where the families had assembled. I found my parked car, and after stashing my rucksack and seabag next to it I searched around for Ashley. She stood next to a group of wives, desperately scanning the crowd for me. I walked up behind her and put my hands on her shoulders. She turned around and jumped into my arms. I was home. The war was over for me.

Then a different war began.

✦ ✧ ✦

The weeks passed quickly for us. Ashley and I flew east to see my family and spend a quiet week together on the Caribbean island of Saint Lucia. After the interruption of September 11, after more than a year and a half of marriage, we were finally spending a real honeymoon together. But the peace and quiet of the island resort did little to calm my nerves, and our vacation was strained with words unspoken. I did my best to share my experiences with her, but in the end I simply handed her my journal and told her to read it for herself. There was no other way to convey my feelings.

Upon my return to Virginia, my brother threw a welcome back party for me. Friends I hadn't seen in years showed up, but throughout the celebration I was uncomfortable and edgy. People asked questions. *How many people did you kill? Did you lose any Marines?* Rather than answer, I handed them the album of photographs I had taken while in Iraq. When my brother led a toast in my honor and asked me to make a speech, I couldn't find the words. For the first time in my life, my friends and family saw me speechless. My parents also hosted a welcome home reception, in my old neighborhood. Yet even amid the kind words of encouragement offered by my neighbors, the feelings of discomfort persisted for me. Being back home in the quiet, sterile environment of suburbia was a change for which I hadn't been prepared.

I also took the opportunity to visit the Marine Corps memorial in Arlington. The giant bronze statue depicting the flag-raising on Iwo Jima had always been something of a shrine for me, and after my experiences abroad I felt the urge to go and pay my respects. Accompanied by my parents, I walked past the white gravestones of Arlington National Cemetery and approached the massive monument. Emblazoned across the front of it were the hallowed words

> In honor and in memory of the men of the United States Marine Corps
> who have given their lives to their country since November 10, 1775.

My parents standing beside me, I stared at the engraving. After all those years, they were no longer merely words to me. One singular thought filled my head: I had been unable to bring all my boys home. As I mourned the loss of Lance Corporal Jésus Suarez del Solar, the energy I had summoned for so long to maintain my composure in front of my men leaked from my body like water through a sieve. The tears finally came.

✦ ✧ ✦

Returning to San Diego, Ashley and I packed up our belongings and moved north to the Naval Postgraduate School (NPS). Sunny San Diego gave way to foggy, cloudy Monterey, and soon I was in school working on a master's degree and preparing to become a South Asian foreign area officer. I had foolishly allowed myself to be misled into believing that a year in Monterey would be a relaxed respite from the rigors of duty in the operating forces. Nothing could have been further from the truth. My undergraduate years at the University of Virginia, where I had majored less in foreign affairs than in partying, were far in the past. I suddenly found myself shackled in an environment where making the grade was far more important than it had been a decade earlier, and my days and nights were spent locked in the campus library studying and writing papers. In the sedentary lifestyle of a student that I had unwittingly forced myself into, my ass and waistline competed to see which could widen the most.

I was in hell. As I sat surrounded by officers from all services who had sat out the war, my time with Delta Company became a blurred, distant memory. With few officers around to share my experiences, I turned inward and focused on my studies. Discussions about Iraq reigned supreme in the academic halls of NPS, and I seethed with anger as officers of all ranks and nationalities openly questioned the war's morality and justification. I found myself vehemently defending the war and the reasons for waging it. But as the war progressed along with my analytical abilities, I was forced to observe the conflict roiling in Iraq from a different perspective. The daily news grimly reported the worsening insurgency and escalating American causalities. The only solace I found was in the fact that *my* boys were no longer risking their lives over there.

I maintained sporadic communication with several men from the company and battalion, among them 1stSgt Guzman, SSgt Kappen, and Dave Hudspeth. They relayed stories to me of the boredom and complacency that had taken root within the battalion, and they frequently asked when Ashley and I would return to San Diego to visit. We took them up on their invitations, and over the Labor Day weekend Ashley and I drove south to see them all. Sitting around a bar in Irvine, Guzman, Kappen, Hudspeth, and I traded quips about the battalion and school. Their demeanor told me they sensed something was wrong. I attempted to play it off.

"School has me running ragged," I explained. "I don't know my ass from a hole in the ground."

"Yeah, but compared to the battalion you must be on a vacation up there," one commented.

"Well, I'll be honest with you guys," I said seriously. "You all are in a better situation than I am. You still have each other to lean on down here. Up in Monterey there's no one that understands what we did last spring."

First Sergeant Guzman leaned over. "You ought to come to the battalion's birthday ball in November, sir."

I pondered it momentarily. "I don't think so. I don't want to be like the guy who graduates from college and then comes back every weekend to party. No one likes that guy."

Kappen joined the conversation. "Bullshit, sir. The Marines miss you. They'd love to see you."

I left after telling them I would consider it. More than anything I wanted to see the Marines one last time, but I doubted the feeling was reciprocal. And again, I didn't want to be *that* guy, the burnt-out has-been who has nothing else to do but revel in glory days gone by.

◆ ◇ ◆

The war in Iraq steadily worsened. Comparisons with Vietnam filled the news, and casualties mounted. Rumors began to fly that the Marines would return to Iraq. It seemed impossible. The Marines weren't an occupation force—that was the army's job. But the army was overwhelmed, and one day in class my professor casually commented that he had just heard 1st Marine Division was scheduled to redeploy to Iraq in the spring. In my head I conjured up ridiculous schemes that would get me redeployed with the Division, with 1st LAR Battalion. Realizing the absurdity of my wishes, I told no one of my desires.

But I couldn't hide them from Ashley, who knew the only place I really wanted to be was back in action with my Marines. She tolerated my rants, my emotional outbursts, my quiet brooding. With no one else around to absorb my disintegration, I took my anger out on my wife. I snapped at her, and when she pleaded with me to share my feelings I stormed off to be by myself. I frequently thought of a line John Wayne had uttered in *The Alamo.* He had said, "There's right and there's wrong. You've got to do one or the other. You do the one and you're living. You do the other and you may be walking around, but in reality you're dead." I felt like a zombie, doing the walk of the dead. I was alone, and at night I tossed and turned with nightmares of long, endless highways and shadowy figures hiding in dark tunnels.

Stabbing thoughts of shame plagued me as I felt that I had abandoned my men, as well as the guilt of having returned alive when Suarez del Solar had not. The ignominy of being the only company commander in the battalion to lose a Marine similarly weighed on me. Each time I began to accept his death, I would read another account of his father's crusade for peace. Grieving over the death of his son, he had turned his anger toward the Marine Corps and the Bush Administration. In several public speeches he levied charges of racism within Delta Company. Moreover, he singled me out for the death of his son, telling everyone Jésus's company commander had abandoned him and deliberately denied him medical attention as he lay bleeding to death in the tilled fields east of Ad Diwaniyah. I wanted to see him in person, to convey my condolences for his son's death. But his fury and his public press conferences prevented me from doing so. Knowing that any personal visit with him would turn into a media circus, I avoided what would have routinely been the responsibility of a company commander to visit the family.

Ashley did her best to keep me occupied when I wasn't trapped in the library stacks or drowning in the classroom. Together we took long motorcycle rides down the winding coast highway overlooking Big Sur and through the vineyards of Carmel Valley. We made trips to Santa Cruz and San Francisco, and we hosted friends and family, all of whom found Monterey to be a wonderful place. Many wondered aloud why I disliked the scenic environment of the peninsula so much, particularly since it had been the place of my birth when my father was in graduate school. Ever the observant, spiritual soul, Ashley pointed out to me one day that I would have been unhappy anywhere we went after what I had been through. She even sent me to Las Vegas to spend a weekend with two old fraternity brothers.

It took me months to realize Ashley put up with more than any spouse should have had to. In my ignorance I had forgotten that she too suffered from my deployment. She had endured my absence for six months while I was on my WestPac deployment, and fewer than six weeks after my return in December 2002 I was gone again to Kuwait and Iraq. As she cared for the wives and families of the men of Delta Company, the anguish of not knowing what I was doing or whether I was alive or dead wore her down. Perhaps worst of all, she bore the brunt of dealing with Suarez del Solar's family after his death. The battalion's failure to prepare properly for a Marine's death in combat resulted in Ashley becoming the primary liaison with Suarez del Solar's wife and father. As she accompanied Jésus's wife in viewing the body and making the funeral arrangements, she became trapped in the ensuing family feud instigated by Suarez's father. She brokered arguments over death benefits and funeral preparations. She gave public talks to the battalion's wives on the subject. She too served.

✦ ✧ ✦

The first tangible step in my personal healing process occurred that November. When the invitation to attend 1st LAR Battalion's Marine Corps birthday ball was formally extended, Ashley insisted we attend. To be fair, her motives were not solely focused on me. True, while she believed it would be good for me to see my men once more in the celebratory atmosphere of the birthday ball, she also wanted to see many of the Delta wives with whom she had developed close, personal relationships during our deployments. Just as the men had become my sons and brothers, the young wives had become a part of *her* family. On the first weekend in November we piled into our car and made the long voyage across the southern California desert to Primm Valley, a small casino resort just across the Nevada state line.

After spending the first night drinking in a casino with the by-now promoted Gunnery Sergeant Kappen and his wife, Melissa, the day of the ball

Ashley and I toured the vast outlet mall adjacent to the resort. As we walked up and down the promenade, I heard a familiar shout.

"Captain Folsom!"

I turned to see Chris Stoia, now a sergeant, standing twenty feet away. He ran over to me, his hand extended.

"Hey, sir! We all heard you were coming! Goddamn, it's good to see you."

I beamed. "Man, it's good to see you, too, Sergeant Stoia."

We talked for several minutes and then parted ways. Seeing him and his enthusiasm, my anxiety and apprehension about the coming evening began to dissipate.

Later that evening as the ball went into full swing, I was swamped by Marines and sailors from Delta Company. Like Kappen and Stoia, many had since been promoted to the next rank, and an equal number had moved on from Delta Company to occupy billets in other companies within the battalion. Their uniforms bristled with unit citation ribbons and personal decorations. Most of the awards from the war had been presented already, and my chest swelled with pride to see these young men proudly wearing their shiny, colorful decorations. They were legitimate combat veterans now, and the brilliance of their dress uniforms confirmed it. Many new Marines had since joined the battalion, and the naked smoothness of their uniforms made them stand out in the sea of experience surrounding them.

The Marines from Delta explained to me that 1st LAR Battalion would be redeploying to Iraq in the spring. Most of them would be returning with it. I was unhappy at the news, but tried to hide my disappointment. Marines thrust cigarettes and drinks at me, and many asked to take pictures of us together. I opened a tab at the bar, and as Marines and sailors from different units lined up to get drinks the bartender grew irritated by the confusion.

"Hey," he asked me. "How do I know who's drinking on your tab and who isn't?"

I leaned across the bar and grinned. "Anyone who says they're with Purple-Six can drink on my tab."

The company gathered in a group, and I made one final, brief speech to them.

"You're the veterans now, the ones who know what the hell to do when the shit hits the fan. Teach the new Marines everything you've learned, and remember the most important thing: do your job and take care of each other. I miss all of you. You truly are part of my family now."

Young men lined up to speak with me, and each repeated the same mantra:

"Thanks for everything you did."

"We miss you."

"The company needs you back."

As their expressions of praise enveloped me, the familiar lump of emotion lodged itself deep in my throat. Through their simple words they paid me the highest compliment possible, and I heard what I had silently needed in all those long months since leaving them: *I had done my job the right way.* Ashley was similarly mobbed by Marines and their wives, all paying their respects and thanking her profusely for her help and friendship during the long deployments. She too needed to hear these utterances.

The evening wasn't entirely filled with joyous banter. In conversation with Maj Bodkin, I learned the award I had written for Doug Cullins had been downgraded from a Bronze Star to a Navy-Marine Corps Achievement Medal. The news infuriated me. Somewhere, someone who didn't know Lt Cullins and who never saw his heroism during the ambush at the Elbow had decided he didn't rate the award I had submitted months earlier. Awards for Capt Portiss and Spool had been similarly downgraded, and I vented my frustrations at the battalion XO. He commiserated, telling me many awards in the battalion had been reduced. With sudden finality, he simply told me nothing could be done about it and changed the subject.

Marines also confided in me that the new company commander had surreptitiously changed the call sign for Delta Company. They were no longer the Dragons. Instead, they now answered the radio to "Dagger." I had no right to be angry—it was no longer my company to do with as I pleased. And besides, I too had changed the company's call sign from "Desperado" to "Dragon" shortly after taking command in 2001. But the difference then had been that the Marines in the company had publicly voted on the name change. The men were angry that the call sign they had fought under had been consigned to the history books.

Ashley and I left Primm Valley the following morning. Slightly hungover, I meditated over the events of the previous evening. The revelation that my men felt much the same about me as I did about them eased the burden on my heart. Despite the knowledge that they would soon face danger in Iraq once again, I remembered my thoughts from those heady days of our highway war so many months earlier.

They're big boys now.

Absorbing every moment of the previous evening, I thought back to a passage my father often quoted from John Muir's *The Mountains of California:*

> When the storm began to abate, I dismounted and sauntered down through the calming woods. The storm-tones died away, and, turning

> toward the east, I beheld the countless hosts of the forests hushed and tranquil, towering above one another on the slopes of the hills like a devout audience. The setting sun filled them with amber light, and seemed to say, while they listened, "My peace I give unto you."
> As I gazed on the impressive scene, all the so-called ruin of the storm was forgotten, and never before did these noble woods appear so fresh, so joyous, so immortal.

The storm was over, and for the first time in months the days ahead of me seemed brighter.

✦ ✧ ✦

In the following weeks and months, I continued with my schoolwork and thought often of the men of Delta Company. In sporadic emails they described their preparation for the imminent redeployment to Iraq. A common theme persisted: We're ready to go, but we wish you were going with us again. My replies had a different theme: Keep your heads down.

One Friday morning in February 2004, as 1st LAR Battalion prepared to redeploy overseas, I received an email from the mother of a Delta Company Marine who had maintained contact with me.

"I'm sure you already heard, but in case you haven't, Emery Nyeki was killed this morning from a humvee rollover."

I was stunned. Sergeant Nyeki had been a vehicle commander in 3rd Platoon during the war the previous year. During our WestPac he had suffered shrapnel wounds from the grenade mishap on Range 4 in Kuwait. After the war he went to work for 1st Marine Division Schools, and during a training evolution his humvee had driven off the road and rolled over. The following week I raced to board a plane for San Diego to attend his memorial service in Camp Pendleton. As a lance corporal he had been my first driver when I joined the company. Now, after working his way up through the ranks; after enduring the grenade explosion in Kuwait; after surviving the ambush at the Elbow and four weeks of combat operations in Iraq, he was gone. He had evaded death for a long time, but it had finally found him. The Marines were grief-stricken, and during the course of his memorial service I was able to do what I had not the previous year at LCpl Suarez del Solar's service—I wept.

Nyeki's death hurt the Marines of Delta Company in a different way from the pain of Suarez del Solar's loss. For many, it cast a dark shadow on their coming deployment. Later, when the company had returned to Iraq and began taking casualties, several Marines confided in me their fears that Delta Company was cursed. But they continued to do their jobs as the battalion patrolled the Syrian border, and through their emails and letters the Marines relayed stories of the company's exploits abroad. Every day I hoped for their safety as I checked the Coalition casualties website, praying I would see no names I recognized. Despite my prayers, however, it wasn't long before the news was bad. As the long months of 1st LAR Battalion's second deployment stretched out and American casualties mounted, I anguished over the fate of my men patrolling the barren deserts of Iraq. Time couldn't go fast enough.

✦ ✧ ✦

But life carried on, and before I knew it my long year in Monterey approached its end. Through personal contacts in Iraq, I continued to trace the activities of 1st LAR Battalion and the men of Delta Company. Accepting the hard reality that I would never again command men the way I had in Iraq during the spring of 2003, I swallowed my pride and prepared to move on.

Reflecting on my time in Iraq, I didn't blame the Marine Corps for what transpired. Bad things happen in war. We understood that when we signed on. It just took some of us longer to accept the realities of war and what happens when you entrust your life and your heart to others. Abraham Lincoln was correct when he said, "There's no honorable way to kill, no gentle way to destroy. There is nothing good in war, except its ending." I would never again look at war through the cavalier, myopic lens of youth of my days before Iraq. But through it all, in the months after leaving the company, my thoughts frequently drifted to words spoken by a soldier named Captain Frank Barron. He had fought on Okinawa in 1945 and years later had said, "I believe fighting for your country in the infantry in battle is the most purifying experience known to man. These men who trained hard together and fought for extended periods together became so completely unselfish, so absorbed with the welfare of the group that their principal concern was for the 'other guy.' I've never wished to die before or since, nor did I wish to die in battle then. But I thought there was a good chance that I would, and I thought then there was no better way to die, and no better men to be buried with." I wish I were capable of such words.

Marines from Delta Company still maintained periodic contact with me, and each time I heard from them I thought about glory days gone by. I thought of long road marches and sandstorms. Of smoky ambushes and booming cannons. Of the smiling, gaunt young faces that filled the long ranks of Delta Company.

No better men, I thought.

✦ ✧ ✦

One day not long before I graduated from school in Monterey, I received an email from a sergeant who had served with me in Delta Company.

He thanked me for my assistance in crafting his application to become a commissioned officer, and as he closed the email he added one final line.

P.S.: I heard a rumor about a message written on a shitter wall in Iraq . . . it said the Delta Marines wanted "Purple-Six" back.

Epilogue

Almost a year to the day after parting ways with Delta Company and returning from Iraq, I once again found myself on a plane back to that blighted place. This time, however, I was returning not as a company commander, but as a student and a researcher. Before 1st Marine Division's redeployment to what had been dubbed Operation Iraqi Freedom-II (OIF-II), I had introduced Dr. Barak Salmoni to the division operations officer. One of my professors, Salmoni was an expert in Middle Eastern affairs and Arabic culture. He was also a fluent Arabic linguist, and he had been providing cultural training to U.S. Army units rotating into Iraq. At my insistence he expanded his training to include 1st Marine Division.

Three months into its deployment, 1st Marine Division asked Salmoni to visit Iraq and assess the impact of the cultural training he had provided. In need of an escort and research assistant, Salmoni asked me to accompany him. After quite a bit of debate and political wrangling, he convinced the division and my superintendent to allow me to go with him. Overnight I went from unknown status to a special guest of the commanding general himself.

My decision to return to Iraq was one born of many factors. Salmoni's plan included visiting several battalions in the field to interview Marines about their interaction with the Iraqi populace. First Light Armored Reconnaissance Battalion was among his list of visits, and while I had no expectations of a Delta Company reunion in the desert along the Syrian border, I knew there was still a chance at seeing some of my Marines in the field.

Life as a student had softened me, and I longed to get back to an environment where there was meaning and a sense of urgency in day-to-day operations. It would have been ridiculous of me to expect to return to Iraq as a commander, or even a trigger-puller. Those days were over for me, and I knew it. But as miserable as I had often been during our push toward Baghdad,

I also realized that I had never felt more alive, more engaged, than I had during those chaotic weeks. The chance to return, even if only for a brief stint, brought with it the hope that some of those feelings would reignite after smoldering for a year in the academic setting of the Naval Postgraduate School.

Salmoni *needed* an escort, too. His area of expertise and language ability notwithstanding, the fact remained that he wasn't a Marine. He needed someone who spoke the lingo and knew his way around the division. My role as a research assistant would be minimal—my skills in gathering information and conducting research paled in comparison to his. Instead, I would serve as his liaison with the different units and personnel we would encounter. There was also a security issue surrounding the trip. Salmoni knew the division wouldn't intentionally put him in danger, but he also knew that we would be in a combat zone. Although I had no illusions that I was going as Salmoni's personal bodyguard, a mutual understanding existed between us that I would be armed throughout the trip and he would not be armed. Like I have always said, sometimes shit happens. I just wanted him to be prepared for it if it did.

When I finally told Ashley about my chance to go, I was surprised by her response. Although I had known about the possibility for several weeks, I had postponed telling her about it while the trip was still in the planning phase. The division's decision to approve my going had been up in the air, and I figured there was no need to worry Ashley needlessly until the trip began to look like a reality. Because she had frequently remarked to me that she was glad I wasn't back in the middle of what was going on in Iraq, I expected her to react adversely when I finally told her about it. Instead, despite being irritated that I had waited so long to let her know what was going on, she immediately responded by telling me she thought it was a great opportunity. It was her hope that a return trip to Iraq would provide some measure of closure for me. Even when I began to vacillate about my decision, she encouraged me to go through with it. I was once again reminded of the amazing strength possessed by the woman I had married.

✦ ✧ ✦

Getting to Iraq the second time around proved no less complicated than it had been the previous year. There was a requirement to in-process at the division headquarters in Camp Pendleton, and because of the approaching Memorial Day holiday Salmoni and I were required to fly from Monterey more than a week before our actual flight out of the country.

The morning we were to head to the airport I conducted my daily Internet check for Coalition casualties in Iraq. I was startled to see that the latest list of those killed in action included Staff Sergeant Jorgé Molina-Bautista. On 23 May 2004, while on patrol near the town of Ar Ramadi, he had died when an improvised explosive device (IED) detonated next to his LAV. Formerly the platoon sergeant for Delta's Weapons Platoon, Molina had suffered the brunt of my wrath after I relieved Lt Stiller outside of Baghdad. As we had stood on the outskirts of Saddam City, Molina-Bautista had challenged my decision to relieve his platoon commander. I had responded by angrily informing him that his inability to carry out and enforce his lieutenant's orders had contributed significantly to the officer's relief.

Now, grieving silently in my dining room, I felt remorse as I remembered my final conversation with him in Ad Diwaniyah a year earlier. As I had prepared my final fitness reports and counseled each officer and SNCO on his conduct and actions during the war, I had been very stern with Molina. In particular I had told him I was disappointed in his performance. Now he was gone forever and I would never be able to take those words back. It continued to eat at me as I boarded my flight out of Monterey.

Shortly after arriving in Carlsbad, California, near Camp Pendleton later in the afternoon, I received a call from Ashley. She had phoned the wife of a Delta Company Marine, and in the course of the conversation she learned that Corporal Dominique Perez—a gunner in 3rd Platoon during OIF-I—had been on SSgt Molina's LAV and had been seriously wounded.

"How bad is it?" I asked.

"Something happened to his elbow, but they fixed that at the scene. They flew him to Germany. From what he told Tiffanie on the phone, apparently he doesn't have a nose anymore."

"Jesus Christ," I muttered, shutting my eyes. "How is Tiffanie doing?"

Ashley and Tiffanie Perez had become close friends during our deployments, and Ashley frequently spoke of how emotionally strong Cpl Perez's wife was.

"Like a rock," was her reply. "She's just glad he's alive." She went on to explain that Perez would be flown from Germany to Walter Reed Army Hospital in Washington, D.C., to recover. I continued to mull it over throughout the half-hour drive north to Camp Pendleton. Corporal Perez was an outstanding Marine, and I thought highly of him. Although I mourned the loss of SSgt Molina, I was thankful Perez had survived the explosion. I wanted more than anything to see him, but I knew that was unlikely to happen.

After a time-consuming three days spent checking in to the division and signing out equipment, I was finally able to relax for the long Memorial Day weekend. Ashley drove down from Monterey, and the two of us spent the four days visiting our old haunts. We called on friends, ate at our favorite restaurants, and remembered just how much we both missed the San Diego area. Additionally, more than a year after his passing, I was able to visit LCpl Suarez del Solar's grave in Escondido. Even with SSgt Molina's recent death bearing down on my shoulders, finally seeing Suarez del Solar's flower-adorned grave allowed me to begin the process of putting things back together.

As our last hours together approached, there was an absence of the tension that had characterized the final days Ashley and I spent together in February 2003 as I prepared to return to Kuwait and the war. This was partly due to the nature of this trip—not to kill people, but instead to gather data. But I really think the main reason was that Ashley had become a professional at seeing me off. She had accepted that there would always be danger in my job, and she knew I loved what I was doing. My deployment was reminiscent of the many my father had made during my youth. The first couple of separations had been difficult for my mother, but in subsequent years she would simply drop my father off at the airfield and then take my brother and me out for lunch and shopping. It had become business as usual. So, too, had it become with Ashley. The military wife is a peculiar creature, steely and persevering.

That last afternoon a pleasant surprise awaited me at Camp Pendleton. Ashley and I had received word that Cpl Perez had been flown back to San Diego to convalesce, and he was recuperating in a barracks room back at 1st LAR Battalion's compound. We raced across the base to see him before I headed out for March Air Reserve Base. To my astonishment there he was, standing around outside the barracks and hanging out with three other Marines from Delta Company. I walked up to him and gave him a quick once over. Despite being rail-thin and covered in dozens of reddened, healing shrapnel wounds, he looked fine. Malnourished, but fine. Across the bridge of his nose an angry scab throbbed, but that was all. He still had his sniffer after all.

"Well, shit," I proclaimed. "You look fine. Just looks like you were in a bar fight."

For the next hour we sat around and got caught up with each other. He remembered little about what had happened in the explosion, but it was evident the memory of SSgt Molina's death bothered him. He informed me the decision had been made that he would spend his remaining months in the Marine Corps recovering before his enlistment expired. He would not be returning to the battalion in Iraq.

When the time came for Ashley and me to part ways with the Marines, I pulled Cpl Perez aside. His physical injuries would heal rapidly. But a long road faced him in the recovery of his emotional wounds. Looking him in the eyes, I passed on my final words.

"Listen to me. I have an idea what is ahead of you when you return home with Tiffanie. It won't be easy. If you need to talk to anyone, get in touch with me."

"Thanks, sir," he replied. "I appreciate that."

"You're my boy now, Dominique. You're part of my family."

We embraced one last time, and then parted ways. Several hours later Ashley dropped me off for the bus ride to March Air Reserve Base.

◆ ◇ ◆

The long flight from March ARB to Kuwait aboard the DC-10 was a more solemn affair than my trip the previous year. Whereas Delta Company's flight of a year before had had a certain air of nervous excitement to it, the planeload of casualty replacements bound for battalions operating in Iraq was quiet. Many of the young Marines sitting around me had just graduated from the School of Infantry, and the knowledge that they would be filling holes in the ranks caused by repeated IED explosions and RPG attacks darkened their moods. Knowing what they were getting themselves into, I didn't envy them. In the year since we had liberated Baghdad, more than eight hundred servicemen and servicewomen had been killed in Iraq. In the three months since 1st Marine Division had redeployed, it had suffered dozens killed in action and hundreds more wounded—a far cry from the minimal losses sustained in our rapid drive to Baghdad the previous year.

Together with the casualty replacements, Salmoni and I rotated through the military cantonment area adjacent to Kuwait City International Airport. In a matter of hours we had boarded a C-130 Hercules bound for the airstrip at a desert outpost named Al Asad. Under the cover of darkness we flew across the Iraqi countryside. Sitting in the dimly lit cargo hold of the C-130, I felt the familiar sensation of being a sitting duck. The vibrations of the four turboprop engines rattled the fuselage, making conversation impossible. Wrapped in body armor, ears plugged with foam to preserve hearing for later in life, each Marine was left with his own thoughts. I thought of that long period in an amphibious assault when a landing craft leaves the safety of its ship and ventures toward shore. Sitting in the cargo bay of a C-130 flying in the darkness over a hostile country makes you realize that you are, for the moment, completely vulnerable.

A steep dive, an instant of terror as the aircraft slammed to the deck, and suddenly we were on the airfield of Al Asad. Months of dodging antiaircraft fire had really made the pilots learn their business. The human cargo debarked, and as we loaded a small bus waiting on the tarmac a radio inside blared ridiculously appropriate lyrics by Edwin Starr:

War! huh... Yeah!
What is it good for?
Absolutely nothin'!

"Jesus," I said to Salmoni. "Do you believe this shit?" He shook his head in disbelief. *Welcome to a combat zone,* I thought, shaking my head, too. *What is this, "Apocalypse Now?"*

They shuffled us around under the bright lights of the airfield's compound. As the time approached for our flight to the division headquarters in Ar Ramadi, we boarded the bus once again and sat waiting on the airstrip for a helicopter ride. Muted conversations filled the cramped bus compartment, and in the darkness a lieutenant colonel leaned over to Salmoni.

"Hey, Doctor, you ever heard of an author named William Manchester?"

I butted in. "Yes, sir. He's my favorite author. What about him?"

"He died yesterday."

His words silenced me. Manchester, a former Marine and accomplished biographer, had written what I considered the greatest war memoir ever, a tome titled *Goodbye, Darkness.* I remembered my days in 1992 as I prepared to attend OCS for the first time. My father had handed me a worn-out paperback and said, "If you want to know what the Marine Corps is really like, read this." Since that time I had memorized the book cover to cover, reading it dozens of times and envying Manchester's fluent command of the English language. Years later, my father actually found a hardbound first edition signed by Manchester and presented it to me upon my graduation from The Basic School. It remains one of my most cherished possessions. The death of this man I had never met crushed me, and I mourned his loss as I would have a close relative.

✦ ✧ ✦

As dawn broke, our CH-46 Sea Knight touched down in a green field alongside the division command post in Ar Ramadi. The area was quiet, and I quickly surveyed our surroundings. First Marine Division had assumed command of the 82nd Airborne Division's area of responsibility, and the command post was situated in a massive, walled-in palace compound. Across the landing zone, a smashed palace threatened to collapse around itself, the victim of a JDAM strike. On the opposite side of the LZ from the JDAM ruins a second palace stood intact. A forest of antennas jutted from its roof, and camouflage-netted tents and trailers encircled it. It wasn't difficult to figure out which of the two palaces was the division CP.

But something else struck me as odd. Standing there, sweating in my body armor and carrying a loaded rifle and pistol, I noticed Marines walking around in nothing but their camouflage utility uniforms. No body armor, no helmets, no web gear. For sure, they carried their weapons with them, but they were unloaded. Marines and sailors exercised around the camp in T-shirts and shorts, and as the sun rose people walked back and forth to and from a contract chow hall. It was the furthest you could possibly be from combat and still be in a combat zone. I was puzzled.

That first morning, as Salmoni and I discussed our options over breakfast, I looked up to see four Marines from Delta Company sitting at the table next to me. Sergeant Carlos Gutierrez, Corporals Andrew Tipton and Sean Scharf, and Lance Corporal Jeremy Bohlman had been among the six Marines from Delta who had gone to work for the commanding general's mobile command post (Jump CP). With the demise of SSgt Molina and the evacuation of Cpl Perez, only the four of them remained. We spoke briefly and made plans to sit down and get caught up later after my jet-lag was finished with me.

Salmoni and I roamed the compound at Ar Ramadi, searching for Marines to interview. After sessions with the public affairs officer, the information operations officer, and a lieutenant colonel from a combat assessment team, we developed a base of useful information. A subsequent group session with the Marines of the Jump CP platoon likewise provided us with details we had not yet heard. Together we developed a picture of the war in Iraq and how it had evolved since my time there.

We were also afforded the opportunity to attend a series of meetings between the division's commanding general, Major General James Mattis, and several Iraqi generals. On several occasions Mattis happily told the Iraqis, whom he had fought against the previous year, of his willingness to join in partnership with the new Iraqi army. At the close of one of these meetings, MajGen Mattis turned to Salmoni and me and encouraged us to attend a negotiation scheduled to take place outside of Fallujah. Leaping at the invitation, we gathered our body armor and met up with the Jump CP outside the palace. As we prepared to board an armored humvee, I heard a familiar voice from the general's LAV-C2.

"Hey, check it out! Captain Folsom's going with us!"

It was Sgt Gutierrez, now the vehicle commander for the general. He yelled to the other Marines I knew from the Jump, who saw me and grinned. The armored column mounted up and rolled out of the compound's gate, and I found myself participating in one final road march with Marines from Delta Company. The inherent dangers of the long trip to Fallujah aside, I felt safe knowing my Marines were there. The irony struck me. With my status as an observer, this time they were in charge, looking out for me.

The scheduled meeting outside of Fallujah turned into a darker episode than the one that had taken place that morning in Ar Ramadi. I watched first-hand as Mattis attempted to negotiate peace with the mayor of Fallujah and two generals from the suspicious Fallujah Brigade. As Marines from Regimental Combat Team-One sat entrenched in defensive positions around Fallujah, Mattis defined the position of strength from which he argued.

"Gentlemen, after heavy fighting in April we turned over the security of Fallujah to you and the Fallujah Brigade. In those thirty days we have seen no heavy weapons handed over to us. We have seen no foreign fighters handed over to us. There is still no freedom of movement in the streets of Fallujah for my Marines. Your time is running out to ensure peace in Fallujah. Otherwise, I will give the order for my Marines to enter the city, and there will be a battle waged that the people of Fallujah will not forget for one thousand years."

Poised, neither raising his voice nor displaying any visible emotion, MajGen Mattis laid out his demands to the leadership of Fallujah. The Iraqis responded by insisting that the Americans provide more money to compensate for the damage caused by the fighting in their city. It was absurd. They had allowed inflated damage claims from the citizens of Fallujah to build up, and Mattis was faced with millions of dollars worth of fraudulent filings. After informing the Iraqi leaders that he would not consider the damage claims until they had been whittled down to reasonable amounts, Mattis still met with resistance from the three men. Their obstinance, their refusal to accept responsibility for keeping the peace in Fallujah, finally exhausted Mattis. After more than two hours of negotiating, he ended the meeting.

"Gentlemen, we have wasted our time here today. It is clear we are not making any progress. Right now you are the only obstacle to peace in Fallujah. If you do not accept our mandate; if you do not begin turning over heavy weapons; if you do not begin turning over foreign fighters; if you do not ensure freedom of movement in the streets of Fallujah; the time will come when my Marines will move back into the town."

The atmosphere was tense, and as the three Iraqis departed I sensed aggravation in MajGen Mattis's voice. It was evident that he didn't want to send his men back into combat in Fallujah, but he had resigned himself to the likelihood. He was there to accomplish a mission, and he understood the risks it entailed. After witnessing this historic event, I knew that the time would eventually come when the Marines would be required to take the city of Fallujah by force.

Witnessing the negotiations, I had gained a newfound respect for the division commander. But my admiration for him skyrocketed in the minutes following completion of the convoy back from Fallujah. As the vehicles of the Jump CP rolled up to the palace in Ar Ramadi to drop off the general, he gathered the Marines in a tight semicircle and fully briefed them on what he had just been doing. He was a busy man, but he felt it was imperative for him to keep his men informed. He closed by lauding them for a job well-done. It

Outside Fallujah, after stalled negotiations with the mayor and local military commanders, 6 June 2004. (L to R: Capt Folsom, MajGen James Mattis, Dr. Barak Salmoni.)

made my heart rest easy knowing that my Marines, who now worked with the Jump, were in the hands of such compassionate, caring leadership.

◆ ◇ ◆

Our days in Ar Ramadi stretched out, and we finally got the chance to visit units outside the palace compound. We spent a day interviewing Marines from Fox Company, Second Battalion, Fourth Marines, in their outpost, which had been nicknamed "the Snakepit." The "Magnificent Bastards" of 2/4 had sustained terrible losses since the division's redeployment to Iraq, and as Professor Salmoni and I interviewed squads of Marines I was again astonished at the resilience of the young men who were doing the fighting and dying. They spoke freely, describing to us the trials and tribulations of operating in the streets among the Iraqi people. At the day's end I felt approbation for these young fighters similar to what I felt for my own men in Delta Company. Like the Marines of Delta, the young men of Fox Company represented the best the United States had to offer. It was a privilege to be in their presence.

Late the next afternoon, while standing behind the safety of the walls surrounding an army camp, I heard a firefight erupt in the distance. Hours later I learned the Jump had been ambushed, and along with several wounded, there had been one death among the Marines. The following day I returned to the division CP and tracked down a friend who worked on the staff. At my request, he handed me the casualty report from the firefight. I ran my finger down the list of names, and at the bottom of the page one line made me freeze.

KIA: LCpl Bohlman, Jeremy L.

I had seen him just two days earlier during our convoy to Fallujah. Now he, too, was gone. I stumbled out of the COC and faced the "Wall of Heroes" at the command post's entrance. Emblazoned on great, white posters were the names of all the Marines and sailors of 1st Marine Division who had been wounded or killed since the redeployment began in February. The roll amounted to nearly one thousand names. Scanning it carefully, I noticed the list of casualties incurred by 1st LAR Battalion. There were more than a dozen, and among them were the names of at least five Marines from Delta. I did a double take. Lance Corporal Aaron Merrill, who during OIF-I had been Capt Portiss's driver, had already been wounded three times. *Three times.* It was unimaginable. The war had changed beyond my comprehension—I didn't even recognize it anymore.

Roaming the division compound, I found the last three Marines from Delta Company who remained with the Jump. That evening we sat down together around a small fire and paid tribute to LCpl Bohlman and SSgt Molina. We reminisced about days past and Delta's highway war of the previous year, when it had pushed to Baghdad and beyond. After several hours together we said our good-byes, and I departed to prepare for my flight out of Ar Ramadi the following morning. As I made the long walk through the darkness back to my tent, the image of their faces haunted me. Gutierrez, Tipton, and Scharf—three young men who had fought their way through Iraq with Delta Company and me only one year before—all now looked ten years older. Their cryptic words and mannerisms indicated to me that, like the Marines of Fox Company, they too believed it was merely a matter of time until they got theirs somewhere along the dusty roads of Ar Ramadi.

✦ ✧ ✦

Having parted ways with Salmoni to allow him to continue his research (and to enable me to get back to Monterey in time to finish my final exams), I boarded a helicopter for the return trip out of Iraq to Kuwait. A conspicuous absence of hassle and administrative paperwork aided my departure as Marines from the division staff funneled me through the checkout procedure. Before I knew it, I was on a Boeing 747 headed home. Like my arrival in theater nearly a year and a half earlier with Delta Company, my departure from Kuwait City took place at night. But, unlike my previous departure, this

Last night with Delta Company Marines in Ar Ramadi, 9 June 2004. (L to R: Cpl Sean Scharf, Capt Folsom, Cpl Andrew Tipton, Sgt Carlos Gutierrez.)

time the plane teemed with families and businessmen. Troops like me returning home from Iraq were the minority.

After a long flight from Kuwait, I found myself sitting in a smoky bar in the Amsterdam airport, waiting for a connecting flight to the United States. Staring at a half-full drink in front of me and struggling to put words down on paper, I thought about my quest of the previous year to find an answer to the disquiet that plagued me. I remembered Manchester's words:

You can't drown your troubles, not the real ones, because if they are real they can swim.

Something had happened to me that first time in Iraq. Some unknown, invisible specter had attached itself to me. In my haste to return to my prewar life, I had brought it home with me. For one long year I had brooded about the war, about my actions during those four weeks between Kuwait and Tikrit. I had second-guessed myself time and time again, questioning not only my subordinates and contemporaries, but my superiors as well. I had replayed decisions made, and words said or unsaid. And I had agonized over the fate of that company of young men I had left behind, all the while feeling extremely proud of my service to the Marine Corps and my county.

But as I prepared for the final leg of my flight home, I recognized something else. My return to Iraq had, in some bizarre, divine way, helped to exorcise the demons I had smuggled back with me a year earlier. The losses of Suarez del Solar, Molina-Bautista, and Bohlman still stung my soul like needles piercing flesh. But I knew they had gone to their deaths like heroes, standing up. Like the other men of Delta Company, they had joined the Corps with their eyes open, and with their hearts dedicated to serving their country. So too had I. The burden I had carried on my shoulders for so long was finally lifted. I realized that whatever it was I had carried back with me had been left behind somewhere in the swirling wind and shifting sands of Iraq.

I boarded my flight back to the United States, *a free man.*

Acknowledgments

Many people assisted me in the writing of this book, and to each and every one of them I owe a debt of gratitude. First and foremost I would like to thank my wife, Ashley, for her love, support, and editing assistance, as well as her indefatigable patience with me during all the long days and nights I put into this work. Additional thanks go to my parents, Captain and Mrs. B. F. Folsom, Jr., U.S. Navy (Retired), for their editing suggestions and unwavering support. Gracious thanks to Mike Andrews, friend and former Marine, for his words of encouragement and moral support. Special recognition also goes to the staff at Potomac Books, Inc., especially Don McKeon, John Church, Claire Noble, and Katie Freeman. Their editing suggestions, patience, and tolerance of my constant "author absenteeism," is greatly appreciated. To all the above people, I am grateful for the hours they spent reading the pile of garbage that was the first draft of this book.

As for the Marines of Delta Company, this is as much their book as it is my own. Among them, I am particularly indebted to Stephen Bright, Doug Cullins, Josh Davis, Carlos Gutierrez, Ruben Guzman, Jason Kappen, Daniel Kunkel, Isaac McCorkle, Joshua Nour, Chad Parment, Thomas Reeves, James Thyden, and José Vargas. Without their assistance this book would not have been possible. Special thanks go to Andrew Roufs, whose scores of beautifully shot and framed combat camera photographs assisted so much in the writing of this book. Thanks also to my colleagues Byron Harper and Andrew Manson, whose assistance in the security and policy review of this book greatly aided the process of getting Delta Company's story published.

I am grateful for the assistance of Dr. Barak Salmoni, Ph.D., without whom I could not have made my return to Iraq and thus completed this book. Thanks also go to the many senior officers whose words of wisdom persuaded me to proceed with my story. Among them are Brigadier General Joseph

Dunford USMC, Brigadier General John Toolan USMC, and Colonel Mike Shupp USMC—all leaders of Marines.

Glossary

2.75-inch rocket: rocket fired from a pod carried on AH-1W Cobra and UH-1W Huey helicopters
3rd ID: U.S. Army's Third Infantry Division
4th ID: U.S. Army's Fourth Infantry Division
A-10 Warthog: U.S. Air Force's heavily armed, low-flying tank-killer attack aircraft
AAA: anti-aircraft artillery (also known as "triple-A," AA, or anti-aircraft)
AAV: amphibious assault vehicle (also known as an "amtrack")
abayah: long, flowing garment traditionally worn by Middle Eastern women
ACE: armored combat excavator
AH-1W Cobra: principal attack helicopter for the Marine Corps
AK-47: Russian-designed assault rifle. Fires 7.62-millimeter rounds
amtrack: nickname for amphibious assault vehicle, or AAV
AN/PAS-13: Thermal viewer capable of being mounted on various weapons systems
AN/VVS-2 "Fishbowl": Night vision scope for LAV drivers
AO: area of operations
APC: armored personnel carrier
ASAP: as soon as possible
AT: antitank (when referring to LAV antitank variant)
AT-4: 84-millimeter disposable antitank rocket
ATF: amphibious task force
Australian Peel: maneuver designed by which vehicles break contact while under fire
AV-8B Harrier: Marine Corps attack jet capable of vertical takeoff and landing
BBC: British Broadcasting Corporation
BDA: battle damage assessment

Black: call sign designator for vehicles in Headquarters Platoon
Blue: call sign designator for vehicles in 3rd Platoon
BM-21: Russian-designed, truck-mounted rocket artillery
BMP-1: Russian-designed infantry fighting vehicle
BMP-2: Russian-designed infantry fighting vehicle (follow-on to BMP-1)
BP: Battle position
Bravo Zulu: Jargon for "A job well-done"
Break, break: brevity code alerting all personnel to clear the radio net
Brown: call sign designator for vehicles in mortar section
C-130 Hercules: multipurpose, four-engine aircraft used by Marine Corps and other services
C2: command and control
CACO: casualty assistance calls officer
Camelbak: commercial hydration system used by Marines
CAS: close air support
CAX: combined arms exercise
CEB: combat engineer battalion
CH-46 Sea Knight: medium-lift transport Marine Corps helicopter
Chaos: call sign for Major General James Mattis
CO: commanding officer
coax: slang for M240 coaxially-mounted machine gun
COC: combat operations center
combat trains: vehicles and personnel designated to provide immediate combat support
CP: command post
CSSC: combat service support company
CVC: combat vehicle crewman helmet
DA: dispersal area
dinar: Iraqi monetary unit
dishdasha: traditional long, flowing garment worn by many Middle Eastern men
DMZ: demilitarized zone
DPICM: dual-purpose, improved conventional munitions
Dragon: call sign for Delta Company
Dragon Eye: small unmanned aerial vehicle (UAV)
eastings: vertical grid lines on a map
EMI: extra military instruction, also known as "NCO justice"
EOD: explosive ordnance disposal
EPW: enemy prisoner of war
F/A-18 Hornet: fighter attack aircraft used by Navy and Marine Corps

F-14 Tomcat: carrier-based fighter aircraft used by Navy
F-15 Eagle: fighter aircraft used by Air Force
F-16 Falcon: fighter aircraft used by Air Force
FAC: forward air controller
FAO: foreign area officer
FARP: forward arming and refueling point
FDC: fire direction center
field trains: vehicles and personnel designated to provide sustained administrative, logistical, and maintenance support
fire in the hole: jargon used by drivers to announce vehicle engine ignition (also used to announce a planned detonation of explosives)
fire-capped: ready to initiate an indirect fire mission
FiST: fire support team
five-five-six: slang for 5.56 millimeter
Forward: principal battalion command element led by battalion commander and operations officer
FPOL: forward passage of lines
frag order: basic operations order that contains minimum amount of information required to accomplish a mission
GOSP: gas-oil separation plant
GPS: global positioning system
Green: call sign designator for vehicles in antitank platoon
Grizzly: call sign for 5th Marine Regiment
Guidons: term used to denote unit leaders
H&S: Headquarters and Service
HEI-T: high explosive incendiary, tracer
Hellfire: laser-guided air-to-ground missile
herringbone: tactical formation where road-bound vehicles face outboard at forty-five-degree angles
HET: human exploitation team
H-Hour: coordinated time for an operation to begin
Highlander: call sign for 1st Light Armored Reconnaissance Battalion
HMMWV: high mobility, multi-purpose, wheeled vehicle, also known as a humvee
ID: infantry division
IED: improvised explosive device
Imam: a male spiritual leader in the Islamic religion
IV line: intervisibility line, a point on the battlefield beyond which you (or the enemy) cannot observe (e.g., a ridgeline or depression that hides the ground behind it)

JDAM: Joint Direct Attack Munition
jihad: holy war
jihadi: holy warrior
Jump: the division commanding general's mobile command post
Kevlar: material used in helmets and body armor, also generic term for a helmet
KIA: killed in action
KVN: Key Volunteer Network
LAI: Light Armored Infantry
LAR: Light Armored Reconnaissance
LAV: light armored vehicle
LD: line of departure
Lightning: brevity code for an enemy ballistic missile launch
LogPack: logistics package, a task-organized group of logistics vehicles and personnel designed to support an operation
LSA: logistics support area
LZ: landing zone
M-16A2: standard semiautomatic rifle issued to Marines that fires 5.56-millimeter rounds
M1A1 Abrams: 63-ton main battle tank that fires 120-millimeter rounds
M240: medium machine gun that fires 7.62-millimeter rounds
M242 Bushmaster: main armament for LAV-25 that fires 25-millimeter rounds
M-249 SAW: squad automatic weapon, a light machine gun for the rifle squad that fires belted 5.56-millimeter rounds
M256: compact chemical detector kit that tests for the presence of chemical agents
M-4: carbine version of M-16A2 with a shortened barrel and stock that makes it ideal for use by vehicle crewmen
M-9: standard sidearm that is issued for the Marine Corps and fires 9-millimeter rounds
Main: alternate battalion command element, led by battalion executive officer and assistant operations officer
MAW: Marine Air Wing
MDACT: Marine data automated communications terminal
Medevac: medical evacuation
MEF: Marine Expeditionary Force
MEU: Marine Expeditionary Unit
mike-mike: slang for "millimeter"
Mk-83: standard 1,000-pound bomb
MLRS: multiple launch rocket system

MOPP: mission oriented protective posture
MPF: maritime prepositioning force
MRE: meal, ready to eat
MTLB: Russian-designed armored personnel carrier
NBC: nuclear, biological, and chemical
NCO: non-commissioned officer
northings: horizontal grid lines on a map
NPS: Naval Postgraduate School
NVG: night vision goggles
OCS: Officer Candidates School
OE-254: adjustable-height antenna designed to increase the communications range of radio systems
OIF: Operation Iraqi Freedom
OODA: orientation, observation, decision, action
Oscar Mike: jargon for "On the move"
PA: position area (for artillery batteries)
Phraselator: Electronic translation device
POW: prisoner of war
PsyOps: psychological operations
RCT: regimental combat team
Red: call sign designator for vehicles in 1st Platoon
Red zone: area surrounding Baghdad in which it was believed the Republican Guard was most likely to employ chemical or biological weapons
RedCon: readiness condition
RPG: rocket propelled grenade
S-1: battalion or regimental personnel and administrative section; also chief personnel officer
S-2: battalion or regimental intelligence section; also chief intelligence officer
S-3: battalion or regimental operations section; also chief operations officer
S-3A: assistant operations officer
S-4: battalion or regimental logistics section; also chief logistics officer
S-6: battalion or regimental communications section; also chief communications officer
S-60: Russian-designed anti-aircraft artillery piece that fires 57-millimeter rounds
SA-2: Russian-designed surface-to-air missile
SA-6: Russian-designed surface-to-air missile
SAPI: small arms protective insert
Scud: Iraqi ballistic missile

SDZ: surface danger zone
SEAL: sea, air, and land; Navy Special Forces team
shamal: Arabic for "north wind," referring to the blinding sandstorms characteristic of the region
sheikh: village leader in Islamic communities
shemagh: multipurpose headscarf worn by Middle Eastern men, adopted by many Marines to protect them from the harsh environment of the desert
short-count: coordinated ignition or shut-down of all engines, designed to mask the number of vehicles in a unit
Slingshot: brevity code to indicate that a friendly unit is about to be overrun
SMAW: shoulder-mounted assault weapon, a reusable rocket launcher that fires 83-millimeter rounds
SNAFU: situation normal all fucked up
SNCO: staff non-commissioned officer
SOP: standard operating procedure
SSO: Special Security Organization
stop-loss: policy that prevents service members from exiting the military during times of war
SUV: sport utility vehicle
T-55: Russian-designed main battle tank
T-62: Russian-designed main battle tank, follow-on to T-55
T-72: Russian-designed main battle tank, follow-on to T-62
TAA: tactical assembly area
TBS: The Basic School
TC-6: Italian-designed antitank land mine
technical: civilian vehicle mounted with either heavy machine gun or recoilless rifle
time: now: jargon for "commence operation immediately"
Tomahawk: surface-to-surface precision-guided missile
TOW: tube-launched, optically tracked, wire-guided missile
UN: United Nations
UAV: unmanned aerial vehicle
UH-1N Huey: multipurpose utility helicopter used by Marine Corps
UXO: unexploded ordnance
VC: vehicle commander
Victor: military jargon for "vehicle"
VS-17: two-sided nylon fabric panel designed to assist friendly aircraft in identifying friendly vehicles
wadi: A dry gully or streambed

Warlord: call sign for Weapons Company
WestPac: Western Pacific deployment
White: call sign designator for vehicles in 2nd Platoon
Wolfpack: call sign for 3rd Light Armored Reconnaissance Battalion
XO: executive officer
ZU-23: Russian-designed, twin-barreled anti-aircraft gun that fires 23-millimeter rounds
Zulu: Greenwich Mean Time, used to coordinate the efforts of many military units operating simultaneously in different time zones

Index

About the Author

An active duty infantry officer, **Maj. Seth William Bell Folsom** joined the U.S. Marine Corps in 1992. After earning a bachelor's degree in international relations from the University of Virginia in 1994, he was commissioned as a second lieutenant. He has served as both a platoon commander and company commander in the First Marine Division's First Light Armored Reconnaissance Battalion. Additional billets have included roles as a platoon commander, company executive officer, and a principal staff officer at the USMC Officer Candidates School. His operational experience includes two overseas deployments with Marine Expeditionary Units and one combat deployment to Operation Iraqi Freedom. Currently a South Asia foreign area officer, Major Folsom has a master's degree in South Asian National Security Affairs from the U.S. Naval Postgraduate School and is a recent graduate of the U.S. State Department's Foreign Service Institute.

CPSIA information can be obtained
at www.ICGtesting.com
Printed in the USA
LVHW091738180621
690597LV00002B/38

9 781597 971065